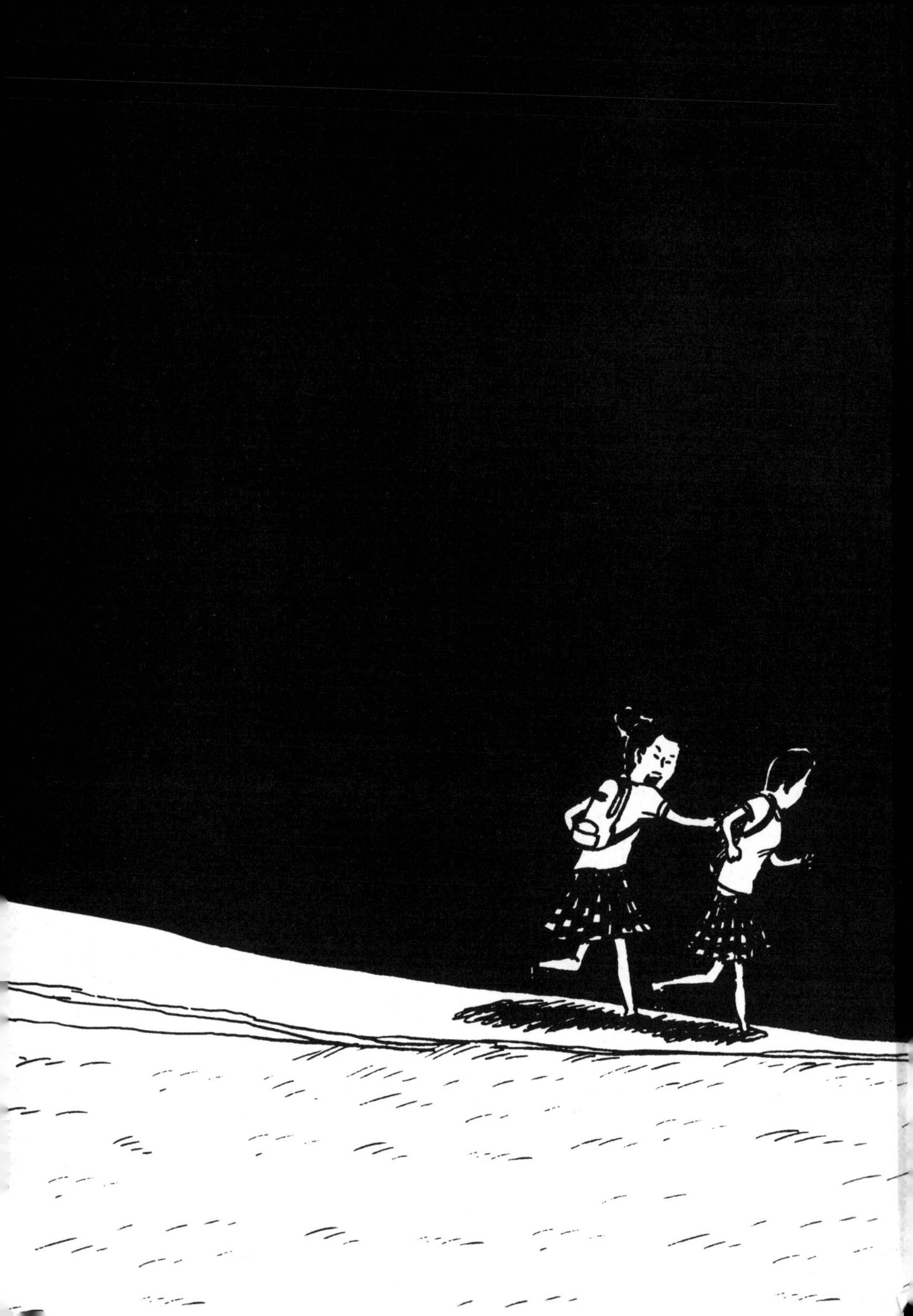

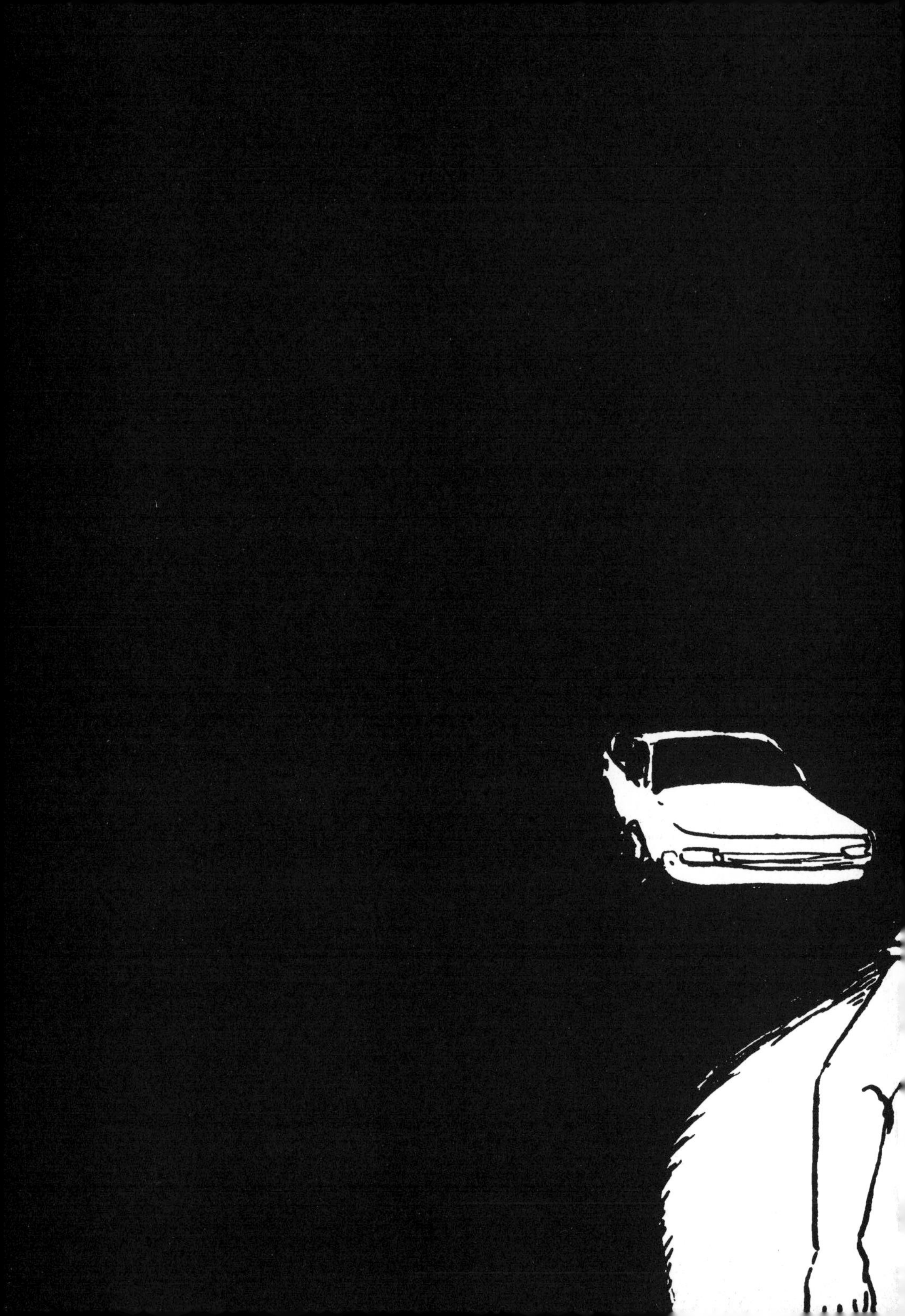

nineteen / ancco

translated by janet hong

drawn & quarterly

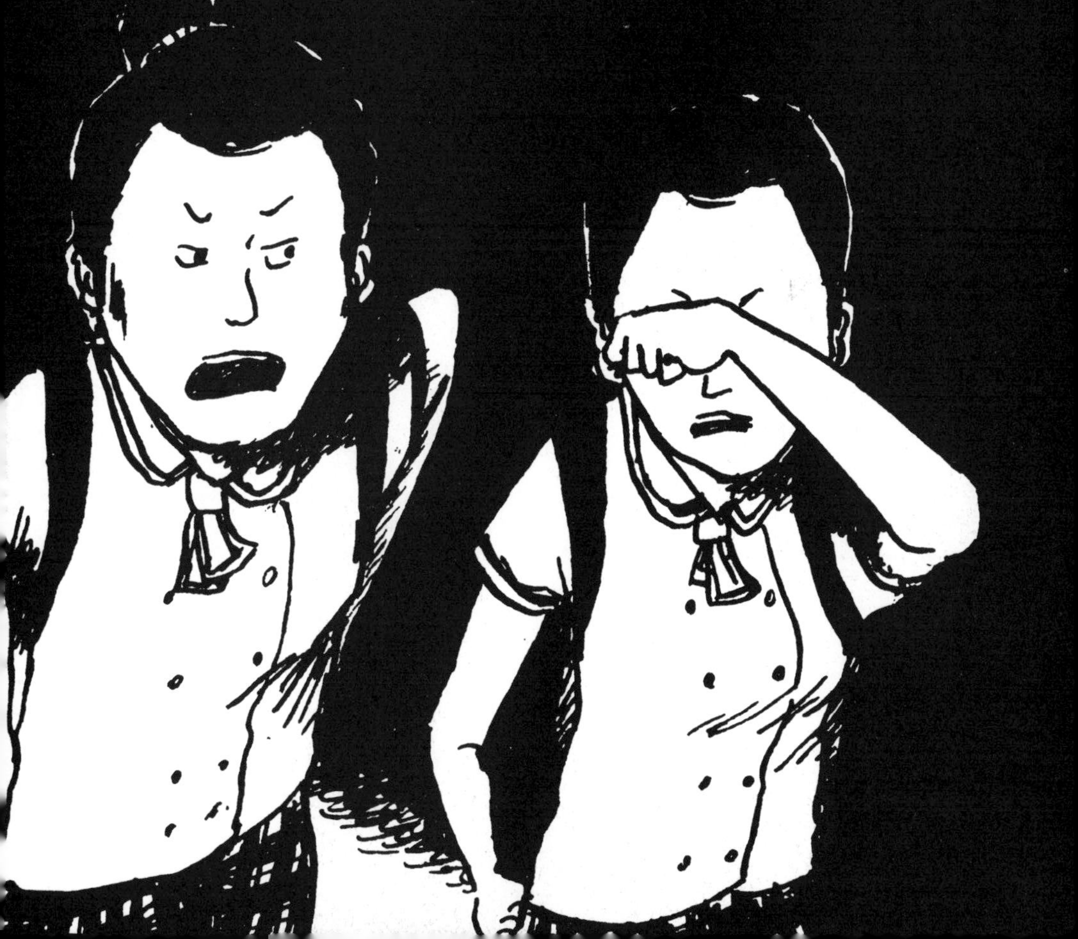

drawnandquarterly.com

978-1-77046-410-0 l First edition: September 2020 l Printed in Canada l 10 9 8 7 6 5 4 3 2 1

Cataloguing data available from Library and Archives Canada.

Published in the USA by Drawn & Quarterly, a client publisher of Farrar, Straus and Giroux. Published in Canada by Drawn & Quarterly, a client publisher of Raincoast Books. Published in the United Kingdom by Drawn & Quarterly, a client publisher of Publishers Group UK.

Nineteen is published under the support of Literature Translation Institute of Korea (LTI Korea).

Canadä Drawn & Quarterly acknowledges the support of the Government of Canada and the Canada Council for the Arts for our publishing program.

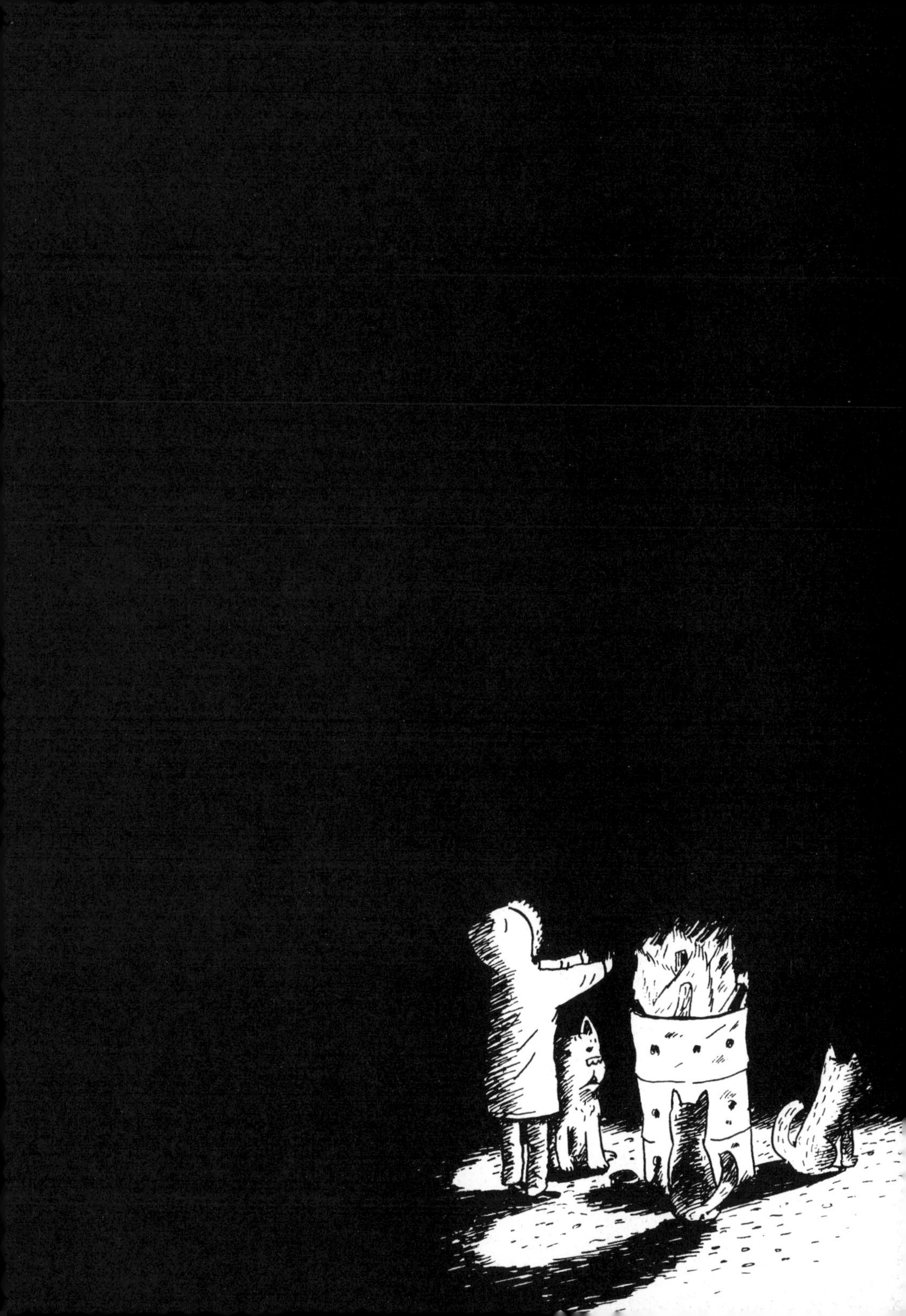

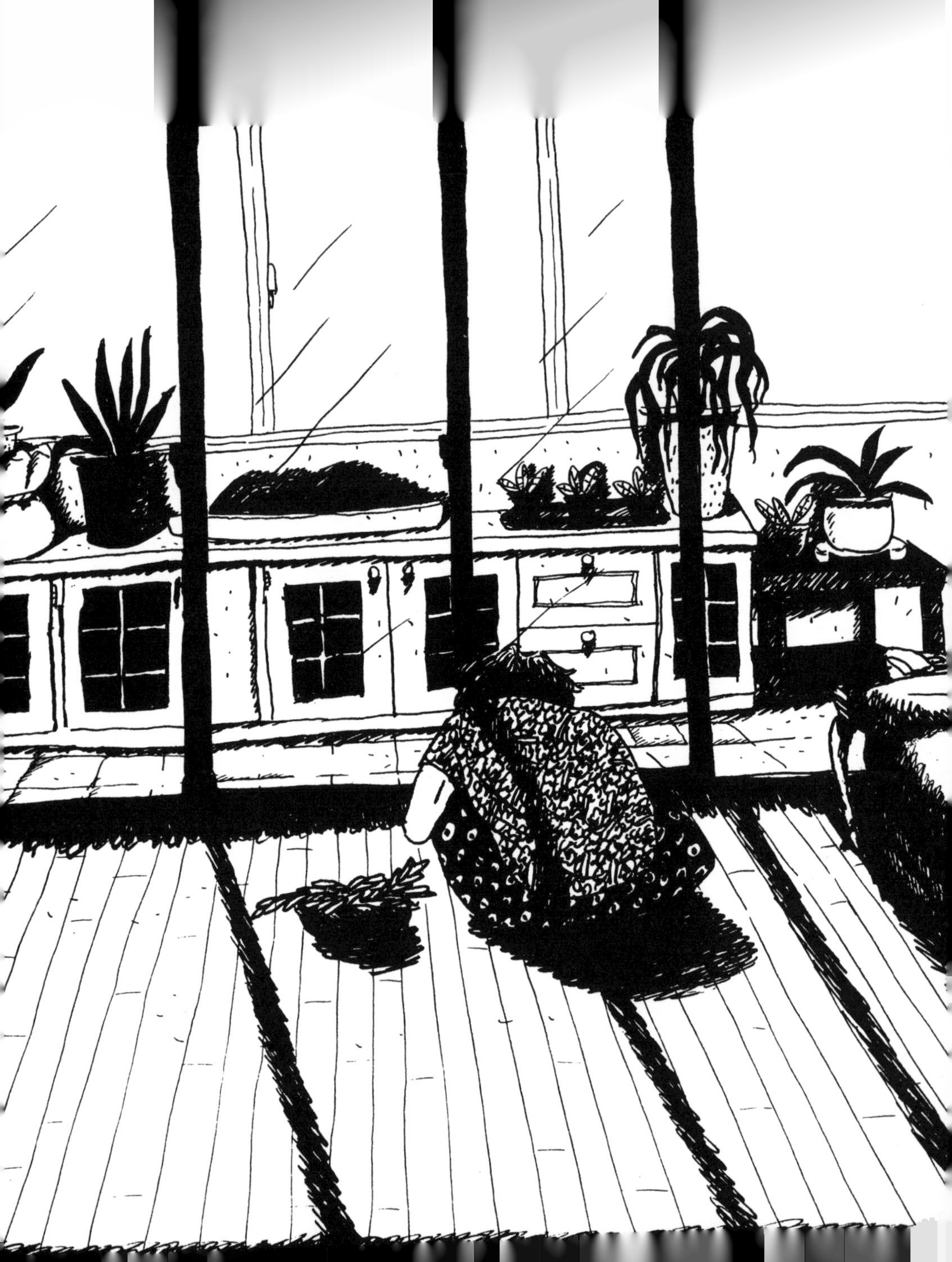

Only days after my grandmother's funeral, I pulled out the original manuscript of *Nineteen* to rescan all the pages for Drawn & Quarterly, who had gotten in touch about publishing the English translation. The book was first released in Korea more than ten years ago, but to make a long story short, the scans of the original art had gone missing when the Korean publisher went out of business.

Nineteen contains comics about my grandmother, as well as things I worked on in my early twenties. Back then, I had been serializing my diary comics online, but I'd started drawing short stories to publish in print magazines. While my diary comics were light-hearted sketches I'd drawn every day, my short stories were experiences I didn't record right away, but pondered for some time before committing them to paper. It took about five years to complete the stories in this book. Those five years in my early twenties felt awfully long, but my worldview and emotions changed rapidly. In the same way, I found my artistic style, and even my interests and subject matter, evolving with each new story. At first, I tried to keep the visuals consistent by mimicking my earlier style, but I wasn't happy with the results. In the end, I decided to just let things be.

My grandmother spent her last year in a nursing home, and toward the end, she had trouble recognizing anyone. Sometimes she managed to get my name right, but most of the time, she asked me who I was. Before she moved into the nursing home, before she became a different person almost overnight and tried to beat me, she'd lived with my family. After several incidents where she tried to hit me, she began to suffer from bowel and urinary incontinence, and had to leave.

Through the process of rescanning this book, I was glad to meet my healthy grandmother once more. Seeing the grandmother I remembered as a child—the way she used to greet me before she forgot my name—it felt as if she'd come back to life. These comics don't simply exist in my imagination. They make my past come alive again. Despite so much time having passed, through these drawings and words, I revisit the world I believed would never change, things I witnessed and took for granted. I revisit feelings, people, a world that's now gone. I feel truly blessed that I can, if only for a brief period, relive these moments.

With the publication of *Nineteen* in English, things beyond reach are finding new life. It's my hope that readers will recognize something of themselves in these stories.

June 2, 2020
Ancco

mom

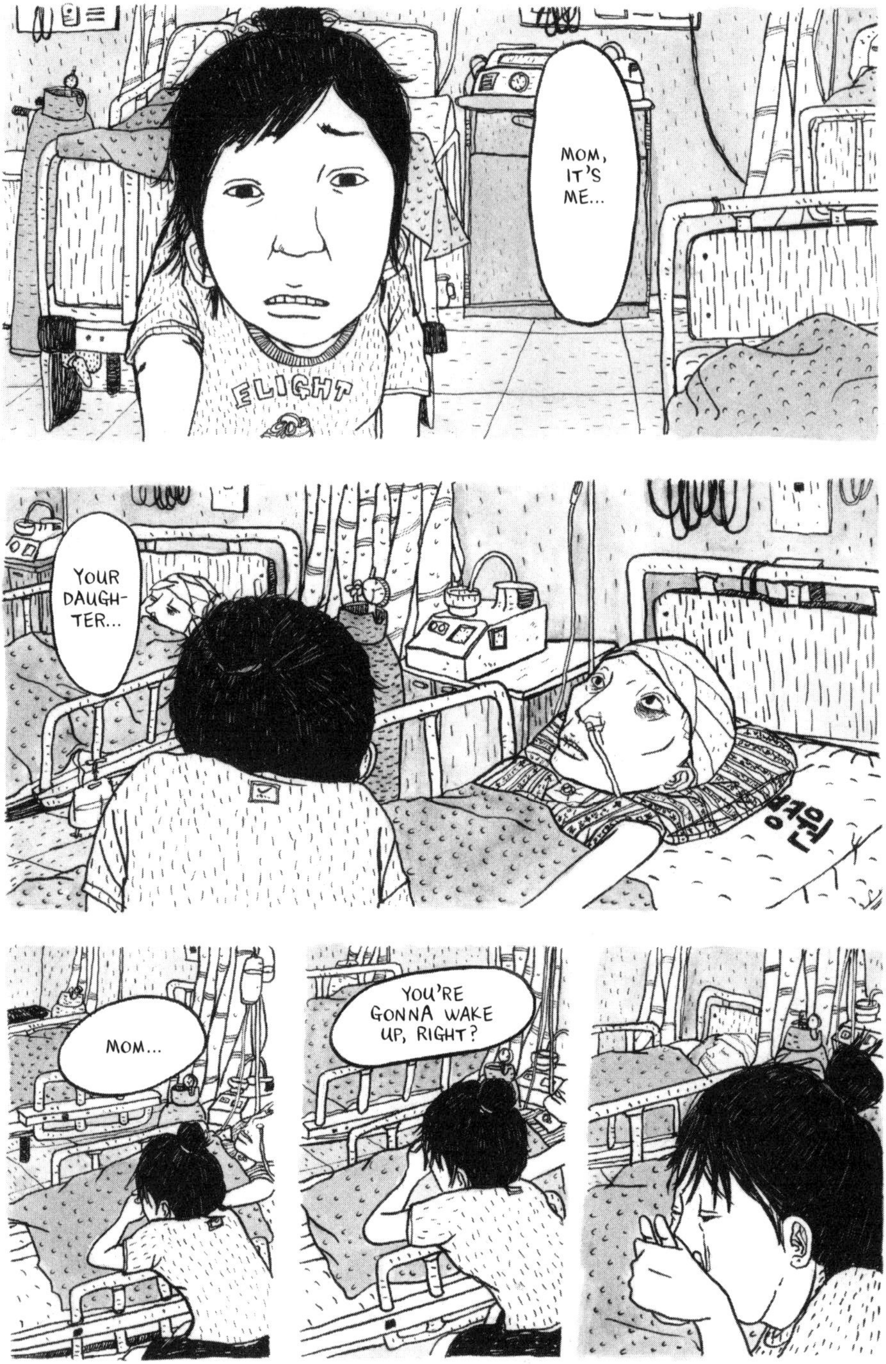
MOM, IT'S ME...
YOUR DAUGHTER...
MOM...
YOU'RE GONNA WAKE UP, RIGHT?

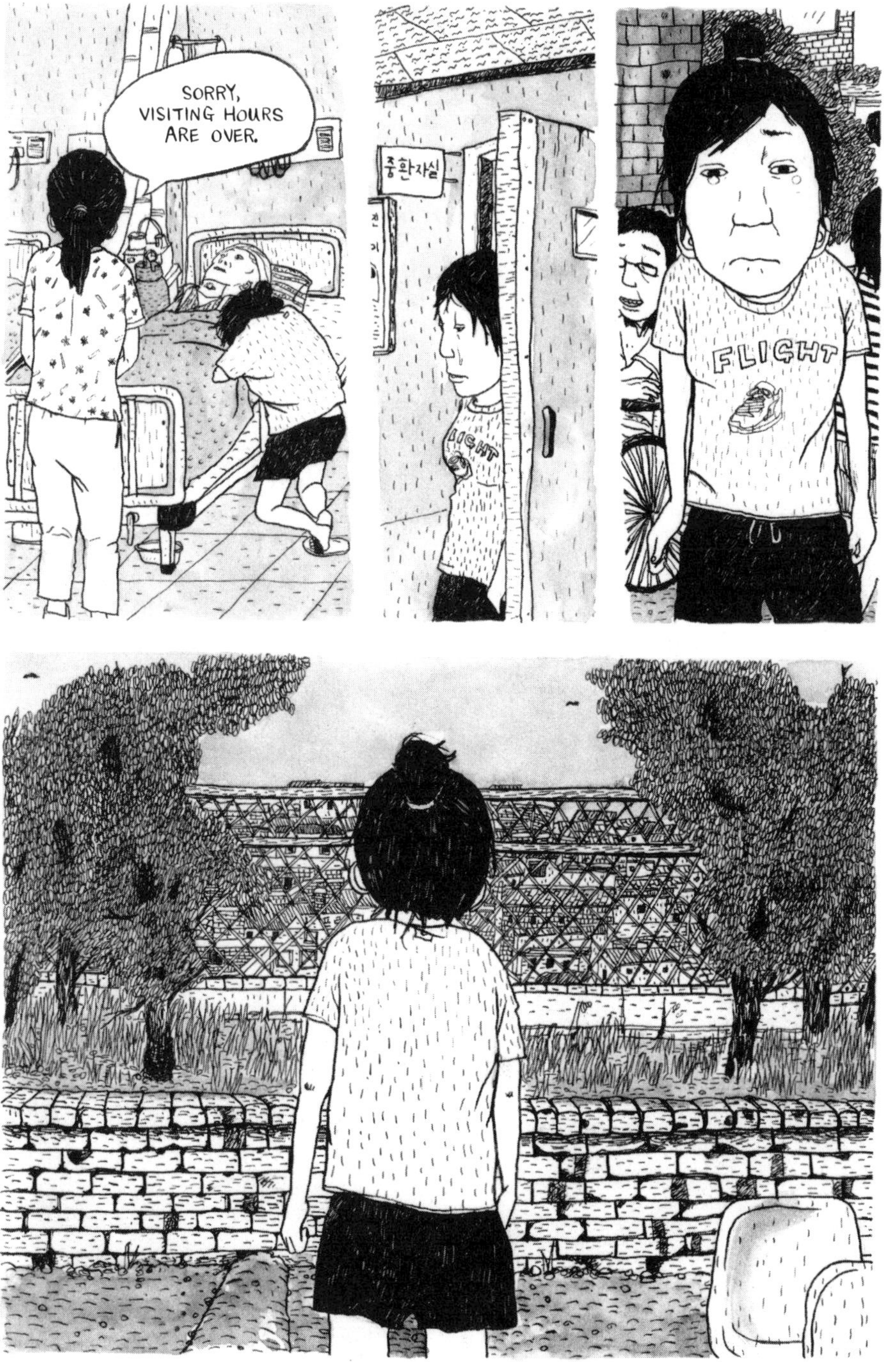
SORRY, VISITING HOURS ARE OVER.
중환자실
FLIGHT

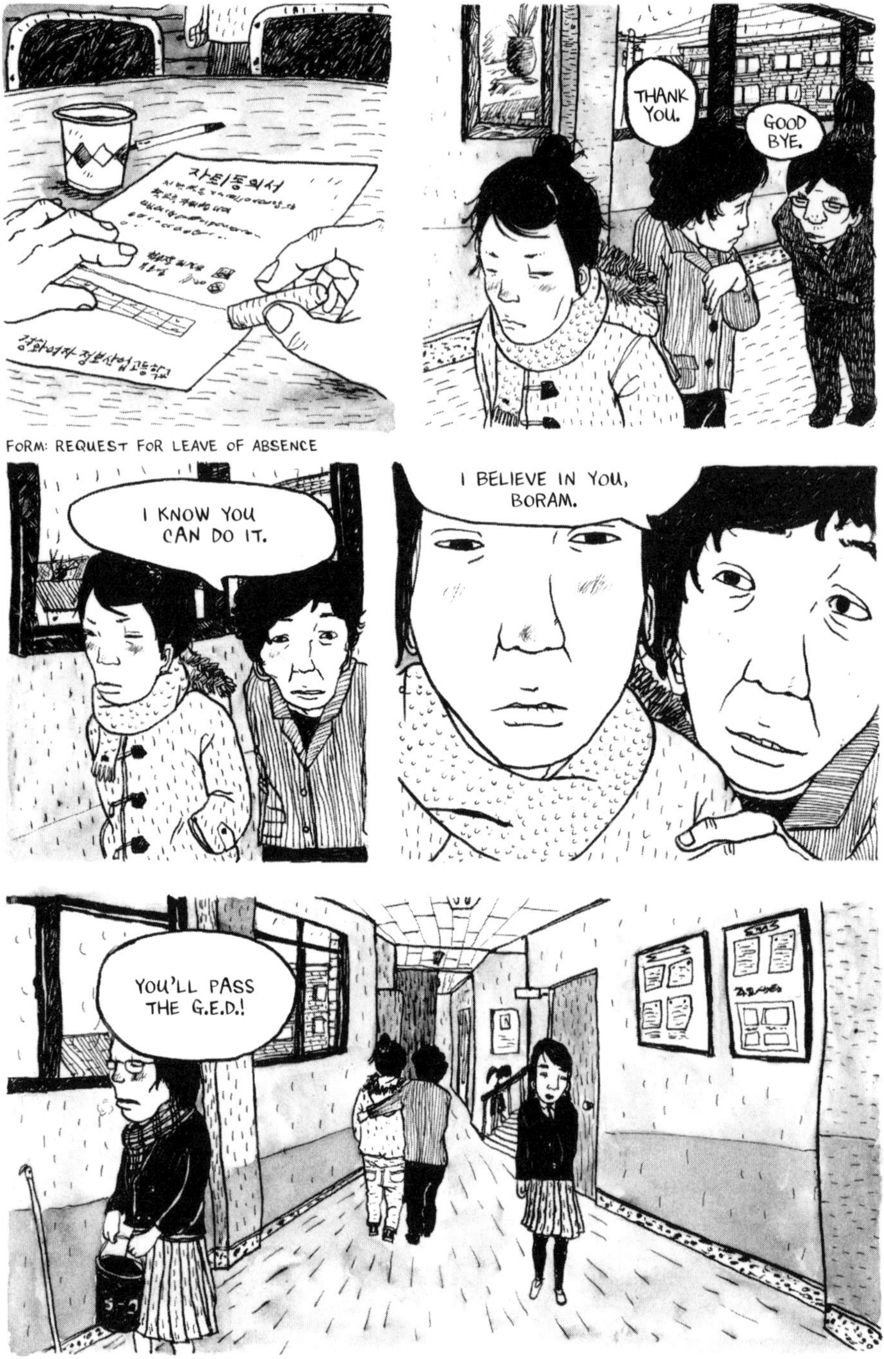

자퇴동의서
FORM: REQUEST FOR LEAVE OF ABSENCE
THANK YOU.
GOOD BYE.
I KNOW YOU CAN DO IT.
I BELIEVE IN YOU, BORAM.
YOU'LL PASS THE G.E.D.!

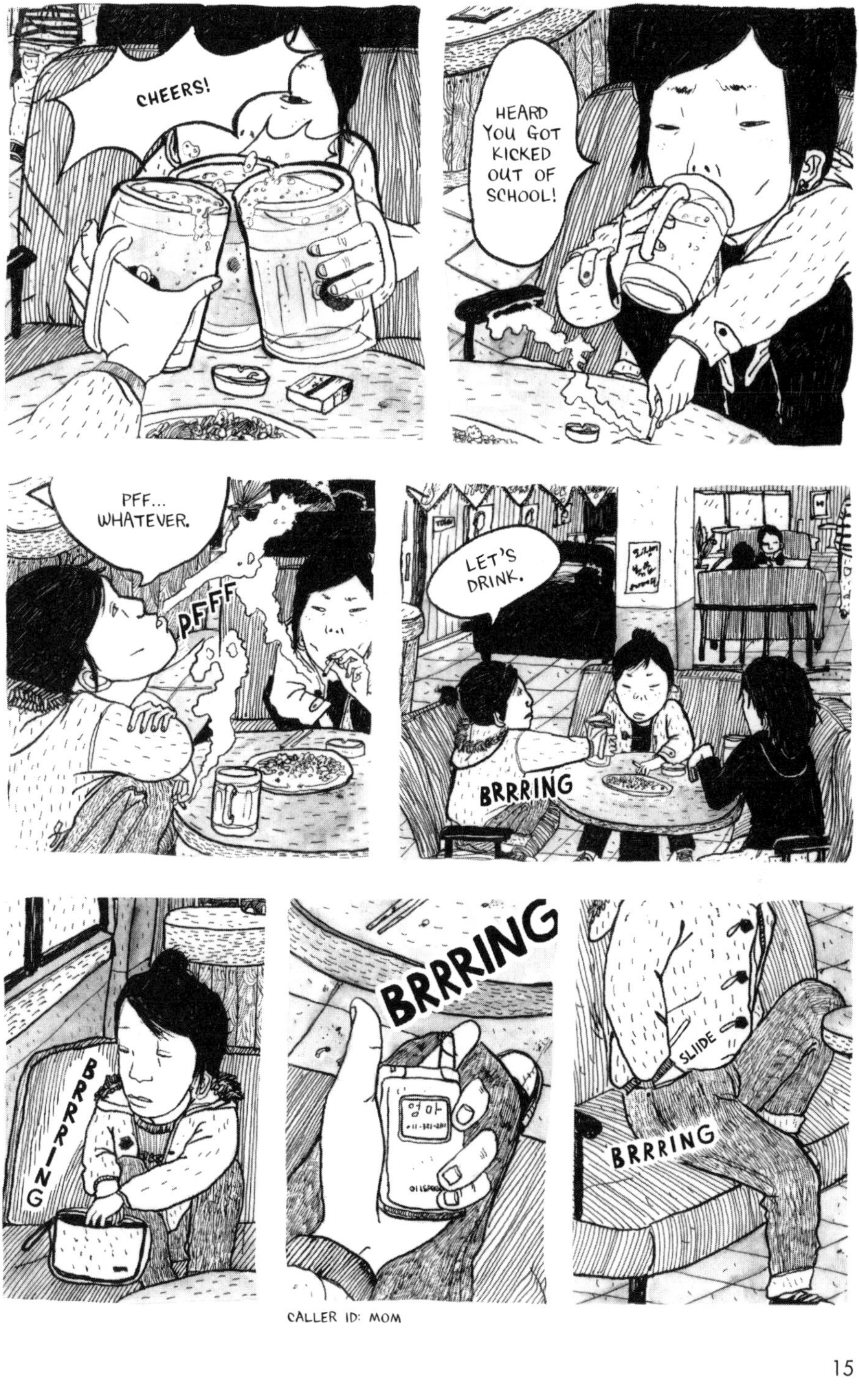
CHEERS!
HEARD YOU GOT KICKED OUT OF SCHOOL!
PFF... WHATEVER.
PFFF
LET'S DRINK.
BRRRING
BRRRING
BRRRING
SLIIDE
BRRRING

CALLER ID: MOM

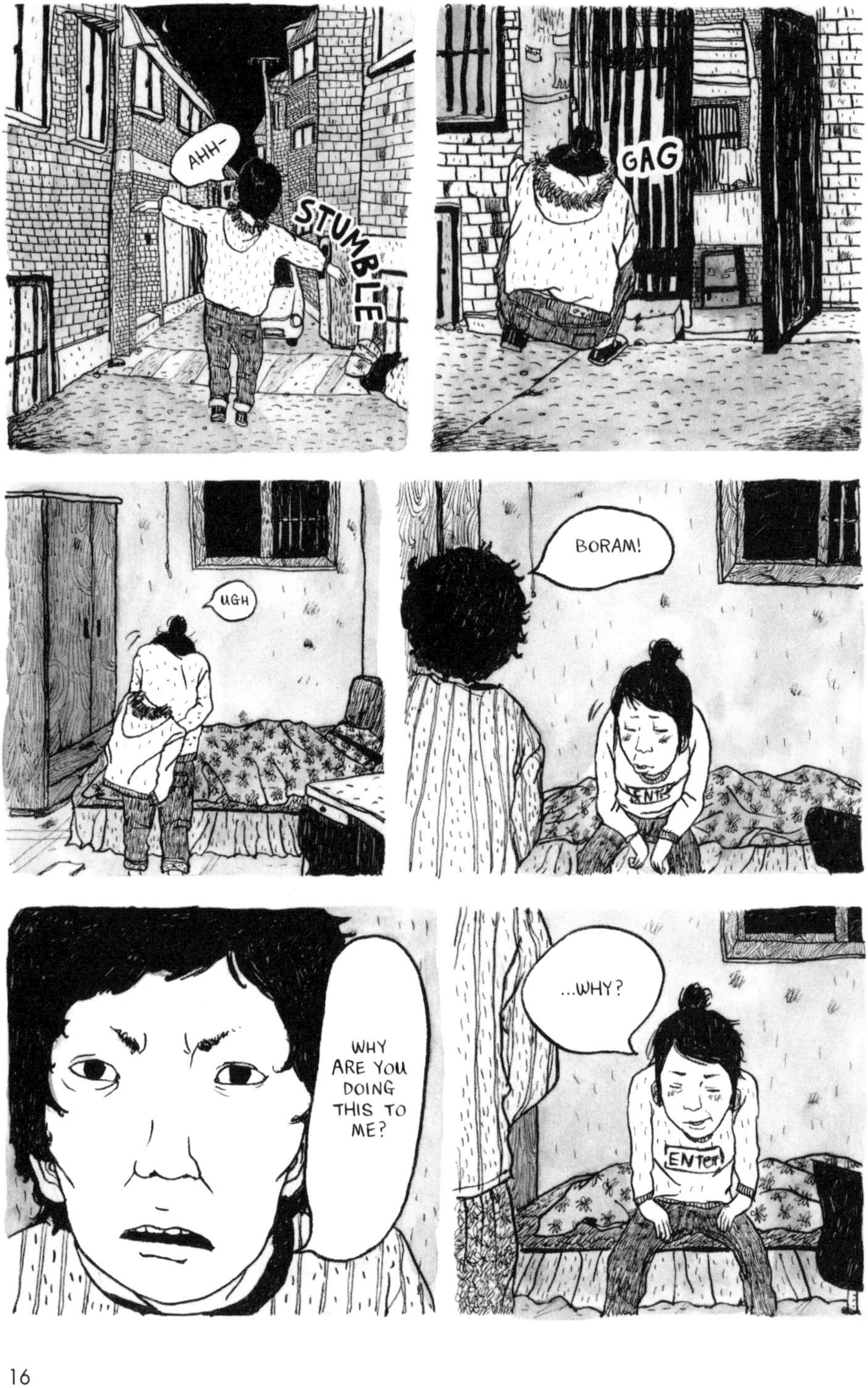
AHH-
STUMBLE
GAG
UGH
BORAM!
WHY ARE YOU DOING THIS TO ME?
...WHY?

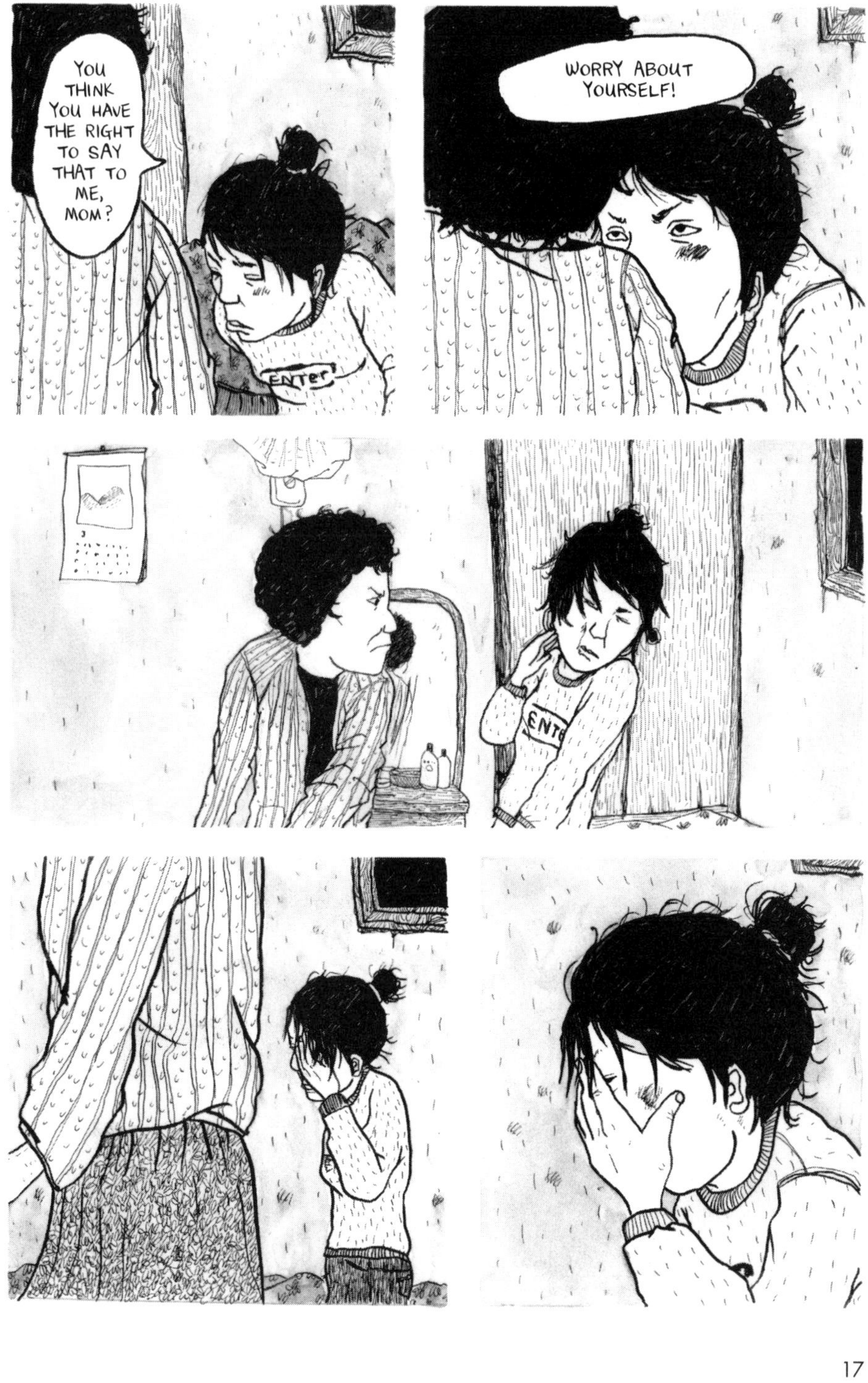
YOU THINK YOU HAVE THE RIGHT TO SAY THAT TO ME, MOM?
ENTer
WORRY ABOUT YOURSELF!

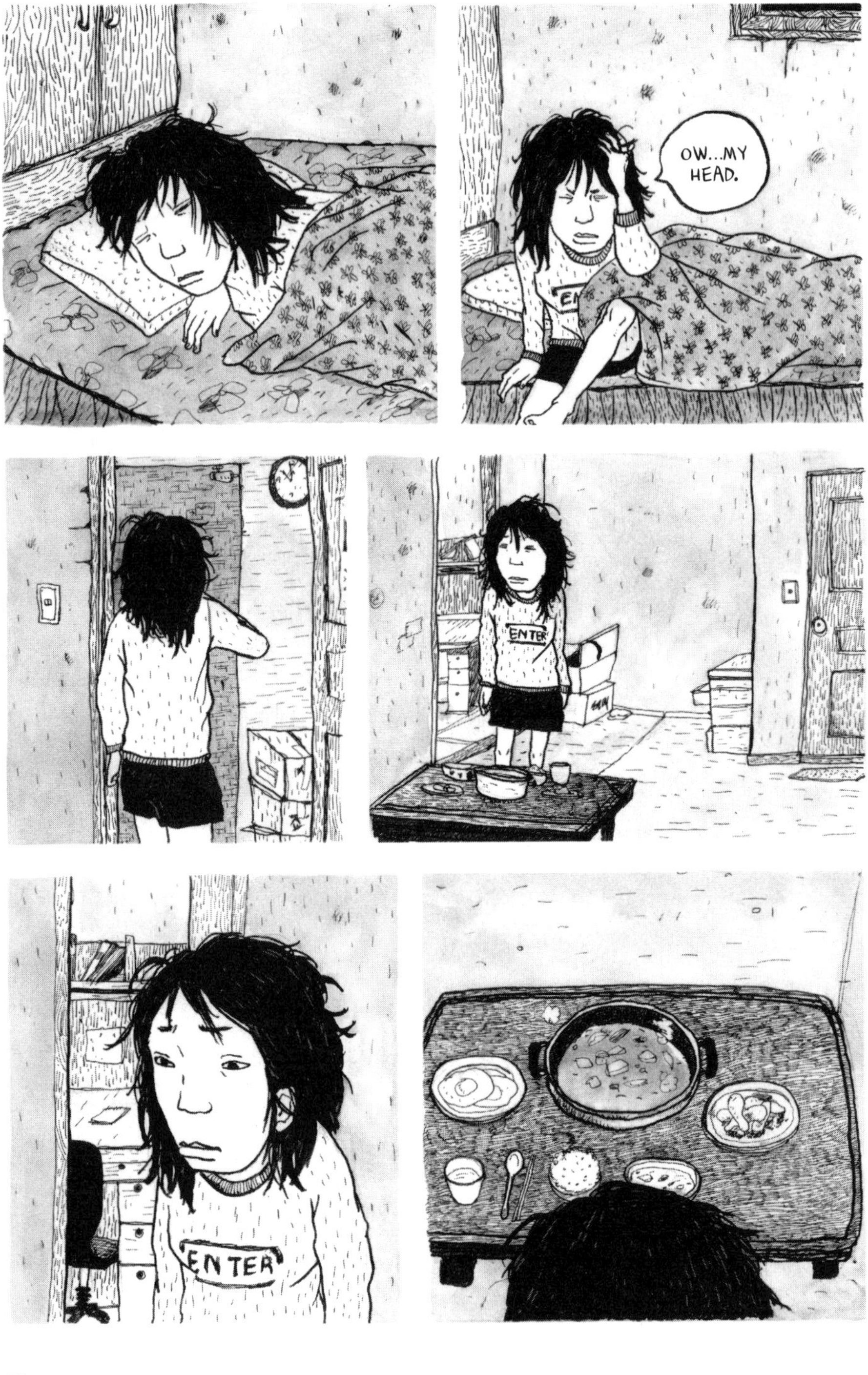
OW...MY HEAD.
ENTER
ENTER

ENTER
SEE YA TOMOR-ROW!
BYE.
I HAVE TO PASS!
STUMBLE
IS MY BORAM STUDY-ING?

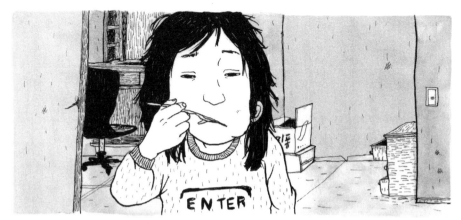

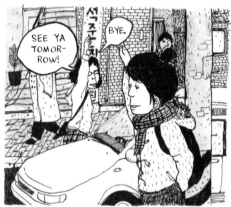

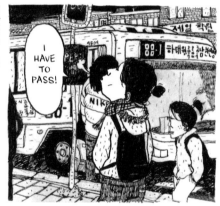

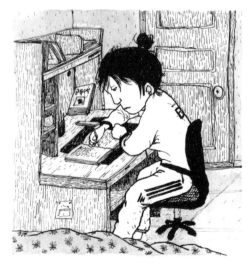

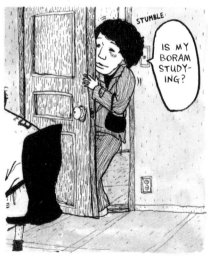

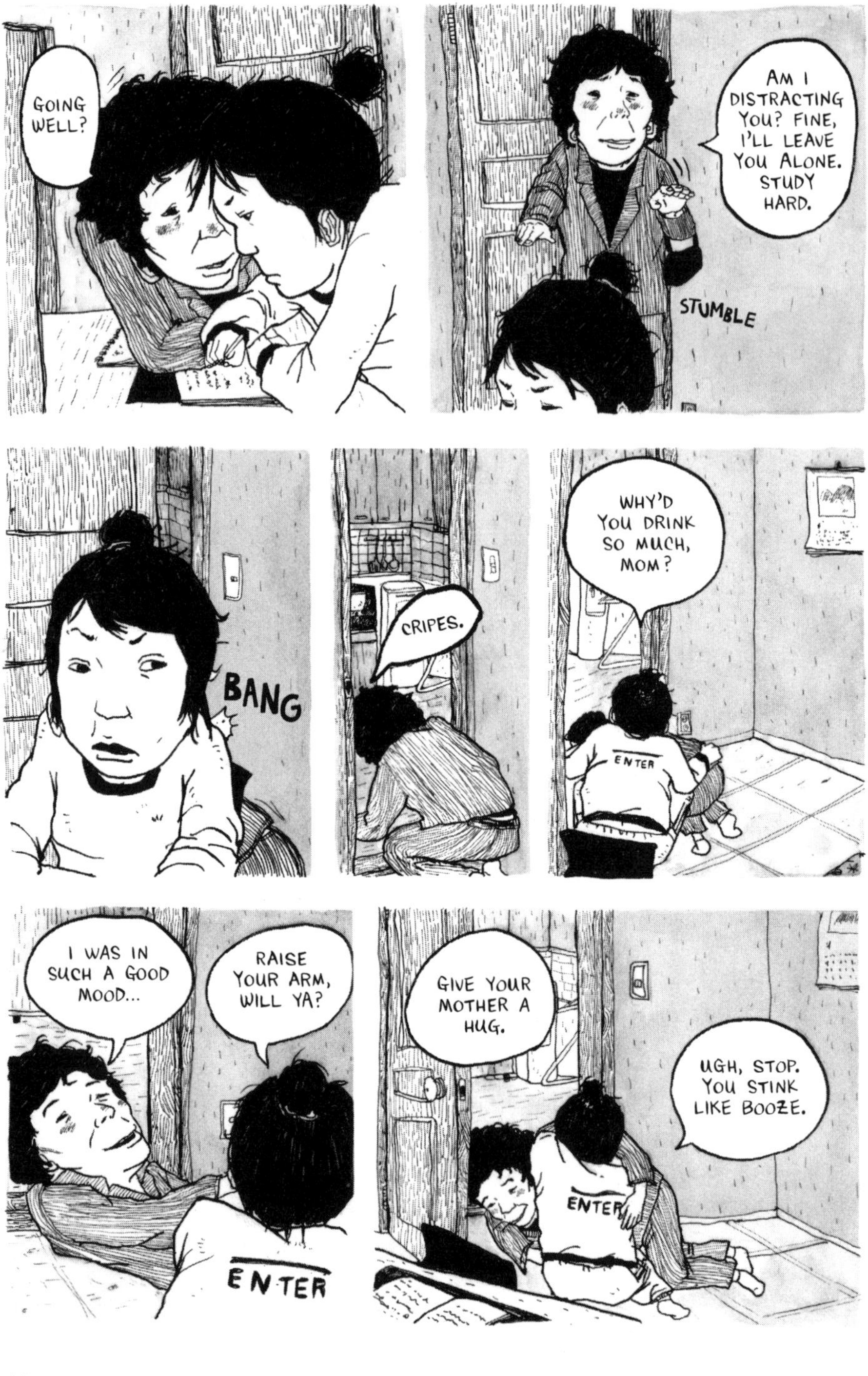
GOING WELL?
AM I DISTRACTING YOU? FINE, I'LL LEAVE YOU ALONE. STUDY HARD.
STUMBLE
BANG
CRIPES.
WHY'D YOU DRINK SO MUCH, MOM?
ENTER
I WAS IN SUCH A GOOD MOOD...
RAISE YOUR ARM, WILL YA?
ENTER
GIVE YOUR MOTHER A HUG.
UGH, STOP. YOU STINK LIKE BOOZE.
ENTER

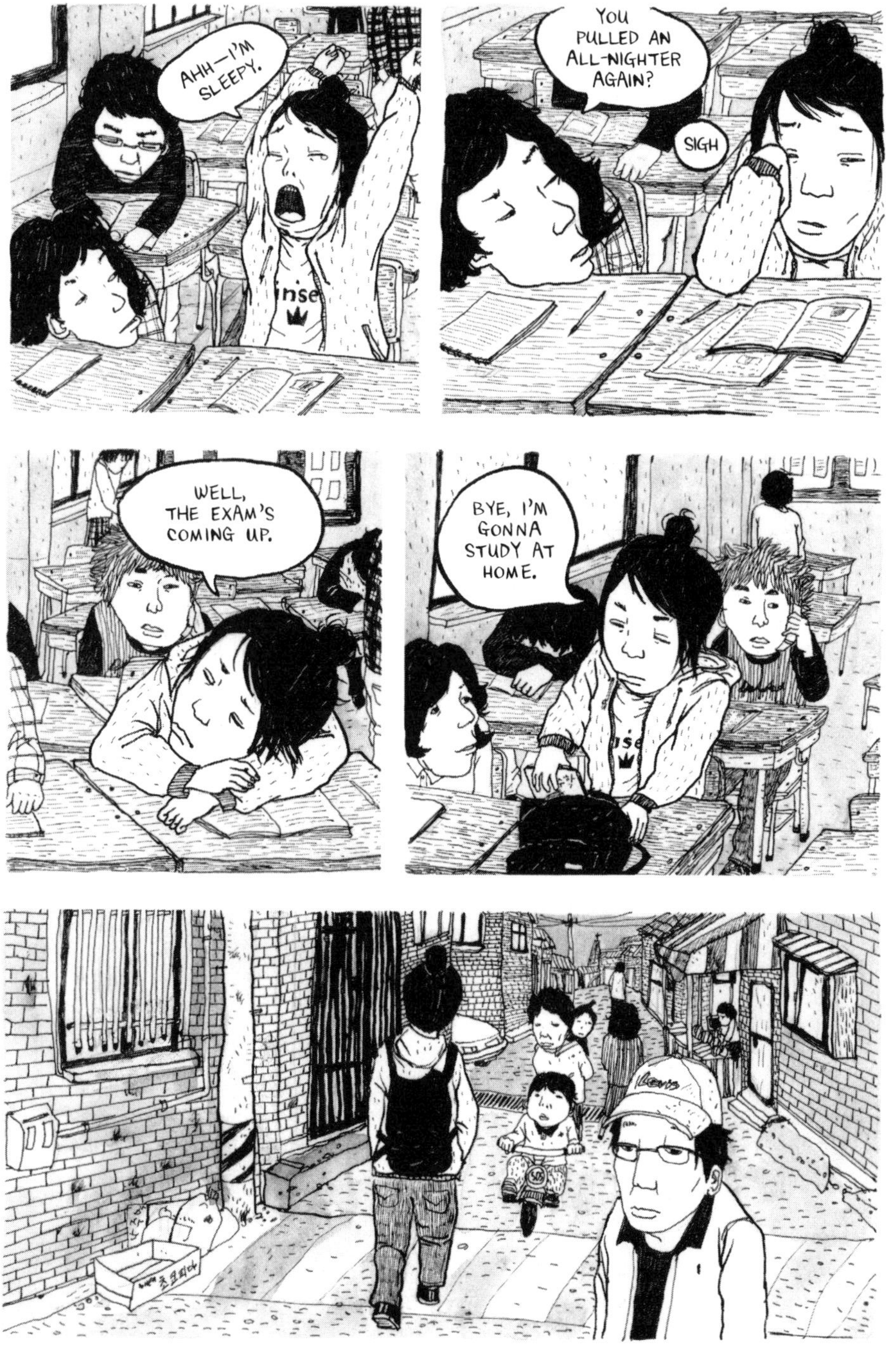
AHH—I'M SLEEPY.
YOU PULLED AN ALL-NIGHTER AGAIN?
SIGH
WELL, THE EXAM'S COMING UP.
BYE, I'M GONNA STUDY AT HOME.

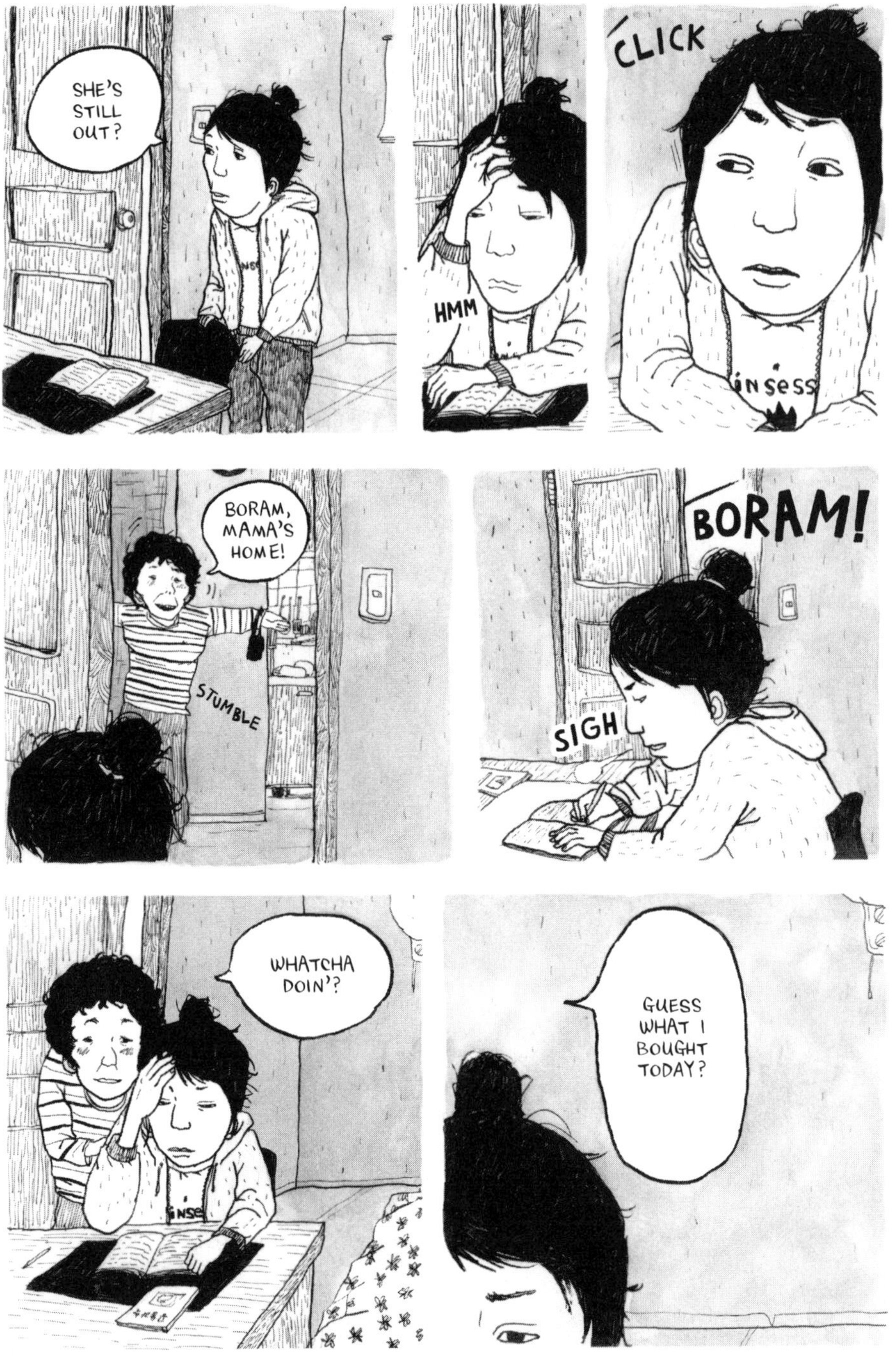
SHE'S STILL OUT?
HMM
CLICK
INSESS
BORAM, MAMA'S HOME!
STUMBLE
BORAM!
SIGH
WHATCHA DOIN'?
GUESS WHAT I BOUGHT TODAY?

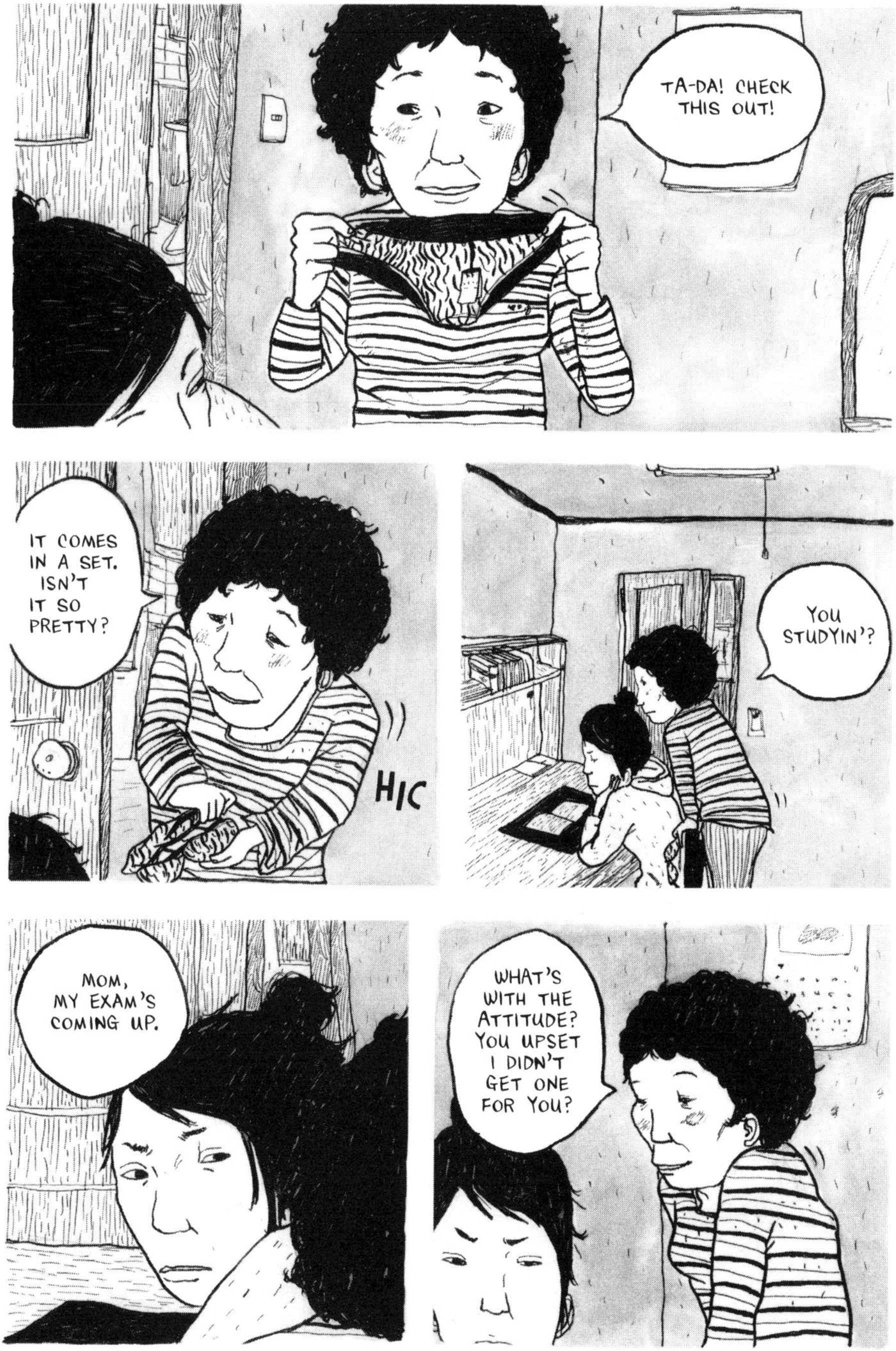
TA-DA! CHECK THIS OUT!
IT COMES IN A SET. ISN'T IT SO PRETTY?
HIC
YOU STUDYIN'?
MOM, MY EXAM'S COMING UP.
WHAT'S WITH THE ATTITUDE? YOU UPSET I DIDN'T GET ONE FOR YOU?

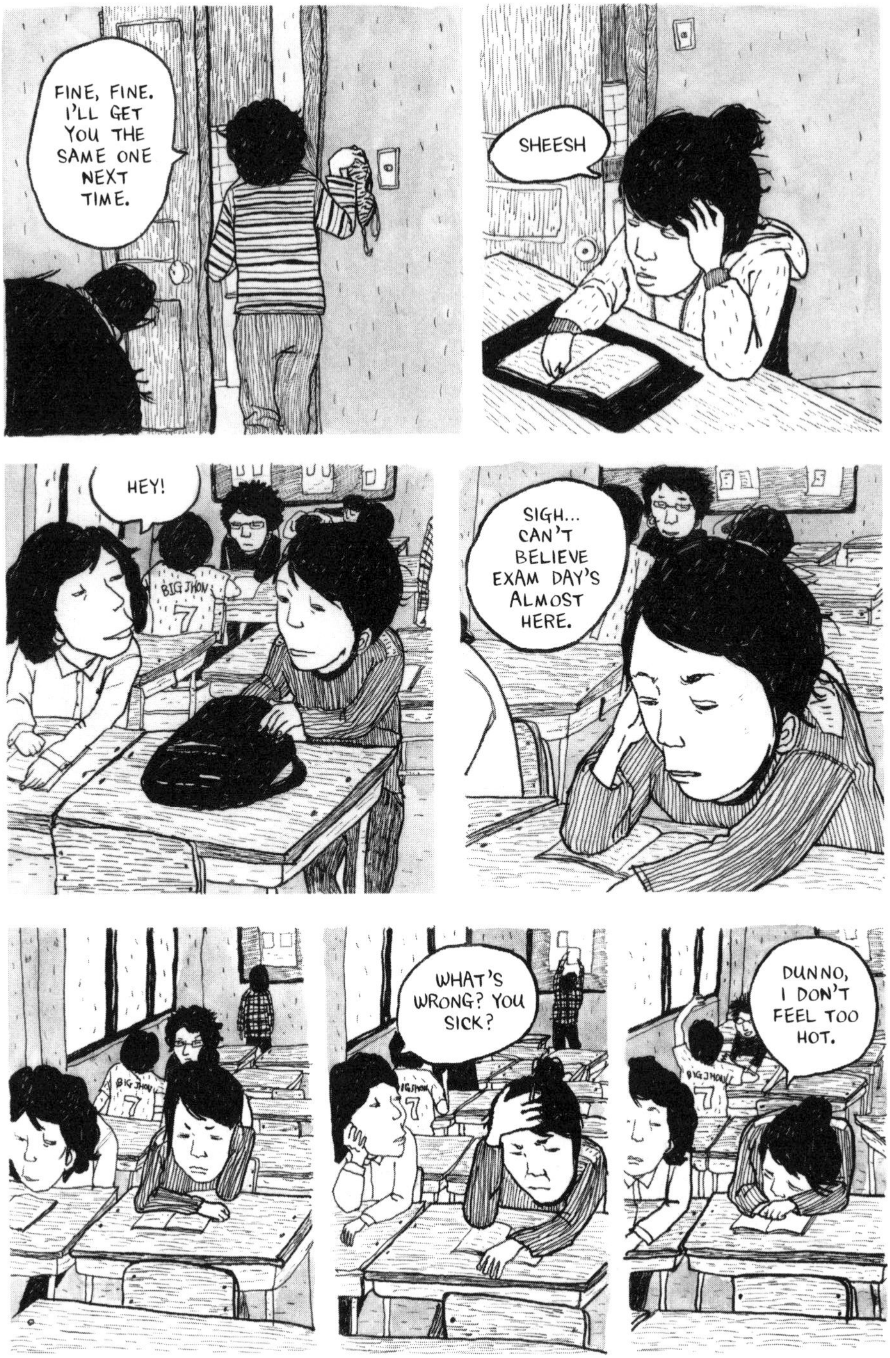
FINE, FINE. I'LL GET YOU THE SAME ONE NEXT TIME.
SHEESH
HEY!
BIG JHON
7
SIGH... CAN'T BELIEVE EXAM DAY'S ALMOST HERE.
BIG JHON
7
WHAT'S WRONG? YOU SICK?
DUNNO, I DON'T FEEL TOO HOT.

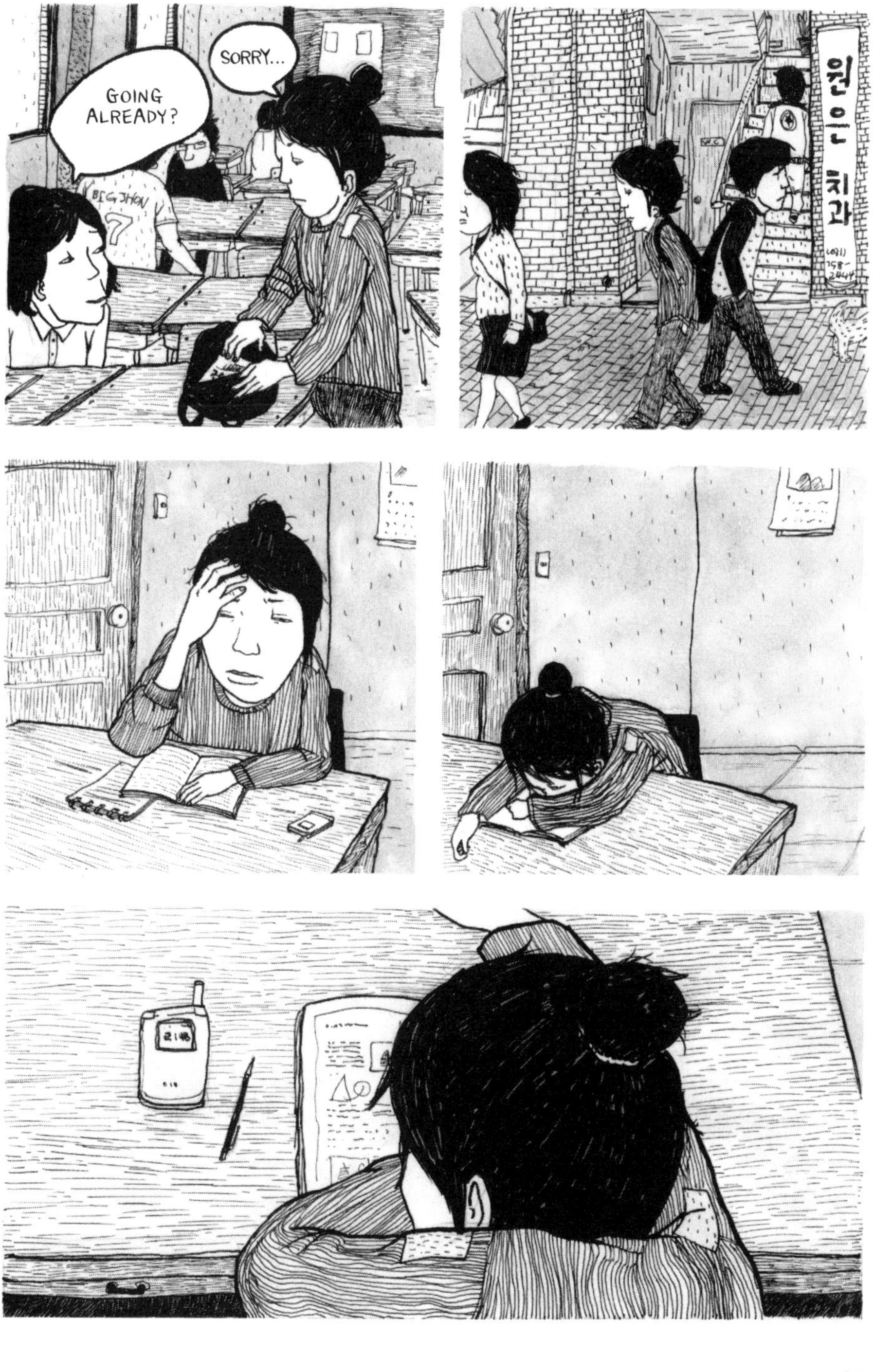
GOING ALREADY?
SORRY...
원은 치과

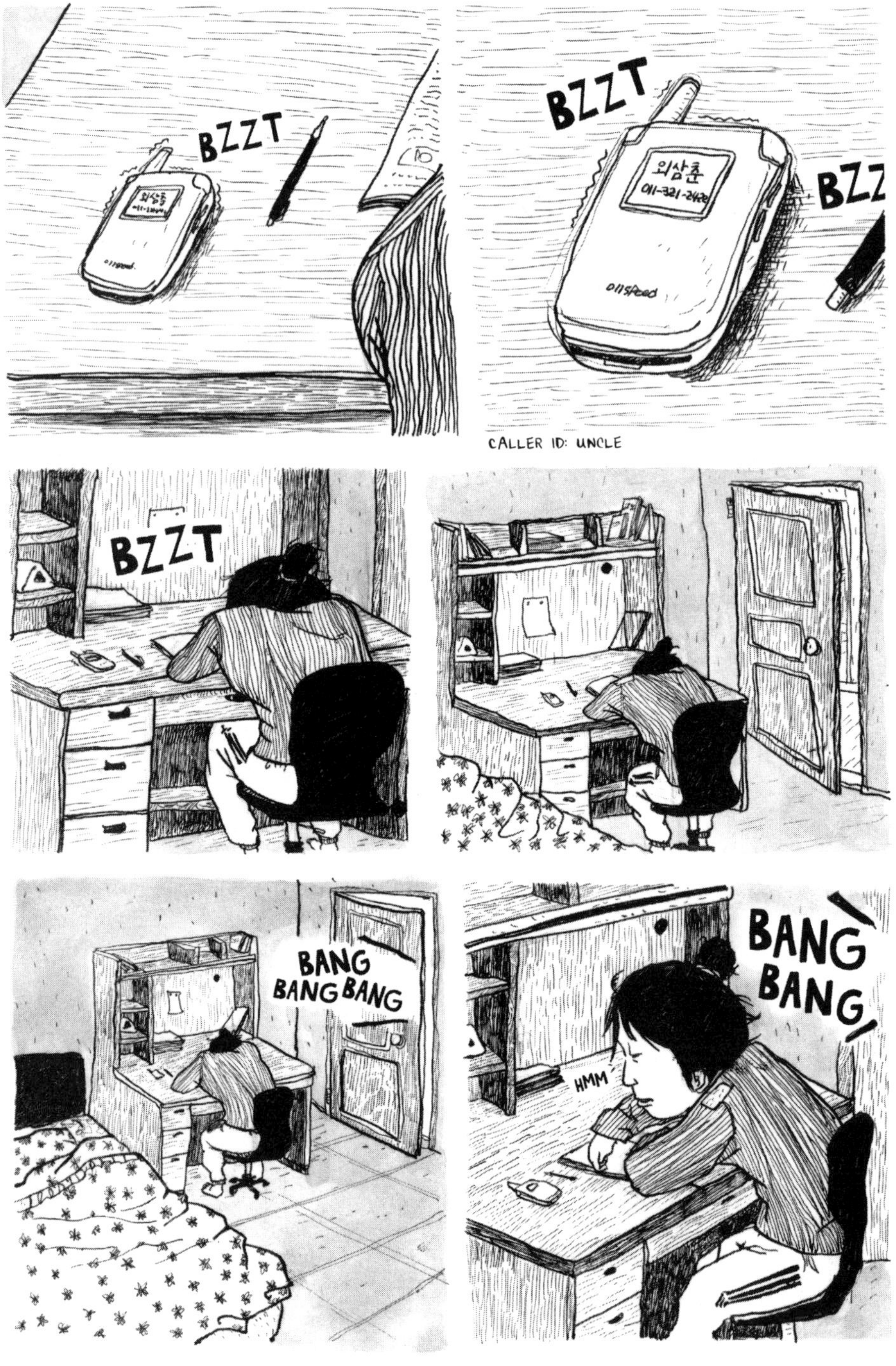
BZZT
BZZT
외삼촌
BZZ
CALLER ID: UNCLE
BZZT
BANG
BANG BANG
BANG
BANG
HMM

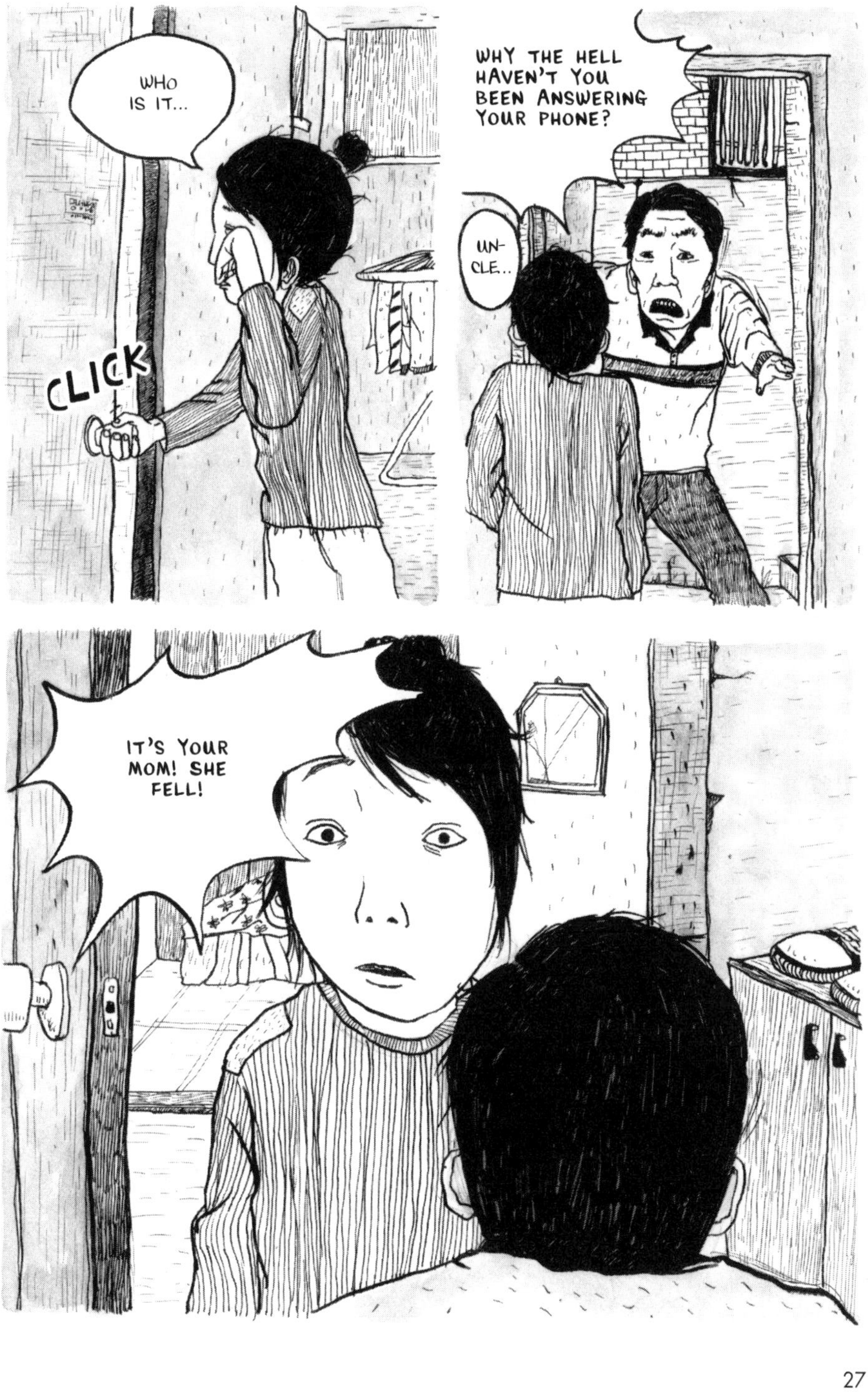
WHO IS IT...
CLICK
WHY THE HELL HAVEN'T YOU BEEN ANSWERING YOUR PHONE?
UN- CLE...
IT'S YOUR MOM! SHE FELL!

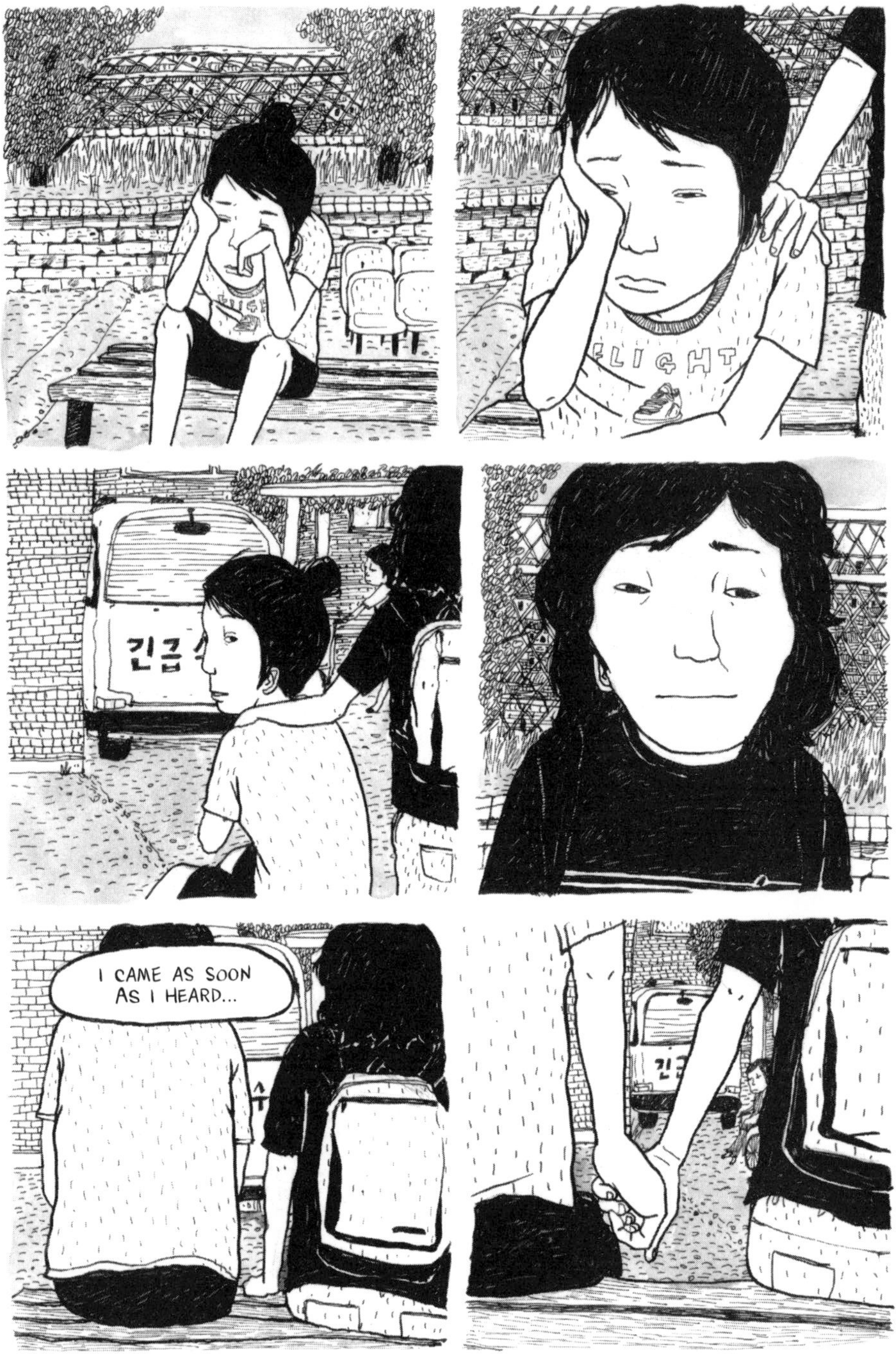
FLIGHT
긴급
I CAME AS SOON AS I HEARD...

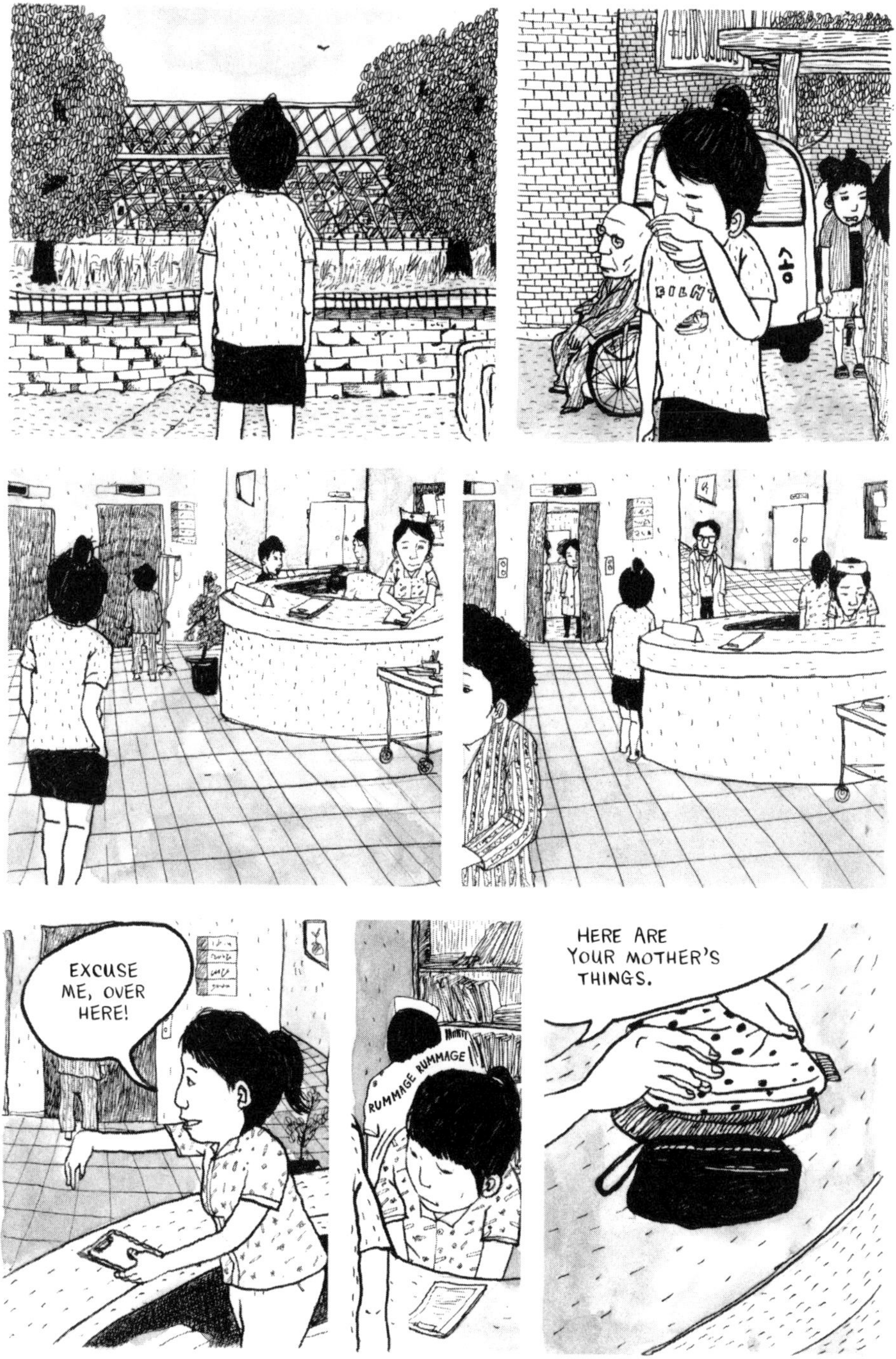
EXCUSE ME, OVER HERE!
RUMMAGE RUMMAGE
HERE ARE YOUR MOTHER'S THINGS.

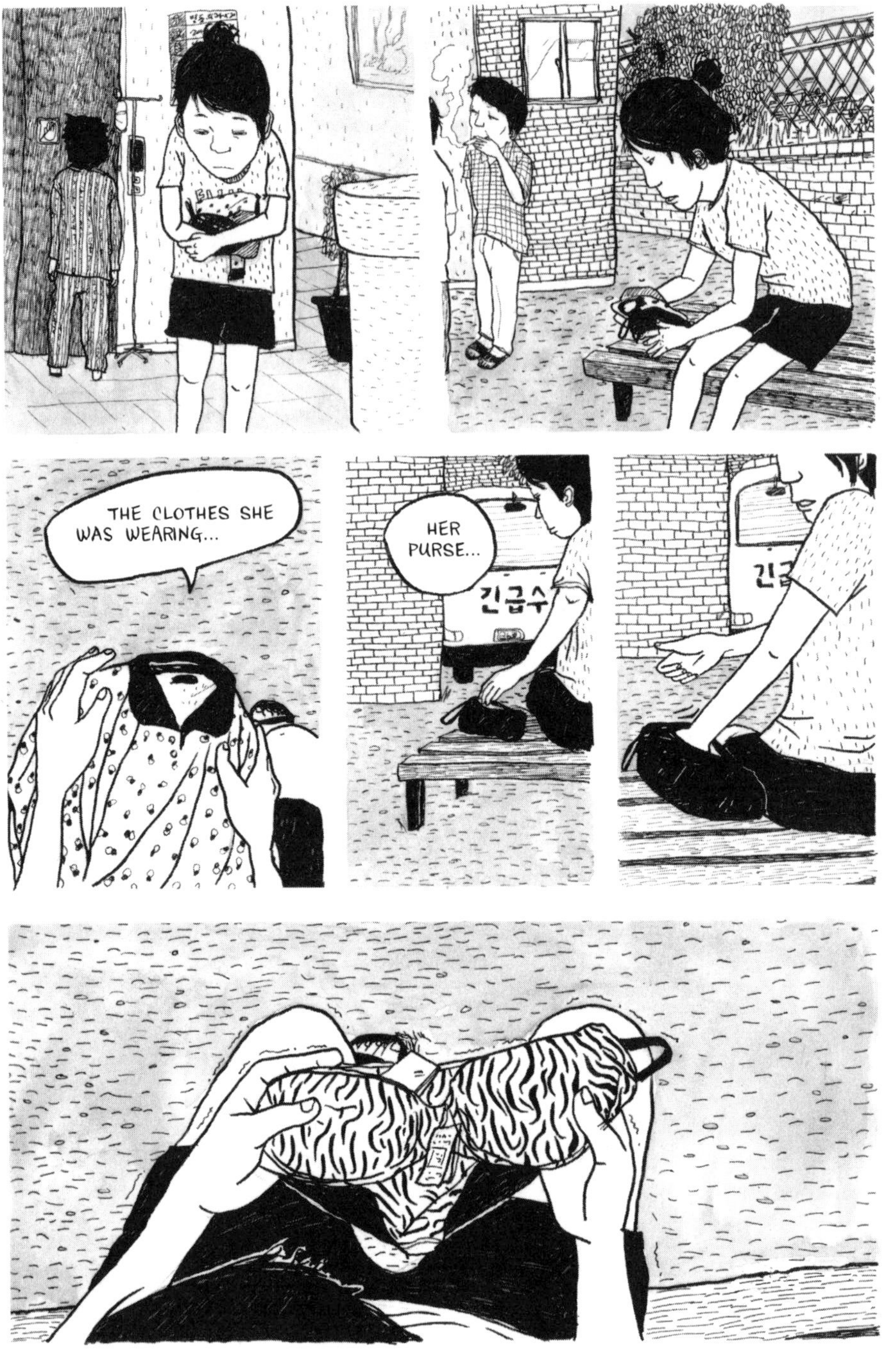
THE CLOTHES SHE WAS WEARING...
HER PURSE...
긴급수

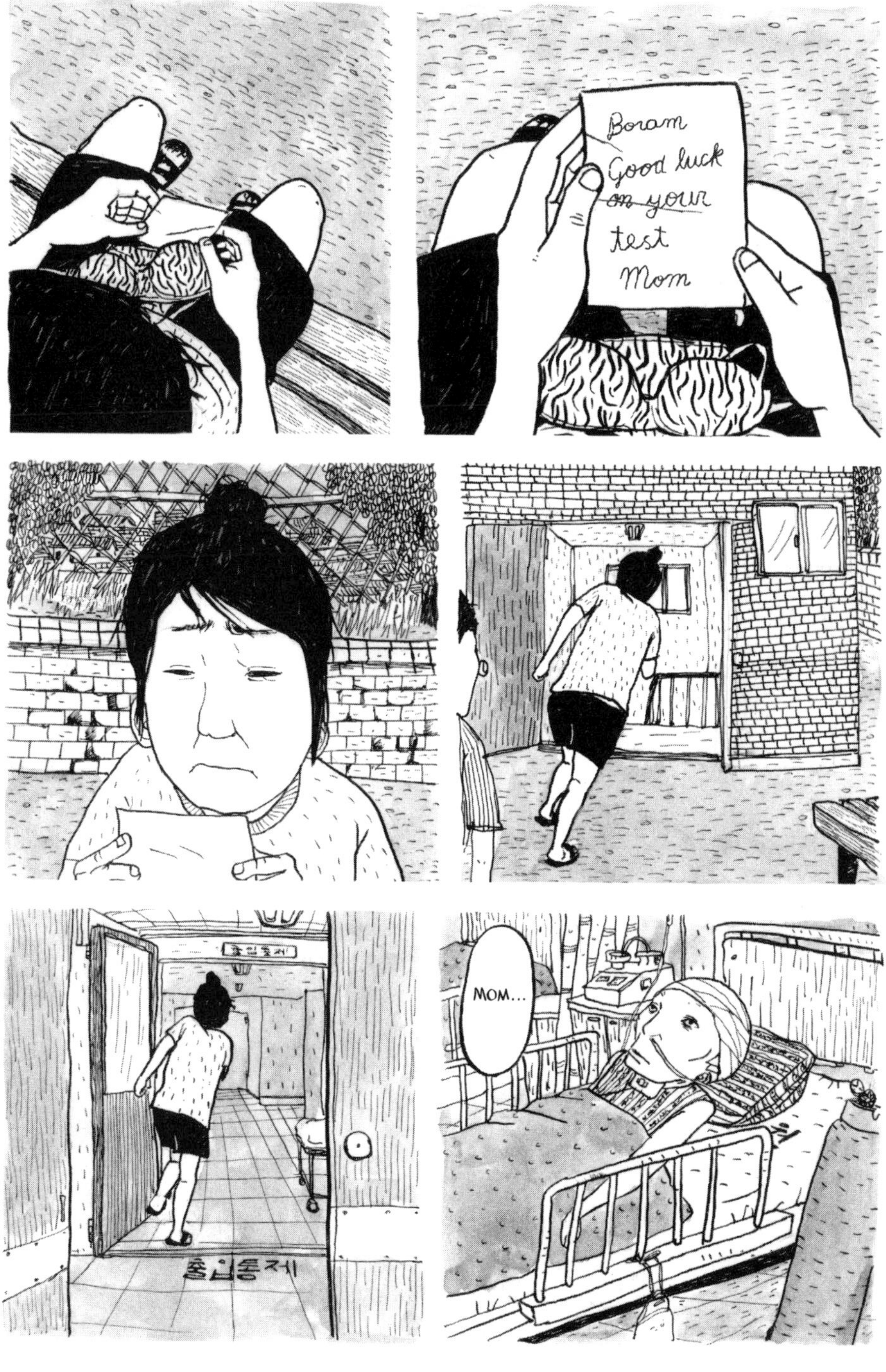
Boram
Good luck
on your
test
Mom
출입통제
MOM...
출입통제

MOM...

I PASSED...

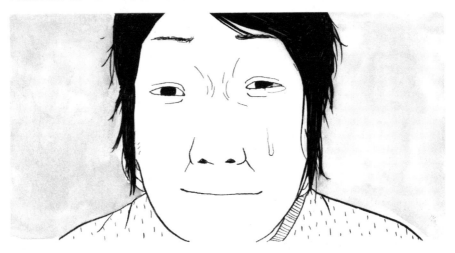

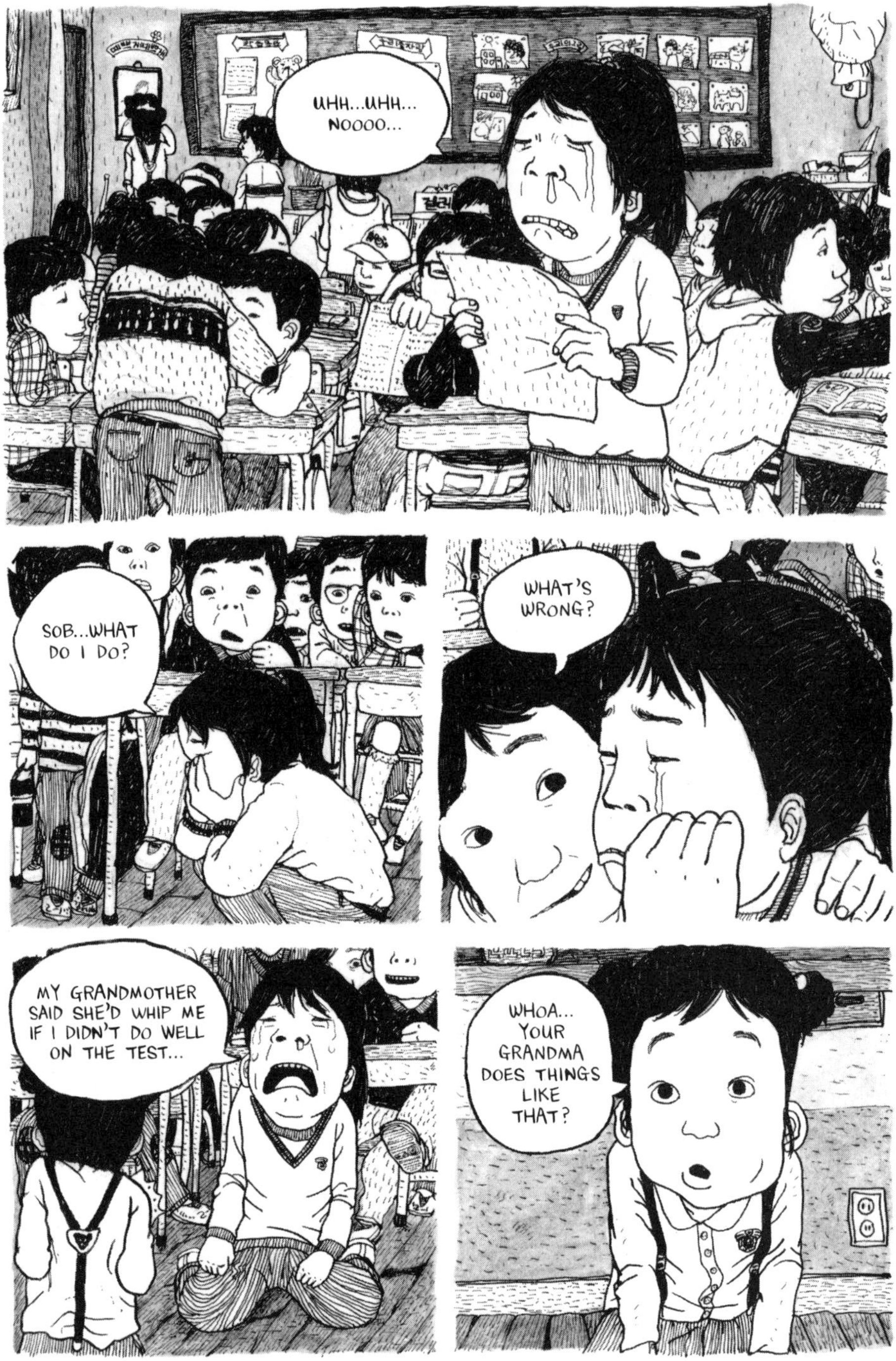
UHH...UHH... NOOOO...
SOB...WHAT DO I DO?
WHAT'S WRONG?
MY GRANDMOTHER SAID SHE'D WHIP ME IF I DIDN'T DO WELL ON THE TEST...
WHOA... YOUR GRANDMA DOES THINGS LIKE THAT?

grandma

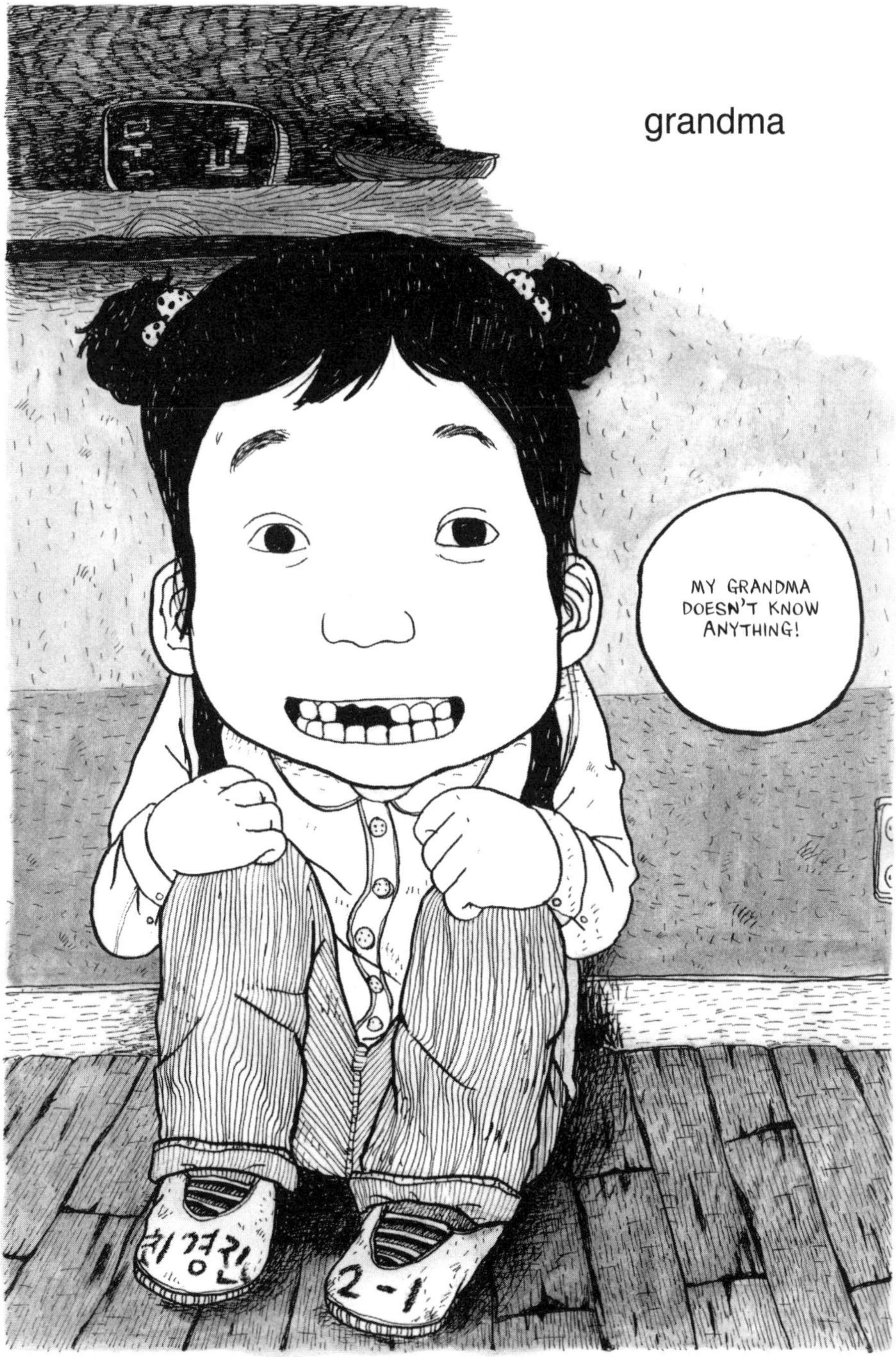
MY GRANDMA DOESN'T KNOW ANYTHING!
최경진
2-1

NAME ON SHOE: CHOI KYUNG-JIN

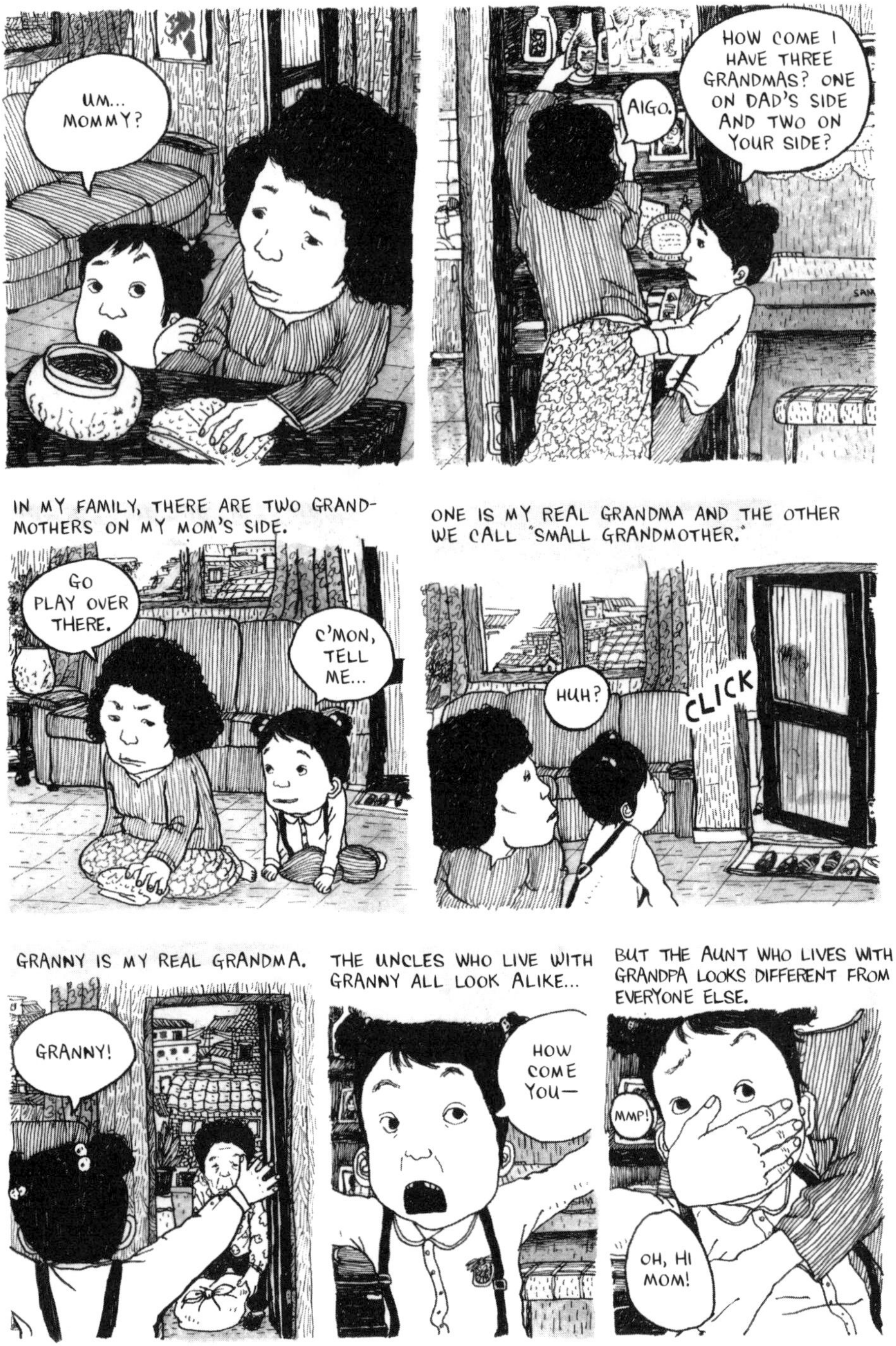

UM... MOMMY?
AIGO.
HOW COME I HAVE THREE GRANDMAS? ONE ON DAD'S SIDE AND TWO ON YOUR SIDE?
IN MY FAMILY, THERE ARE TWO GRAND-MOTHERS ON MY MOM'S SIDE.
GO PLAY OVER THERE.
C'MON, TELL ME...
ONE IS MY REAL GRANDMA AND THE OTHER WE CALL "SMALL GRANDMOTHER."
HUH?
CLICK
GRANNY IS MY REAL GRANDMA.
GRANNY!
THE UNCLES WHO LIVE WITH GRANNY ALL LOOK ALIKE...
HOW COME YOU—
BUT THE AUNT WHO LIVES WITH GRANDPA LOOKS DIFFERENT FROM EVERYONE ELSE.
MMP!
OH, HI MOM!

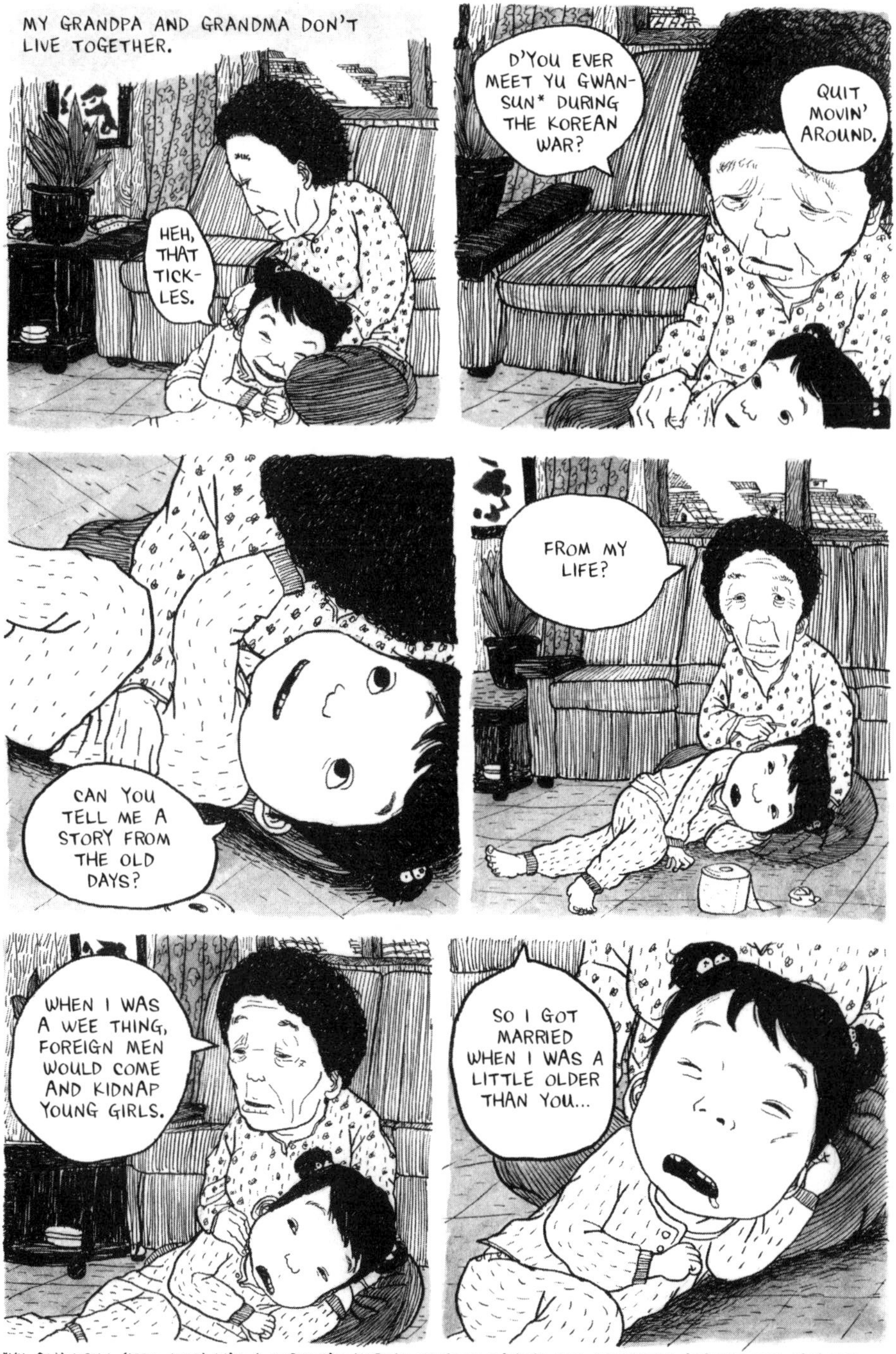
MY GRANDPA AND GRANDMA DON'T LIVE TOGETHER.
HEH, THAT TICK-LES.
D'YOU EVER MEET YU GWAN-SUN* DURING THE KOREAN WAR?
QUIT MOVIN' AROUND.
CAN YOU TELL ME A STORY FROM THE OLD DAYS?
FROM MY LIFE?
WHEN I WAS A WEE THING, FOREIGN MEN WOULD COME AND KIDNAP YOUNG GIRLS.
SO I GOT MARRIED WHEN I WAS A LITTLE OLDER THAN YOU...

*YU GWAN-SUN (1902–1920) WAS A CHRISTIAN KOREAN FREEDOM FIGHTER WHO PROTESTED AGAINST THE JAPANESE OCCUPATION OF KOREA. SHE BECAME A SYMBOL OF KOREA'S FIGHT FOR INDEPENDENCE. SHE WAS NOT, HOWEVER, ALIVE DURING THE KOREAN WAR, WHICH BEGAN ON JUNE 25, 1950 AND ENDED ON JULY 27, 1953.

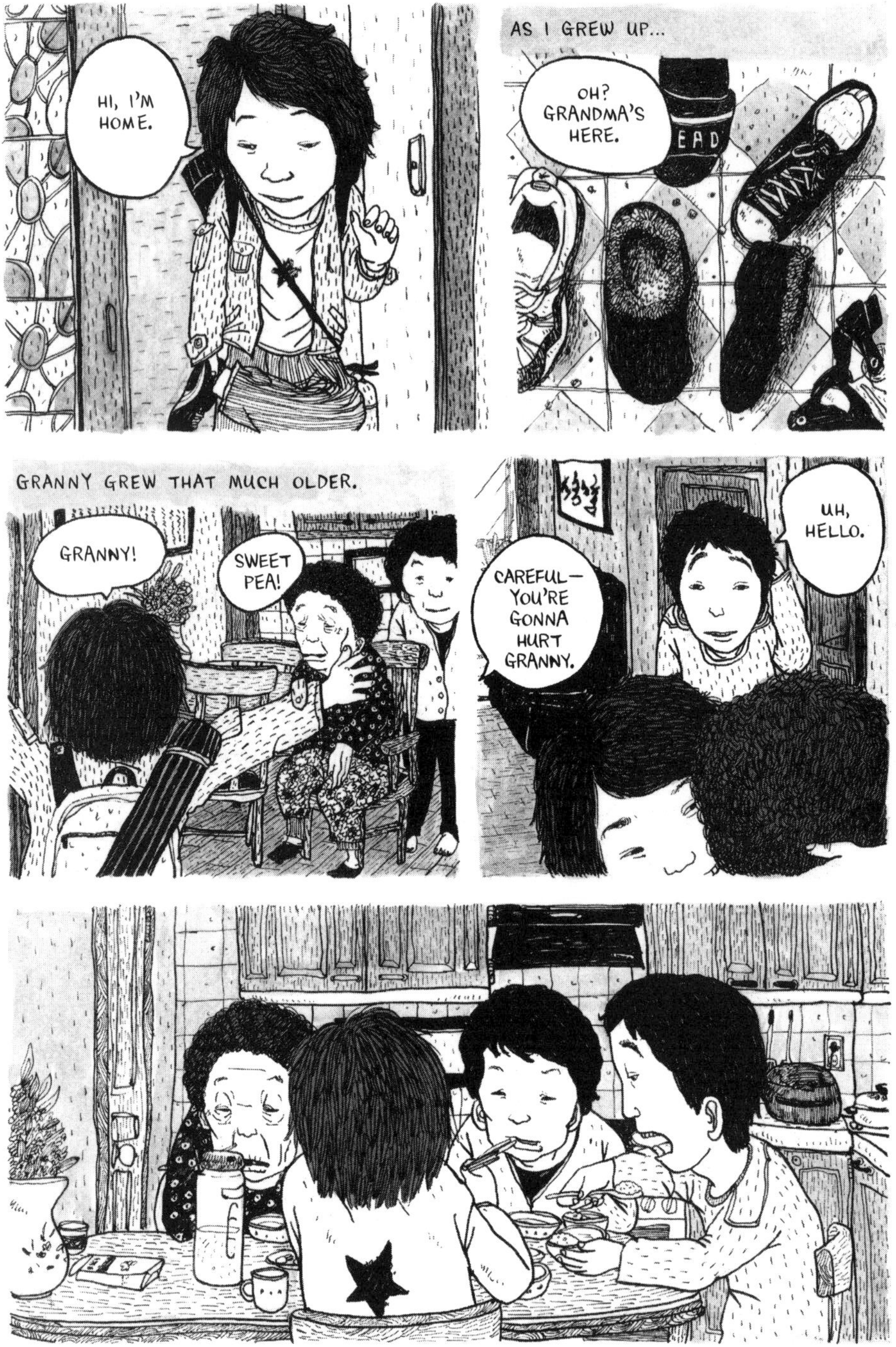
HI, I'M HOME.
AS I GREW UP...
OH? GRANDMA'S HERE.
GRANNY GREW THAT MUCH OLDER.
GRANNY!
SWEET PEA!
UH, HELLO.
CAREFUL— YOU'RE GONNA HURT GRANNY.

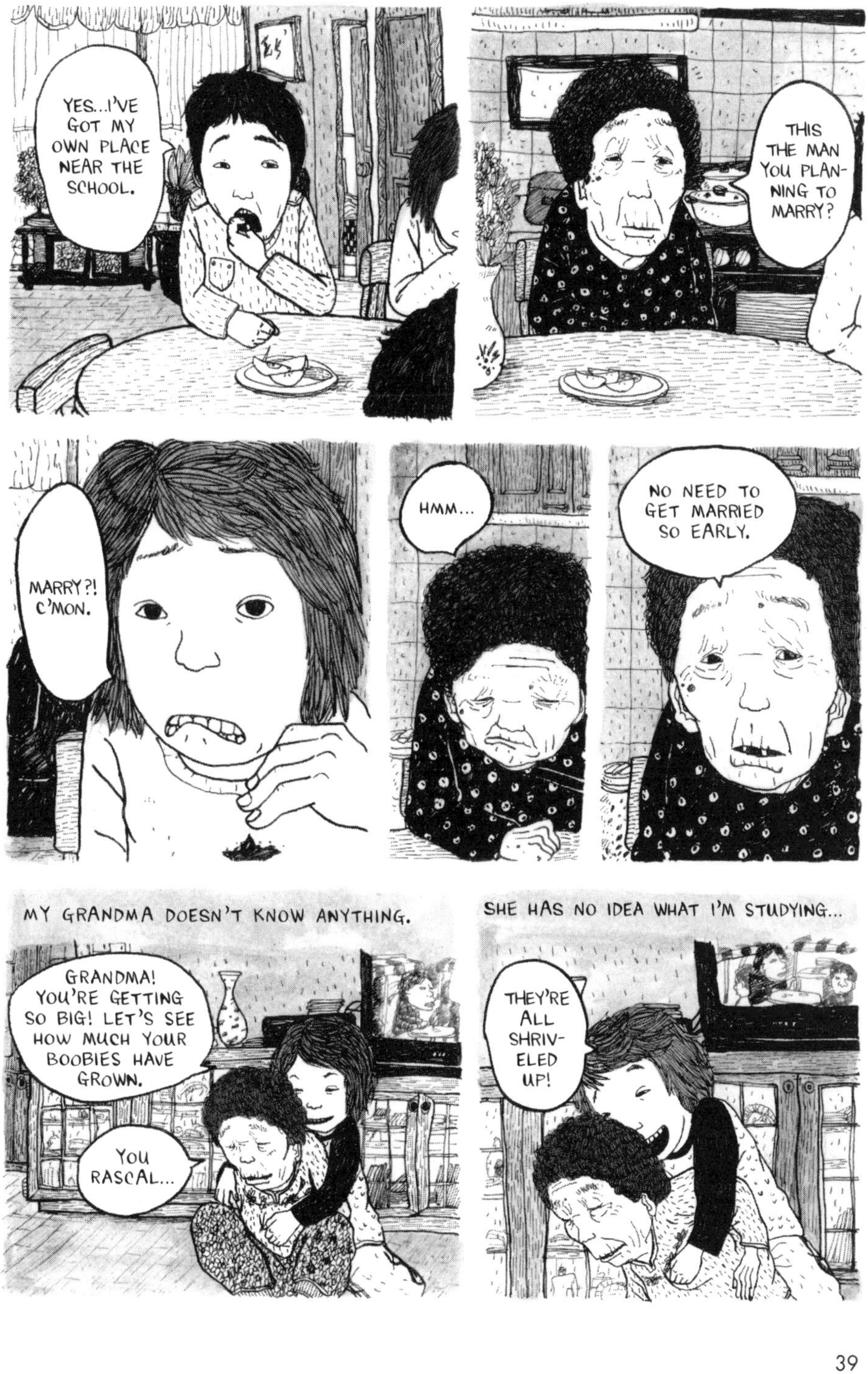

YES...I'VE GOT MY OWN PLACE NEAR THE SCHOOL.
THIS THE MAN YOU PLAN-NING TO MARRY?
MARRY?! C'MON.
HMM...
NO NEED TO GET MARRIED SO EARLY.
MY GRANDMA DOESN'T KNOW ANYTHING.
GRANDMA! YOU'RE GETTING SO BIG! LET'S SEE HOW MUCH YOUR BOOBIES HAVE GROWN.
YOU RASCAL...
SHE HAS NO IDEA WHAT I'M STUDYING...
THEY'RE ALL SHRIV-ELED UP!

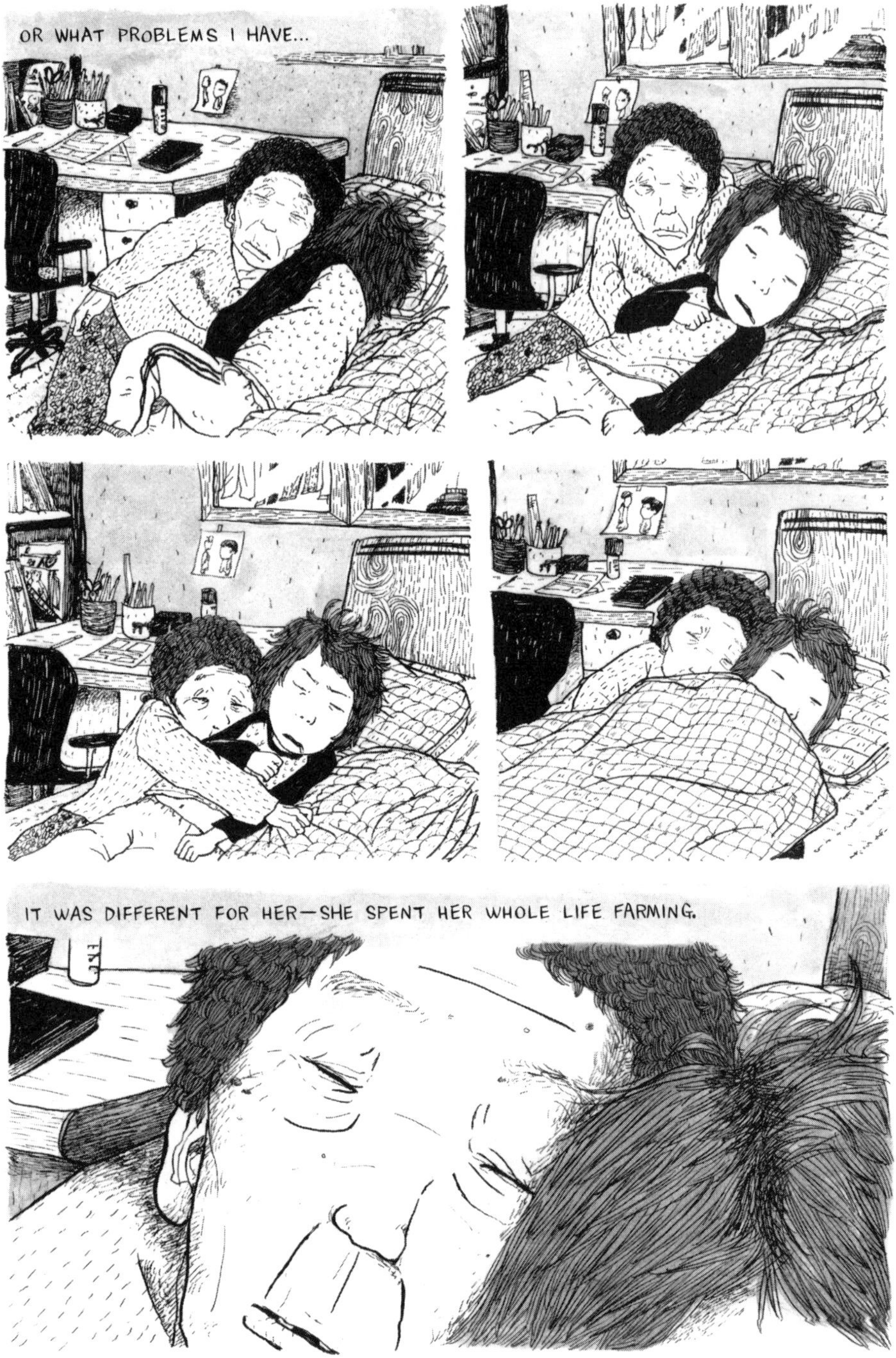
OR WHAT PROBLEMS I HAVE...
IT WAS DIFFERENT FOR HER—SHE SPENT HER WHOLE LIFE FARMING.

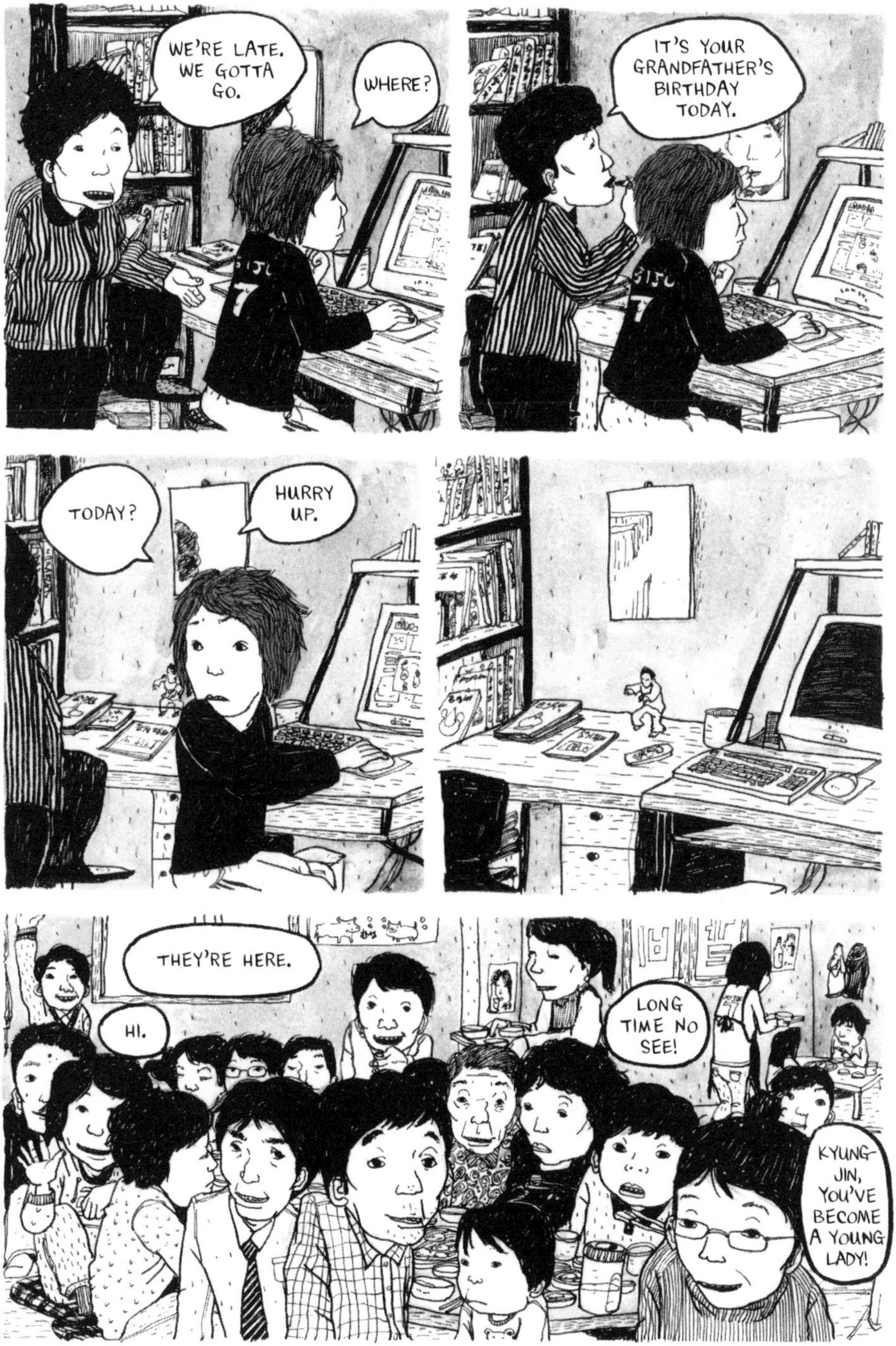

WE'RE LATE. WE GOTTA GO.
WHERE?
IT'S YOUR GRANDFATHER'S BIRTHDAY TODAY.
TODAY?
HURRY UP.
THEY'RE HERE.
HI.
LONG TIME NO SEE!
KYUNG-JIN, YOU'VE BECOME A YOUNG LADY!

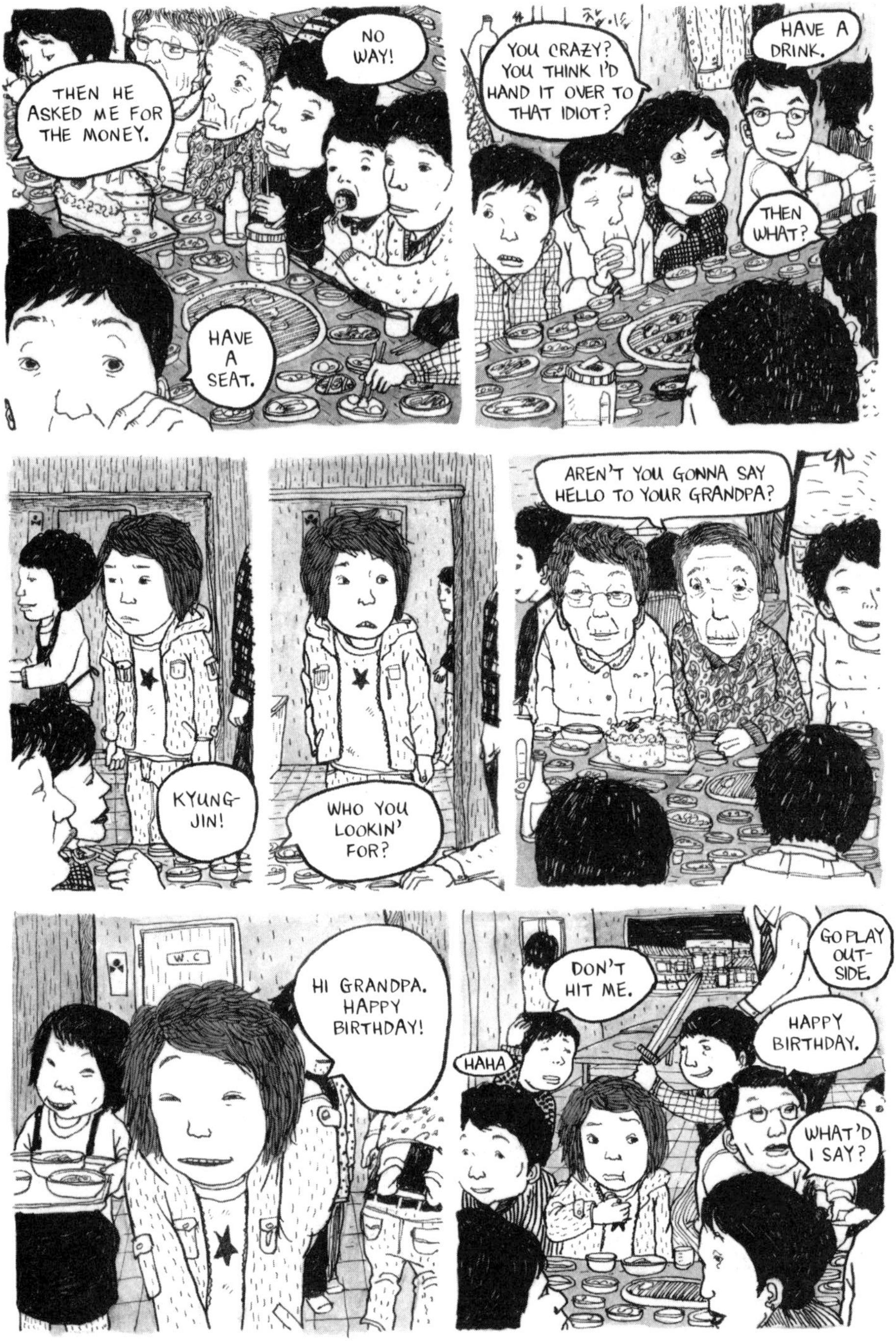
THEN HE ASKED ME FOR THE MONEY.
NO WAY!
HAVE A SEAT.
YOU CRAZY? YOU THINK I'D HAND IT OVER TO THAT IDIOT?
HAVE A DRINK.
THEN WHAT?
KYUNG-JIN!
WHO YOU LOOKIN' FOR?
AREN'T YOU GONNA SAY HELLO TO YOUR GRANDPA?
W.C
HI GRANDPA. HAPPY BIRTHDAY!
DON'T HIT ME.
GO PLAY OUT-SIDE.
HAHA
HAPPY BIRTHDAY.
WHAT'D I SAY?

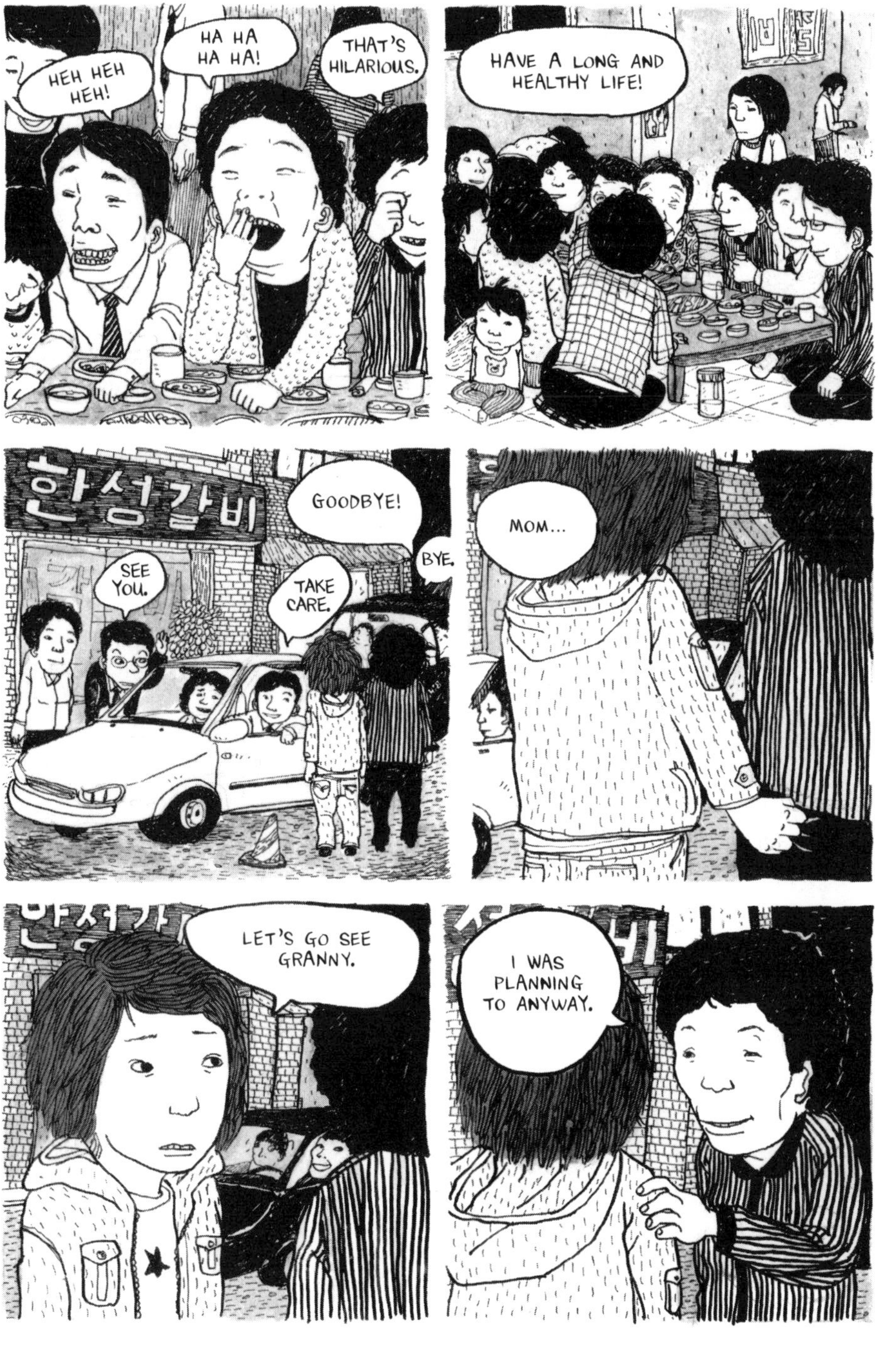
HEH HEH HEH!
HA HA HA HA!
THAT'S HILARIOUS.
HAVE A LONG AND HEALTHY LIFE!
한성갈비
GOODBYE!
SEE YOU.
TAKE CARE.
BYE.
MOM...
LET'S GO SEE GRANNY.
I WAS PLANNING TO ANYWAY.

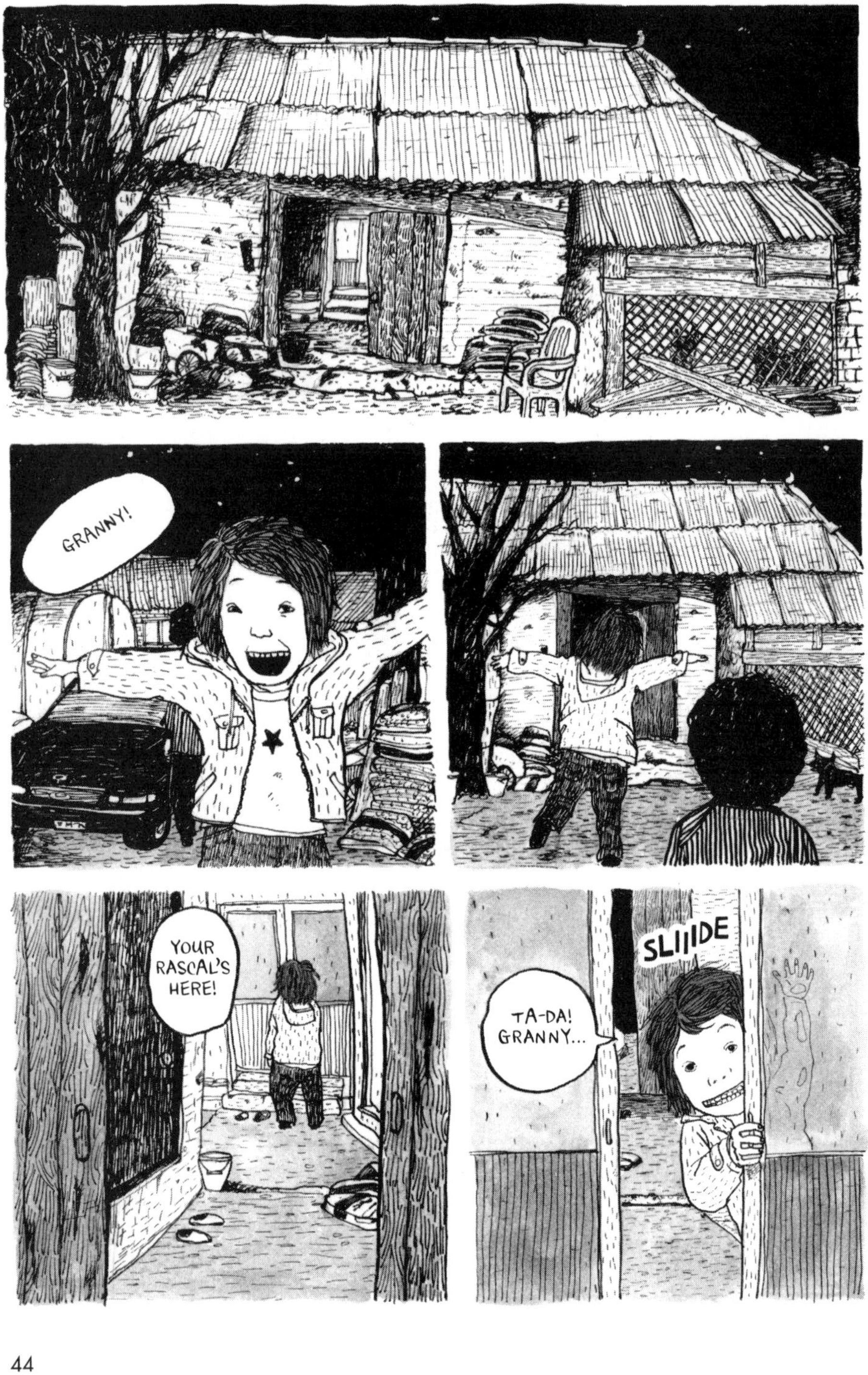
GRANNY!
YOUR RASCAL'S HERE!
SLIIIDE
TA-DA! GRANNY...

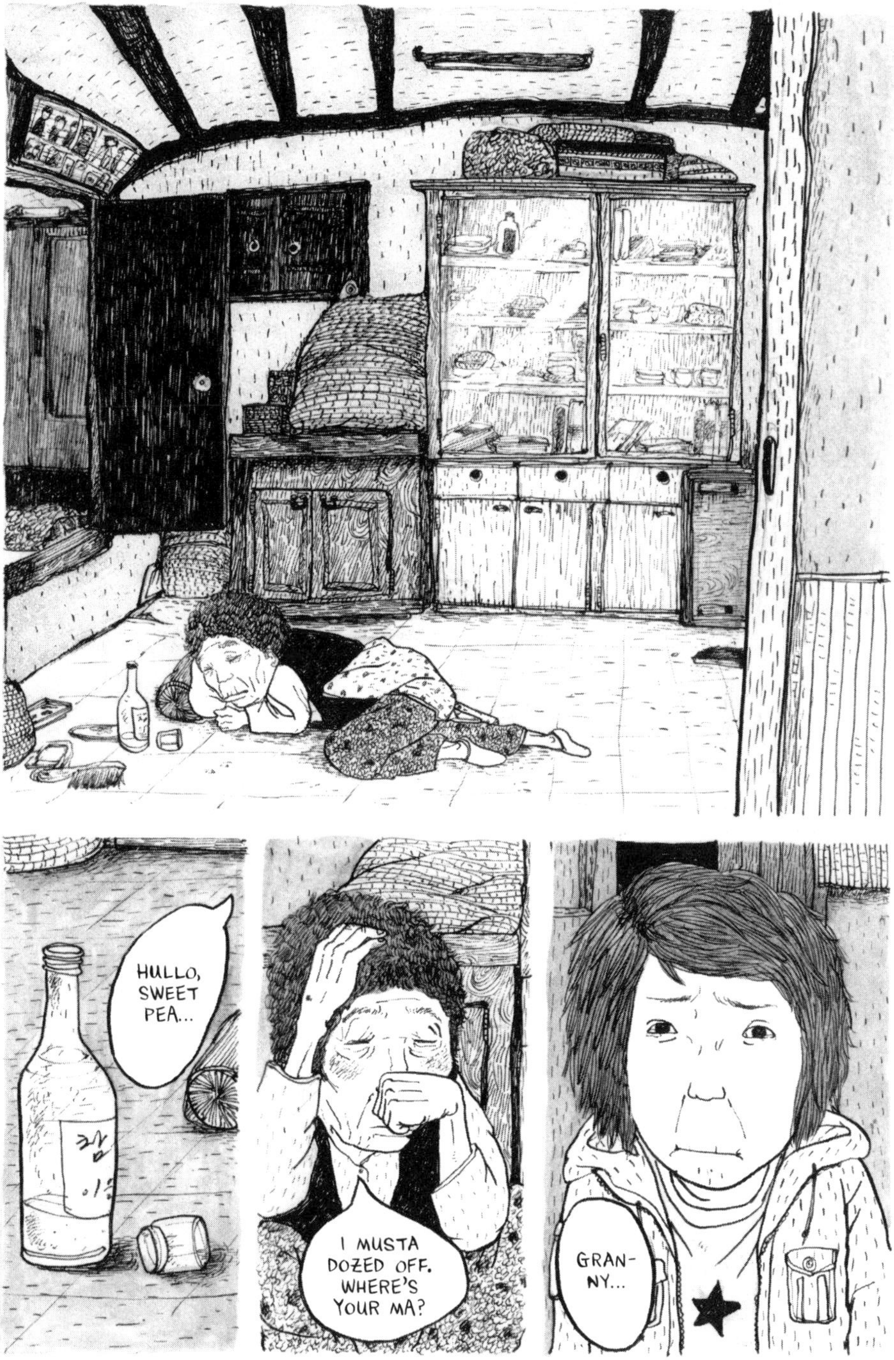
HULLO, SWEET PEA...
I MUSTA DOZED OFF. WHERE'S YOUR MA?
GRAN-NY...

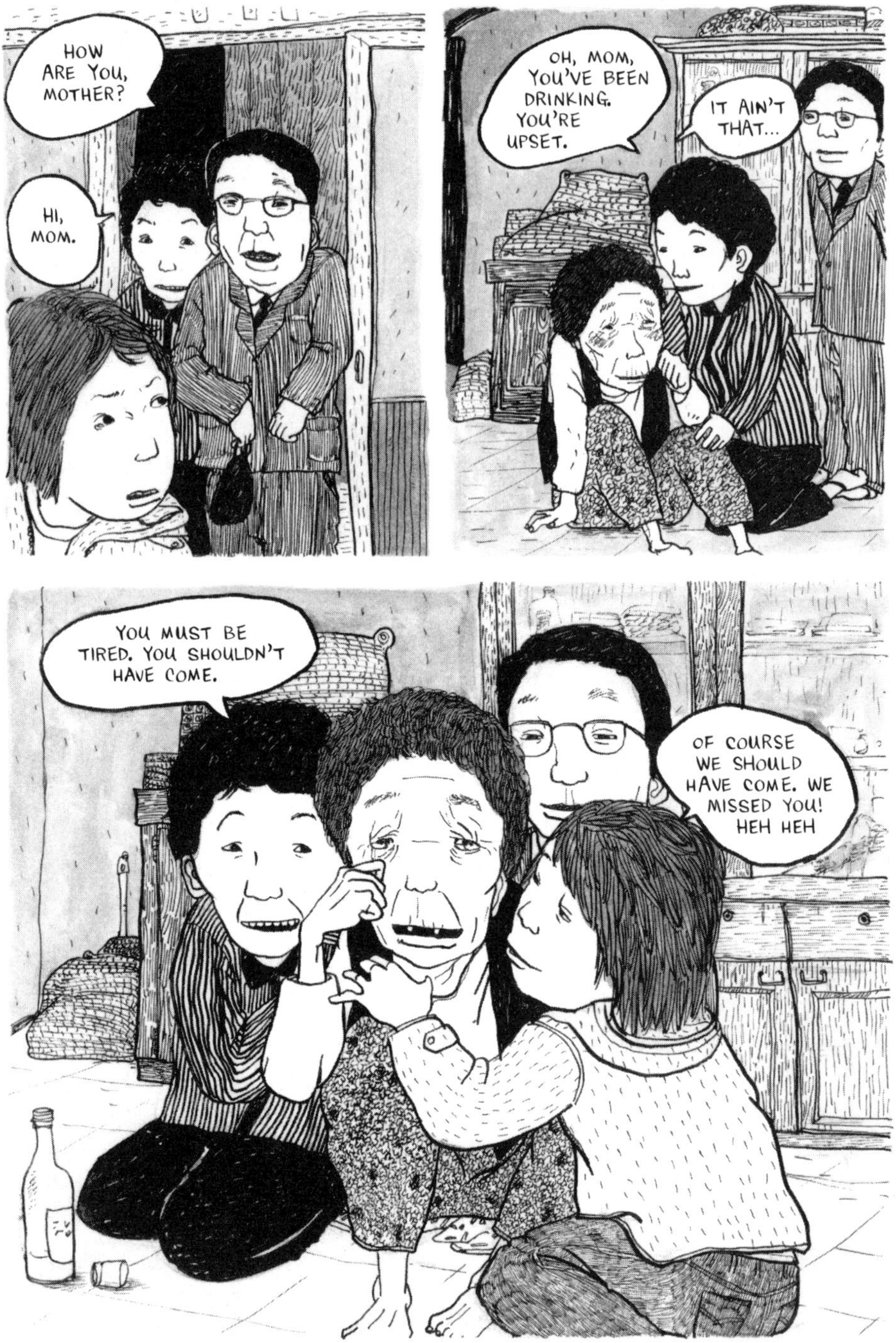
HOW ARE YOU, MOTHER?
HI, MOM.
OH, MOM, YOU'VE BEEN DRINKING. YOU'RE UPSET.
IT AIN'T THAT...
YOU MUST BE TIRED. YOU SHOULDN'T HAVE COME.
OF COURSE WE SHOULD HAVE COME. WE MISSED YOU! HEH HEH

i'm sorry

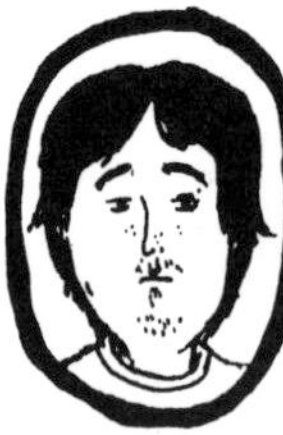

YONGDEUK IS MY BOYFRIEND. RECENTLY WE STARTED SHARING A STUDIO NEAR MY APARTMENT.

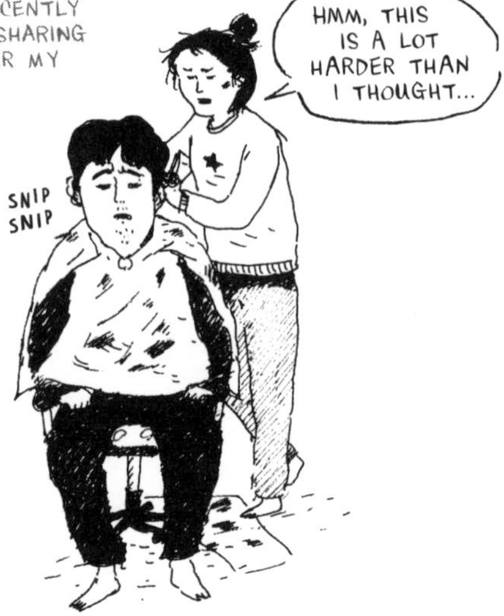
HMM, THIS IS A LOT HARDER THAN I THOUGHT...
SNIP SNIP

HE'S BEEN FEELING DOWN THESE DAYS AND HIS HAIR IS GETTING LONG. I THOUGHT IT'D BE NICE TO CHEER HIM UP AND TRY SOMETHING NEW, SO I DECIDED TO GIVE HIM A HAIRCUT.

HE LOOKED IN THE MIRROR HALFWAY THROUGH...

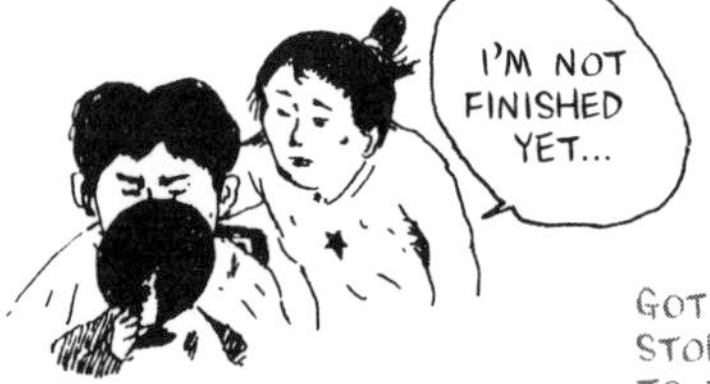
I'M NOT FINISHED YET...

GOT ANGRY AND STORMED BACK TO THE STUDIO.

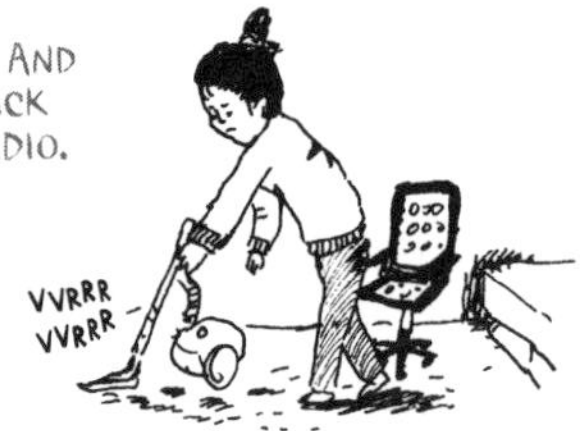
VVRRR VVRRR

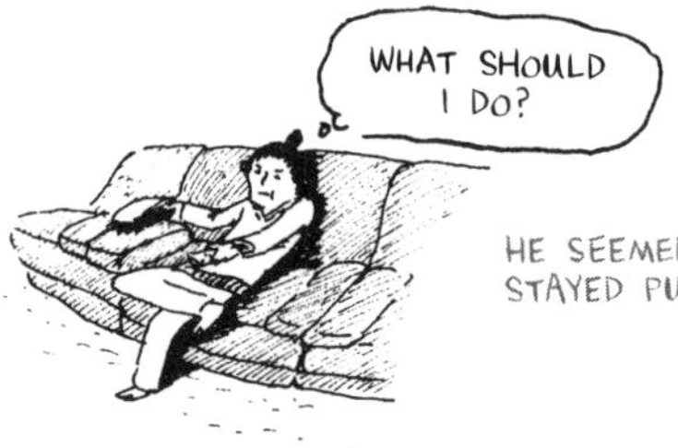
WHAT SHOULD I DO?

HE SEEMED REALLY ANGRY, SO I STAYED PUT FOR ABOUT TWO HOURS.

WHEN I GOT TO THE STUDIO, HE'D JUST WOKEN UP AND WAS HAVING A SMOKE. HE WAS STILL PISSED.

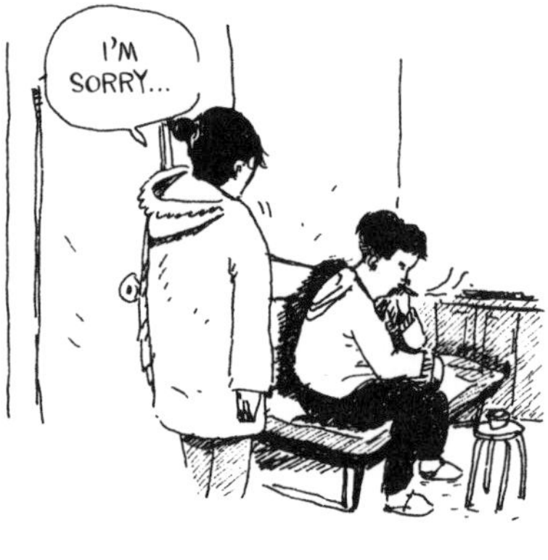
I'M SORRY...

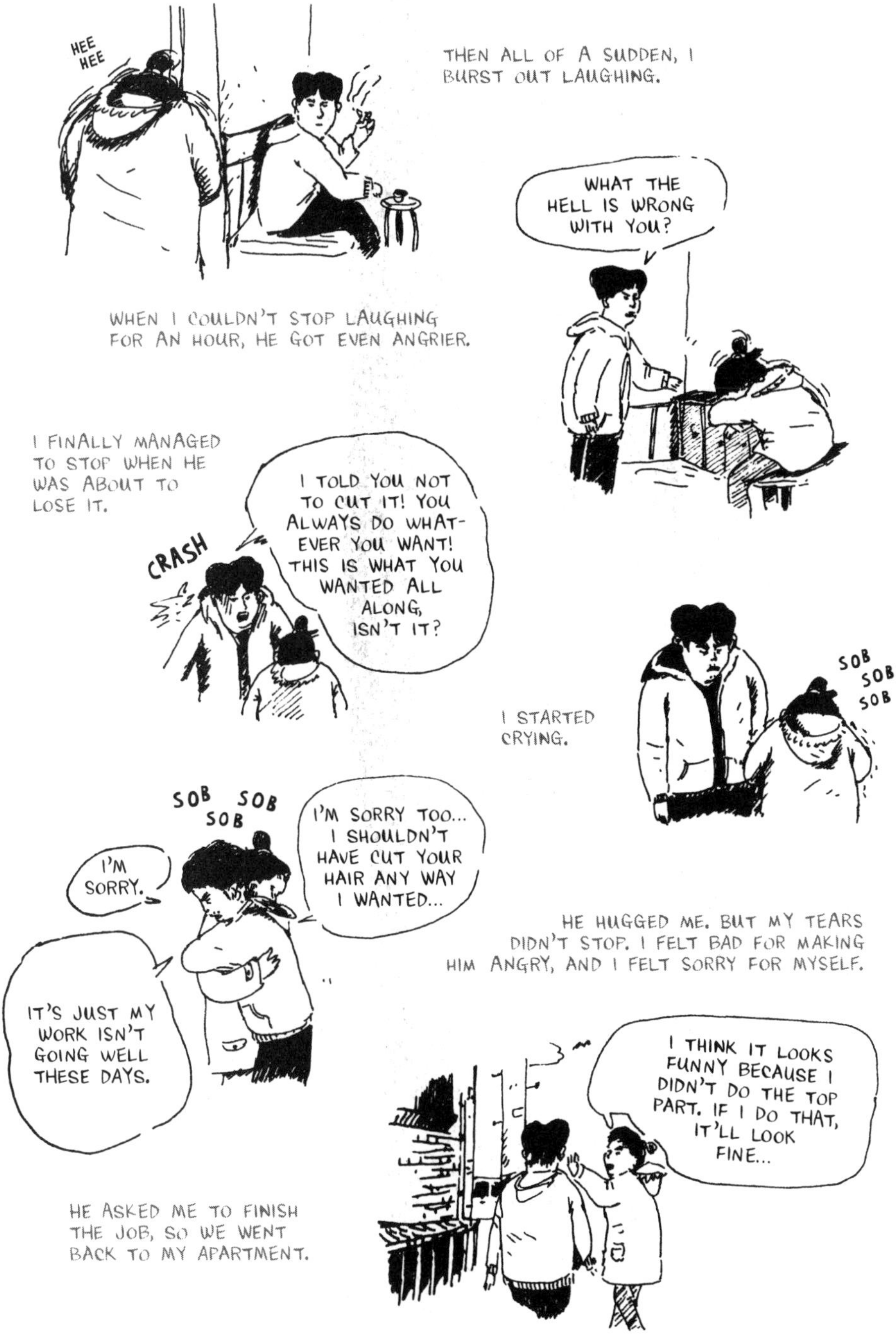
HEE HEE
THEN ALL OF A SUDDEN, I BURST OUT LAUGHING.
WHAT THE HELL IS WRONG WITH YOU?
WHEN I COULDN'T STOP LAUGHING FOR AN HOUR, HE GOT EVEN ANGRIER.
I FINALLY MANAGED TO STOP WHEN HE WAS ABOUT TO LOSE IT.
CRASH
I TOLD YOU NOT TO CUT IT! YOU ALWAYS DO WHAT-EVER YOU WANT! THIS IS WHAT YOU WANTED ALL ALONG, ISN'T IT?
I STARTED CRYING.
SOB SOB SOB
SOB SOB SOB
I'M SORRY.
I'M SORRY TOO... I SHOULDN'T HAVE CUT YOUR HAIR ANY WAY I WANTED...
IT'S JUST MY WORK ISN'T GOING WELL THESE DAYS.
HE HUGGED ME. BUT MY TEARS DIDN'T STOP. I FELT BAD FOR MAKING HIM ANGRY, AND I FELT SORRY FOR MYSELF.
HE ASKED ME TO FINISH THE JOB, SO WE WENT BACK TO MY APARTMENT.
I THINK IT LOOKS FUNNY BECAUSE I DIDN'T DO THE TOP PART. IF I DO THAT, IT'LL LOOK FINE...

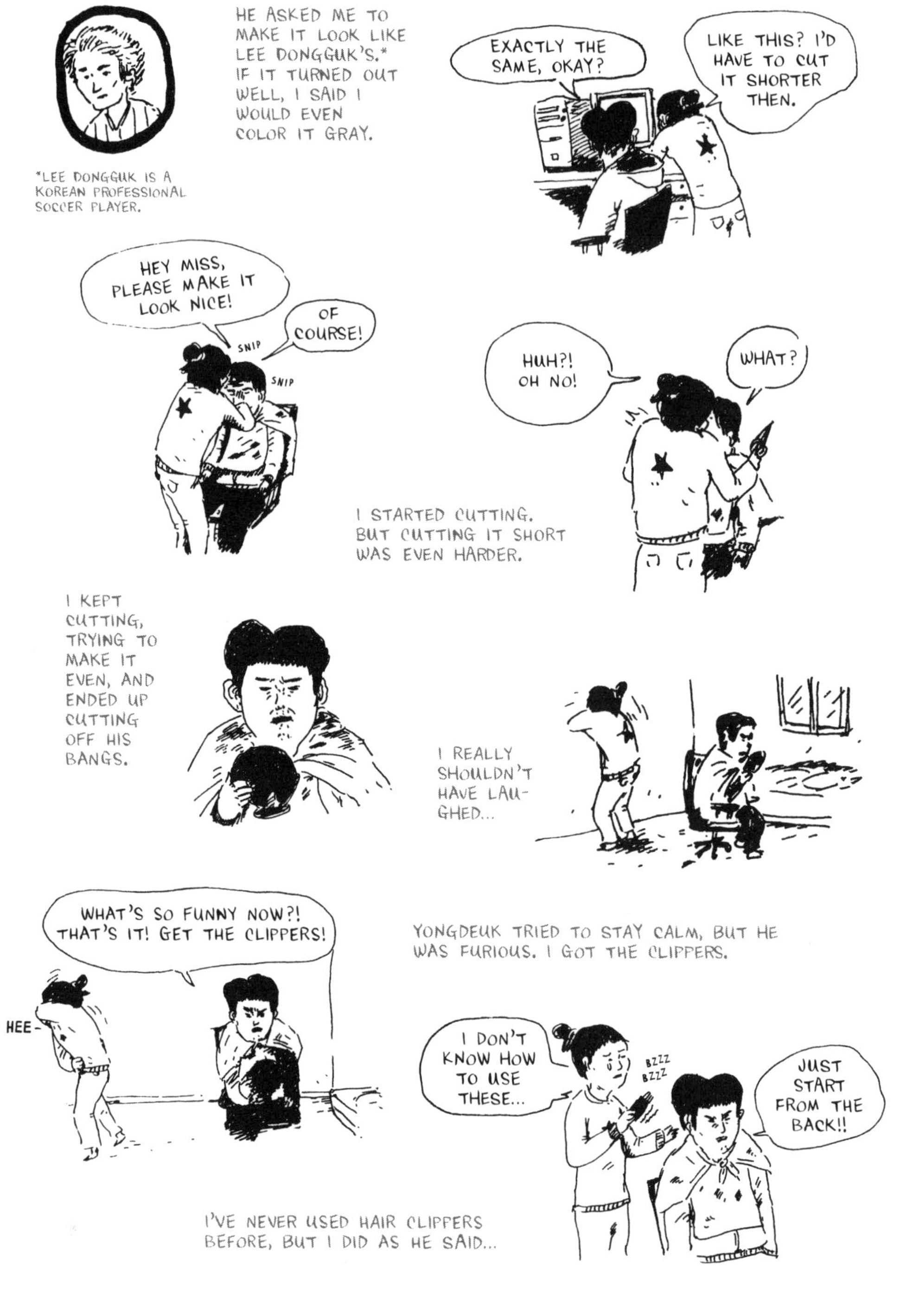
*LEE DONGGUK IS A KOREAN PROFESSIONAL SOCCER PLAYER.
HE ASKED ME TO MAKE IT LOOK LIKE LEE DONGGUK'S.* IF IT TURNED OUT WELL, I SAID I WOULD EVEN COLOR IT GRAY.
EXACTLY THE SAME, OKAY?
LIKE THIS? I'D HAVE TO CUT IT SHORTER THEN.
HEY MISS, PLEASE MAKE IT LOOK NICE!
OF COURSE!
SNIP
SNIP
I STARTED CUTTING. BUT CUTTING IT SHORT WAS EVEN HARDER.
HUH?! OH NO!
WHAT?
I KEPT CUTTING, TRYING TO MAKE IT EVEN, AND ENDED UP CUTTING OFF HIS BANGS.
I REALLY SHOULDN'T HAVE LAU-GHED...
WHAT'S SO FUNNY NOW?! THAT'S IT! GET THE CLIPPERS!
HEE-
YONGDEUK TRIED TO STAY CALM, BUT HE WAS FURIOUS. I GOT THE CLIPPERS.
I DON'T KNOW HOW TO USE THESE...
BZZZ BZZZ
JUST START FROM THE BACK!!
I'VE NEVER USED HAIR CLIPPERS BEFORE, BUT I DID AS HE SAID...

BZZZ — BZZZ —

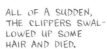

OH SHIT!

BZZZ —

CLUNK!

ACK!

ALL OF A SUDDEN, THE CLIPPERS SWALLOWED UP SOME HAIR AND DIED.

OH NO! I THINK IT'S THE BATTERY...

TACK TACK

WHAT DO YOU MEAN "OH NO?" WE HAVE TO GO TO THE SALON!

IN THE END, I FOUND THE CHARGER AND WAS ABLE TO SHAVE THE REST OF HIS HAIR.

—RUSTLE

ZZZ —

ZZZ —

I JUST FEEL BAD FOR YONGDEUK, THAT'S ALL.

life

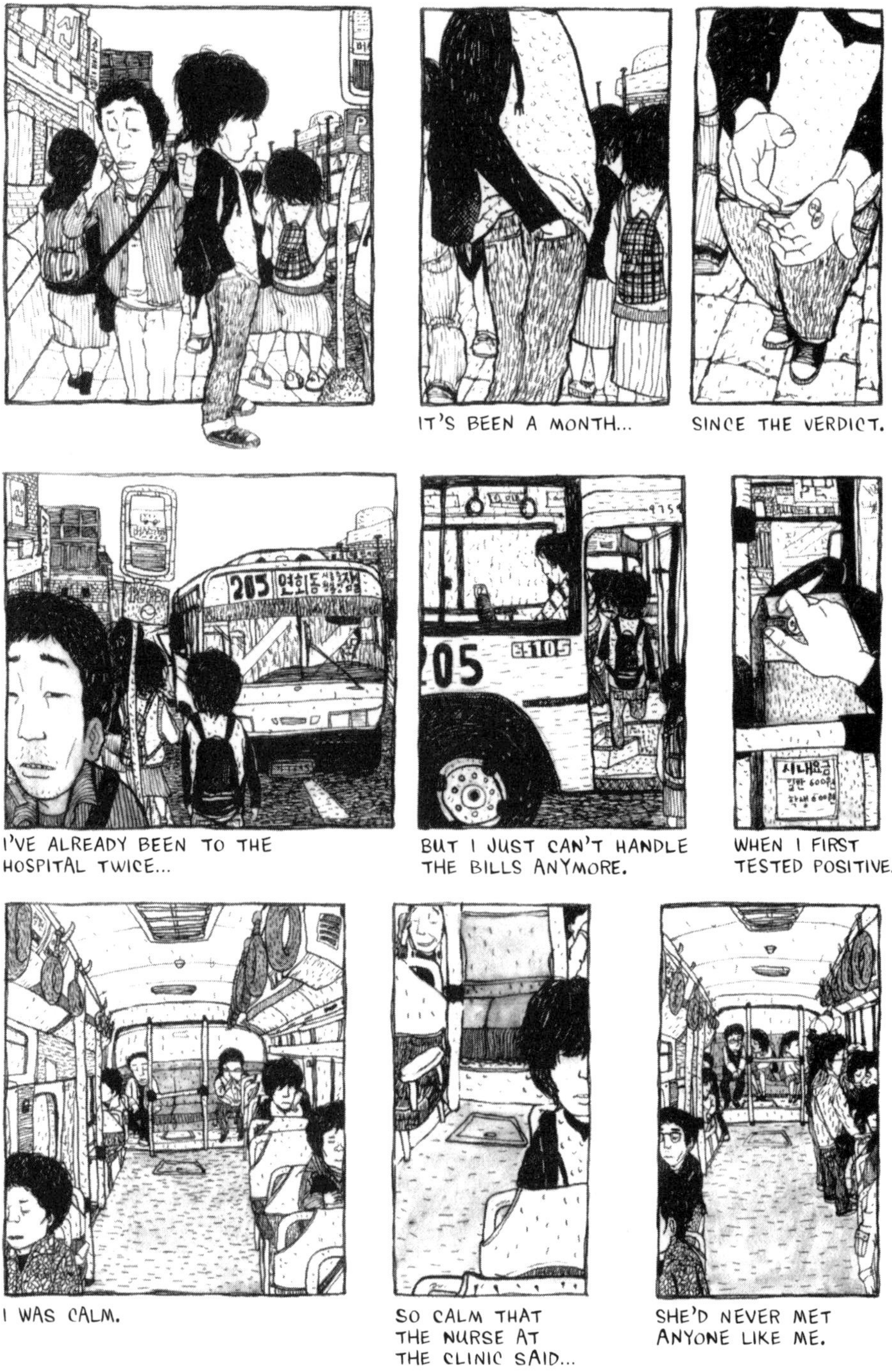
IT'S BEEN A MONTH...
SINCE THE VERDICT.
I'VE ALREADY BEEN TO THE HOSPITAL TWICE...
BUT I JUST CAN'T HANDLE THE BILLS ANYMORE.
WHEN I FIRST TESTED POSITIVE...
I WAS CALM.
SO CALM THAT THE NURSE AT THE CLINIC SAID...
SHE'D NEVER MET ANYONE LIKE ME.

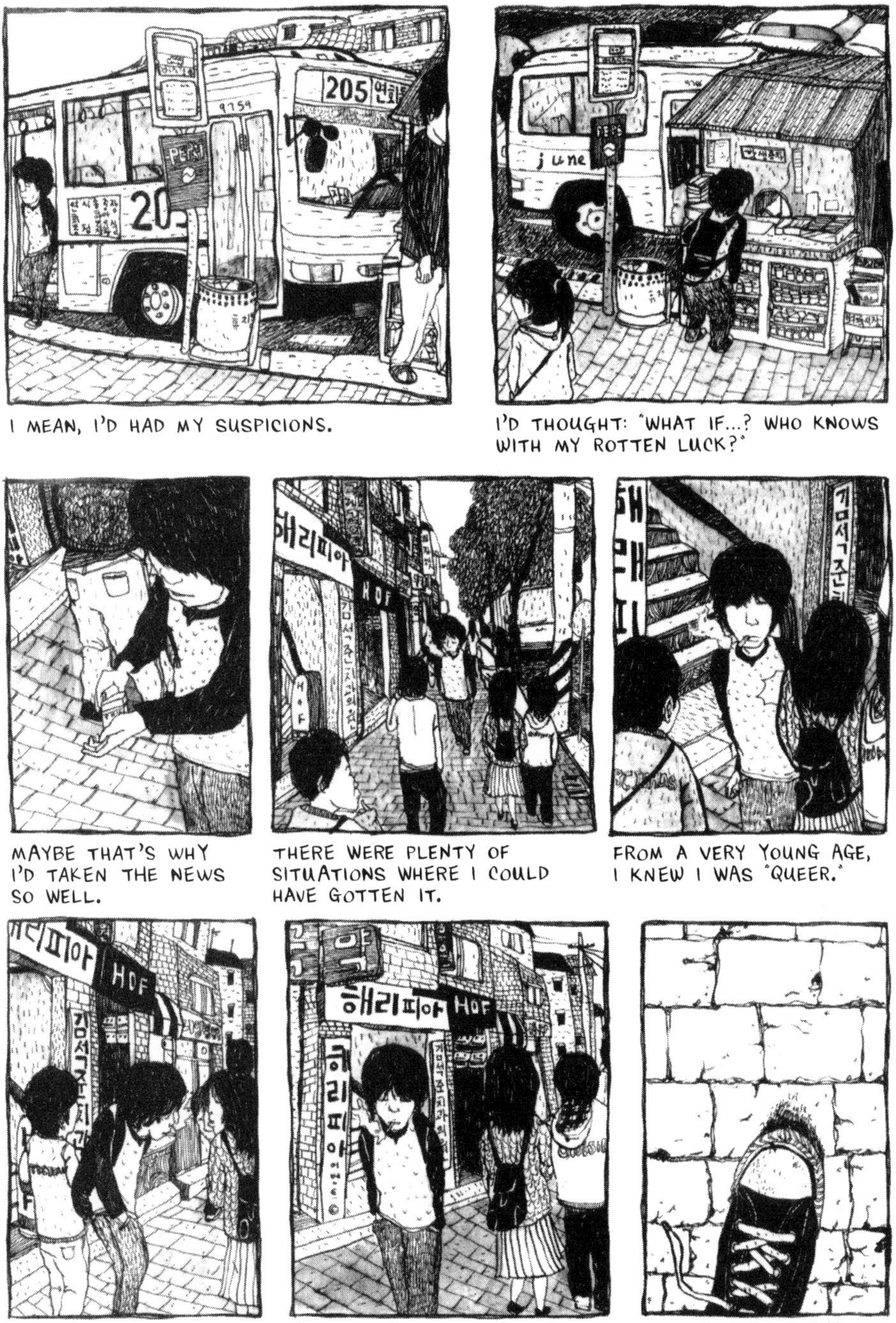
I MEAN, I'D HAD MY SUSPICIONS.
I'D THOUGHT: "WHAT IF...? WHO KNOWS WITH MY ROTTEN LUCK?"
MAYBE THAT'S WHY I'D TAKEN THE NEWS SO WELL.
THERE WERE PLENTY OF SITUATIONS WHERE I COULD HAVE GOTTEN IT.
FROM A VERY YOUNG AGE, I KNEW I WAS "QUEER."
I DIDN'T HAVE ANY PROBLEMS...
ACCEPTING MY SEXUALITY.
I LIVED RECKLESSLY.

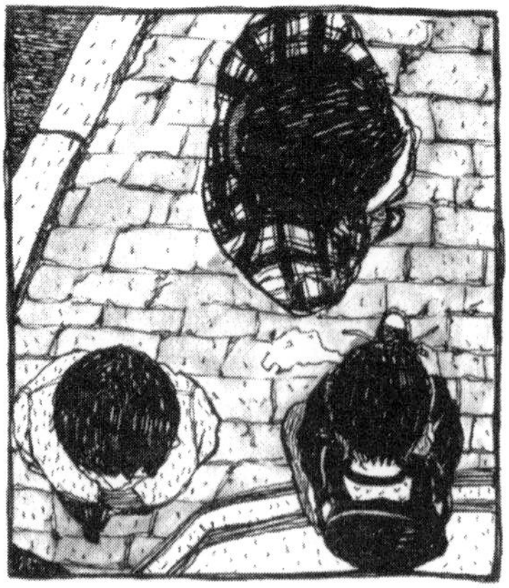

INSTEAD OF A STEADY RELATIONSHIP...

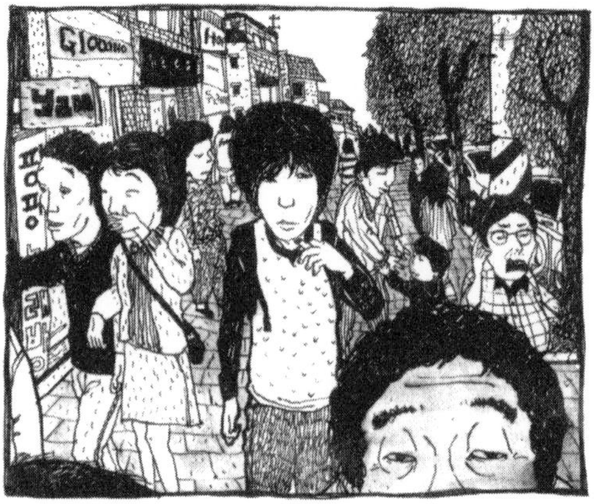
Yam

I HAD A LOT OF ONE-NIGHT STANDS.

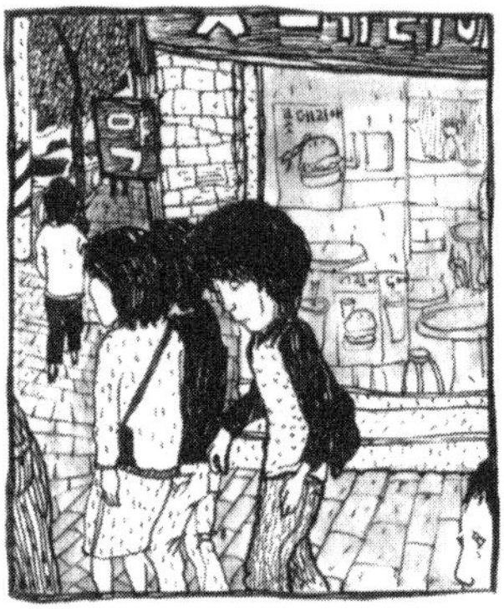

UNABLE TO TELL ANYONE...

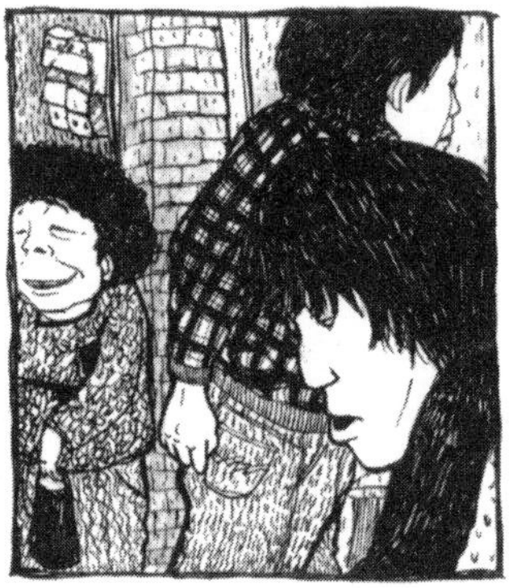

I'M NOW CARRYING THIS BURDEN ALONE.

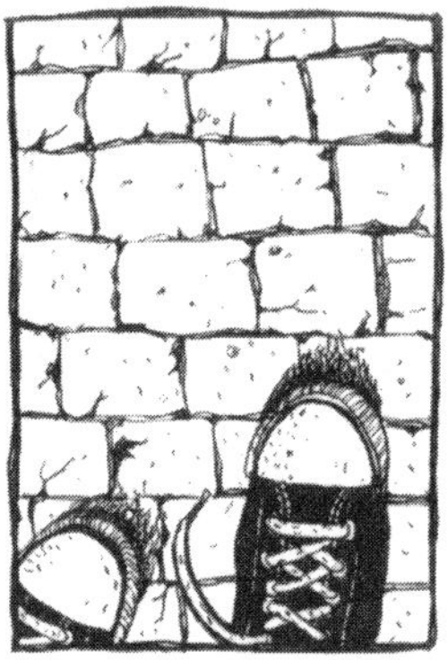

THE THING IS, I'M WORRIED ABOUT MY FAMILY.

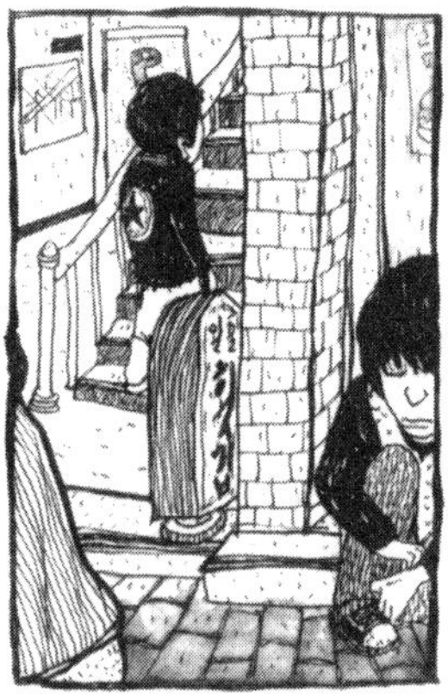

THEY HAVE NO IDEA.

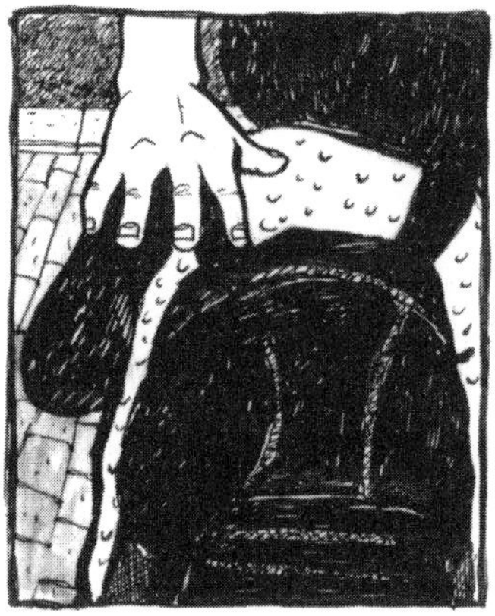

WHAT IF I GIVE IT TO THEM?

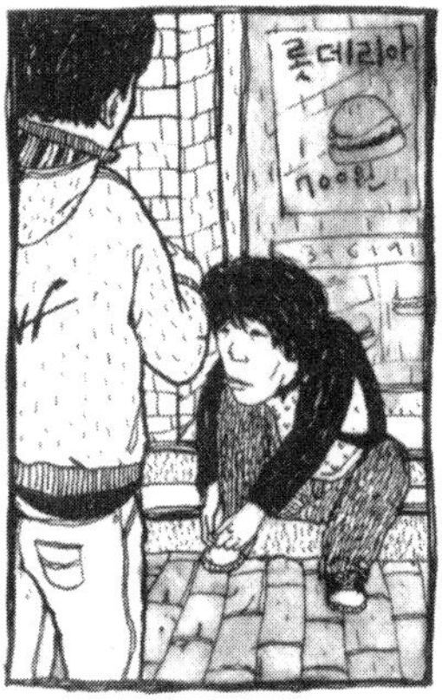
롯데리아

THAT'S MY BIGGEST FEAR.

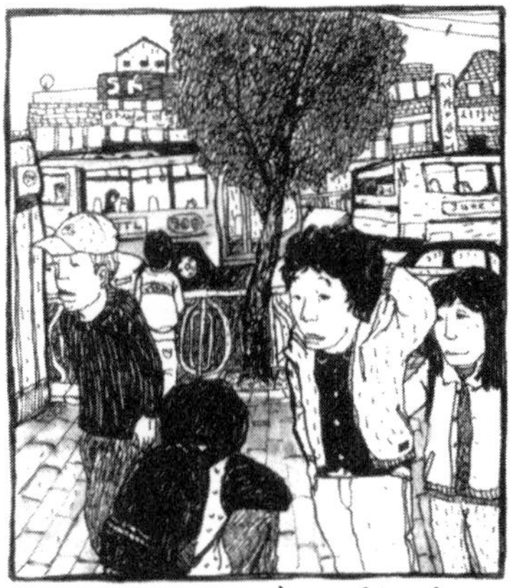

AS LONG AS I DON'T SHARE A RAZOR OR TOOTHBRUSH, THE NURSE SAID I DON'T HAVE TO WORRY.

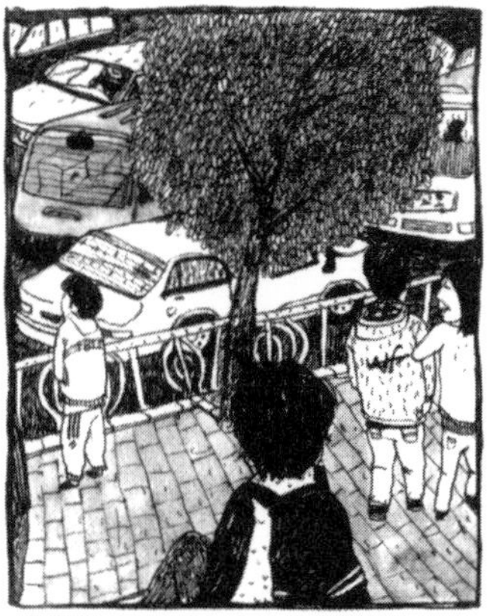

BUT I STILL FEEL SO ANXIOUS...

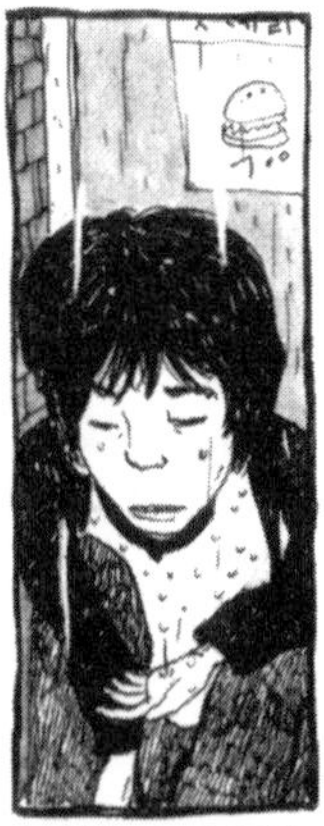

EVERY TIME I EAT WITH MY FAMILY.

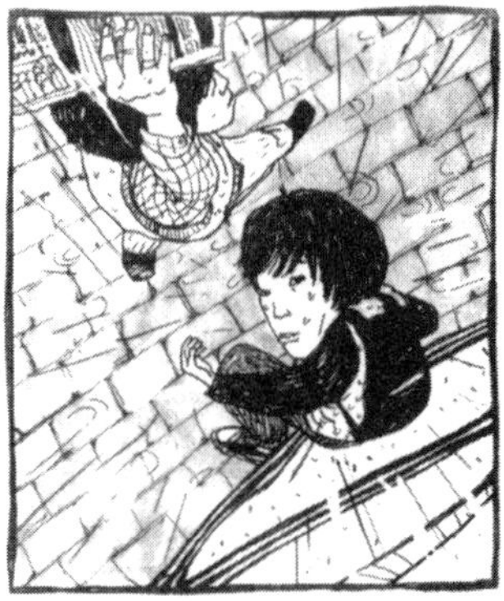

I FEEL BAD EVEN DIPPING MY SPOON IN THE STEW.

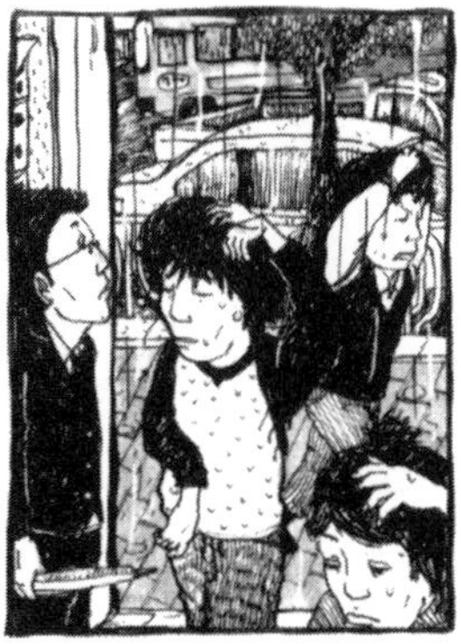

IF I KEPT THIS A SECRET...

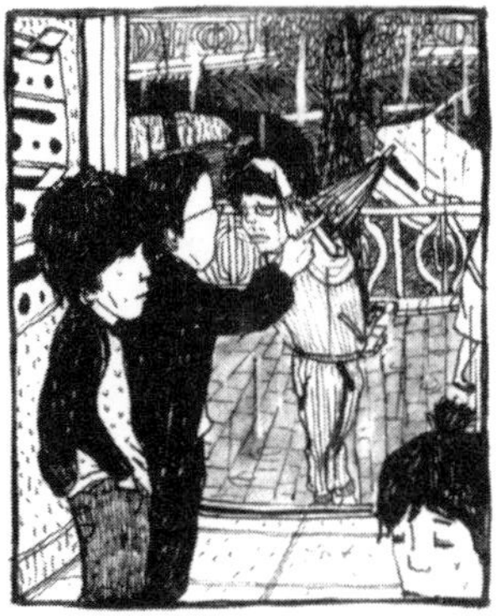

AND QUIETLY SLIPPED AWAY...

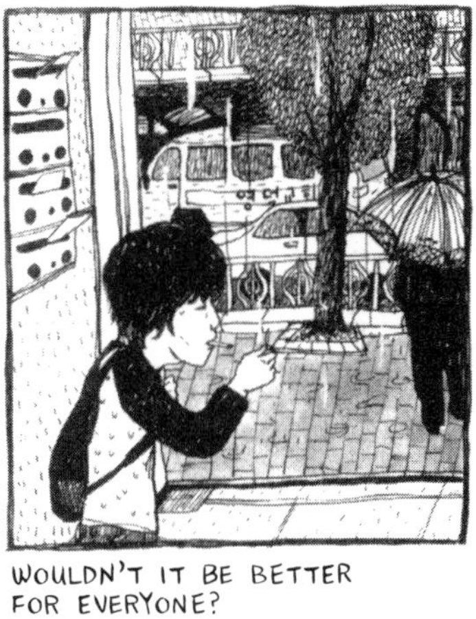

WOULDN'T IT BE BETTER FOR EVERYONE?

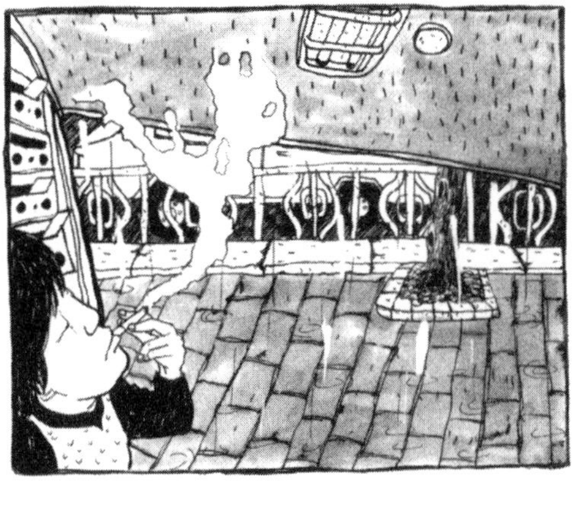

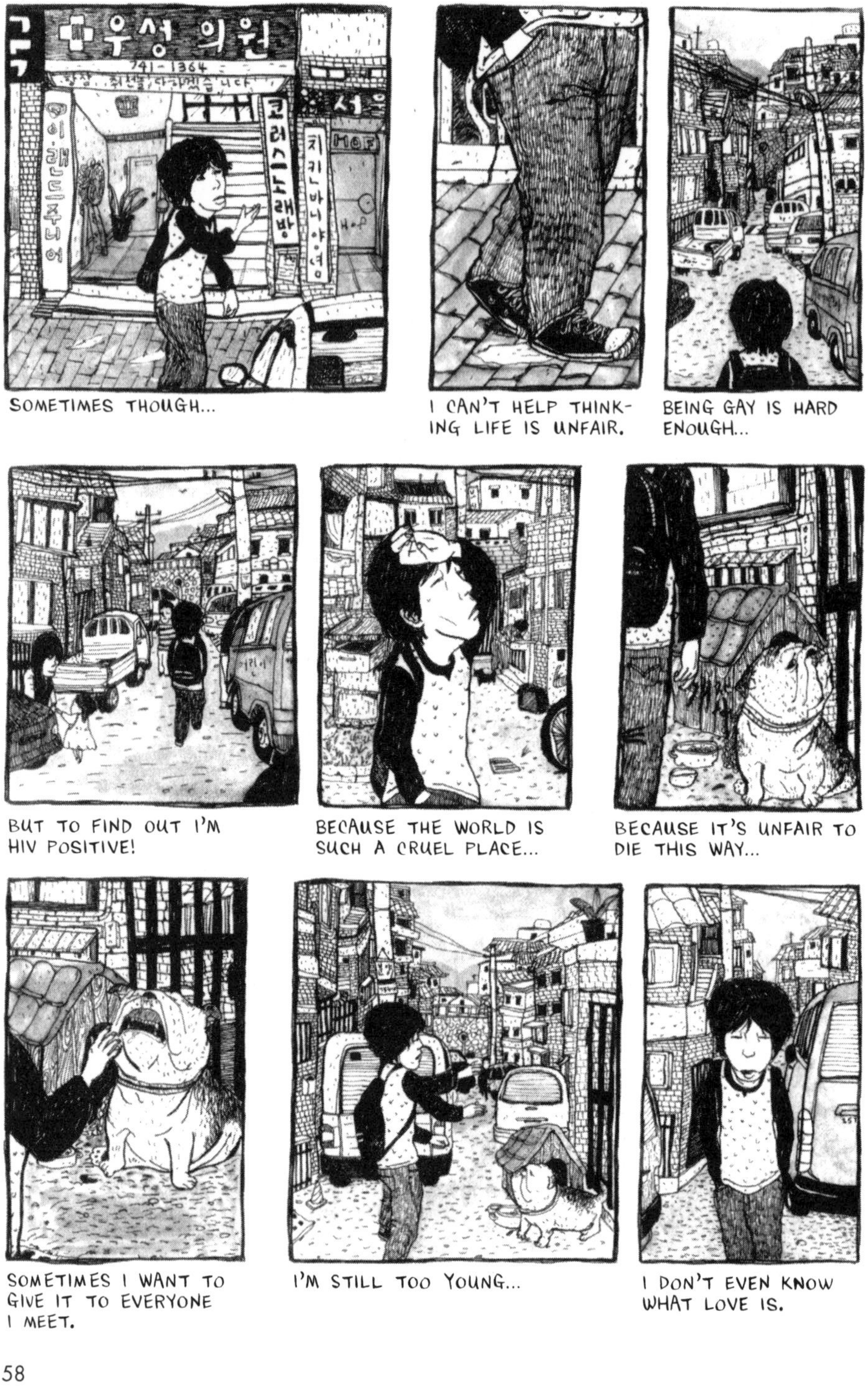
우성의원
741-1364
코러스노래방
HOF
SOMETIMES THOUGH...
I CAN'T HELP THINKING LIFE IS UNFAIR.
BEING GAY IS HARD ENOUGH...
BUT TO FIND OUT I'M HIV POSITIVE!
BECAUSE THE WORLD IS SUCH A CRUEL PLACE...
BECAUSE IT'S UNFAIR TO DIE THIS WAY...
SOMETIMES I WANT TO GIVE IT TO EVERYONE I MEET.
I'M STILL TOO YOUNG...
I DON'T EVEN KNOW WHAT LOVE IS.

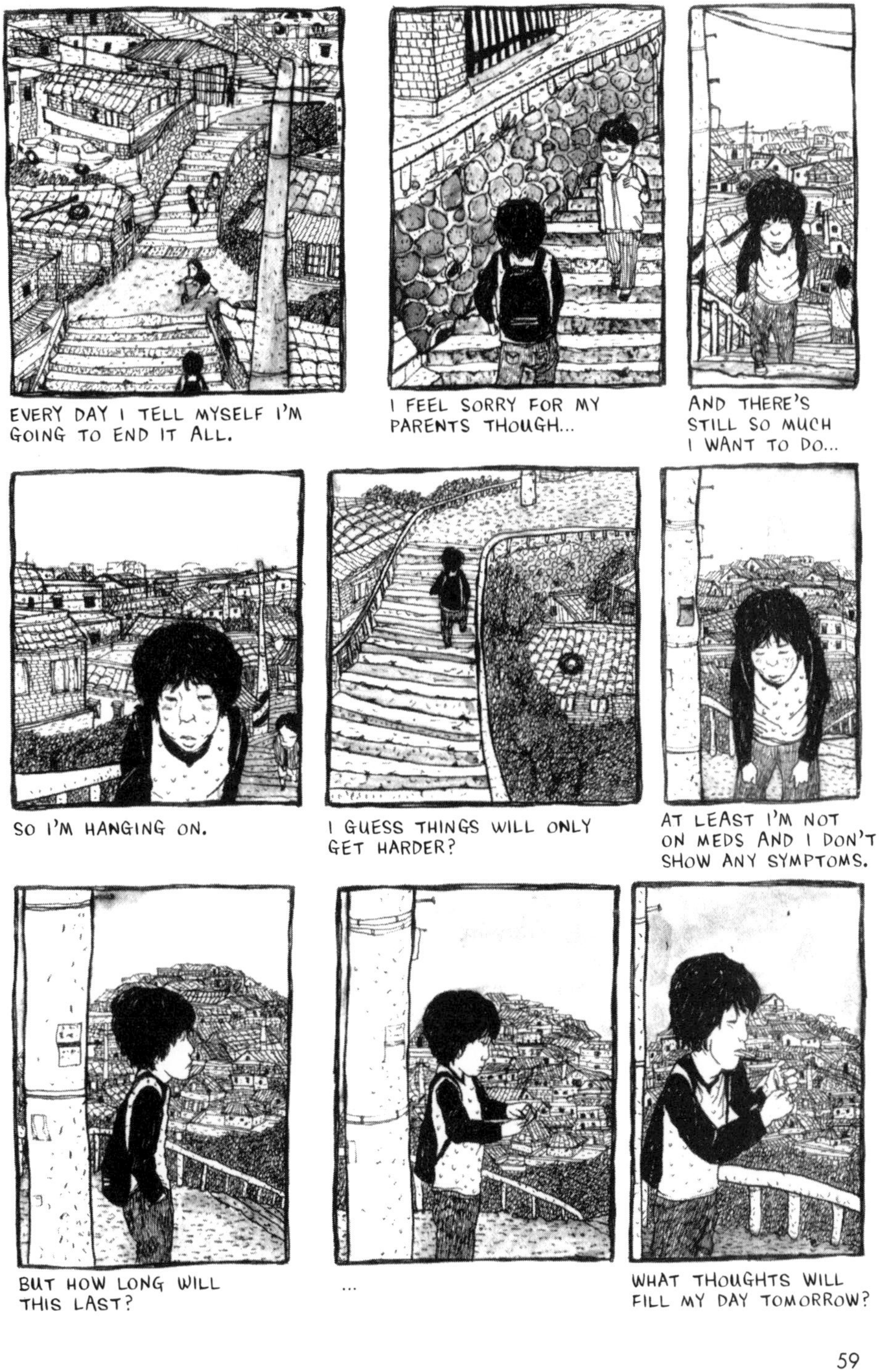
EVERY DAY I TELL MYSELF I'M GOING TO END IT ALL.
I FEEL SORRY FOR MY PARENTS THOUGH...
AND THERE'S STILL SO MUCH I WANT TO DO...
SO I'M HANGING ON.
I GUESS THINGS WILL ONLY GET HARDER?
AT LEAST I'M NOT ON MEDS AND I DON'T SHOW ANY SYMPTOMS.
BUT HOW LONG WILL THIS LAST?
...
WHAT THOUGHTS WILL FILL MY DAY TOMORROW?

MAYBE IT'D BE BETTER IF I JUST DIDN'T WAKE UP...

"LIFE" IS BASED ON AN ANONYMOUS GUEST'S COMMENT
THAT WAS POSTED ON A FORUM ON DAUM.NET IN 2003.

nineteen

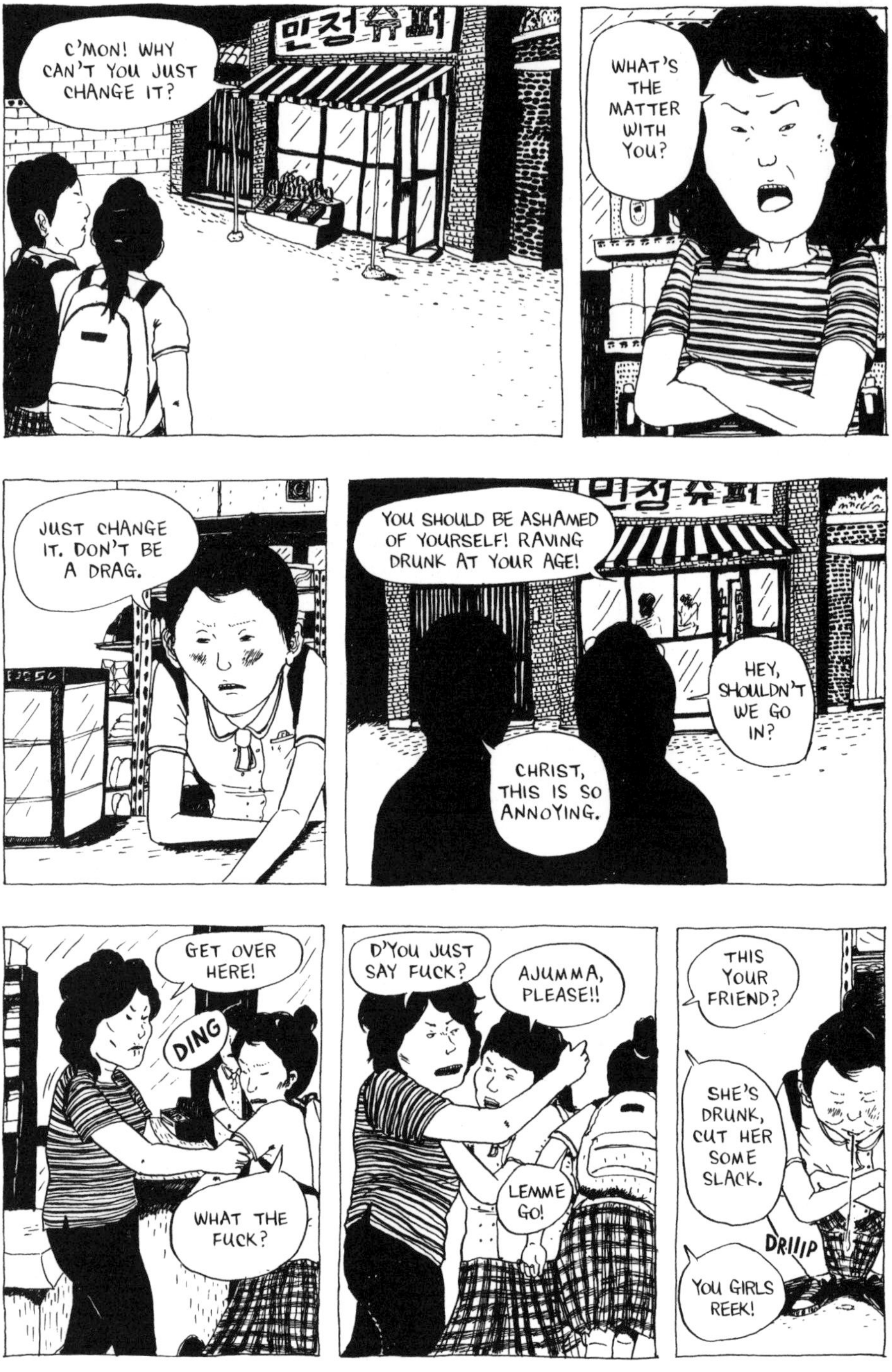
민정슈퍼
C'MON! WHY CAN'T YOU JUST CHANGE IT?
WHAT'S THE MATTER WITH YOU?
JUST CHANGE IT. DON'T BE A DRAG.
YOU SHOULD BE ASHAMED OF YOURSELF! RAVING DRUNK AT YOUR AGE!
민정슈퍼
HEY, SHOULDN'T WE GO IN?
CHRIST, THIS IS SO ANNOYING.
GET OVER HERE!
DING
WHAT THE FUCK?
D'YOU JUST SAY FUCK?
AJUMMA, PLEASE!!
LEMME GO!
THIS YOUR FRIEND?
SHE'S DRUNK, CUT HER SOME SLACK.
DRIIIP
YOU GIRLS REEK!

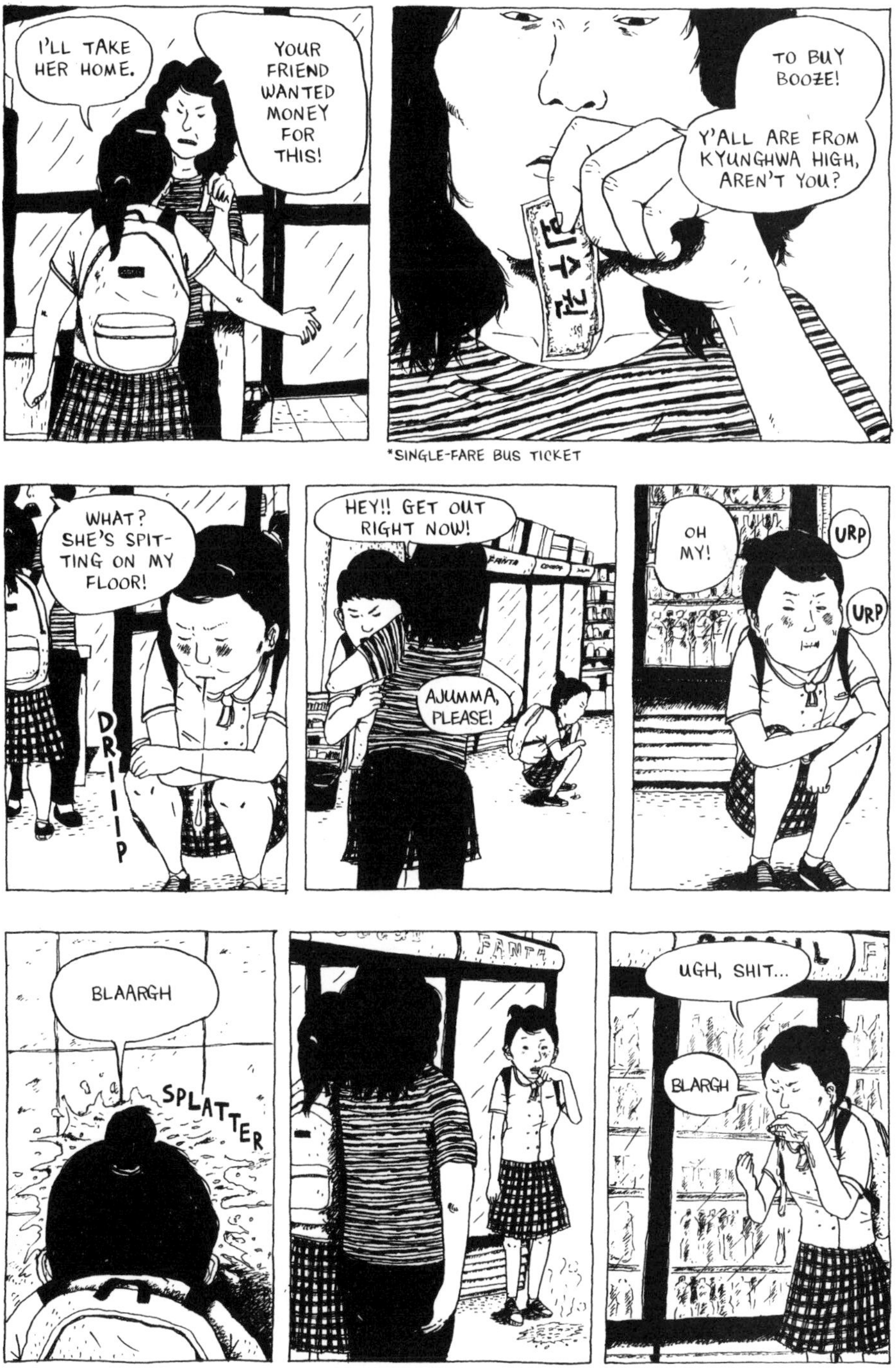
I'LL TAKE HER HOME.
YOUR FRIEND WANTED MONEY FOR THIS!
TO BUY BOOZE!
Y'ALL ARE FROM KYUNGHWA HIGH, AREN'T YOU?
WHAT? SHE'S SPIT-TING ON MY FLOOR!
DRIIIP
HEY!! GET OUT RIGHT NOW!
AJUMMA, PLEASE!
OH MY!
URP
URP
BLAARGH
SPLATTER
UGH, SHIT...
BLARGH

*SINGLE-FARE BUS TICKET

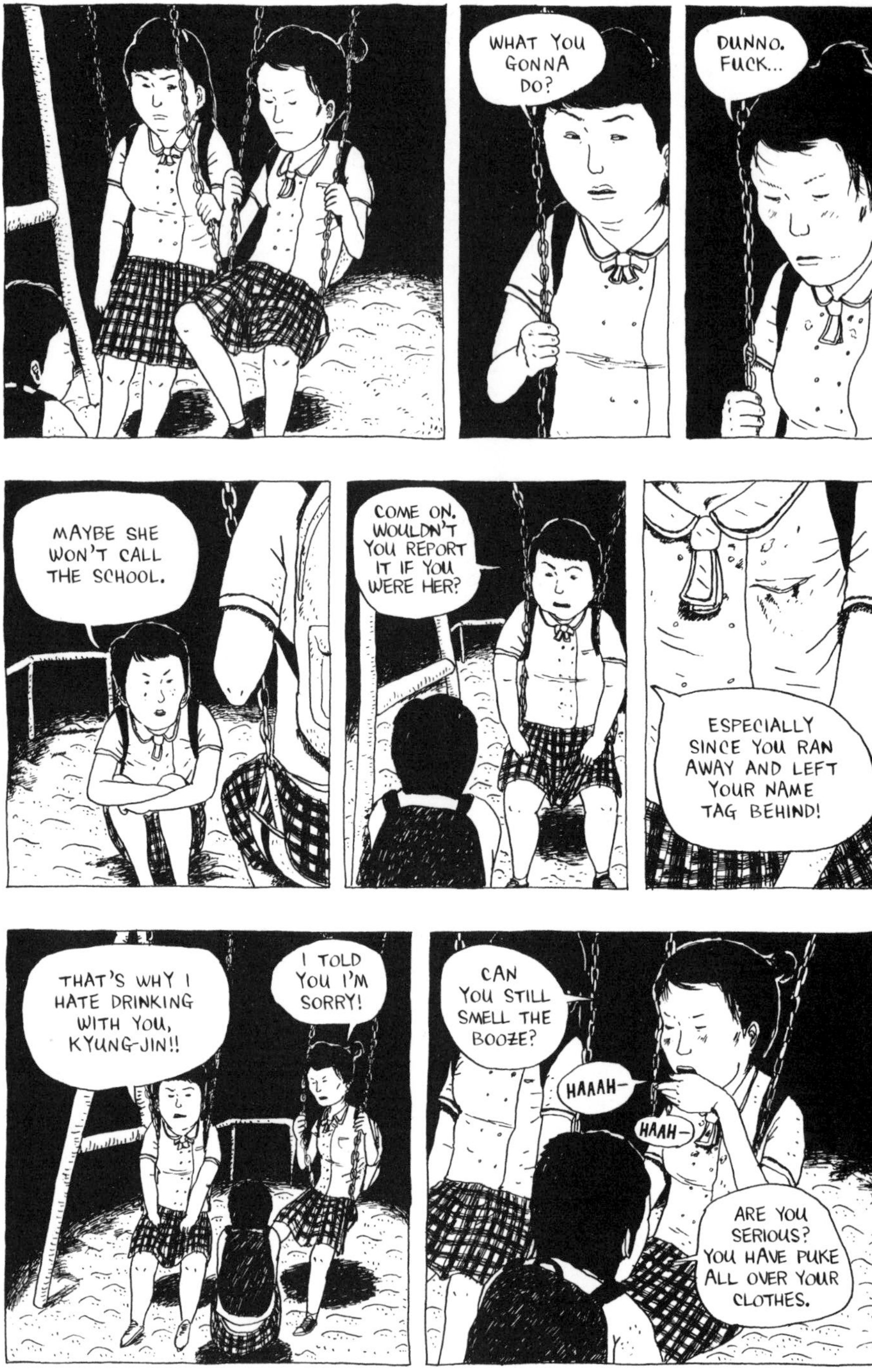
WHAT YOU GONNA DO?
DUNNO. FUCK...
MAYBE SHE WON'T CALL THE SCHOOL.
COME ON. WOULDN'T YOU REPORT IT IF YOU WERE HER?
ESPECIALLY SINCE YOU RAN AWAY AND LEFT YOUR NAME TAG BEHIND!
THAT'S WHY I HATE DRINKING WITH YOU, KYUNG-JIN!!
I TOLD YOU I'M SORRY!
CAN YOU STILL SMELL THE BOOZE?
HAAAH-
HAAH-
ARE YOU SERIOUS? YOU HAVE PUKE ALL OVER YOUR CLOTHES.

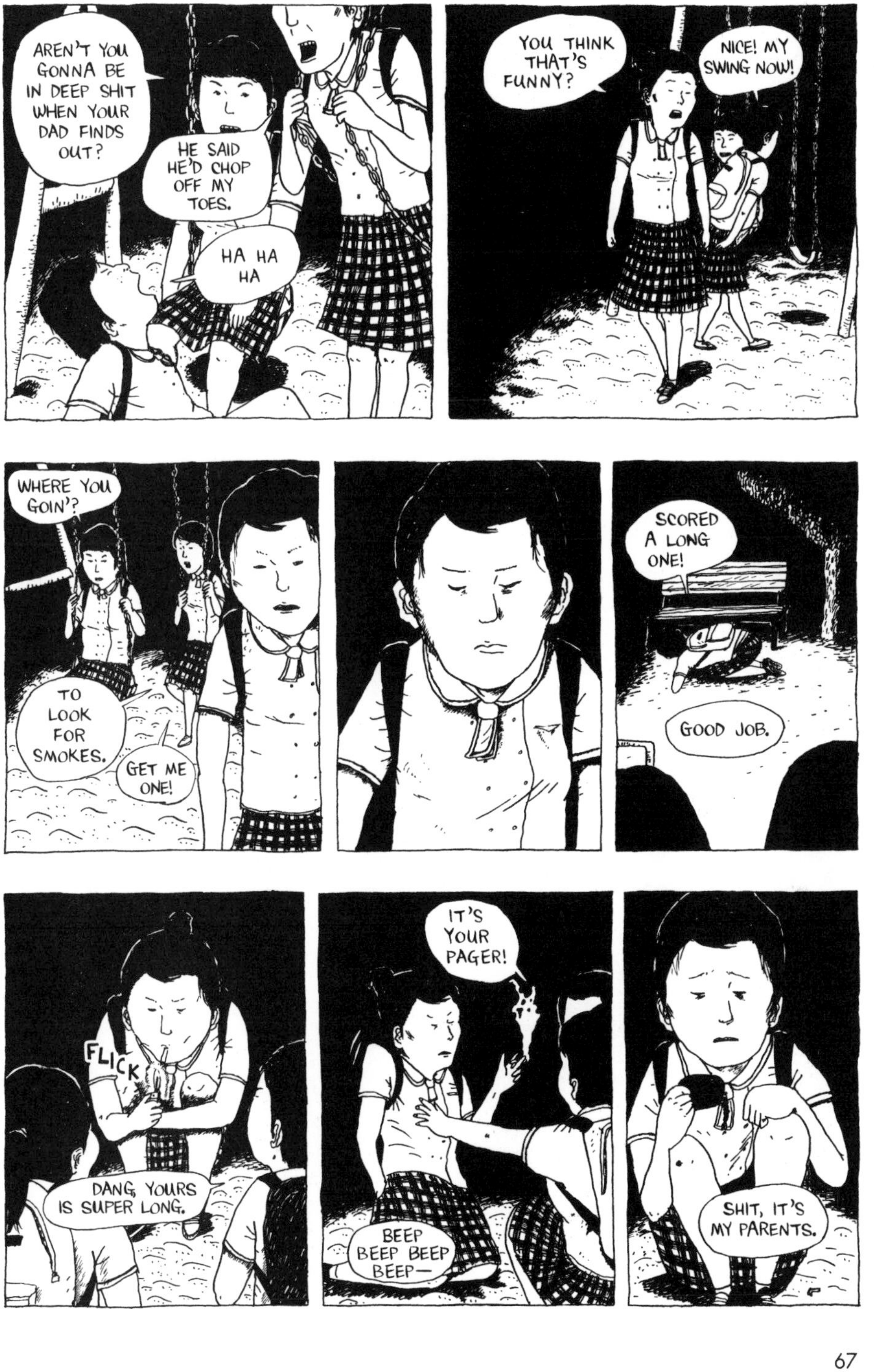
AREN'T YOU GONNA BE IN DEEP SHIT WHEN YOUR DAD FINDS OUT?
HE SAID HE'D CHOP OFF MY TOES.
HA HA HA
YOU THINK THAT'S FUNNY?
NICE! MY SWING NOW!
WHERE YOU GOIN'?
TO LOOK FOR SMOKES.
GET ME ONE!
SCORED A LONG ONE!
GOOD JOB.
FLICK
DANG, YOURS IS SUPER LONG.
IT'S YOUR PAGER!
BEEP BEEP BEEP BEEP—
SHIT, IT'S MY PARENTS.

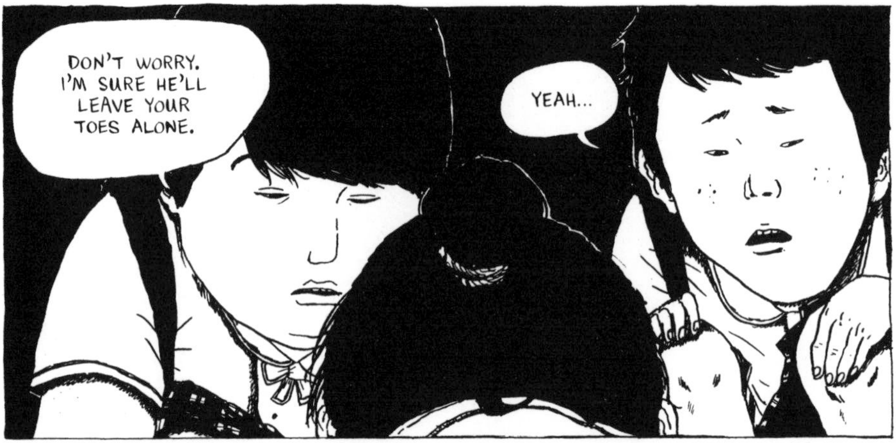
DON'T WORRY. I'M SURE HE'LL LEAVE YOUR TOES ALONE.
YEAH...

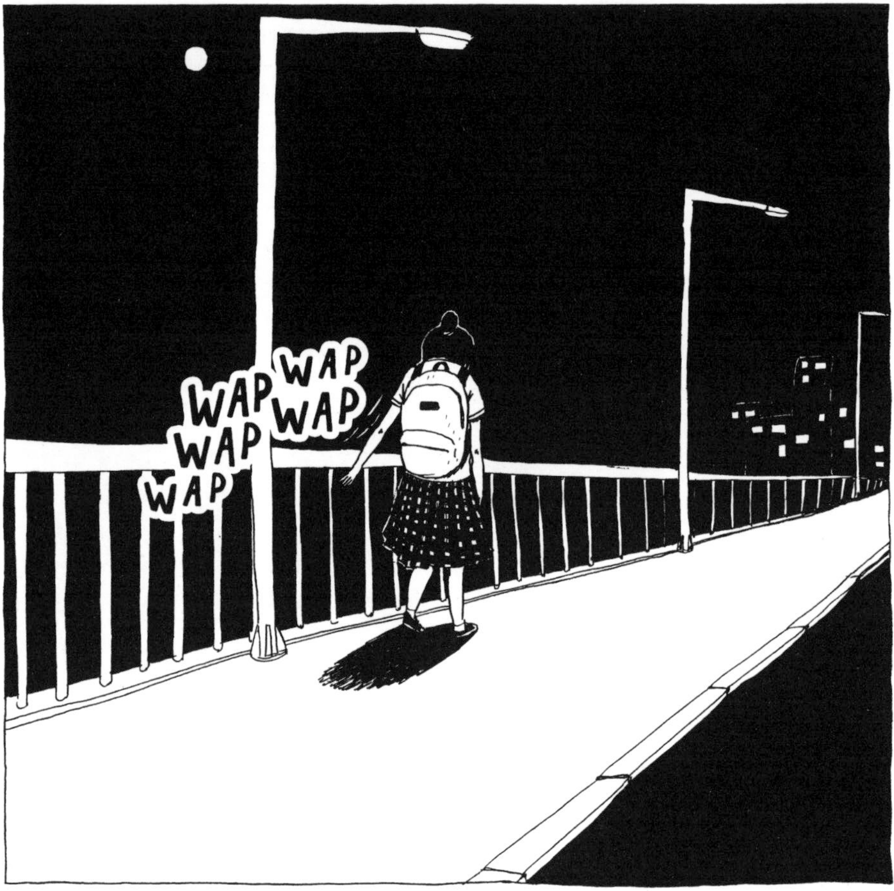
WAP WAP WAP WAP WAP

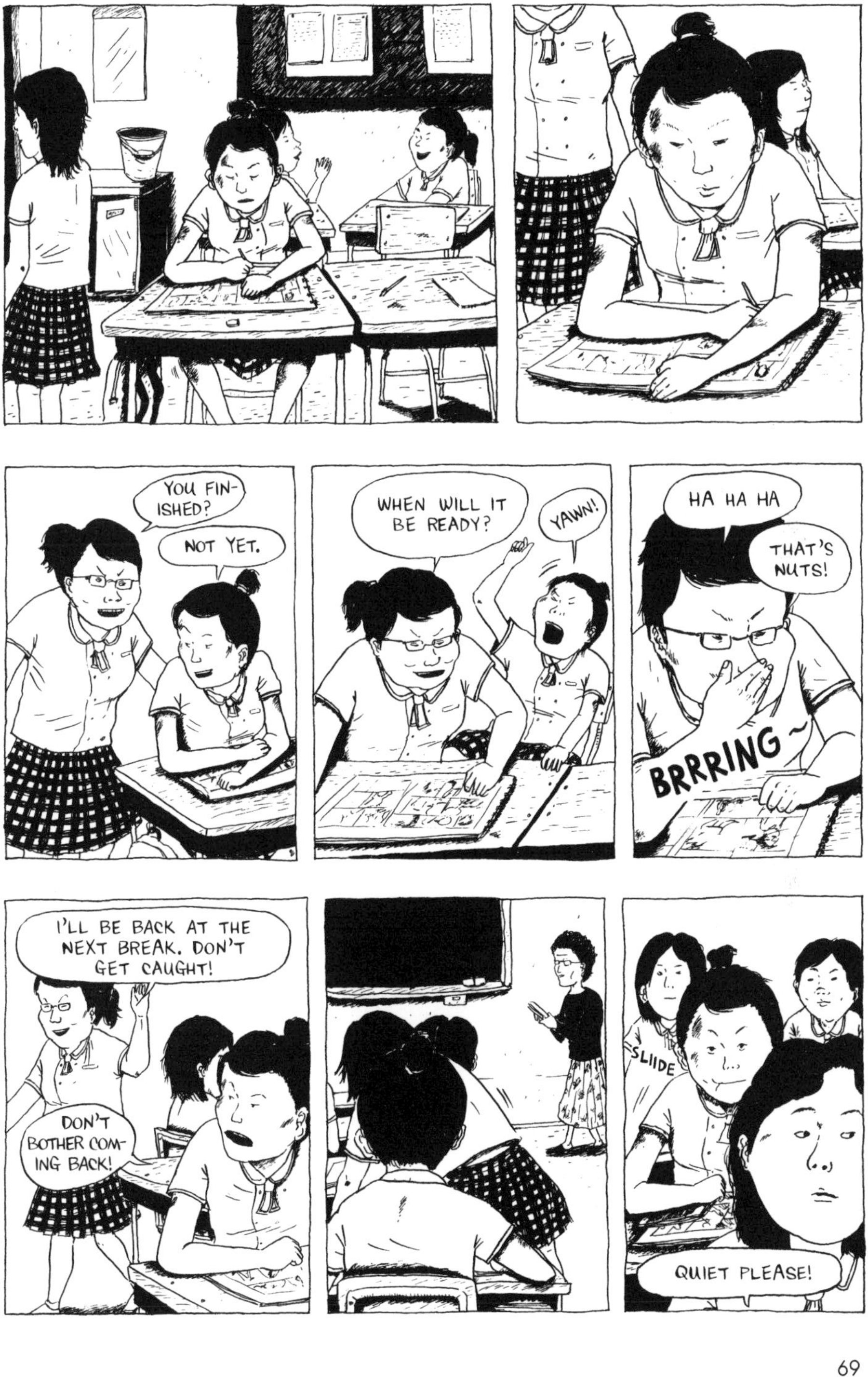
YOU FIN-ISHED?
NOT YET.
WHEN WILL IT BE READY?
YAWN!
HA HA HA
THAT'S NUTS!
BRRRING~
I'LL BE BACK AT THE NEXT BREAK. DON'T GET CAUGHT!
DON'T BOTHER COM-ING BACK!
SLIIDE
QUIET PLEASE!

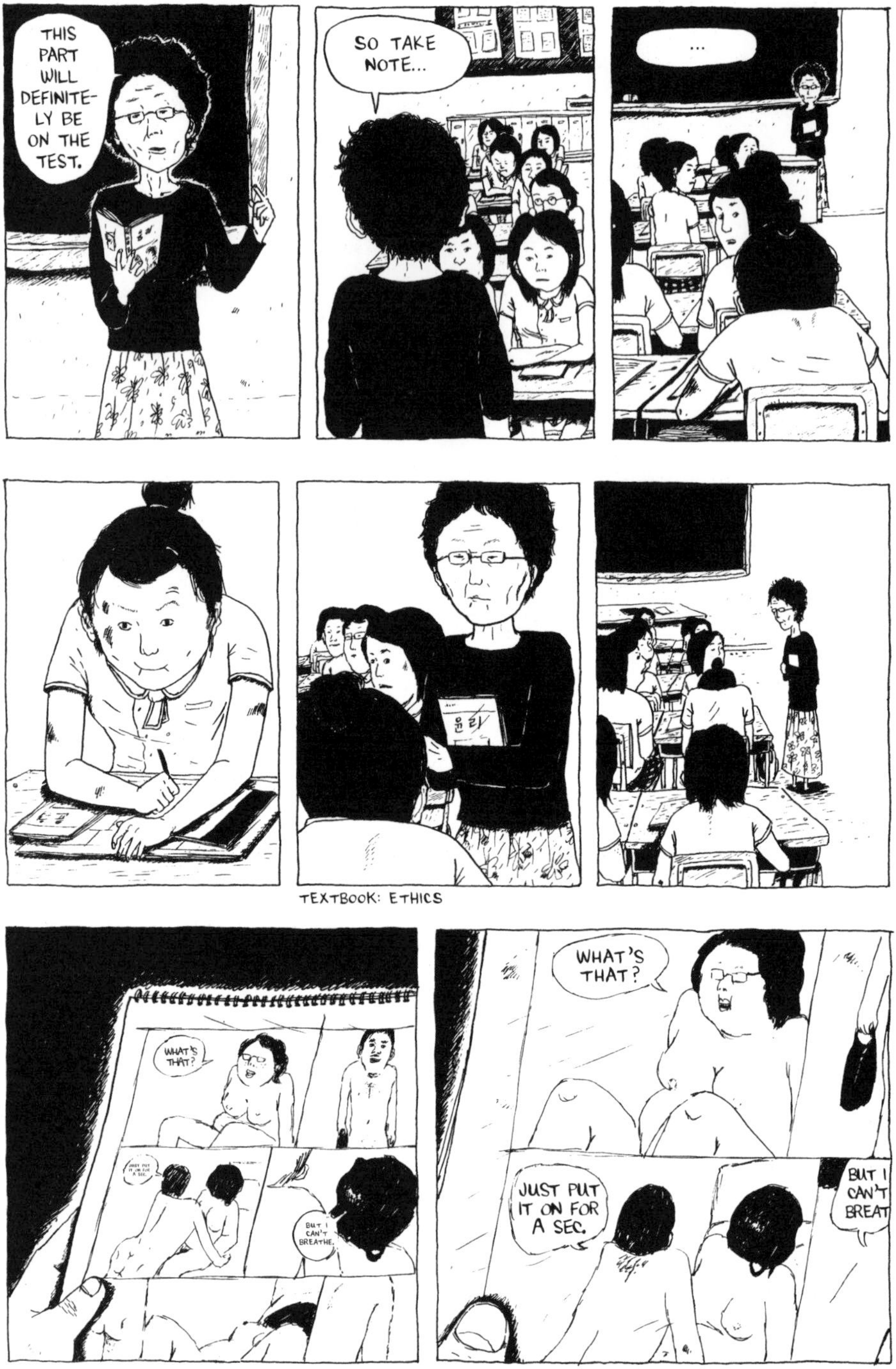
THIS PART WILL DEFINITE-LY BE ON THE TEST.
SO TAKE NOTE...
...
윤리
TEXTBOOK: ETHICS
WHAT'S THAT?
JUST PUT IT ON FOR A SEC.
BUT I CAN'T BREATHE.
WHAT'S THAT?
JUST PUT IT ON FOR A SEC.
BUT I CAN'T BREAT

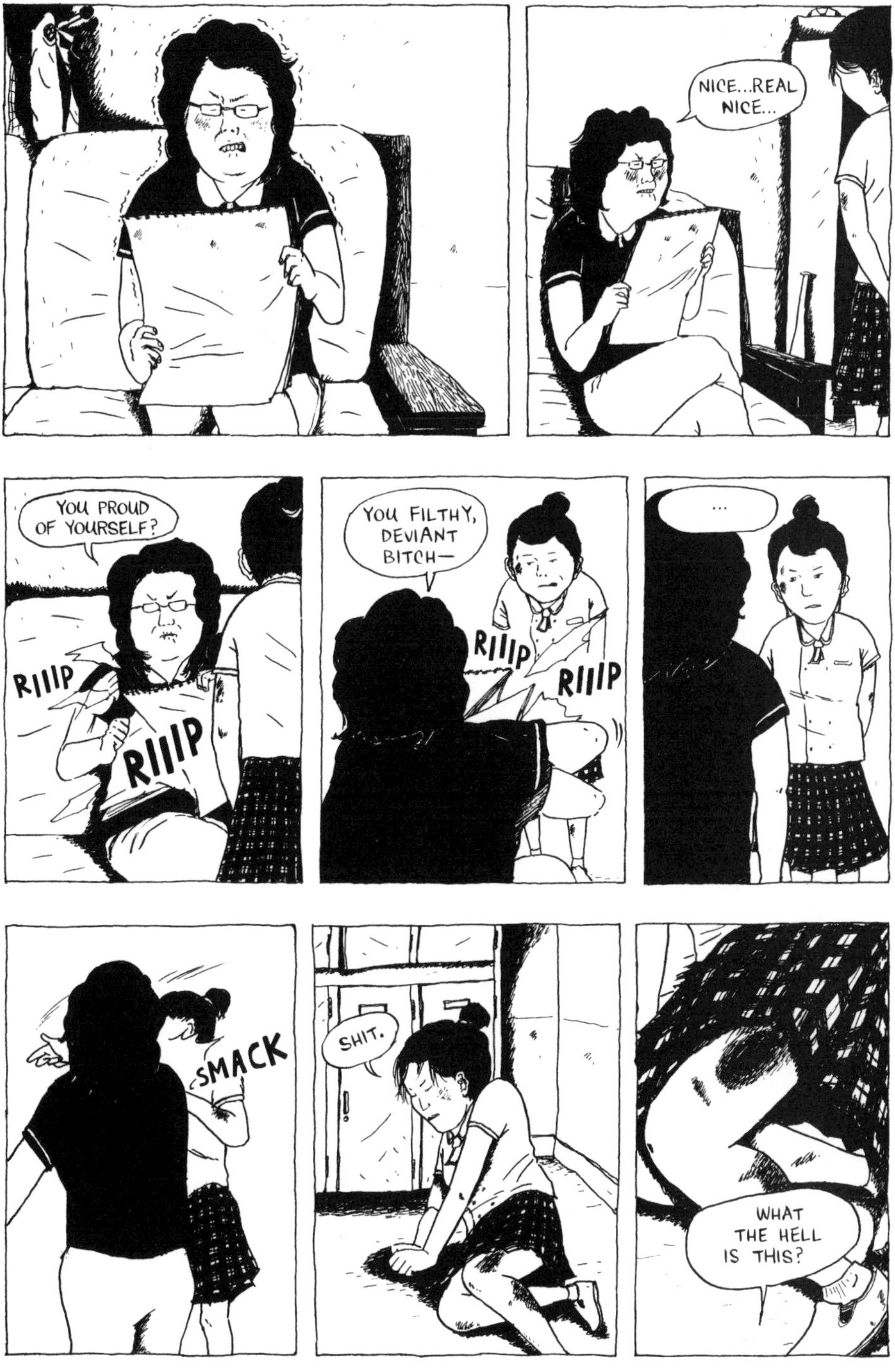
NICE...REAL NICE...
YOU PROUD OF YOURSELF?
RIIIP
RIIIP
YOU FILTHY, DEVIANT BITCH—
RIIIP
RIIIP
...
SMACK
SHIT.
WHAT THE HELL IS THIS?

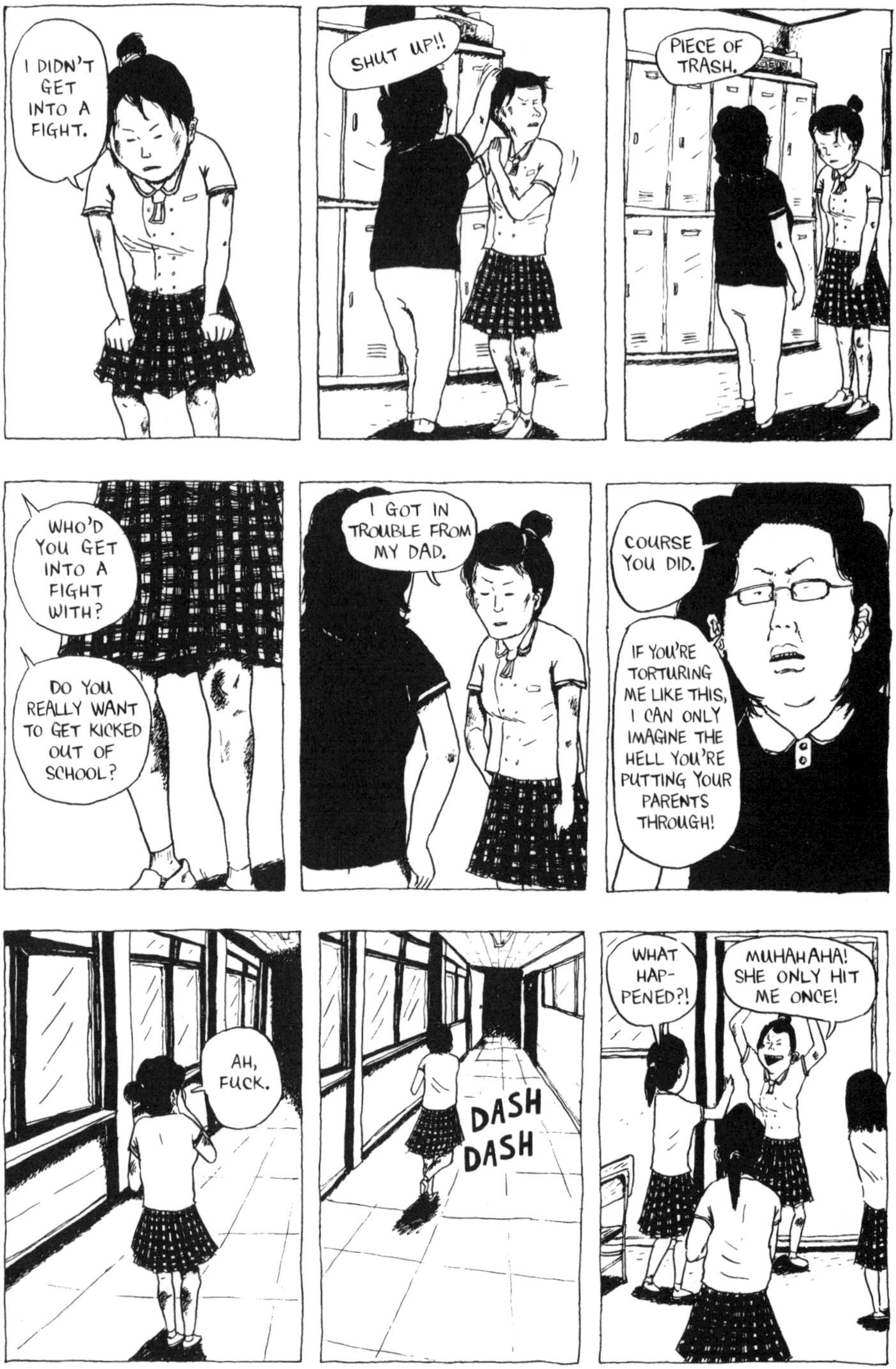
I DIDN'T GET INTO A FIGHT.
SHUT UP!!
PIECE OF TRASH.
WHO'D YOU GET INTO A FIGHT WITH?
DO YOU REALLY WANT TO GET KICKED OUT OF SCHOOL?
I GOT IN TROUBLE FROM MY DAD.
COURSE YOU DID.
IF YOU'RE TORTURING ME LIKE THIS, I CAN ONLY IMAGINE THE HELL YOU'RE PUTTING YOUR PARENTS THROUGH!
AH, FUCK.
DASH DASH
WHAT HAP-PENED?!
MUHAHAHA! SHE ONLY HIT ME ONCE!

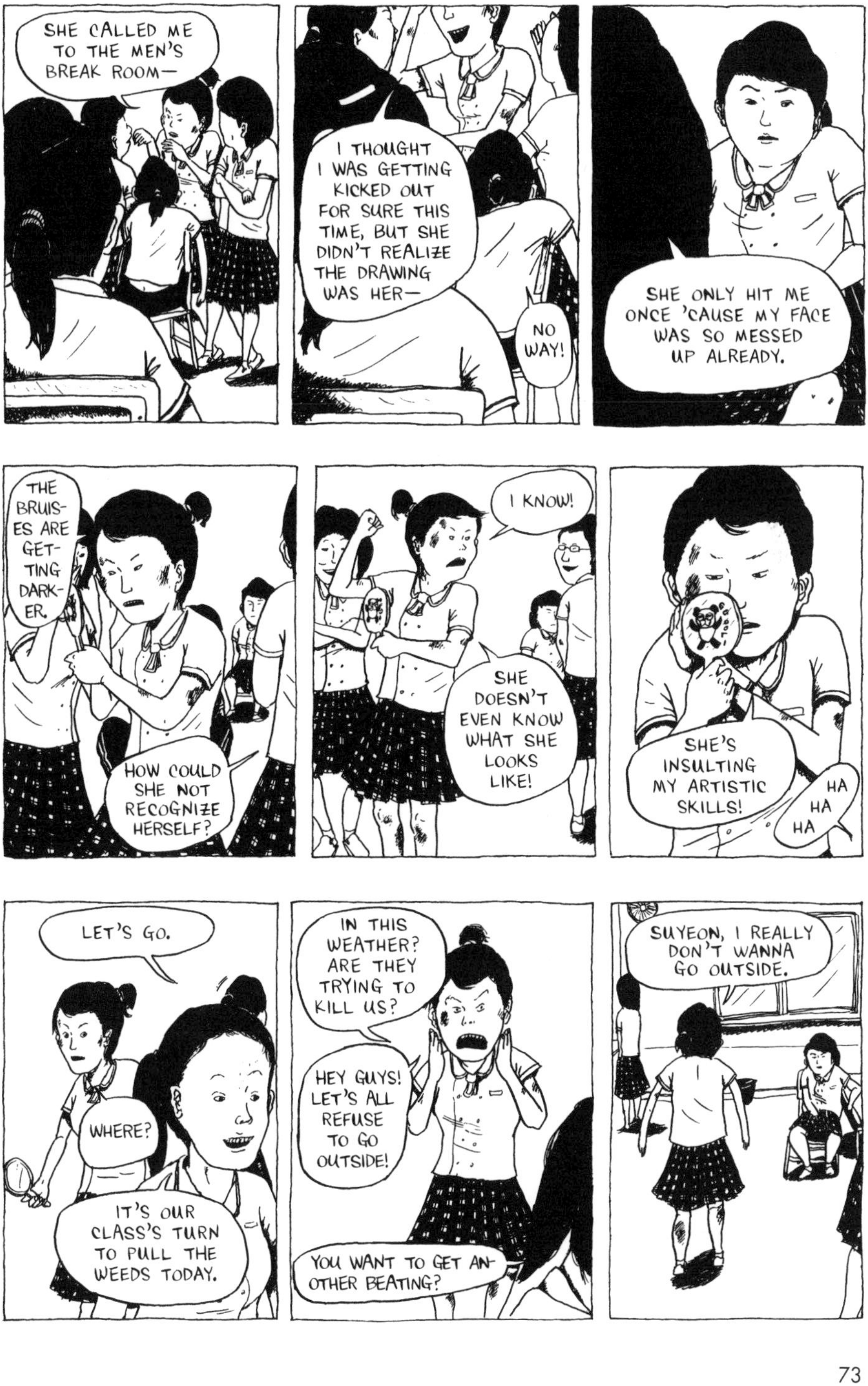

SHE CALLED ME TO THE MEN'S BREAK ROOM—
I THOUGHT I WAS GETTING KICKED OUT FOR SURE THIS TIME, BUT SHE DIDN'T REALIZE THE DRAWING WAS HER—
NO WAY!
SHE ONLY HIT ME ONCE 'CAUSE MY FACE WAS SO MESSED UP ALREADY.
THE BRUISES ARE GETTING DARKER.
HOW COULD SHE NOT RECOGNIZE HERSELF?
I KNOW!
SHE DOESN'T EVEN KNOW WHAT SHE LOOKS LIKE!
SHE'S INSULTING MY ARTISTIC SKILLS!
HA HA HA
LET'S GO.
WHERE?
IT'S OUR CLASS'S TURN TO PULL THE WEEDS TODAY.
IN THIS WEATHER? ARE THEY TRYING TO KILL US?
HEY GUYS! LET'S ALL REFUSE TO GO OUTSIDE!
YOU WANT TO GET ANOTHER BEATING?
SUYEON, I REALLY DON'T WANNA GO OUTSIDE.

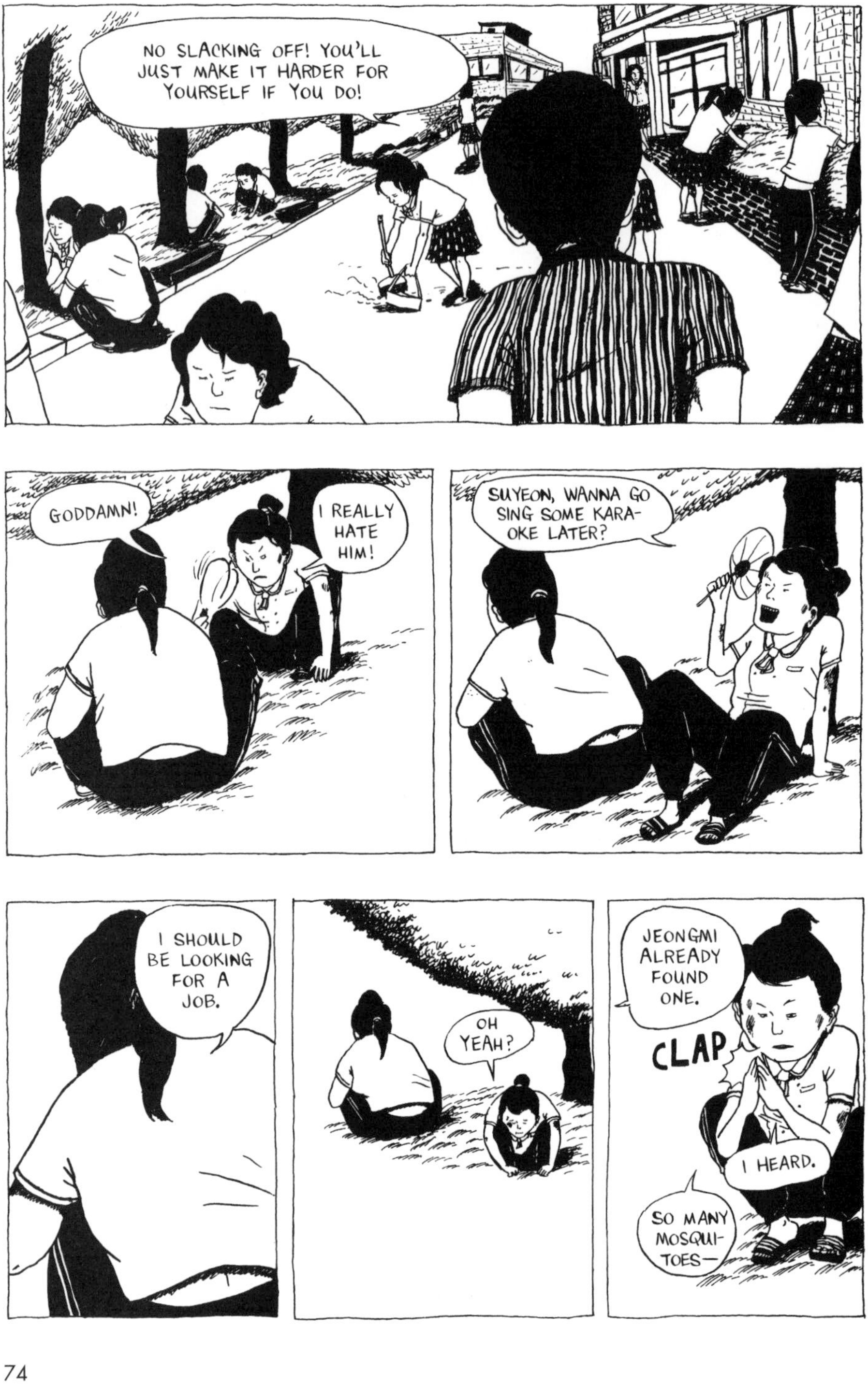
NO SLACKING OFF! YOU'LL JUST MAKE IT HARDER FOR YOURSELF IF YOU DO!
GODDAMN!
I REALLY HATE HIM!
SUYEON, WANNA GO SING SOME KARAOKE LATER?
I SHOULD BE LOOKING FOR A JOB.
OH YEAH?
JEONGMI ALREADY FOUND ONE.
CLAP
I HEARD.
SO MANY MOSQUITOES—

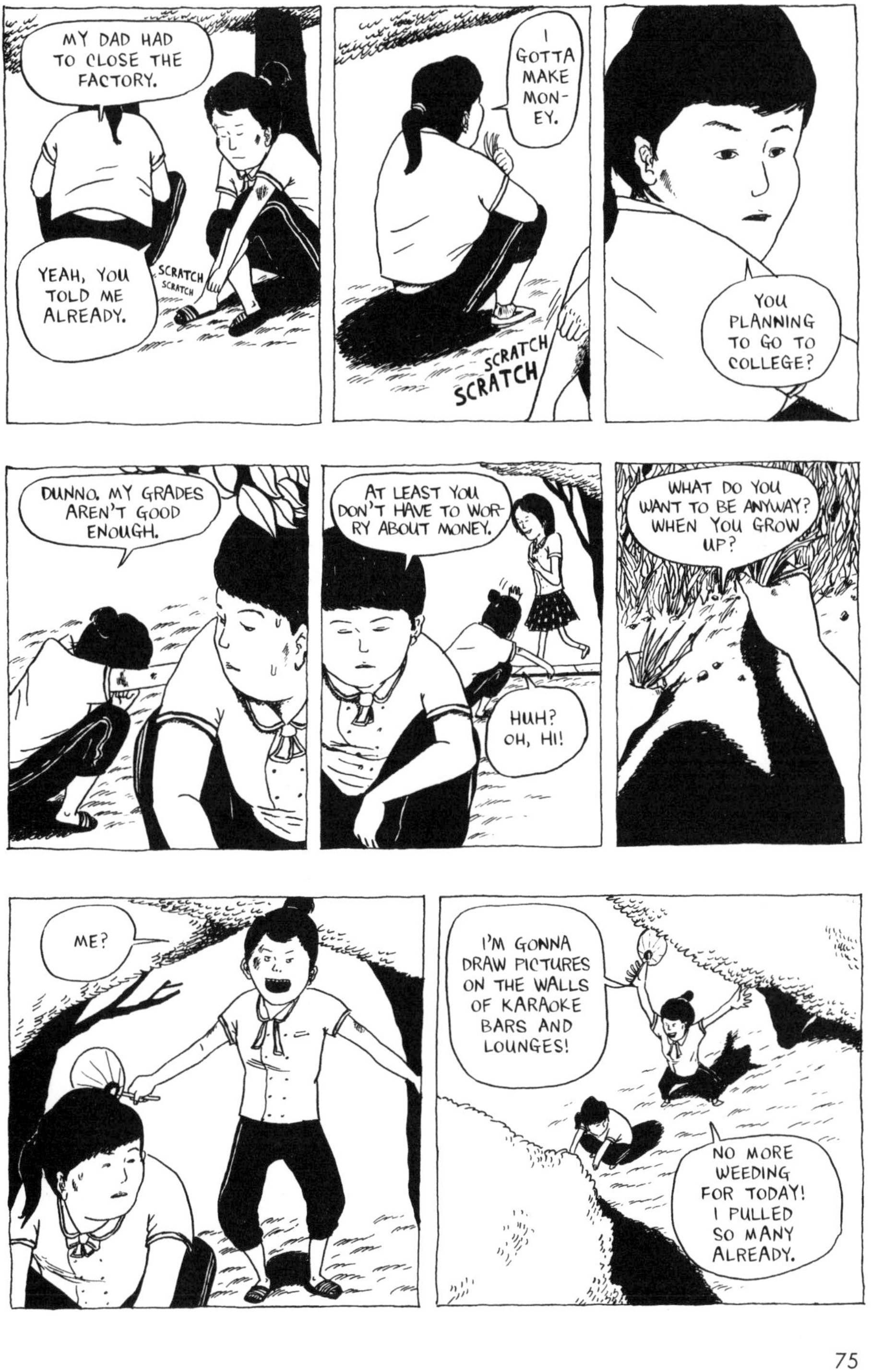
MY DAD HAD TO CLOSE THE FACTORY.
YEAH, YOU TOLD ME ALREADY.
SCRATCH SCRATCH
I GOTTA MAKE MON-EY.
SCRATCH SCRATCH
YOU PLANNING TO GO TO COLLEGE?
DUNNO. MY GRADES AREN'T GOOD ENOUGH.
AT LEAST YOU DON'T HAVE TO WOR-RY ABOUT MONEY.
HUH? OH, HI!
WHAT DO YOU WANT TO BE ANYWAY? WHEN YOU GROW UP?
ME?
I'M GONNA DRAW PICTURES ON THE WALLS OF KARAOKE BARS AND LOUNGES!
NO MORE WEEDING FOR TODAY! I PULLED SO MANY ALREADY.

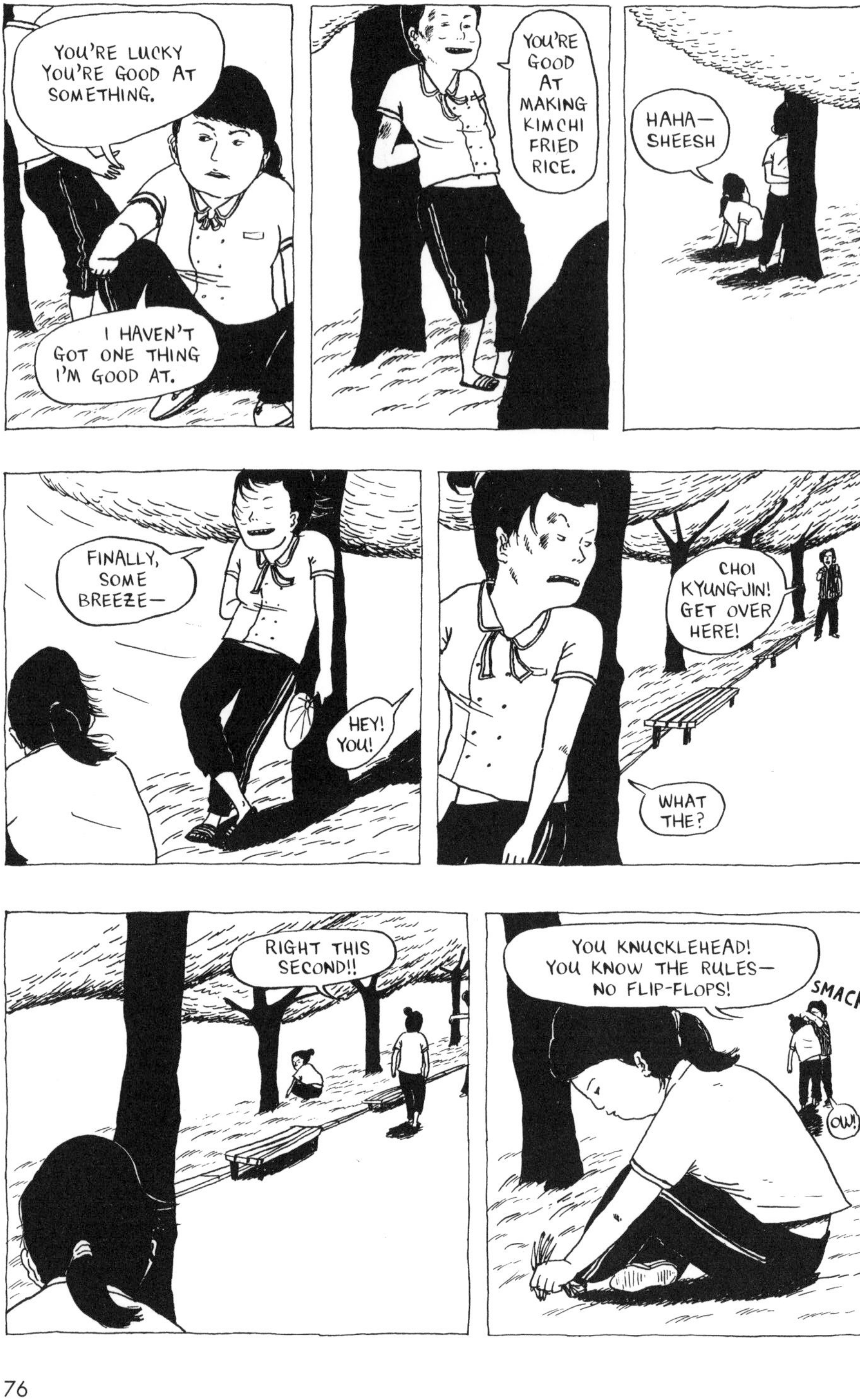
YOU'RE LUCKY YOU'RE GOOD AT SOMETHING.
I HAVEN'T GOT ONE THING I'M GOOD AT.
YOU'RE GOOD AT MAKING KIMCHI FRIED RICE.
HAHA—SHEESH
FINALLY, SOME BREEZE—
HEY! YOU!
CHOI KYUNG-JIN! GET OVER HERE!
WHAT THE?
RIGHT THIS SECOND!!
YOU KNUCKLEHEAD! YOU KNOW THE RULES—NO FLIP-FLOPS!
SMACK
OW!

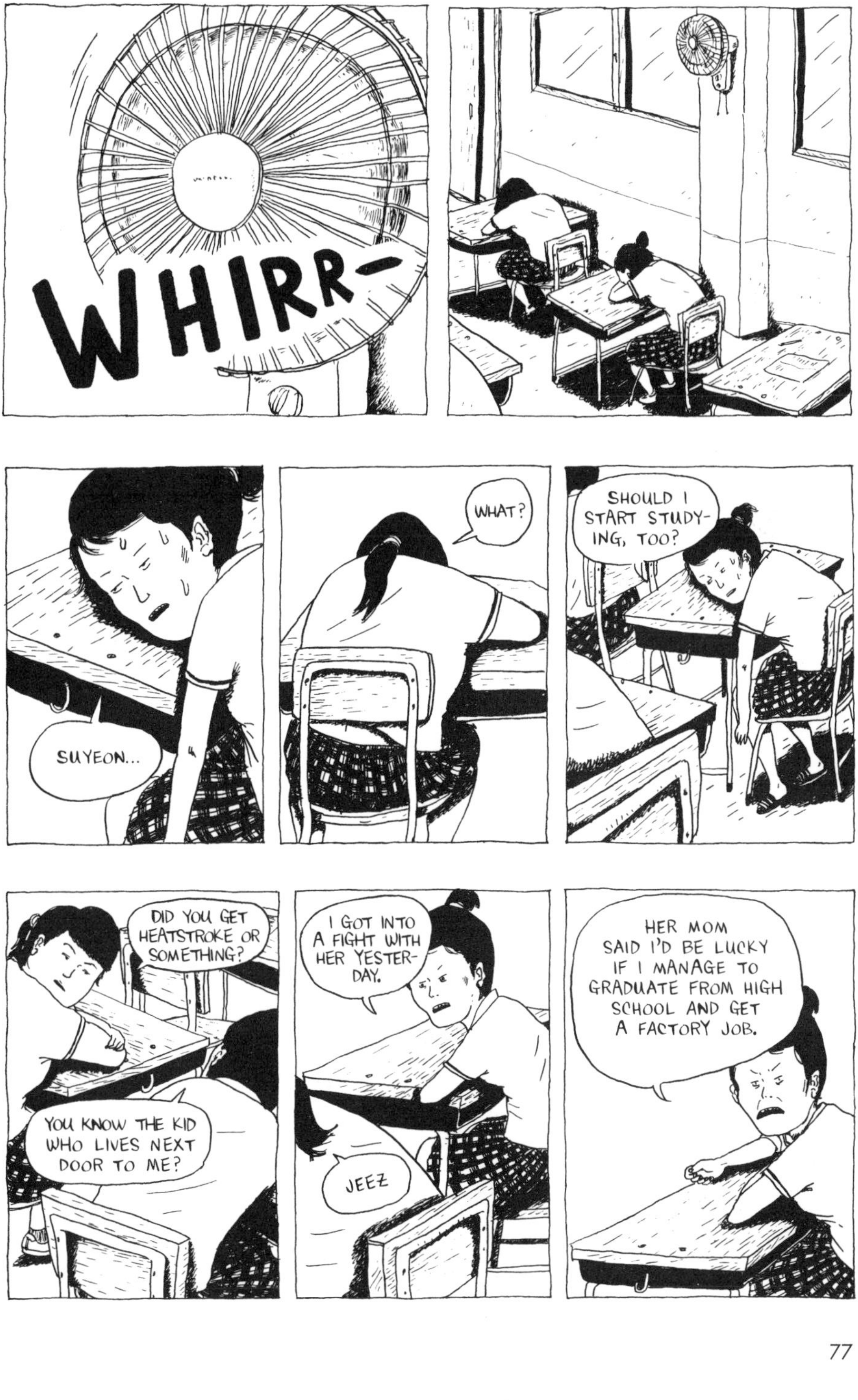
WHIRR-
SUYEON...
WHAT?
SHOULD I START STUDYING, TOO?
DID YOU GET HEATSTROKE OR SOMETHING?
YOU KNOW THE KID WHO LIVES NEXT DOOR TO ME?
I GOT INTO A FIGHT WITH HER YESTERDAY.
JEEZ
HER MOM SAID I'D BE LUCKY IF I MANAGE TO GRADUATE FROM HIGH SCHOOL AND GET A FACTORY JOB.

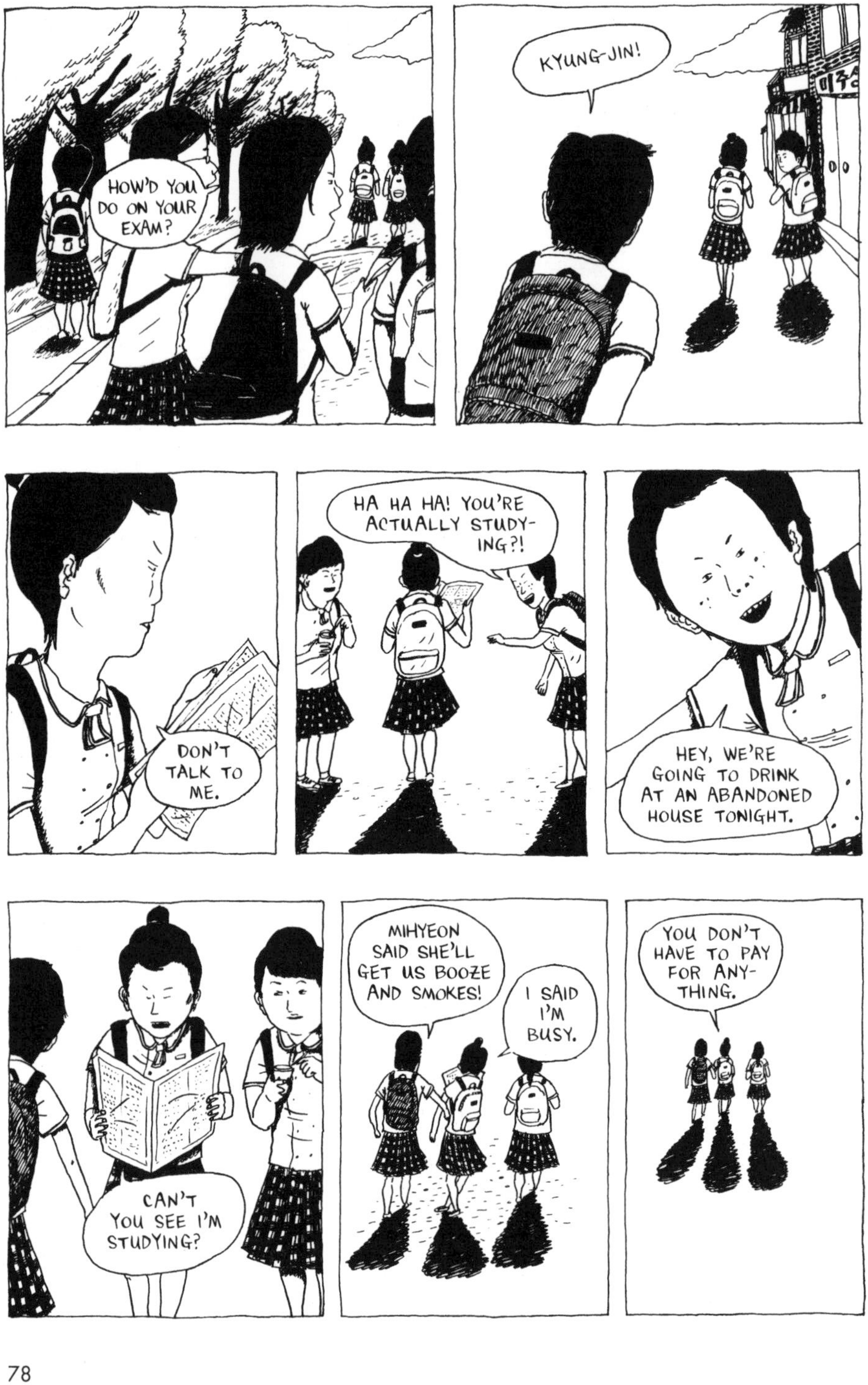
HOW'D YOU DO ON YOUR EXAM?
KYUNG-JIN!
DON'T TALK TO ME.
HA HA HA! YOU'RE ACTUALLY STUDYING?!
HEY, WE'RE GOING TO DRINK AT AN ABANDONED HOUSE TONIGHT.
CAN'T YOU SEE I'M STUDYING?
MIHYEON SAID SHE'LL GET US BOOZE AND SMOKES!
I SAID I'M BUSY.
YOU DON'T HAVE TO PAY FOR ANYTHING.

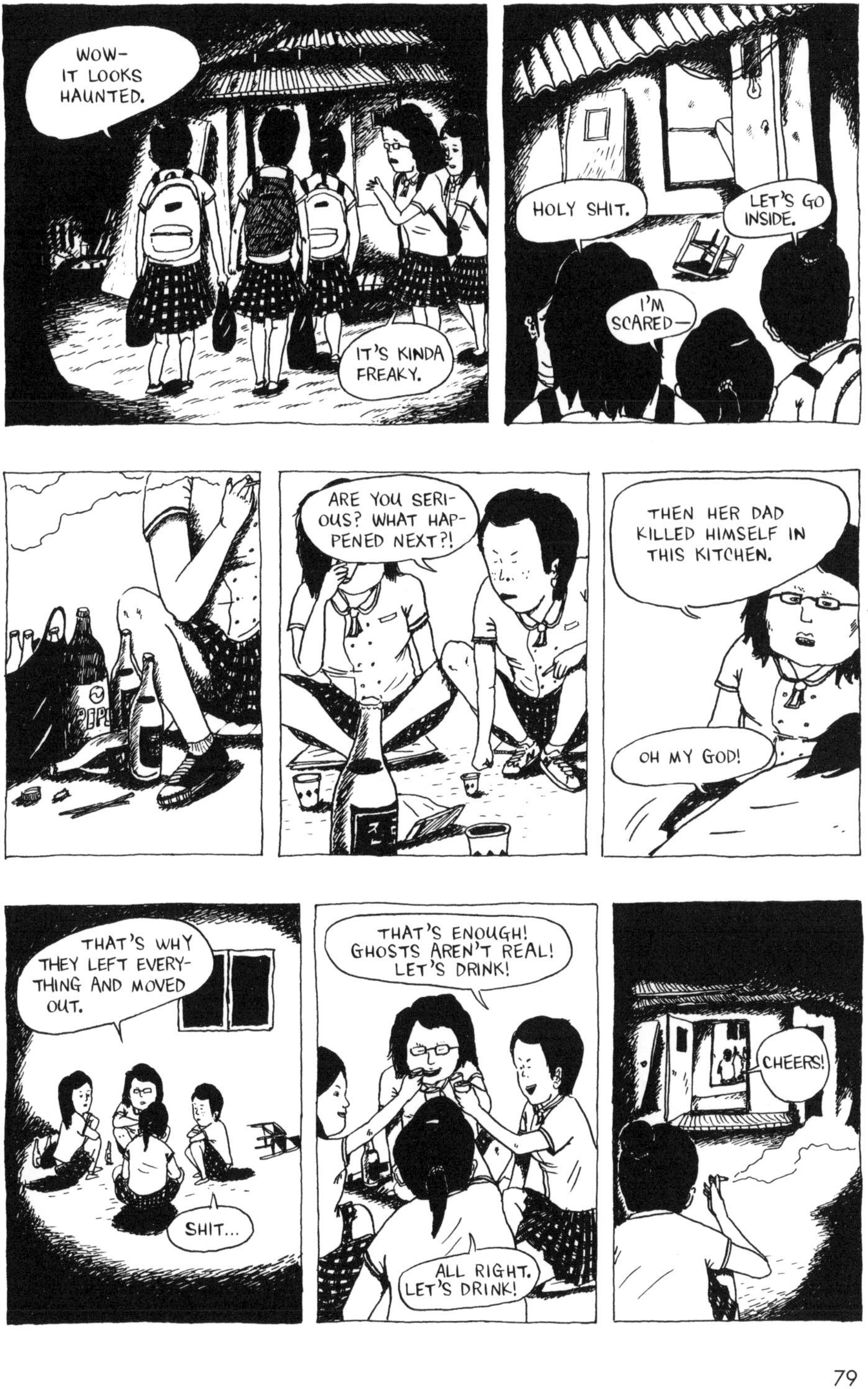
WOW-
IT LOOKS HAUNTED.
IT'S KINDA FREAKY.
HOLY SHIT.
LET'S GO INSIDE.
I'M SCARED—
ARE YOU SERI-OUS? WHAT HAP-PENED NEXT?!
THEN HER DAD KILLED HIMSELF IN THIS KITCHEN.
OH MY GOD!
THAT'S WHY THEY LEFT EVERY-THING AND MOVED OUT.
SHIT...
THAT'S ENOUGH! GHOSTS AREN'T REAL! LET'S DRINK!
ALL RIGHT. LET'S DRINK!
CHEERS!

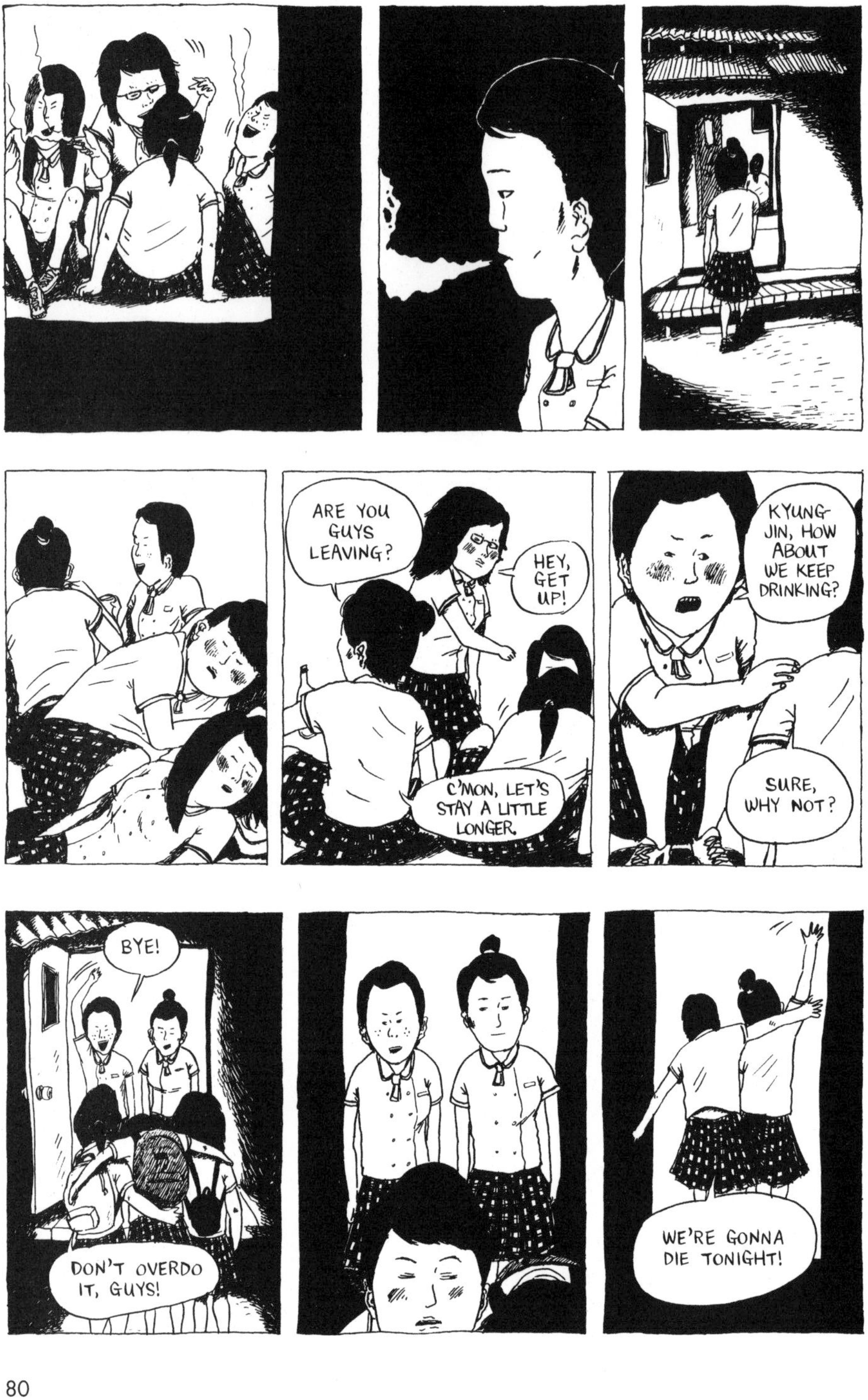
ARE YOU GUYS LEAVING?
HEY, GET UP!
C'MON, LET'S STAY A LITTLE LONGER.
KYUNG-JIN, HOW ABOUT WE KEEP DRINKING?
SURE, WHY NOT?
BYE!
DON'T OVERDO IT, GUYS!
WE'RE GONNA DIE TONIGHT!

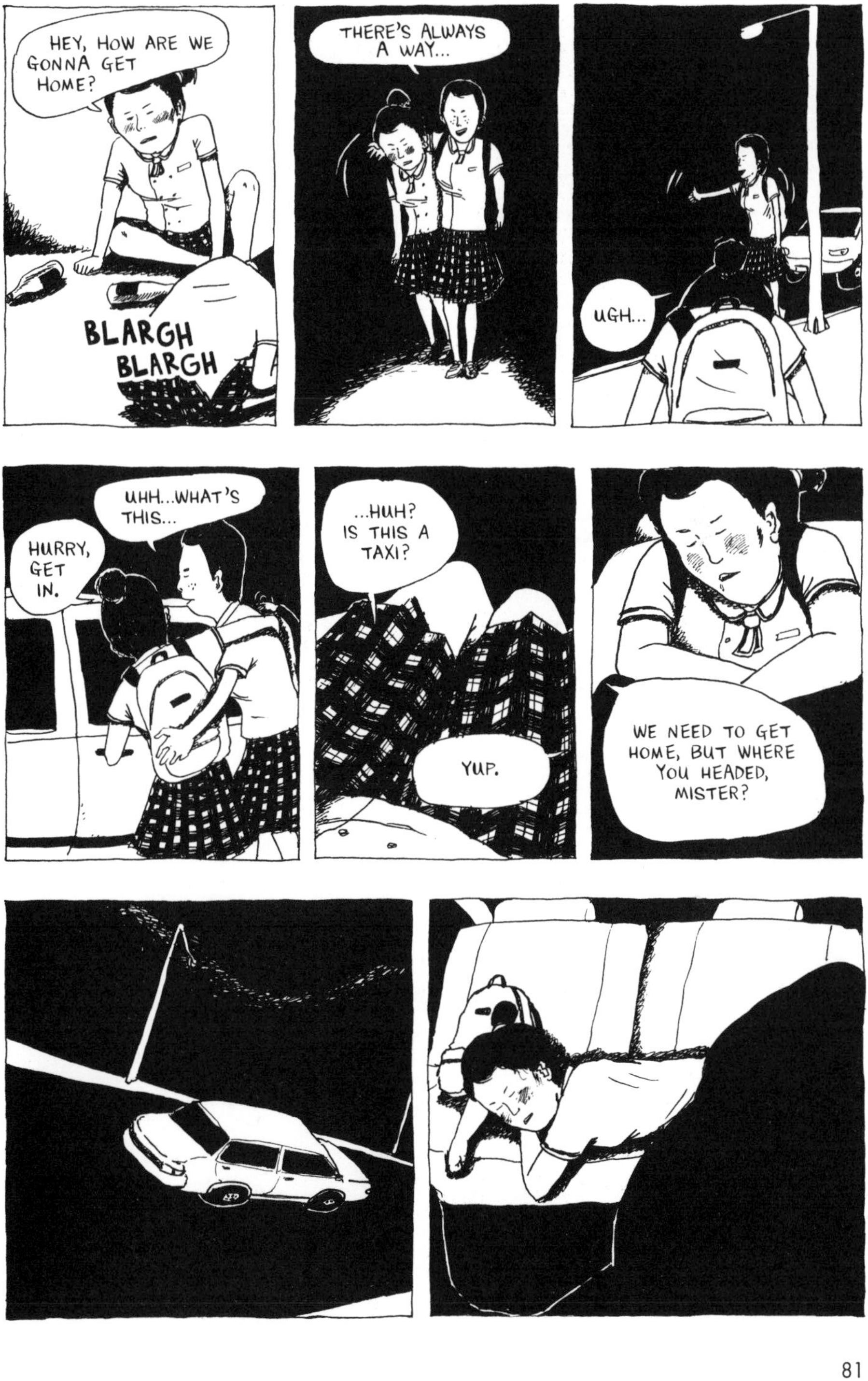
HEY, HOW ARE WE GONNA GET HOME?
BLARGH BLARGH
THERE'S ALWAYS A WAY...
UGH...
UHH...WHAT'S THIS...
HURRY, GET IN.
...HUH? IS THIS A TAXI?
YUP.
WE NEED TO GET HOME, BUT WHERE YOU HEADED, MISTER?

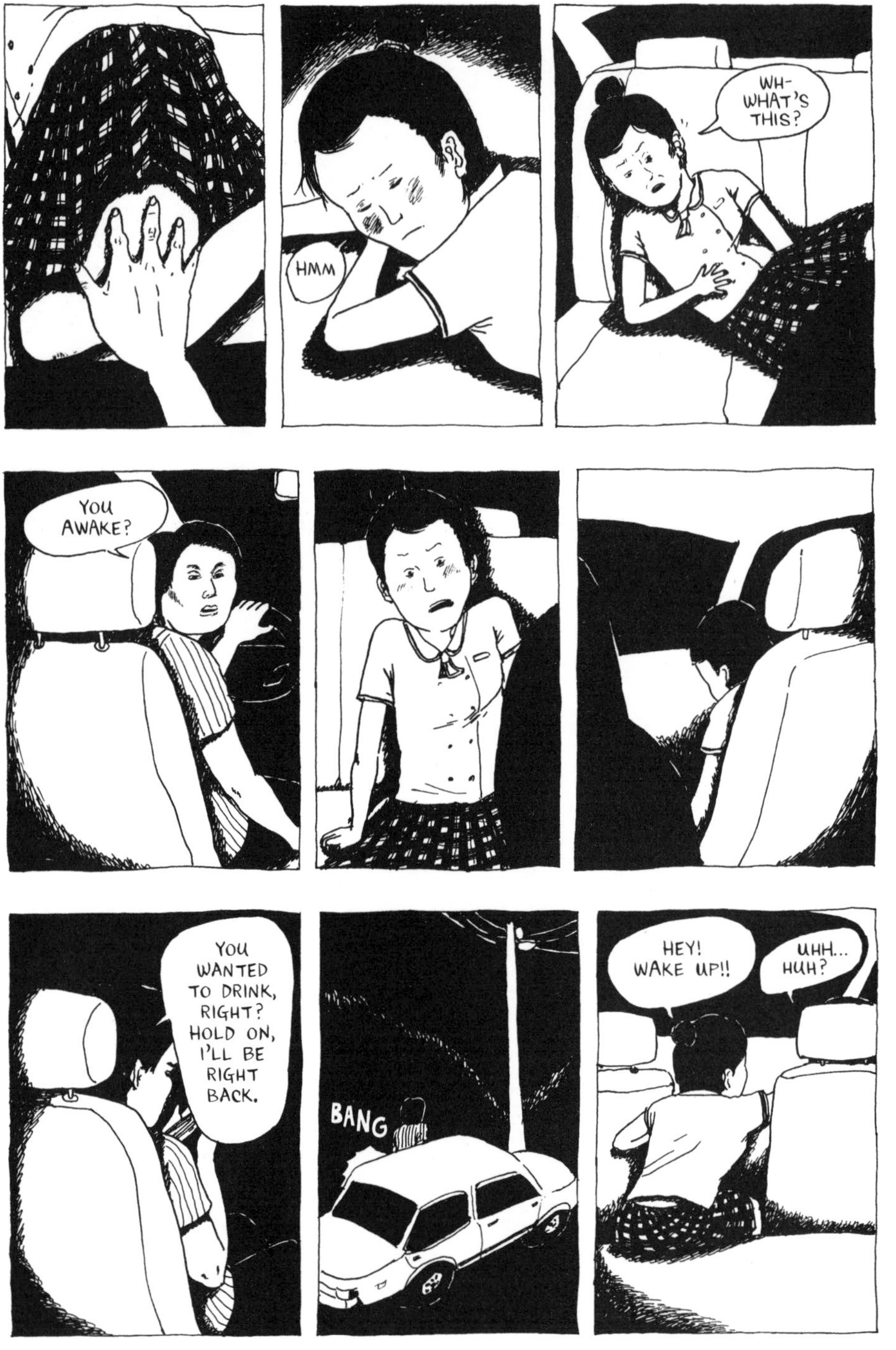
HMM
WH- WHAT'S THIS?
YOU AWAKE?
YOU WANTED TO DRINK, RIGHT? HOLD ON, I'LL BE RIGHT BACK.
BANG
HEY! WAKE UP!!
UHH... HUH?

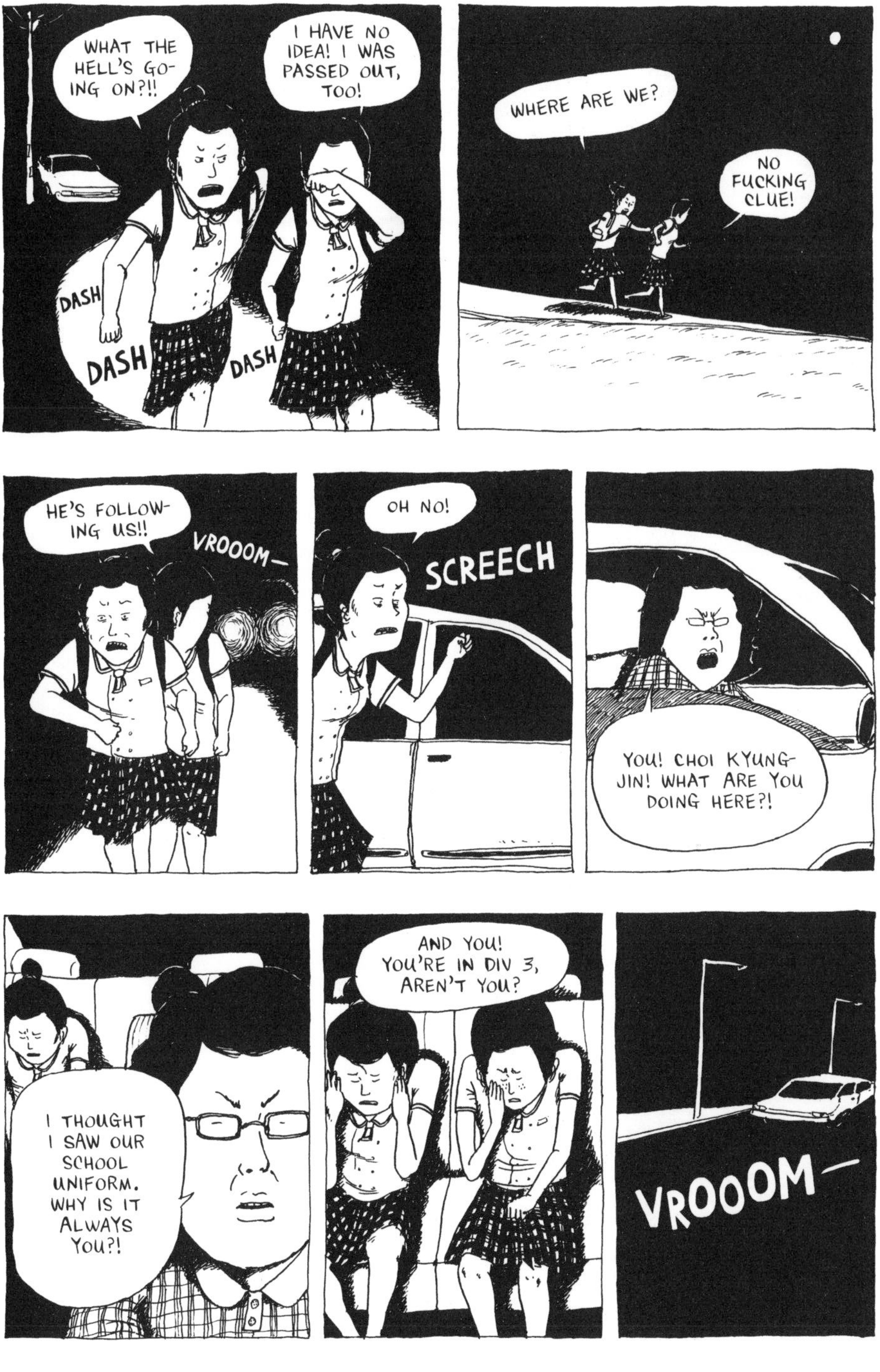
WHAT THE HELL'S GO-ING ON?!!
I HAVE NO IDEA! I WAS PASSED OUT, TOO!
DASH
DASH
DASH
WHERE ARE WE?
NO FUCKING CLUE!
HE'S FOLLOW-ING US!!
VROOOM—
OH NO!
SCREECH
YOU! CHOI KYUNG-JIN! WHAT ARE YOU DOING HERE?!
I THOUGHT I SAW OUR SCHOOL UNIFORM. WHY IS IT ALWAYS YOU?!
AND YOU! YOU'RE IN DIV 3, AREN'T YOU?
VROOOM—

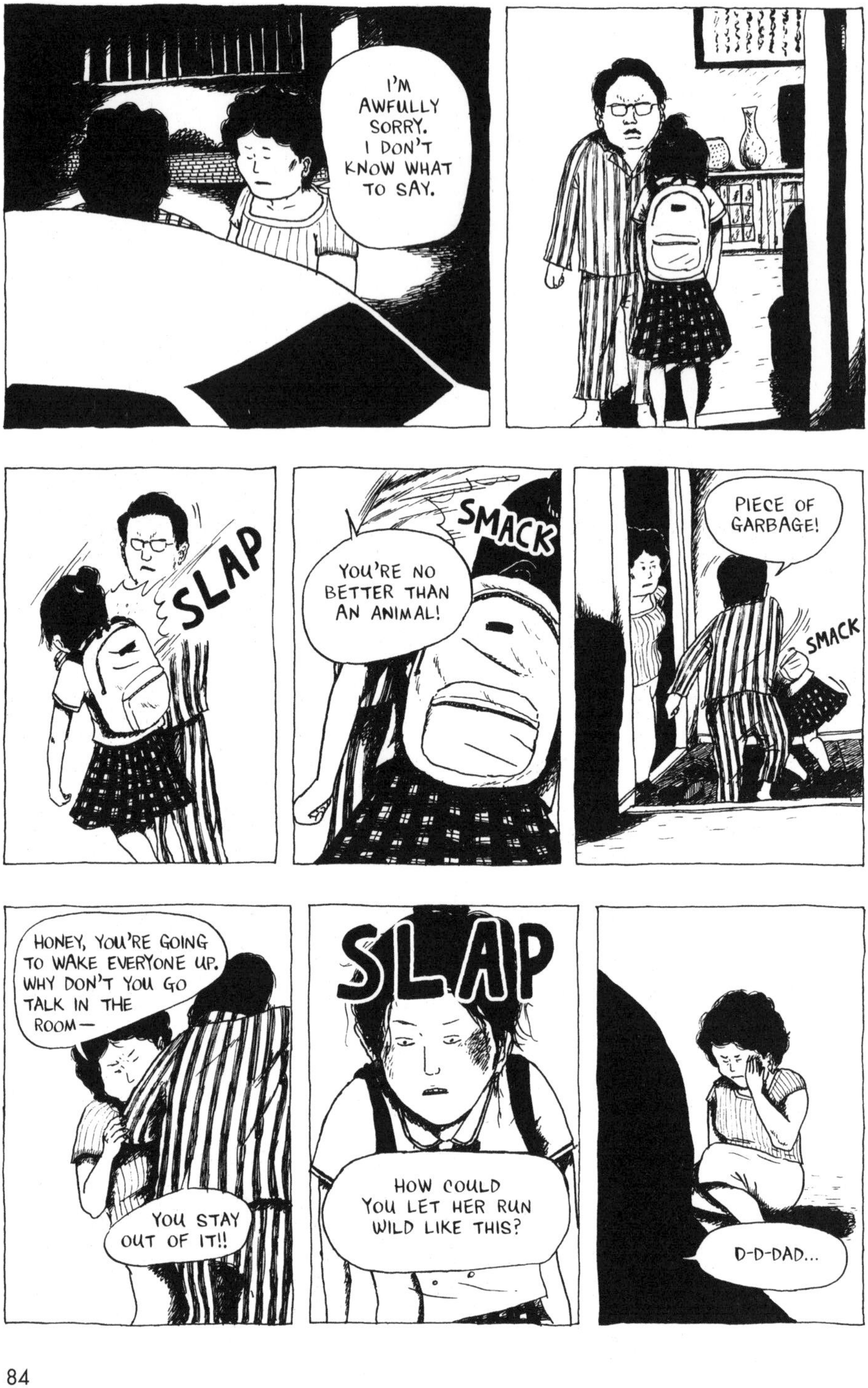
I'M AWFULLY SORRY. I DON'T KNOW WHAT TO SAY.
SLAP
SMACK
YOU'RE NO BETTER THAN AN ANIMAL!
PIECE OF GARBAGE!
SMACK
HONEY, YOU'RE GOING TO WAKE EVERYONE UP. WHY DON'T YOU GO TALK IN THE ROOM—
YOU STAY OUT OF IT!!
SLAP
HOW COULD YOU LET HER RUN WILD LIKE THIS?
D-D-DAD...

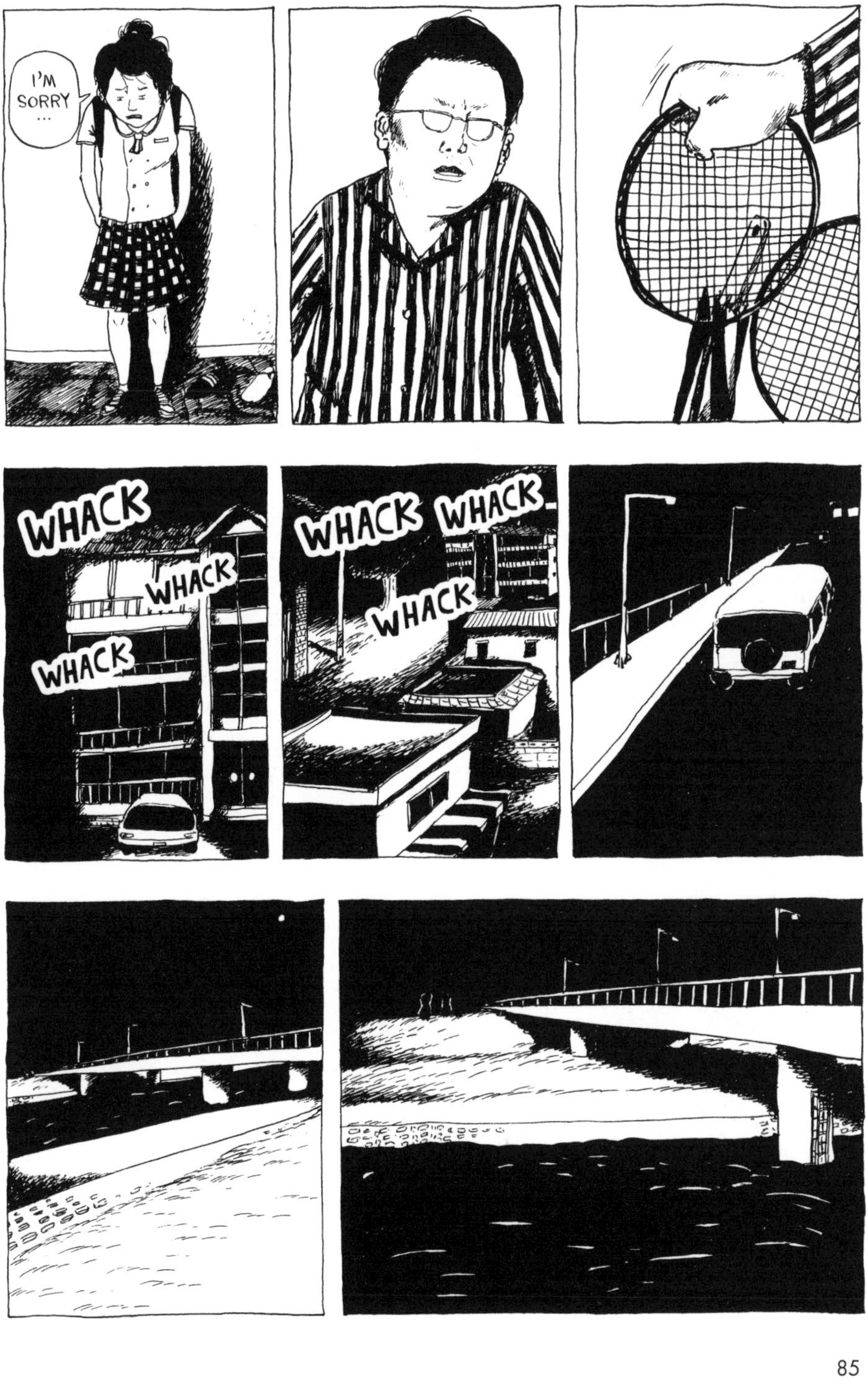
I'M SORRY ...
WHACK
WHACK
WHACK
WHACK WHACK
WHACK

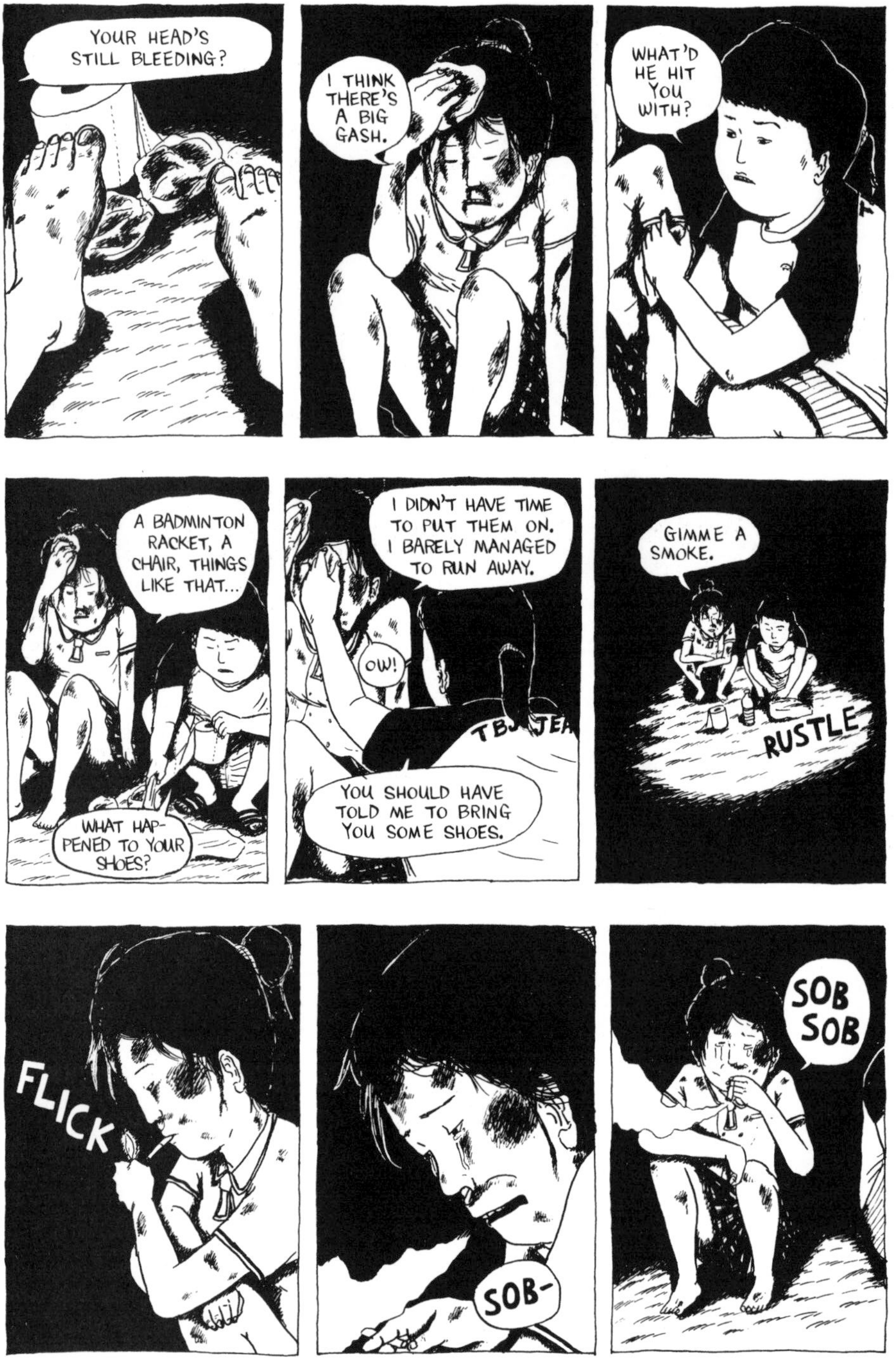
YOUR HEAD'S STILL BLEEDING?
I THINK THERE'S A BIG GASH.
WHAT'D HE HIT YOU WITH?
A BADMINTON RACKET, A CHAIR, THINGS LIKE THAT...
WHAT HAPPENED TO YOUR SHOES?
I DIDN'T HAVE TIME TO PUT THEM ON. I BARELY MANAGED TO RUN AWAY.
OW!
YOU SHOULD HAVE TOLD ME TO BRING YOU SOME SHOES.
GIMME A SMOKE.
RUSTLE
FLICK
SOB-
SOB SOB

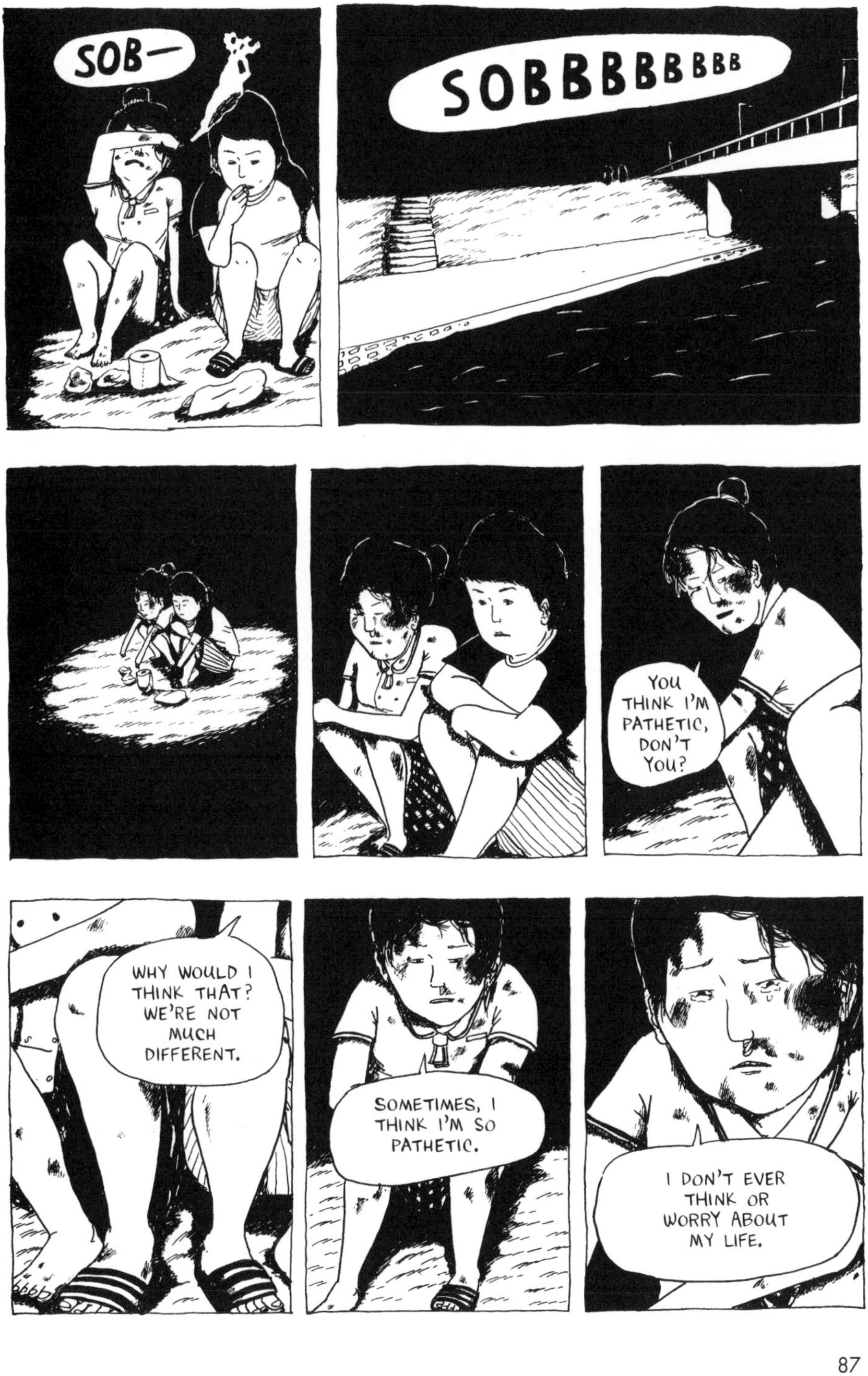
SOB—
SOBBBBBBBB
YOU THINK I'M PATHETIC, DON'T YOU?
WHY WOULD I THINK THAT? WE'RE NOT MUCH DIFFERENT.
SOMETIMES, I THINK I'M SO PATHETIC.
I DON'T EVER THINK OR WORRY ABOUT MY LIFE.

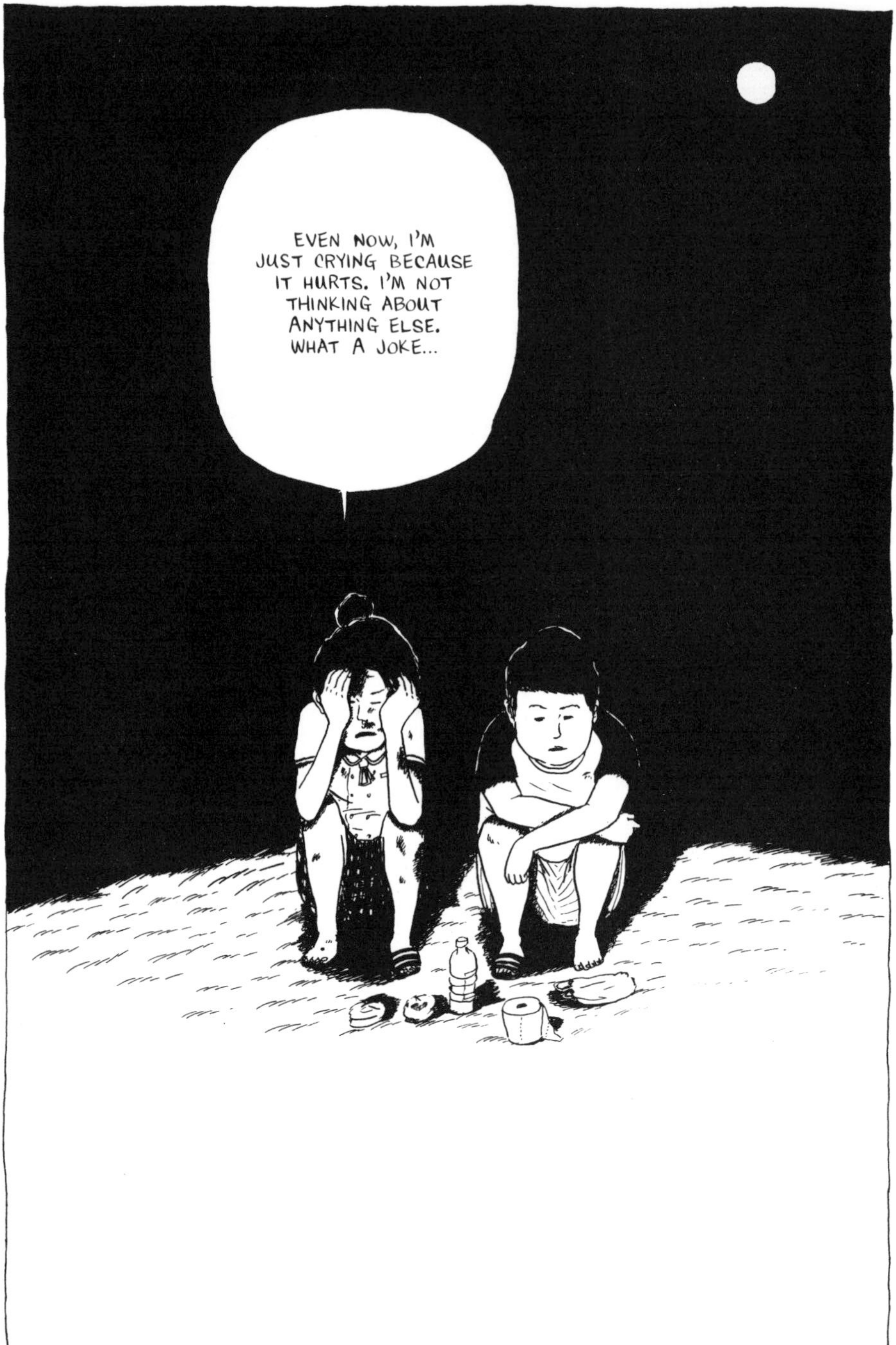
EVEN NOW, I'M JUST CRYING BECAUSE IT HURTS. I'M NOT THINKING ABOUT ANYTHING ELSE. WHAT A JOKE...

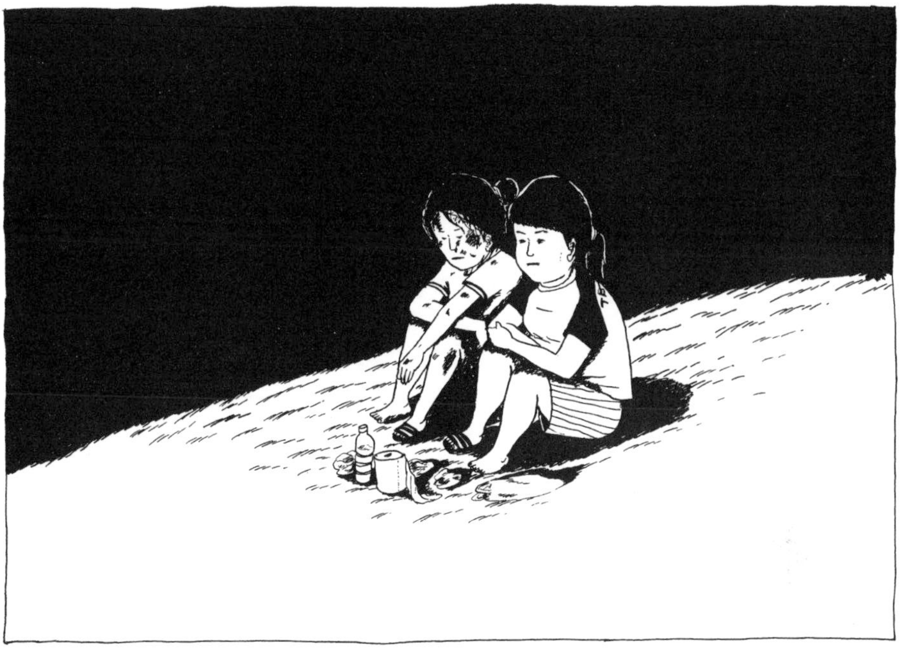

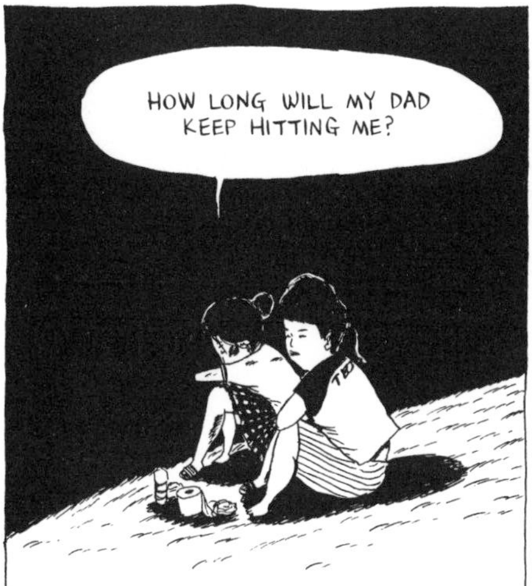
HOW LONG WILL MY DAD KEEP HITTING ME?

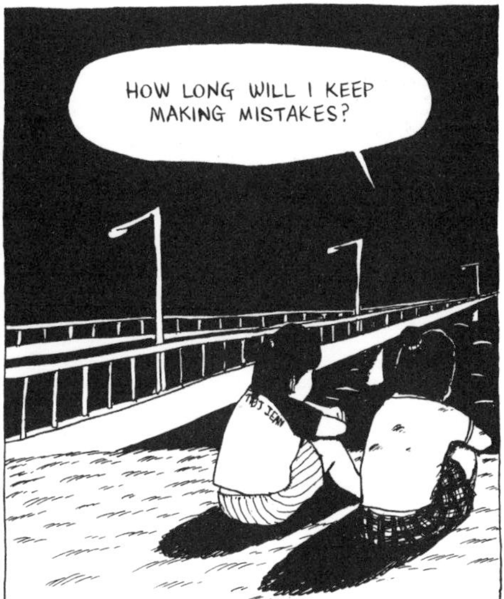
HOW LONG WILL I KEEP MAKING MISTAKES?

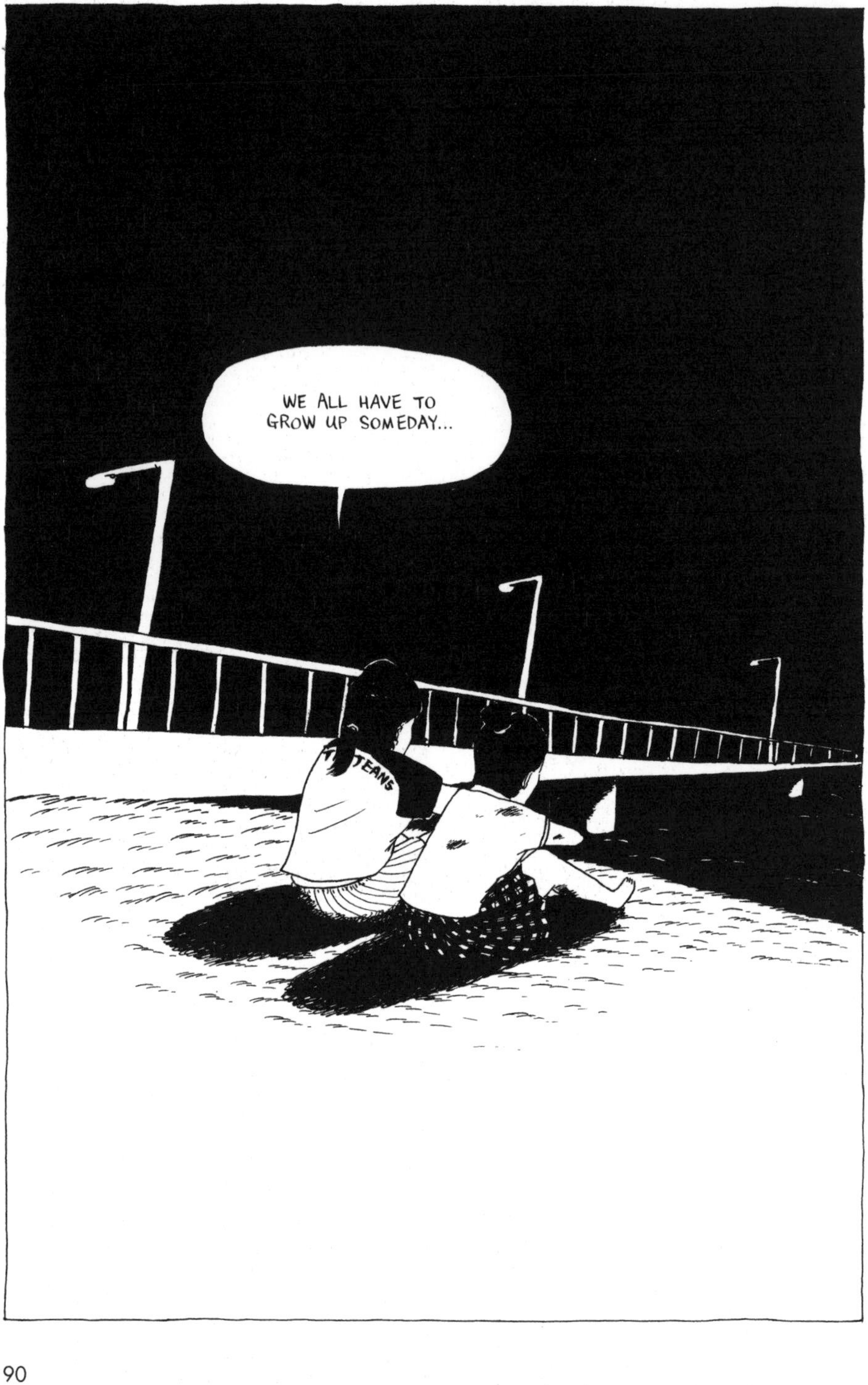
WE ALL HAVE TO GROW UP SOMEDAY...
TEANS

school of kyung-jin

TODAY, I WOULD LIKE TO TALK ABOUT MY SCHOOL.

THE SCHOOL OF KYUNG-JIN, LOCATED IN HADAEWON-DONG, JUNGWON, SEONGNAM, GYEONGGI PROVINCE, CONSISTS OF PRINCIPAL CHOI KYUNG-JIN, TEACHER CHOI KYUNG-JIN, AND STUDENTS CHOI KYUNG-JIN AND KWON YONGDEUK.

STUDENT #2, KWON YONGDEUK

LET'S TAKE A LOOK AT A DAY IN THE LIFE OF MY SCHOOL, SHALL WE?

UHH...GUESS IT'S TIME I GOT UP.

THE FIRST CLASS BEGINS WHENEVER I WAKE UP.

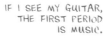

IF I SEE MY GUITAR, THE FIRST PERIOD IS MUSIC.

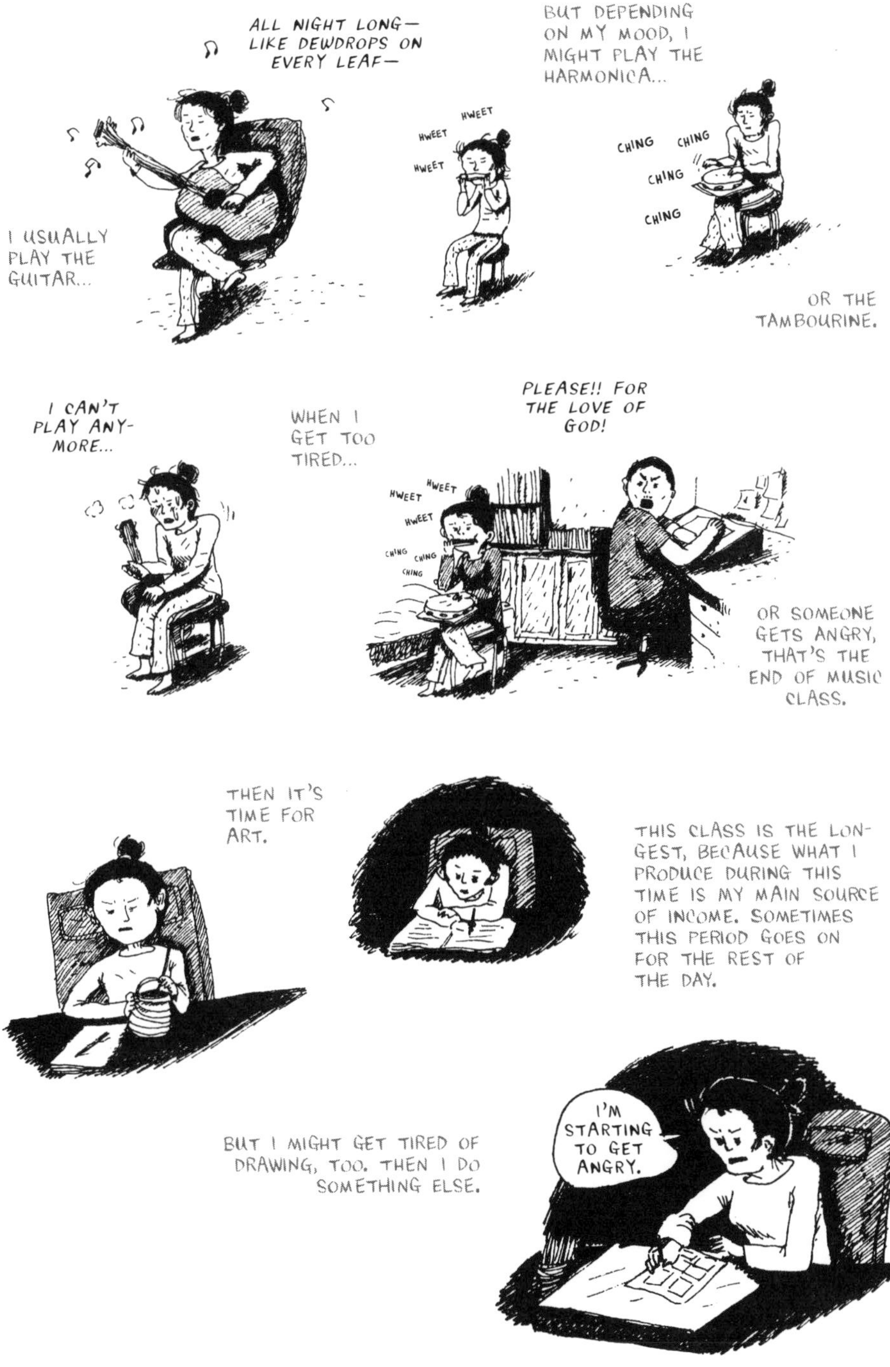
ALL NIGHT LONG— LIKE DEWDROPS ON EVERY LEAF—
I USUALLY PLAY THE GUITAR...
HWEET
HWEET
HWEET
BUT DEPENDING ON MY MOOD, I MIGHT PLAY THE HARMONICA...
CHING
CHING
CHING
CHING
OR THE TAMBOURINE.
I CAN'T PLAY ANY-MORE...
WHEN I GET TOO TIRED...
PLEASE!! FOR THE LOVE OF GOD!
HWEET
HWEET
HWEET
CHING
CHING
CHING
OR SOMEONE GETS ANGRY, THAT'S THE END OF MUSIC CLASS.
THEN IT'S TIME FOR ART.
THIS CLASS IS THE LON-GEST, BECAUSE WHAT I PRODUCE DURING THIS TIME IS MY MAIN SOURCE OF INCOME. SOMETIMES THIS PERIOD GOES ON FOR THE REST OF THE DAY.
BUT I MIGHT GET TIRED OF DRAWING, TOO. THEN I DO SOMETHING ELSE.
I'M STARTING TO GET ANGRY.

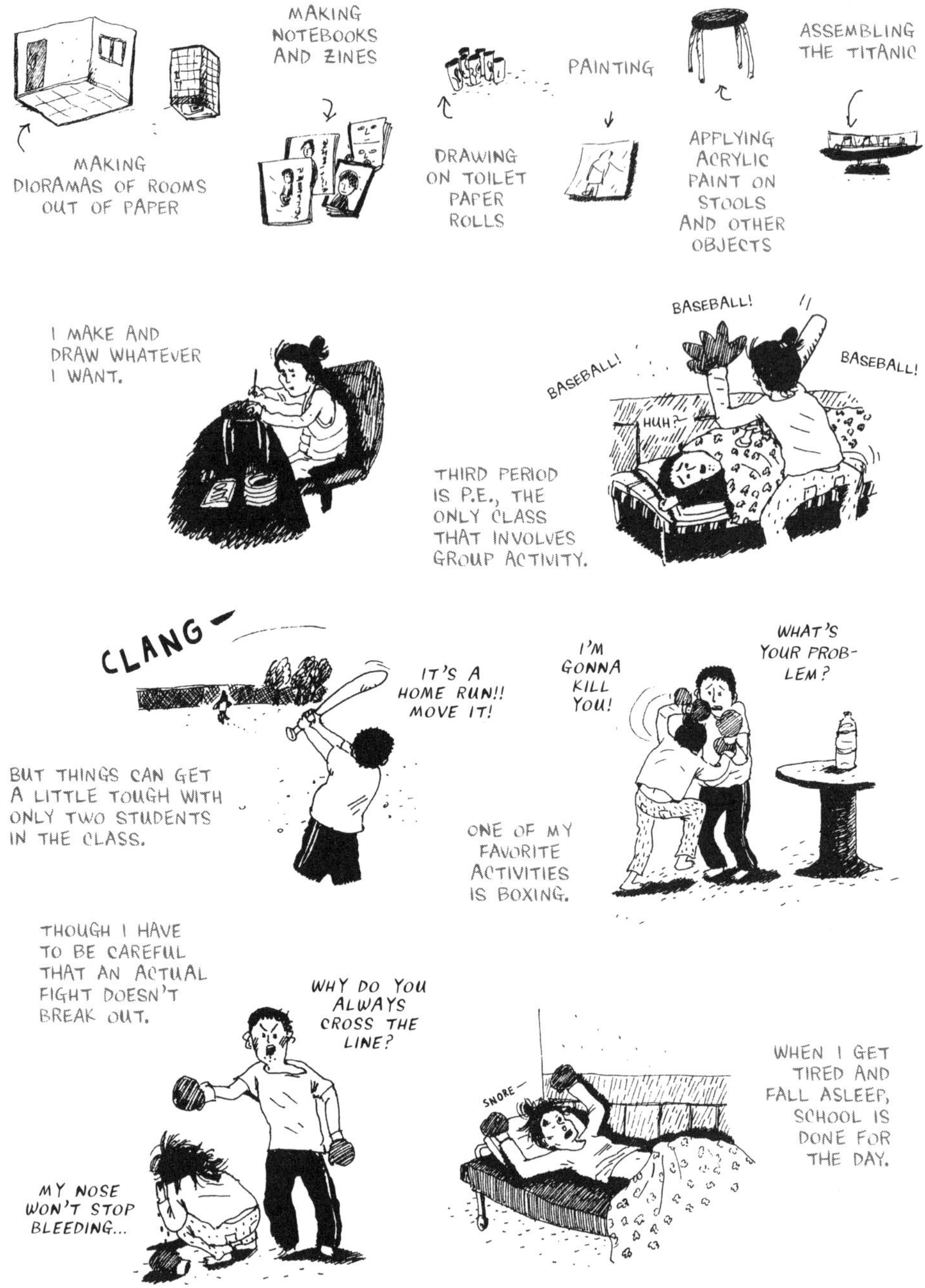
MAKING DIORAMAS OF ROOMS OUT OF PAPER
MAKING NOTEBOOKS AND ZINES
DRAWING ON TOILET PAPER ROLLS
PAINTING
APPLYING ACRYLIC PAINT ON STOOLS AND OTHER OBJECTS
ASSEMBLING THE TITANIC
I MAKE AND DRAW WHATEVER I WANT.
THIRD PERIOD IS P.E., THE ONLY CLASS THAT INVOLVES GROUP ACTIVITY.
BASEBALL!
BASEBALL!
BASEBALL!
HUH?
CLANG-
IT'S A HOME RUN!! MOVE IT!
BUT THINGS CAN GET A LITTLE TOUGH WITH ONLY TWO STUDENTS IN THE CLASS.
I'M GONNA KILL YOU!
WHAT'S YOUR PROB-LEM?
ONE OF MY FAVORITE ACTIVITIES IS BOXING.
THOUGH I HAVE TO BE CAREFUL THAT AN ACTUAL FIGHT DOESN'T BREAK OUT.
WHY DO YOU ALWAYS CROSS THE LINE?
MY NOSE WON'T STOP BLEEDING...
SNORE-
WHEN I GET TIRED AND FALL ASLEEP, SCHOOL IS DONE FOR THE DAY.

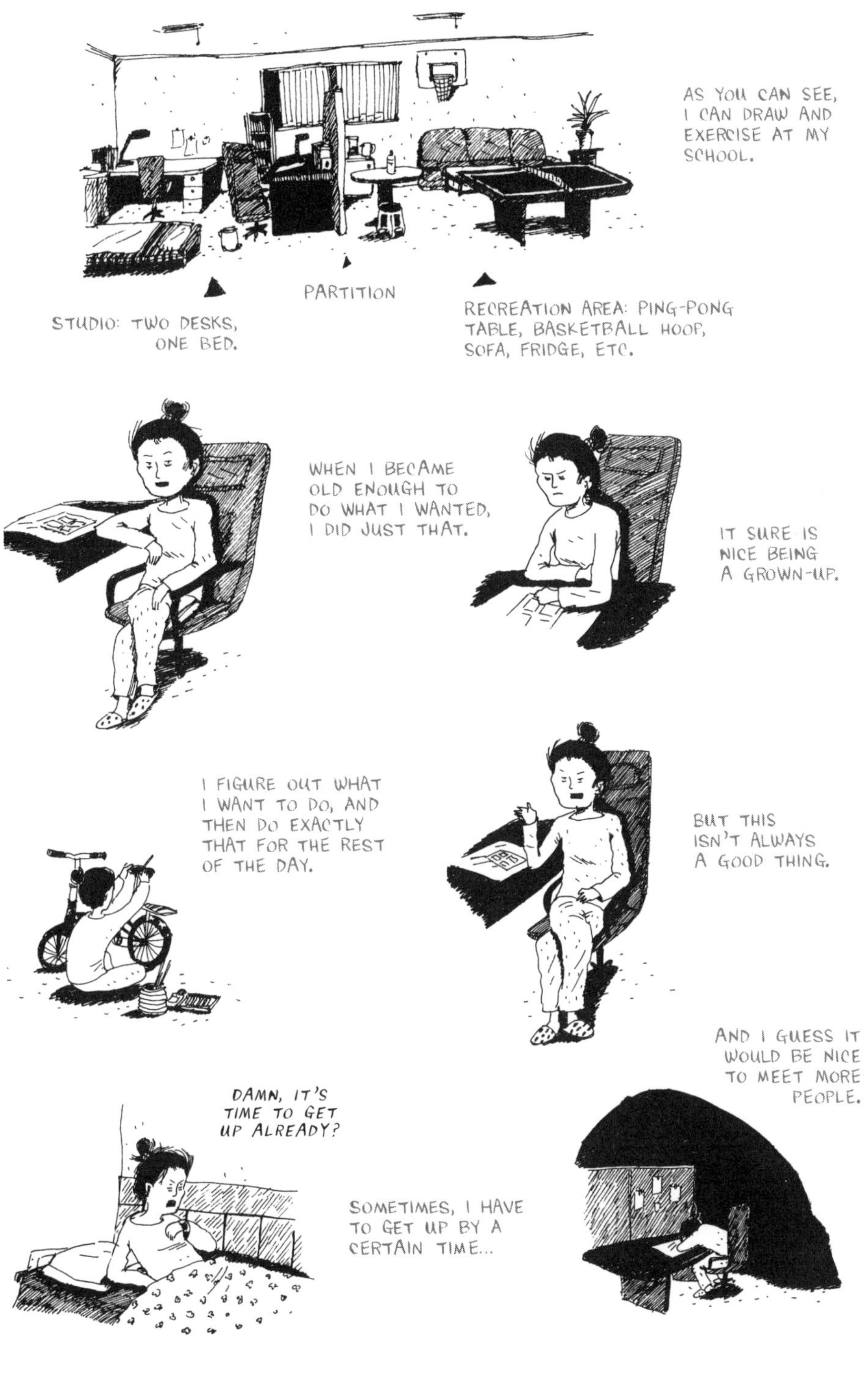
AS YOU CAN SEE, I CAN DRAW AND EXERCISE AT MY SCHOOL.
STUDIO: TWO DESKS, ONE BED.
PARTITION
RECREATION AREA: PING-PONG TABLE, BASKETBALL HOOP, SOFA, FRIDGE, ETC.
WHEN I BECAME OLD ENOUGH TO DO WHAT I WANTED, I DID JUST THAT.
IT SURE IS NICE BEING A GROWN-UP.
I FIGURE OUT WHAT I WANT TO DO, AND THEN DO EXACTLY THAT FOR THE REST OF THE DAY.
BUT THIS ISN'T ALWAYS A GOOD THING.
AND I GUESS IT WOULD BE NICE TO MEET MORE PEOPLE.
DAMN, IT'S TIME TO GET UP ALREADY?
SOMETIMES, I HAVE TO GET UP BY A CERTAIN TIME...

do you know jinsil?

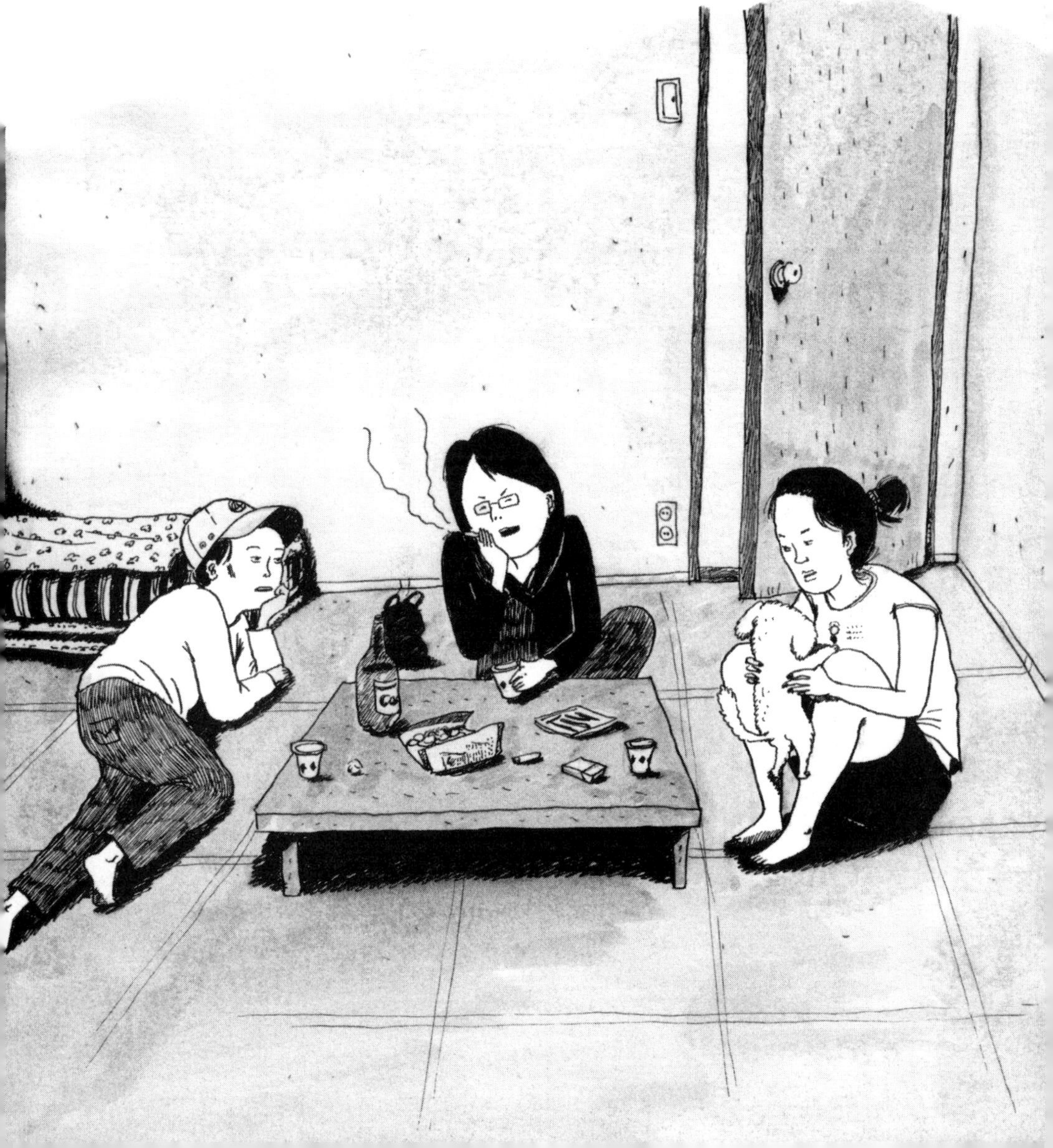

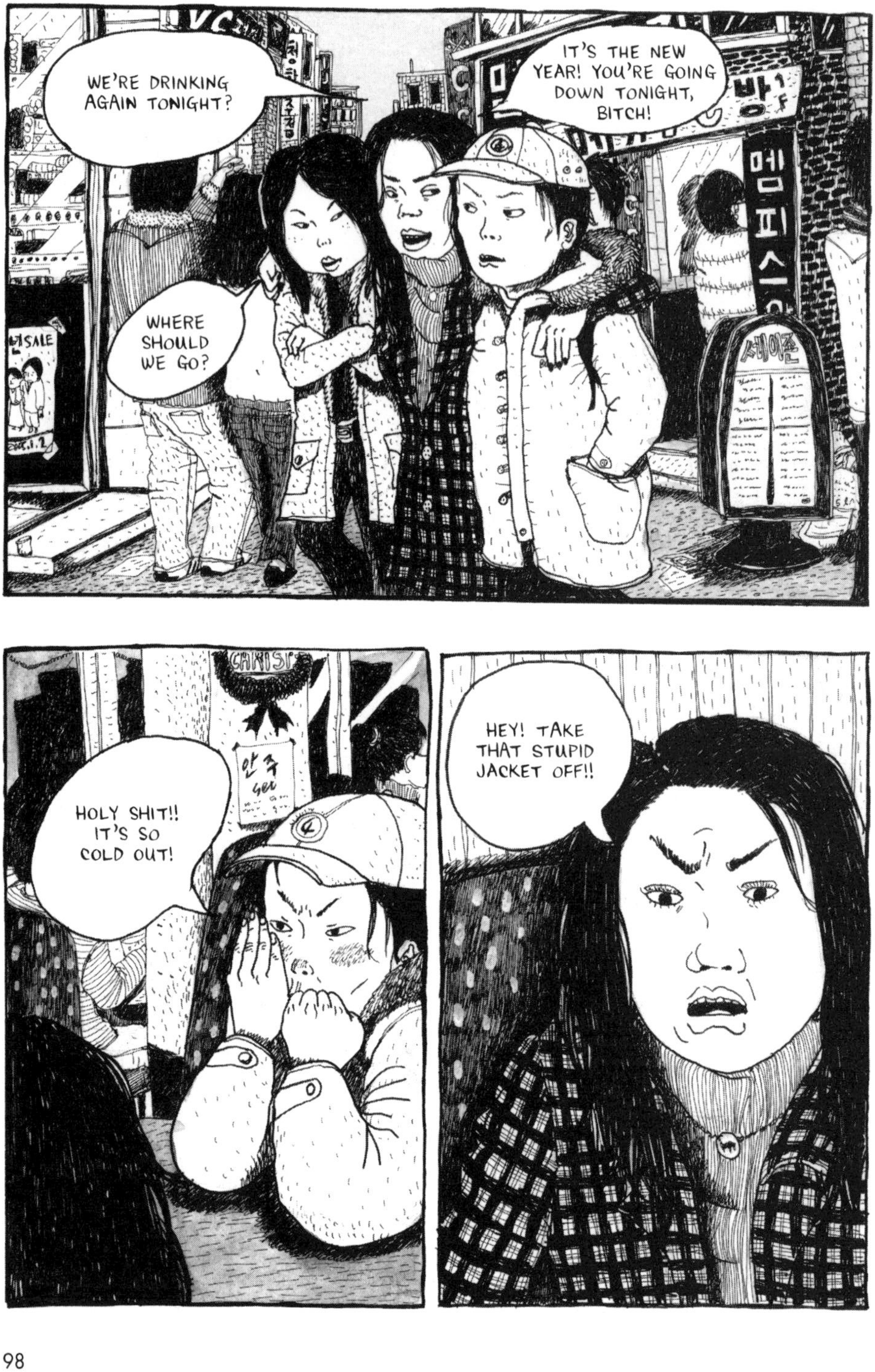
WE'RE DRINKING AGAIN TONIGHT?
IT'S THE NEW YEAR! YOU'RE GOING DOWN TONIGHT, BITCH!
WHERE SHOULD WE GO?
HOLY SHIT!! IT'S SO COLD OUT!
HEY! TAKE THAT STUPID JACKET OFF!!

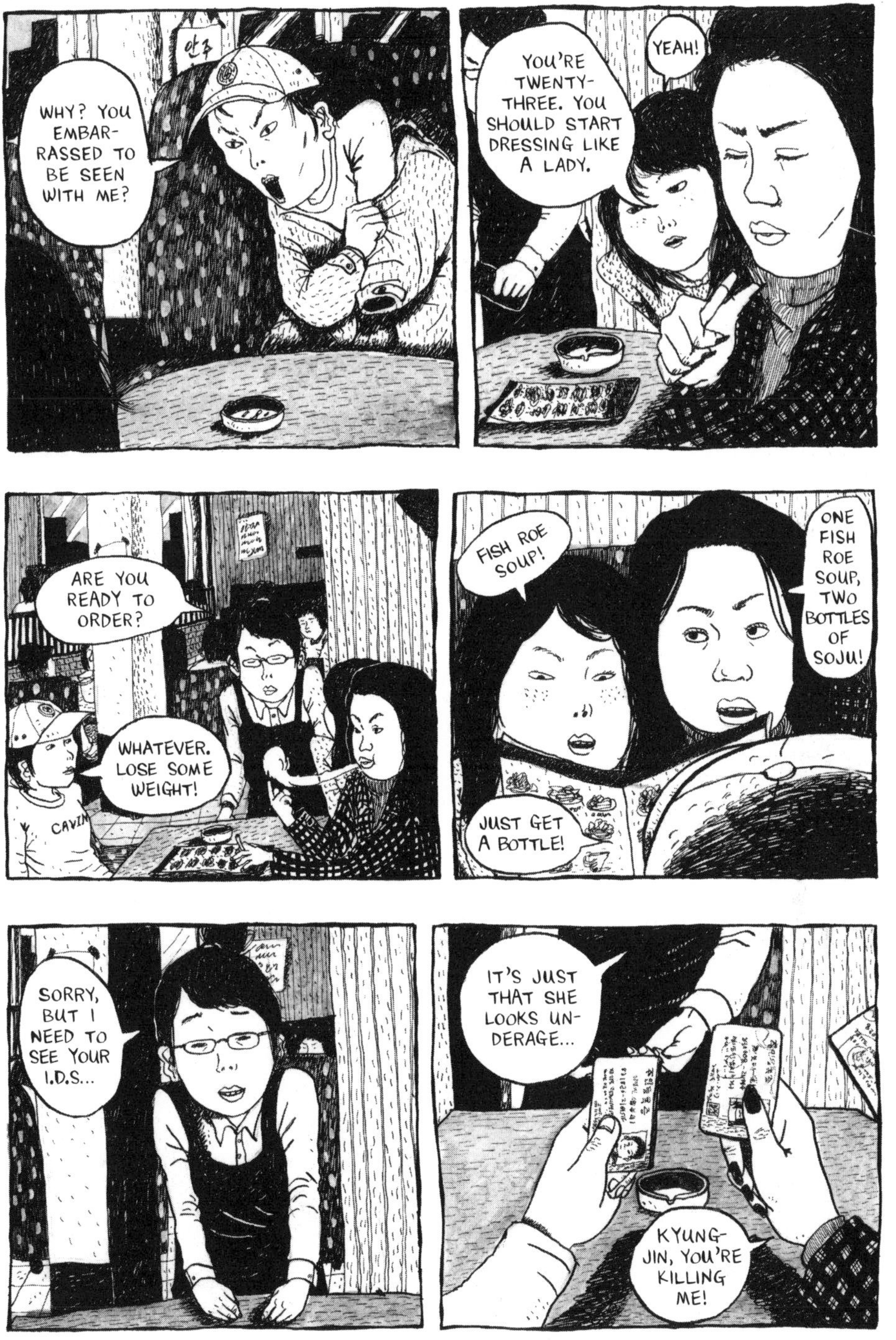
WHY? YOU EMBAR-RASSED TO BE SEEN WITH ME?
YOU'RE TWENTY-THREE. YOU SHOULD START DRESSING LIKE A LADY.
YEAH!
ARE YOU READY TO ORDER?
WHATEVER. LOSE SOME WEIGHT!
CAVIN
FISH ROE SOUP!
ONE FISH ROE SOUP, TWO BOTTLES OF SOJU!
JUST GET A BOTTLE!
SORRY, BUT I NEED TO SEE YOUR I.D.S...
IT'S JUST THAT SHE LOOKS UN-DERAGE...
KYUNG-JIN, YOU'RE KILLING ME!

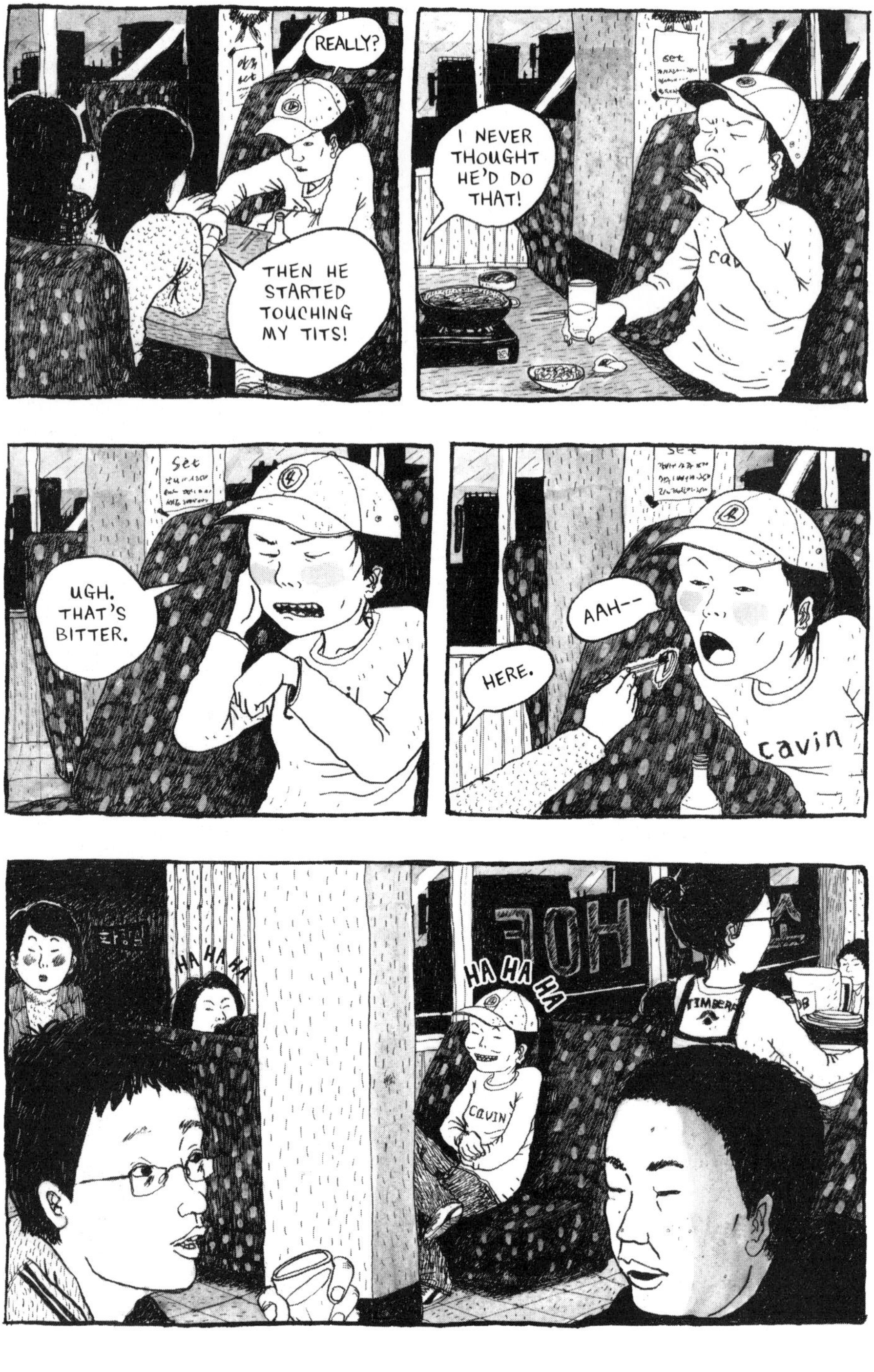
REALLY?
THEN HE STARTED TOUCHING MY TITS!
I NEVER THOUGHT HE'D DO THAT!
cavin
UGH. THAT'S BITTER.
AAH--
HERE.
cavin
HA HA HA
HA HA HA
CAVIN

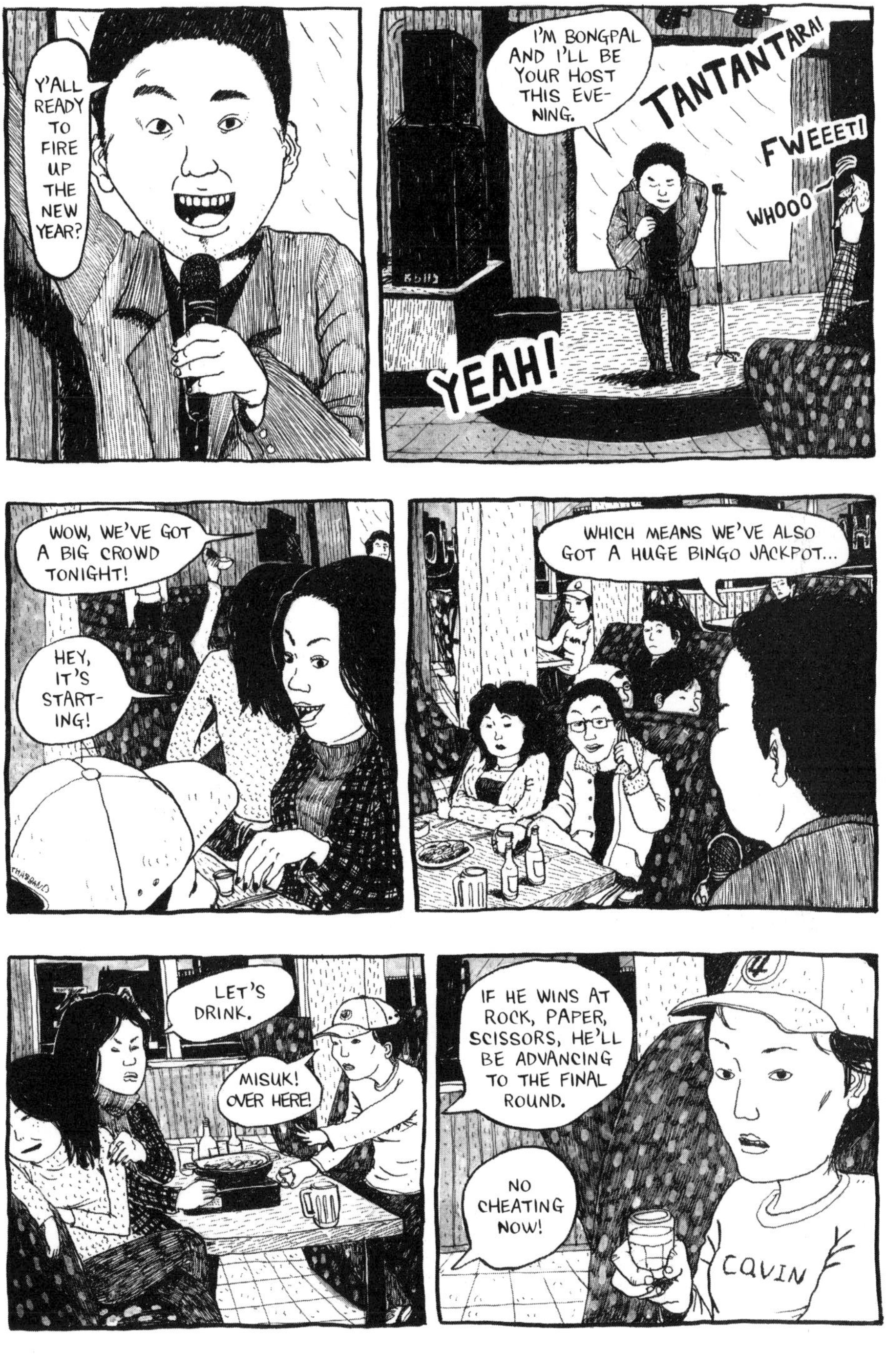
Y'ALL READY TO FIRE UP THE NEW YEAR?
I'M BONGPAL AND I'LL BE YOUR HOST THIS EVE-NING.
TANTANTARA!
FWEEET!
WHOOO
YEAH!
WOW, WE'VE GOT A BIG CROWD TONIGHT!
HEY, IT'S START-ING!
WHICH MEANS WE'VE ALSO GOT A HUGE BINGO JACKPOT...
LET'S DRINK.
MISUK! OVER HERE!
IF HE WINS AT ROCK, PAPER, SCISSORS, HE'LL BE ADVANCING TO THE FINAL ROUND.
NO CHEATING NOW!
CQVIN

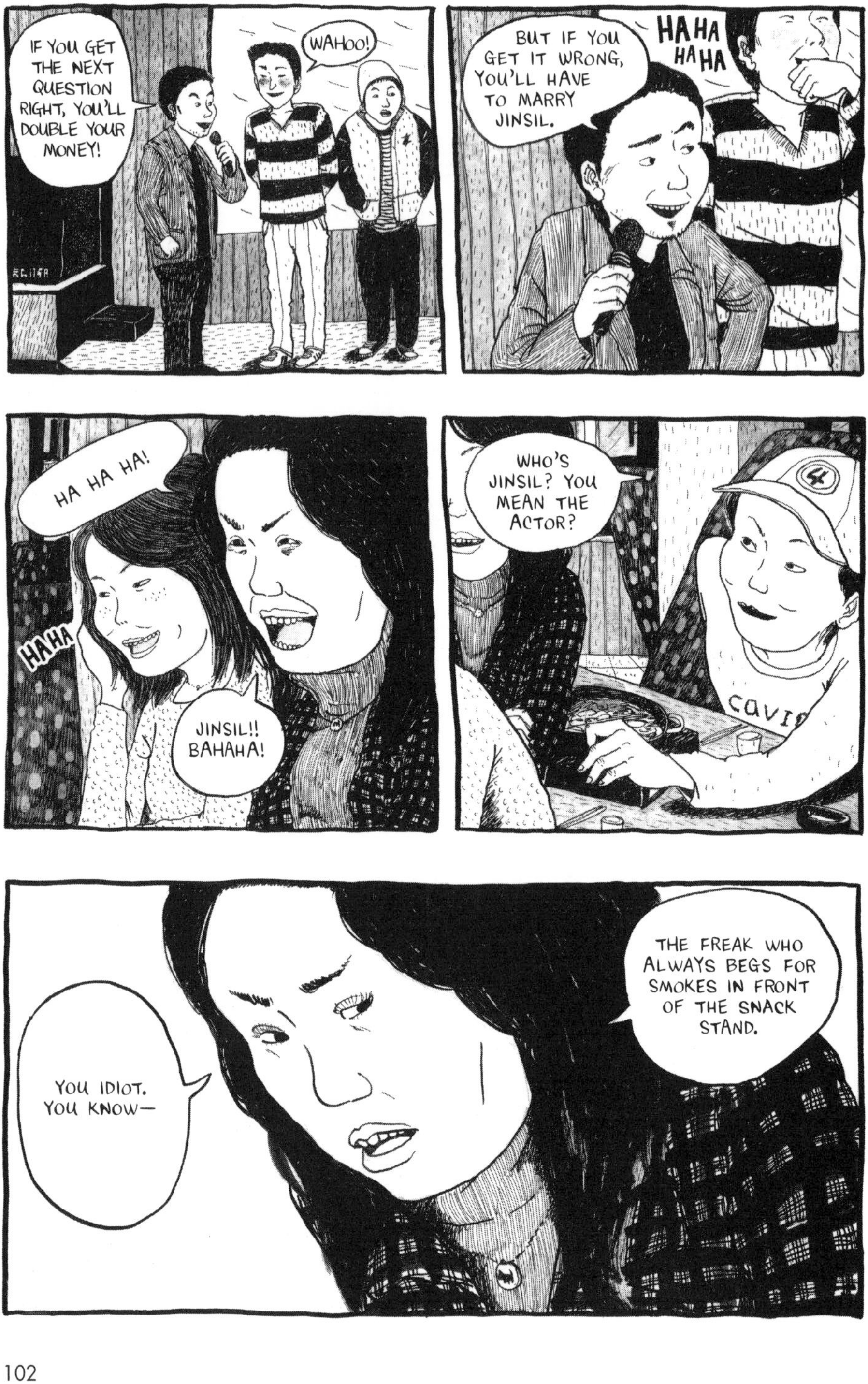
IF YOU GET THE NEXT QUESTION RIGHT, YOU'LL DOUBLE YOUR MONEY!
WAHOO!
BUT IF YOU GET IT WRONG, YOU'LL HAVE TO MARRY JINSIL.
HA HA HA HA
HA HA HA!
HAHA
JINSIL!! BAHAHA!
WHO'S JINSIL? YOU MEAN THE ACTOR?
YOU IDIOT. YOU KNOW—
THE FREAK WHO ALWAYS BEGS FOR SMOKES IN FRONT OF THE SNACK STAND.

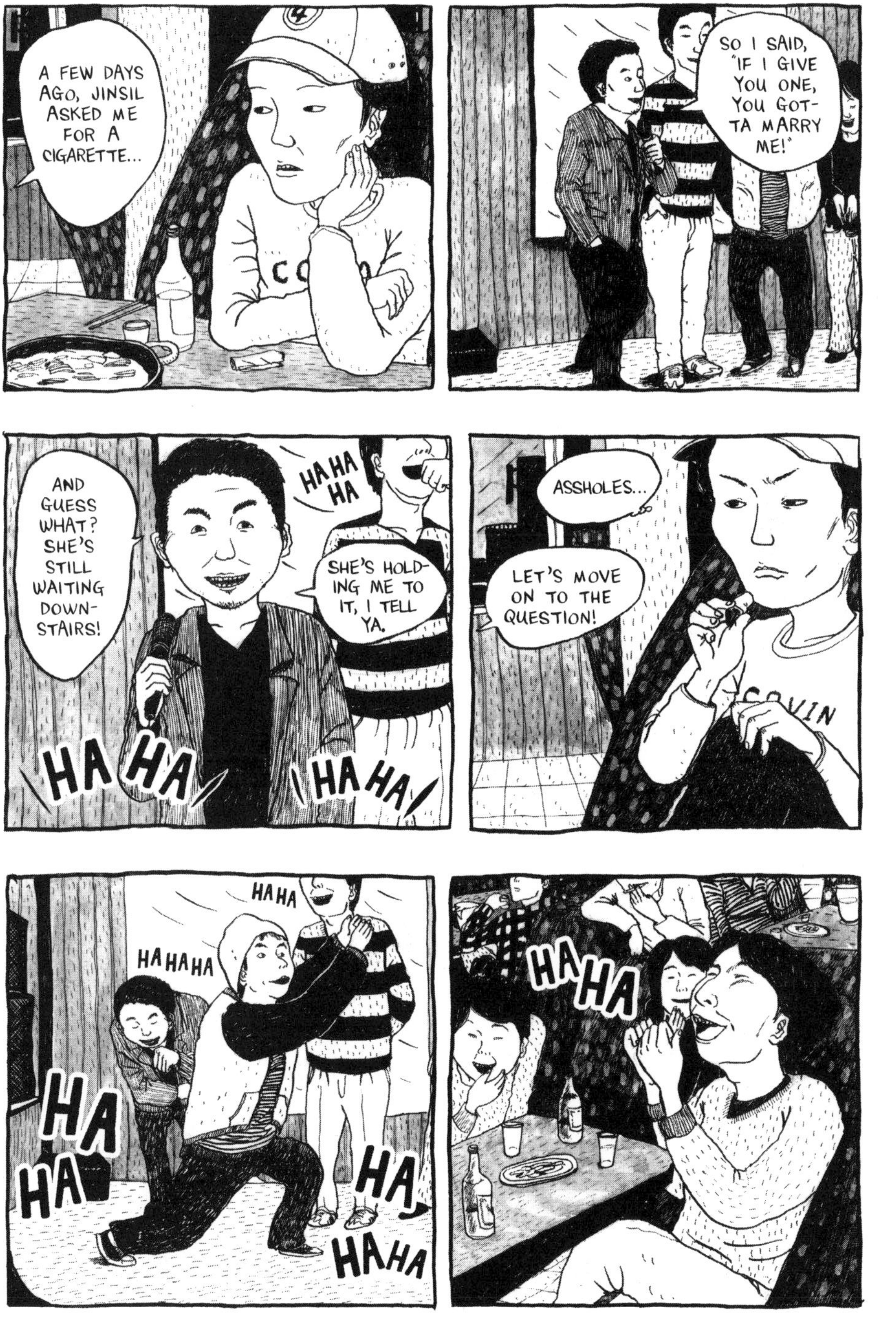
A FEW DAYS AGO, JINSIL ASKED ME FOR A CIGARETTE...
SO I SAID, "IF I GIVE YOU ONE, YOU GOTTA MARRY ME!"
AND GUESS WHAT? SHE'S STILL WAITING DOWN-STAIRS!
HA HA HA
SHE'S HOLD-ING ME TO IT, I TELL YA.
HA HA
HA HA
ASSHOLES...
LET'S MOVE ON TO THE QUESTION!
HA HA
HA HA HA
HA HA
HA HA
HA HA
HA HA

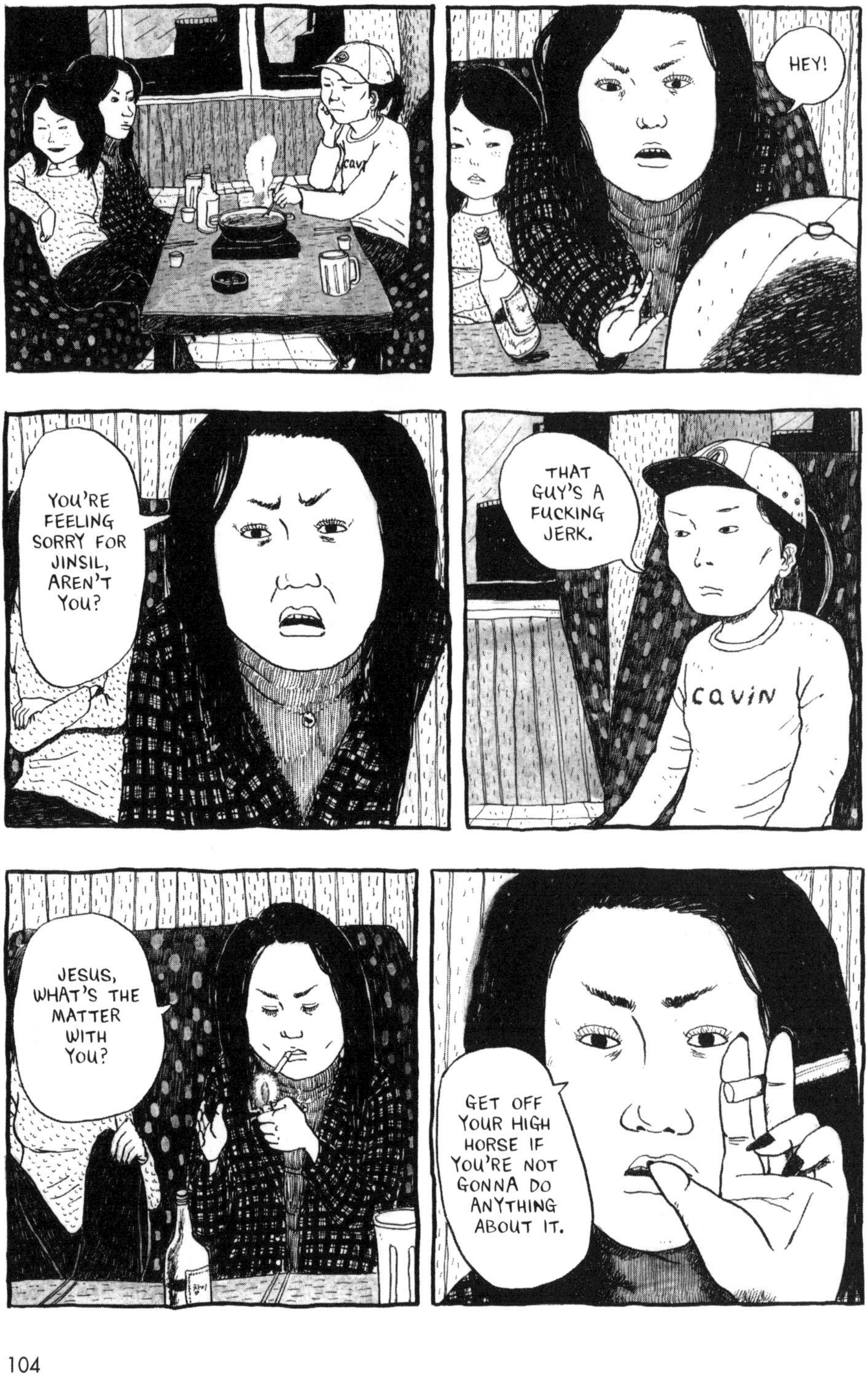
HEY!
YOU'RE FEELING SORRY FOR JINSIL, AREN'T YOU?
THAT GUY'S A FUCKING JERK.
CAVIN
JESUS, WHAT'S THE MATTER WITH YOU?
GET OFF YOUR HIGH HORSE IF YOU'RE NOT GONNA DO ANYTHING ABOUT IT.

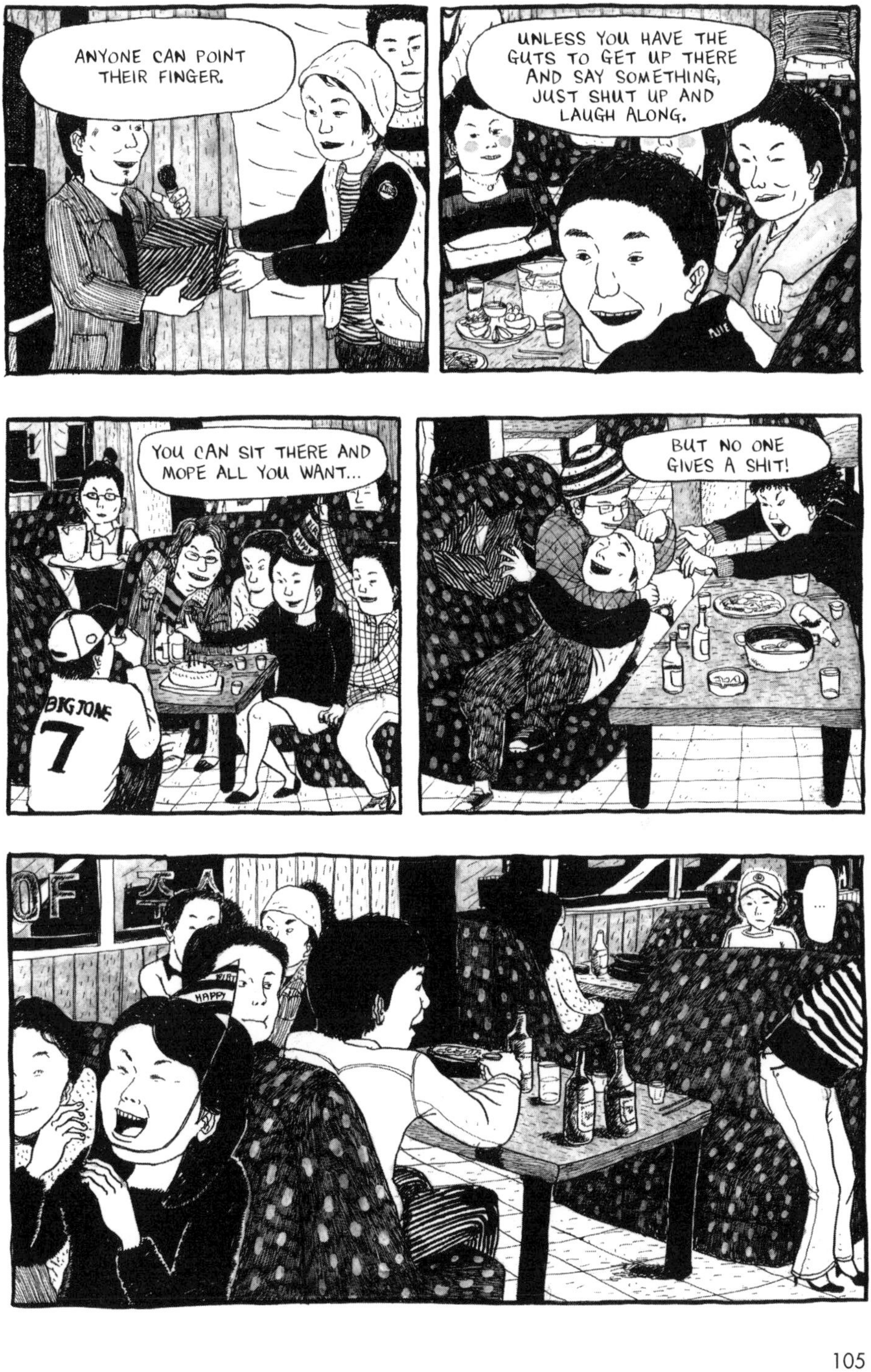
ANYONE CAN POINT THEIR FINGER.
UNLESS YOU HAVE THE GUTS TO GET UP THERE AND SAY SOMETHING, JUST SHUT UP AND LAUGH ALONG.
YOU CAN SIT THERE AND MOPE ALL YOU WANT...
BIG TONE 7
BUT NO ONE GIVES A SHIT!
HAPPY
...

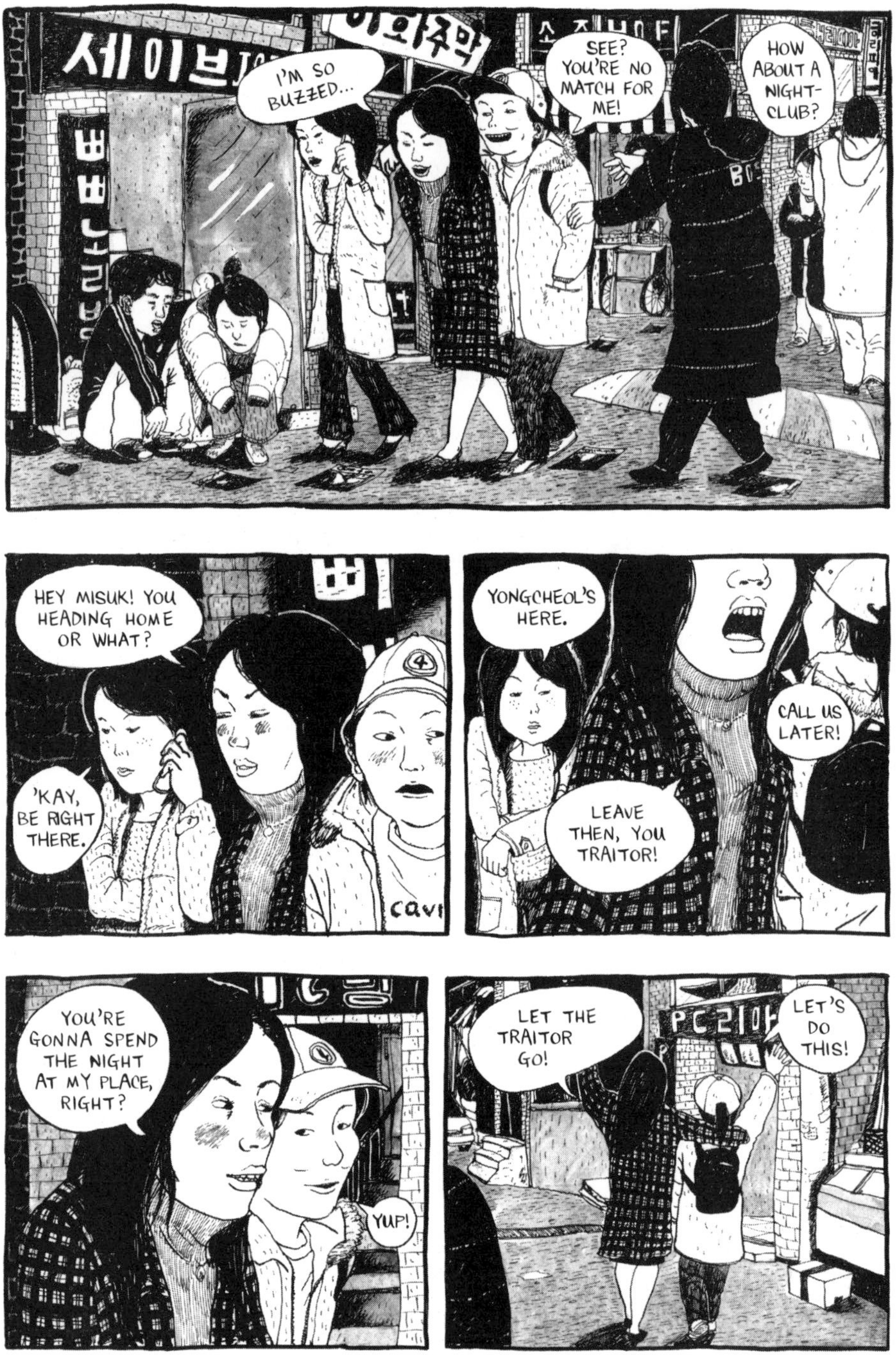
I'M SO BUZZED...
SEE? YOU'RE NO MATCH FOR ME!
HOW ABOUT A NIGHT-CLUB?
HEY MISUK! YOU HEADING HOME OR WHAT?
'KAY, BE RIGHT THERE.
YONGCHEOL'S HERE.
CALL US LATER!
LEAVE THEN, YOU TRAITOR!
YOU'RE GONNA SPEND THE NIGHT AT MY PLACE, RIGHT?
YUP!
LET THE TRAITOR GO!
PC리아
LET'S DO THIS!

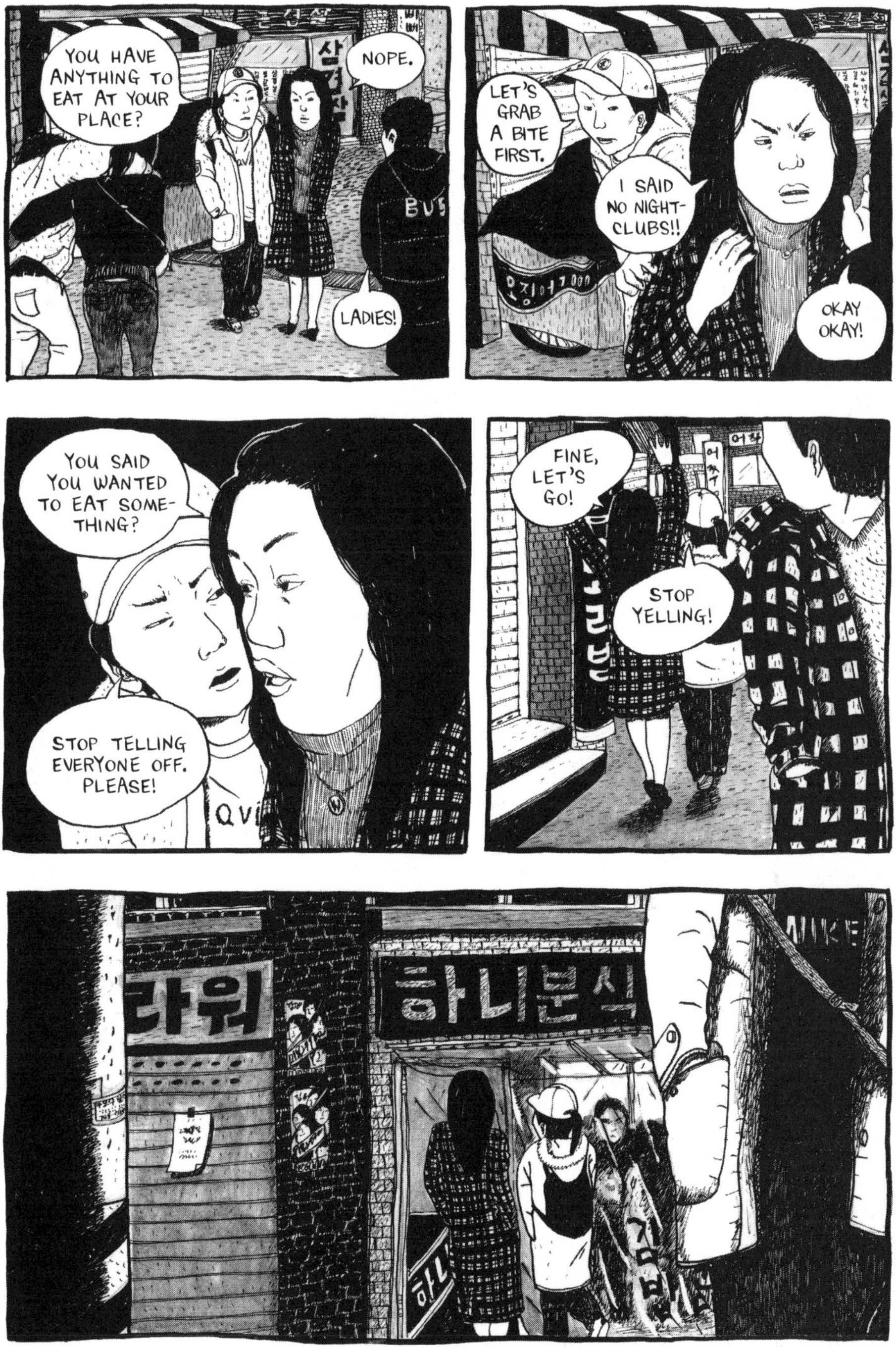
YOU HAVE ANYTHING TO EAT AT YOUR PLACE?
NOPE.
LADIES!
LET'S GRAB A BITE FIRST.
I SAID NO NIGHT-CLUBS!!
OKAY OKAY!
YOU SAID YOU WANTED TO EAT SOME-THING?
STOP TELLING EVERYONE OFF. PLEASE!
FINE, LET'S GO!
STOP YELLING!
하니분식

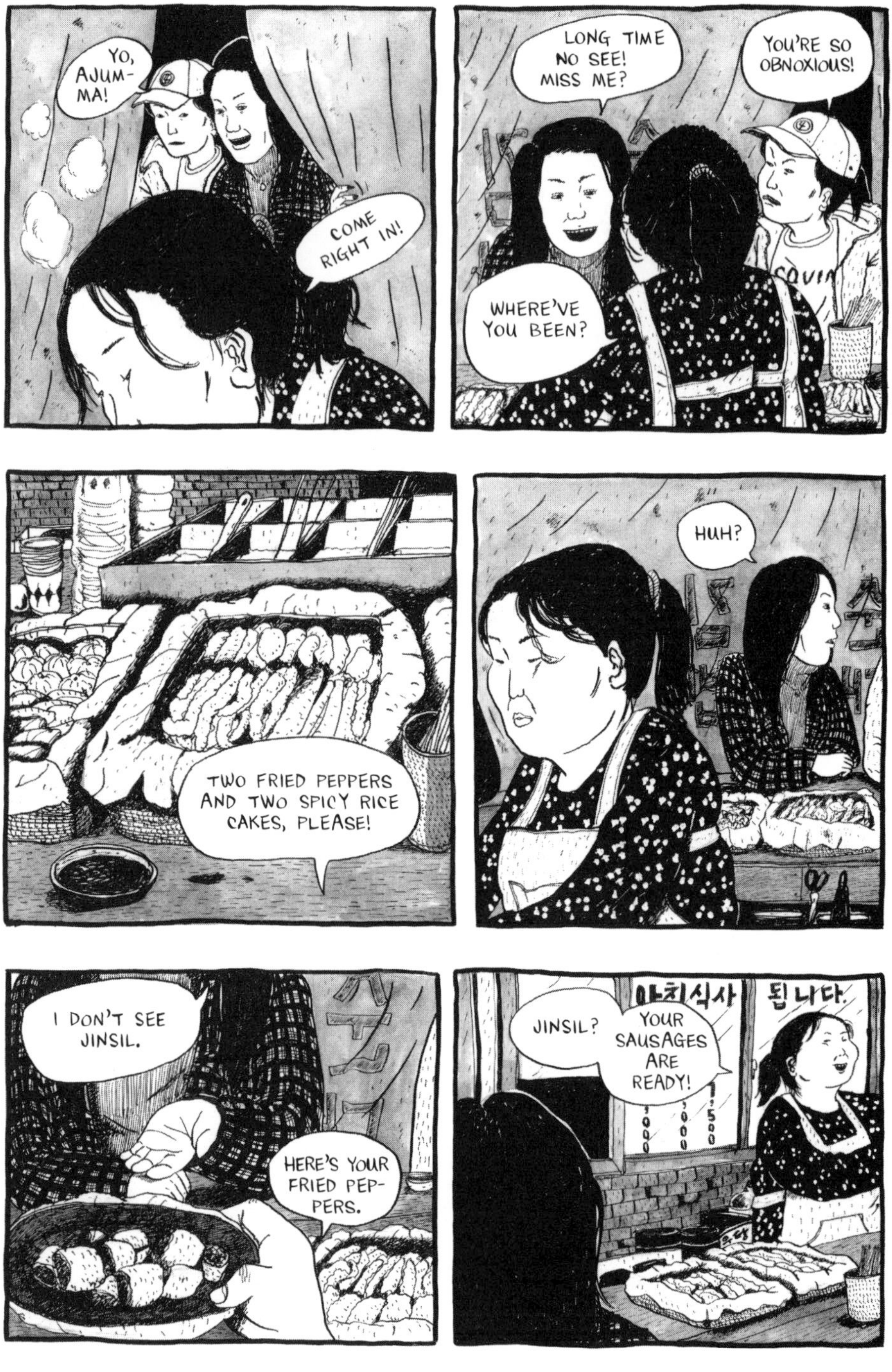
YO, AJUM-MA!
COME RIGHT IN!
LONG TIME NO SEE! MISS ME?
YOU'RE SO OBNOXIOUS!
WHERE'VE YOU BEEN?
TWO FRIED PEPPERS AND TWO SPICY RICE CAKES, PLEASE!
HUH?
I DON'T SEE JINSIL.
HERE'S YOUR FRIED PEP-PERS.
아치식사 됩니다.
JINSIL?
YOUR SAUSAGES ARE READY!

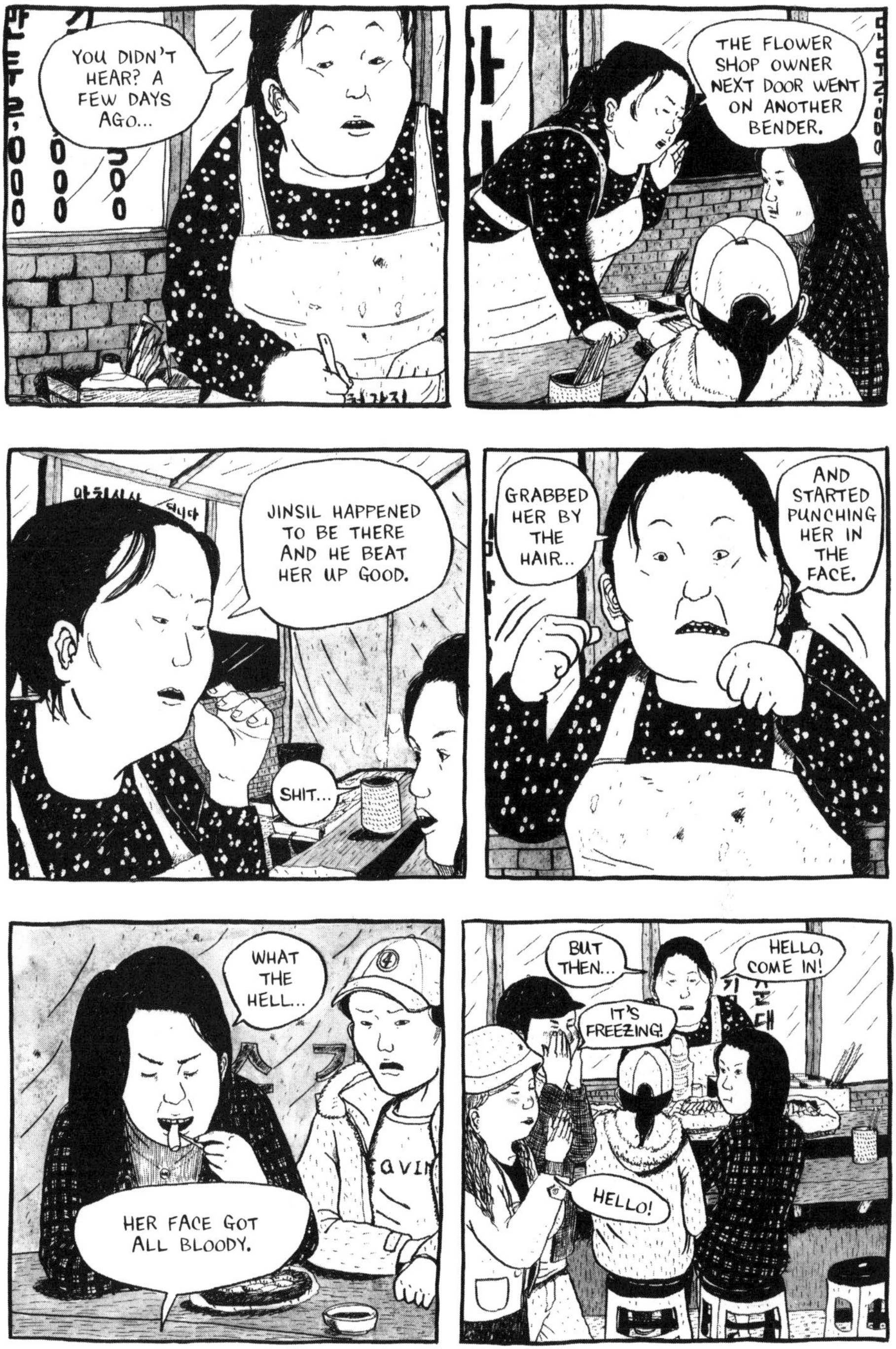
YOU DIDN'T HEAR? A FEW DAYS AGO...
THE FLOWER SHOP OWNER NEXT DOOR WENT ON ANOTHER BENDER.
JINSIL HAPPENED TO BE THERE AND HE BEAT HER UP GOOD.
SHIT...
GRABBED HER BY THE HAIR...
AND STARTED PUNCHING HER IN THE FACE.
WHAT THE HELL...
HER FACE GOT ALL BLOODY.
BUT THEN...
HELLO, COME IN!
IT'S FREEZING!
HELLO!

HE DRAGGED HER OVER TO HIS HOUSE...

HOLY CRAP! WHY?

YOU REALLY DON'T KNOW?

EVER SINCE HIS WIFE RAN OFF, I'VE SEEN HIM TAKE JIN-SIL BACK TO HIS PLACE A FEW TIMES.

AND NO ONE SAID ANY-THING?

YOU GIRLS WANT ANYTHING ELSE?

I TRIED TO STOP HIM, BUT LOOK WHAT HAP-PENED—

SEE THIS BRUISE?

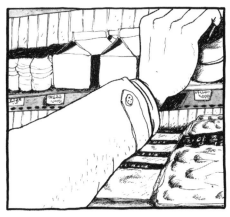

YOU KNOW JINSIL WELL? DOES SHE KNOW WHO YOU ARE?

YOU RE-ALLY DON'T REMEMBER HER?

THESE DRINKS AND A PACK OF THOSE, PLEASE.

HUP!

REMEMBER? IN FRONT OF OUR SCHOOL, "HEY SIS, CAN I BUM A SMOKE?"

CAN I...BUM A SMOKE...?

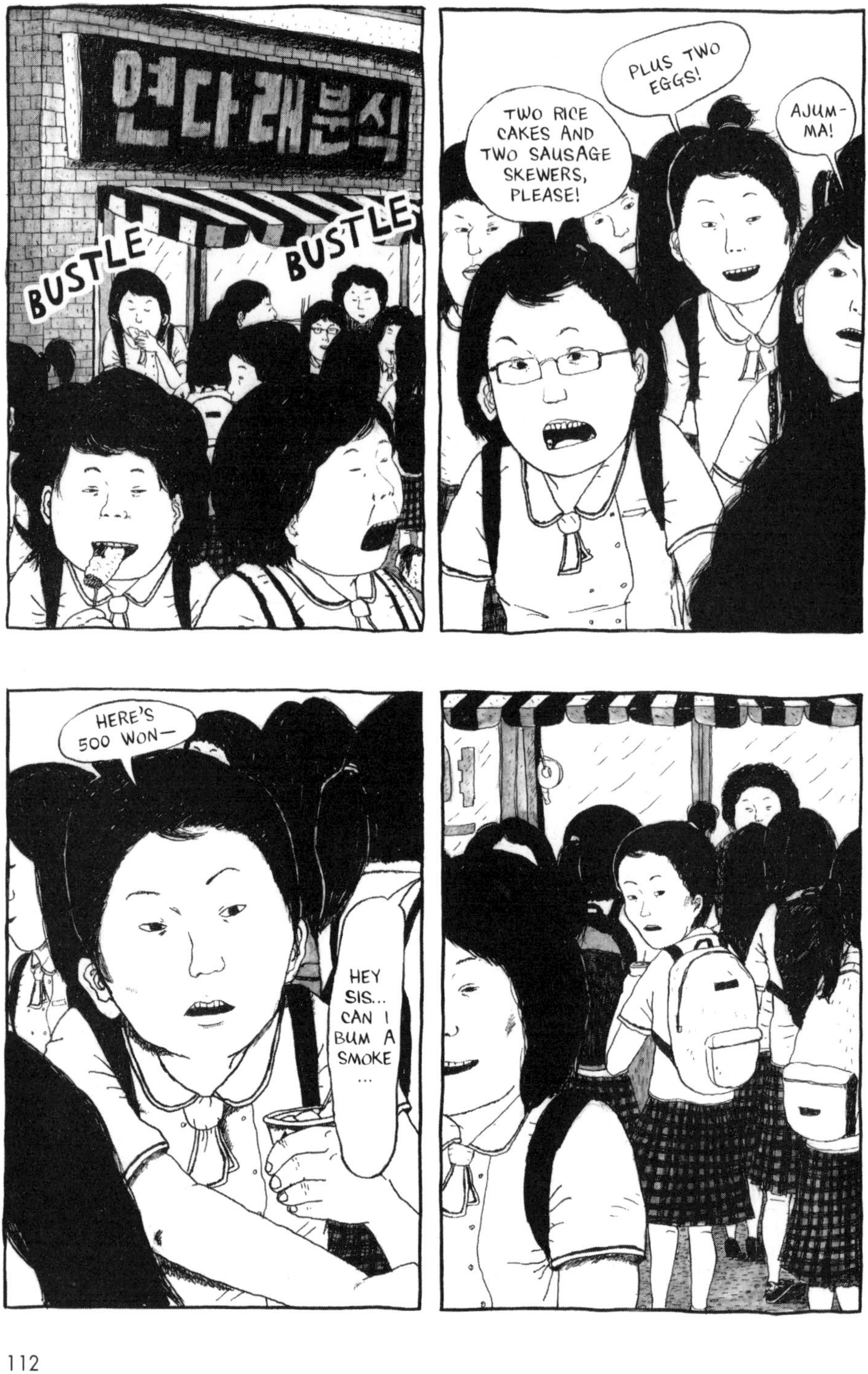
연다래분식
BUSTLE
BUSTLE
TWO RICE CAKES AND TWO SAUSAGE SKEWERS, PLEASE!
PLUS TWO EGGS!
AJUM-MA!
HERE'S 500 WON—
HEY SIS... CAN I BUM A SMOKE ...

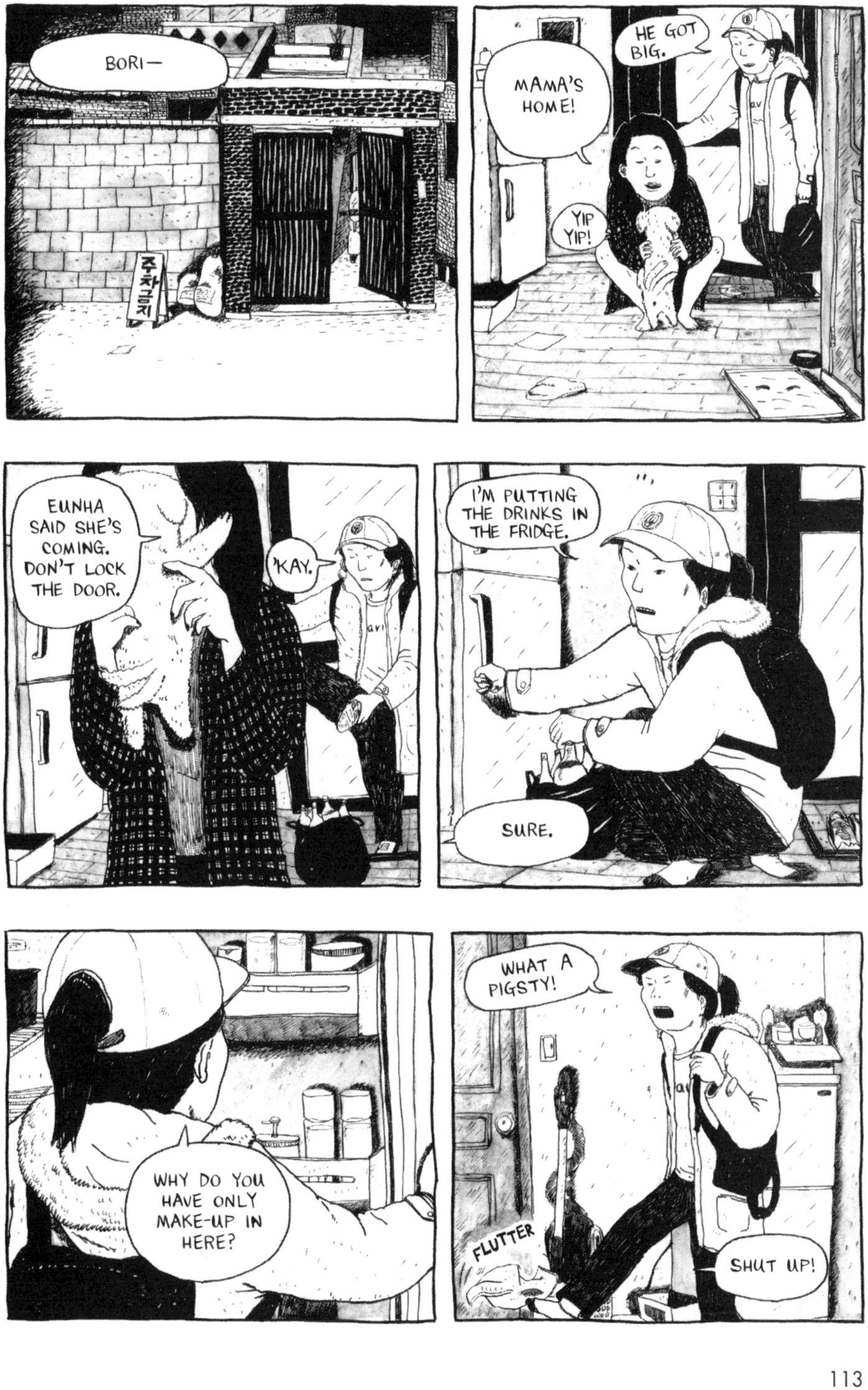
BORI—
주차금지
MAMA'S HOME!
HE GOT BIG.
YIP YIP!
EUNHA SAID SHE'S COMING. DON'T LOCK THE DOOR.
'KAY.
I'M PUTTING THE DRINKS IN THE FRIDGE.
SURE.
WHY DO YOU HAVE ONLY MAKE-UP IN HERE?
WHAT A PIGSTY!
FLUTTER
SHUT UP!

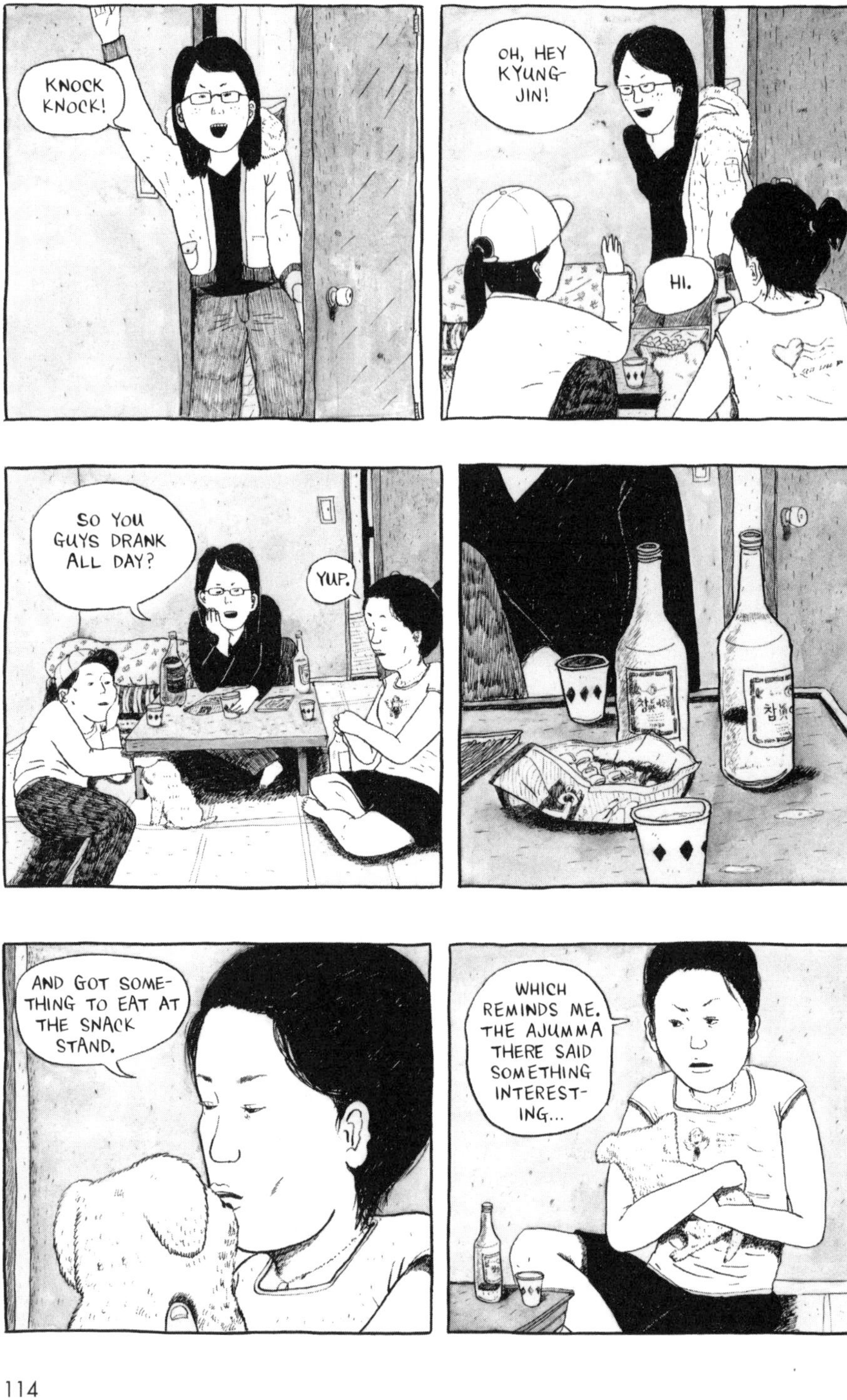
KNOCK KNOCK!
OH, HEY KYUNG-JIN!
HI.
SO YOU GUYS DRANK ALL DAY?
YUP.
AND GOT SOME-THING TO EAT AT THE SNACK STAND.
WHICH REMINDS ME. THE AJUMMA THERE SAID SOMETHING INTEREST-ING...

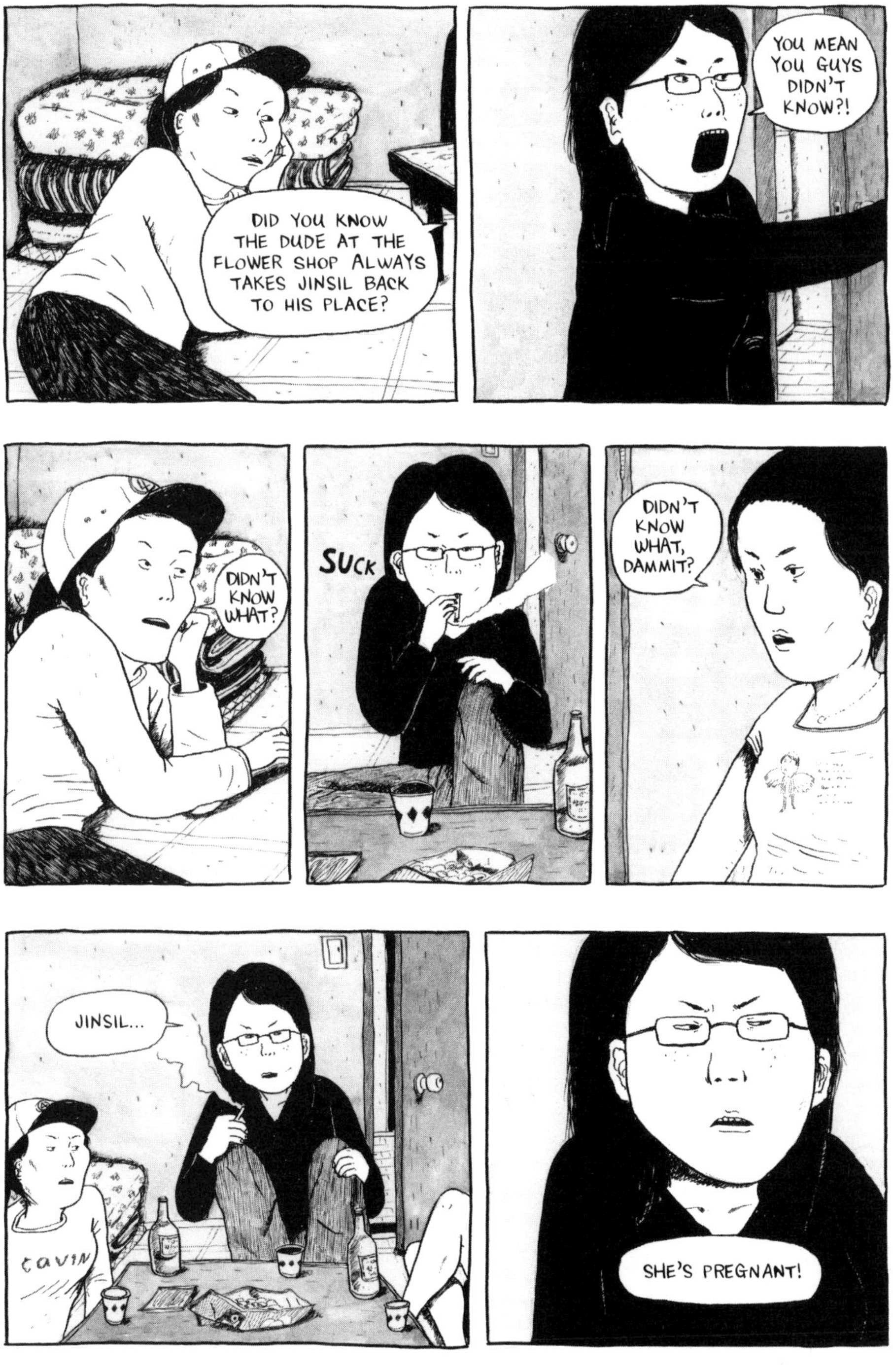
DID YOU KNOW THE DUDE AT THE FLOWER SHOP ALWAYS TAKES JINSIL BACK TO HIS PLACE?
YOU MEAN YOU GUYS DIDN'T KNOW?!
DIDN'T KNOW WHAT?
SUCK
DIDN'T KNOW WHAT, DAMMIT?
JINSIL...
SHE'S PREGNANT!

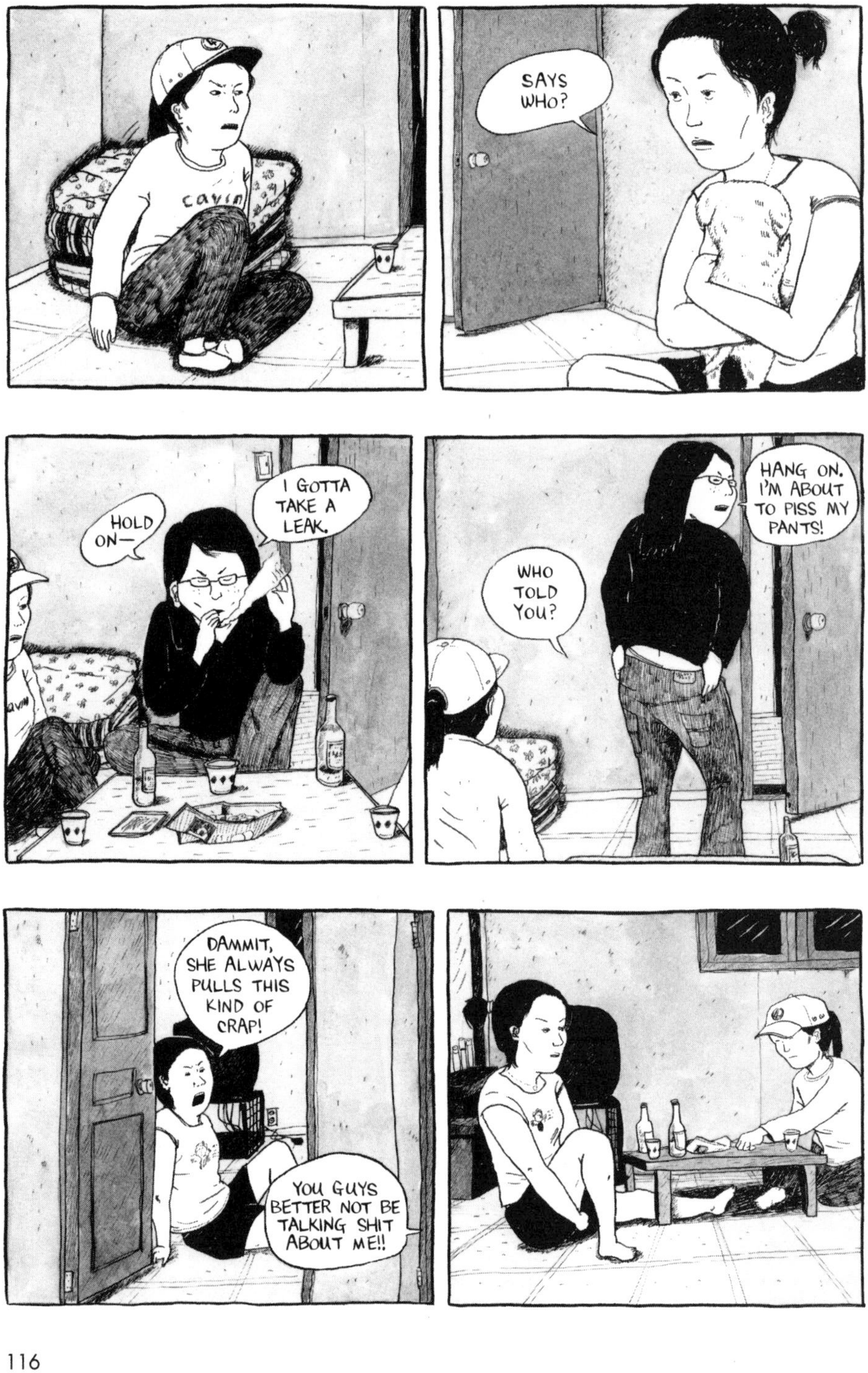
SAYS WHO?
HOLD ON—
I GOTTA TAKE A LEAK.
HANG ON. I'M ABOUT TO PISS MY PANTS!
WHO TOLD YOU?
DAMMIT, SHE ALWAYS PULLS THIS KIND OF CRAP!
YOU GUYS BETTER NOT BE TALKING SHIT ABOUT ME!!

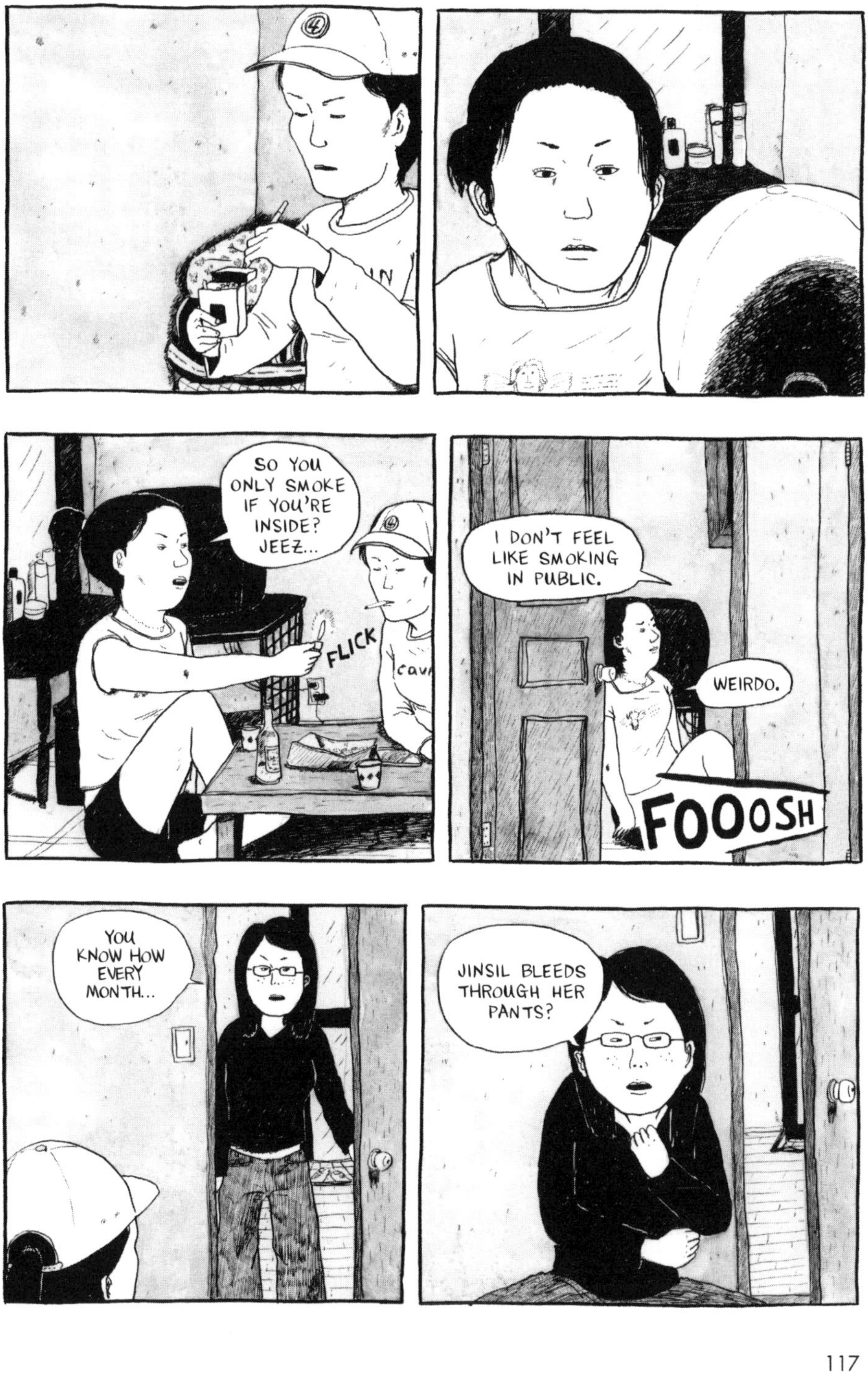
SO YOU ONLY SMOKE IF YOU'RE INSIDE? JEEZ...
FLICK
I DON'T FEEL LIKE SMOKING IN PUBLIC.
WEIRDO.
FOOOSH
YOU KNOW HOW EVERY MONTH...
JINSIL BLEEDS THROUGH HER PANTS?

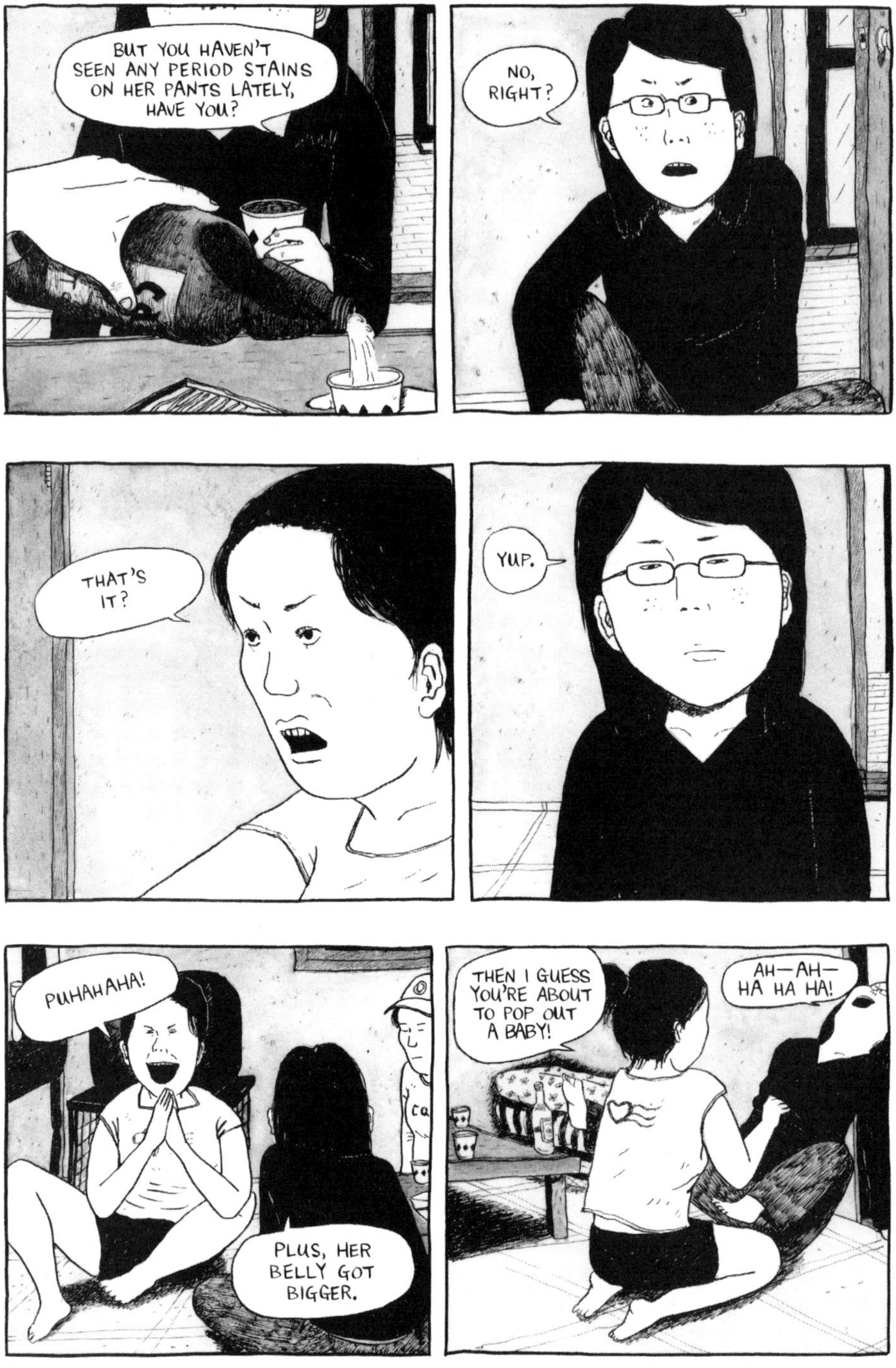
BUT YOU HAVEN'T SEEN ANY PERIOD STAINS ON HER PANTS LATELY, HAVE YOU?
NO, RIGHT?
THAT'S IT?
YUP.
PUHAHAHA!
PLUS, HER BELLY GOT BIGGER.
THEN I GUESS YOU'RE ABOUT TO POP OUT A BABY!
AH—AH—HA HA HA!

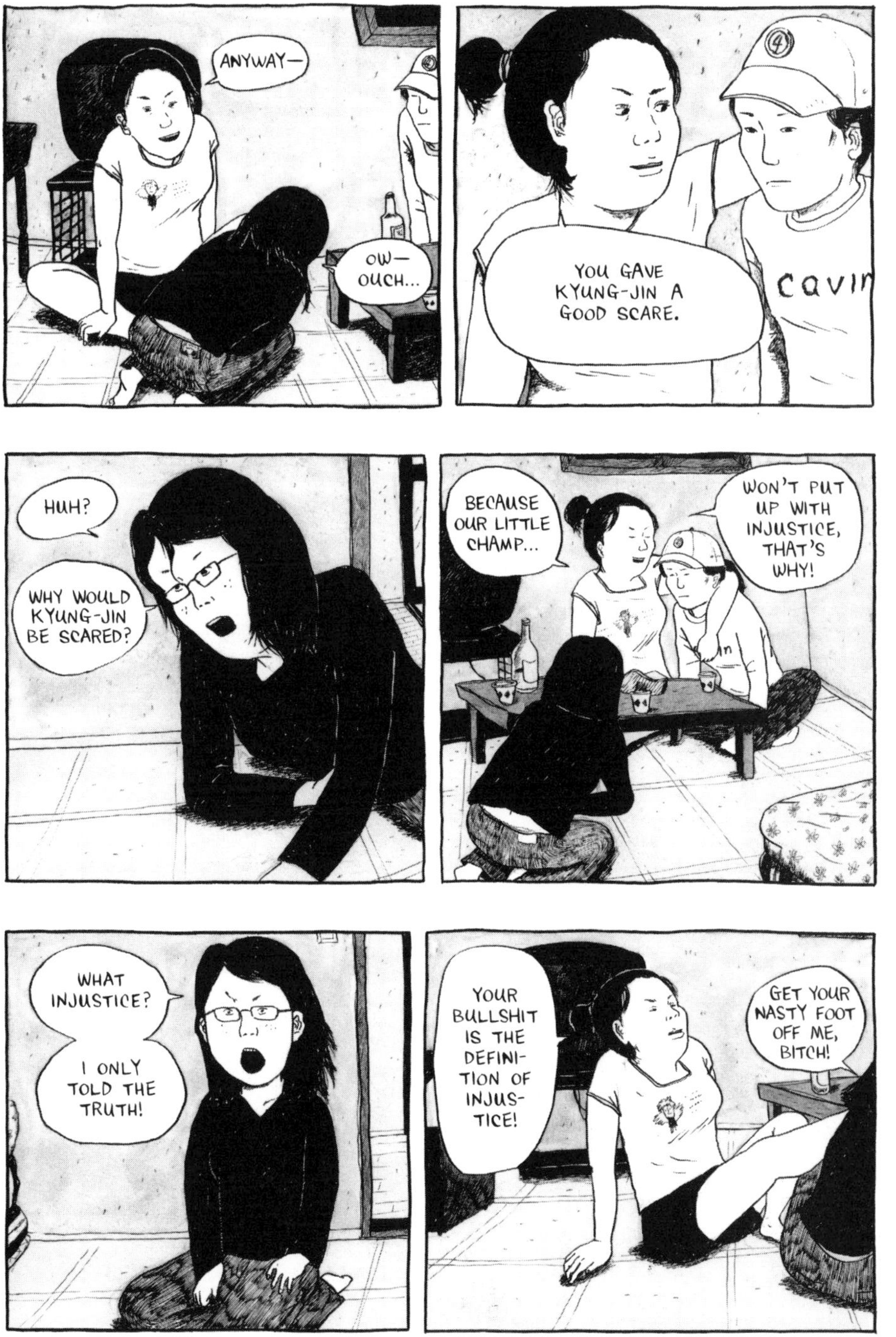
ANYWAY—
OW— OUCH...
YOU GAVE KYUNG-JIN A GOOD SCARE.
cavin
HUH?
WHY WOULD KYUNG-JIN BE SCARED?
BECAUSE OUR LITTLE CHAMP...
WON'T PUT UP WITH INJUSTICE, THAT'S WHY!
WHAT INJUSTICE?
I ONLY TOLD THE TRUTH!
YOUR BULLSHIT IS THE DEFINITION OF INJUSTICE!
GET YOUR NASTY FOOT OFF ME, BITCH!

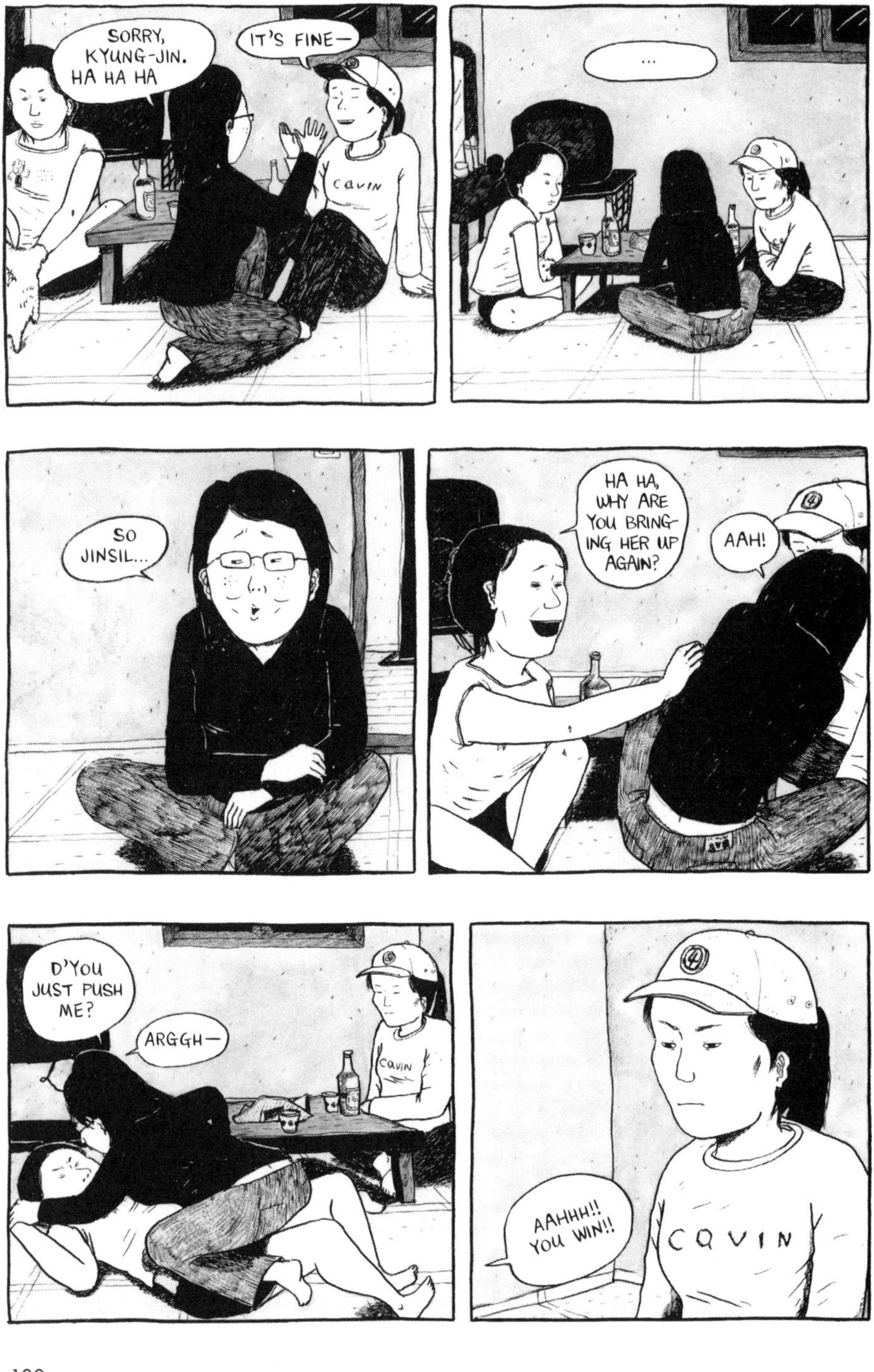
SORRY, KYUNG-JIN. HA HA HA
IT'S FINE—
...
SO JINSIL...
HA HA, WHY ARE YOU BRINGING HER UP AGAIN?
AAH!
D'YOU JUST PUSH ME?
ARGGH—
AAHHH!! YOU WIN!!

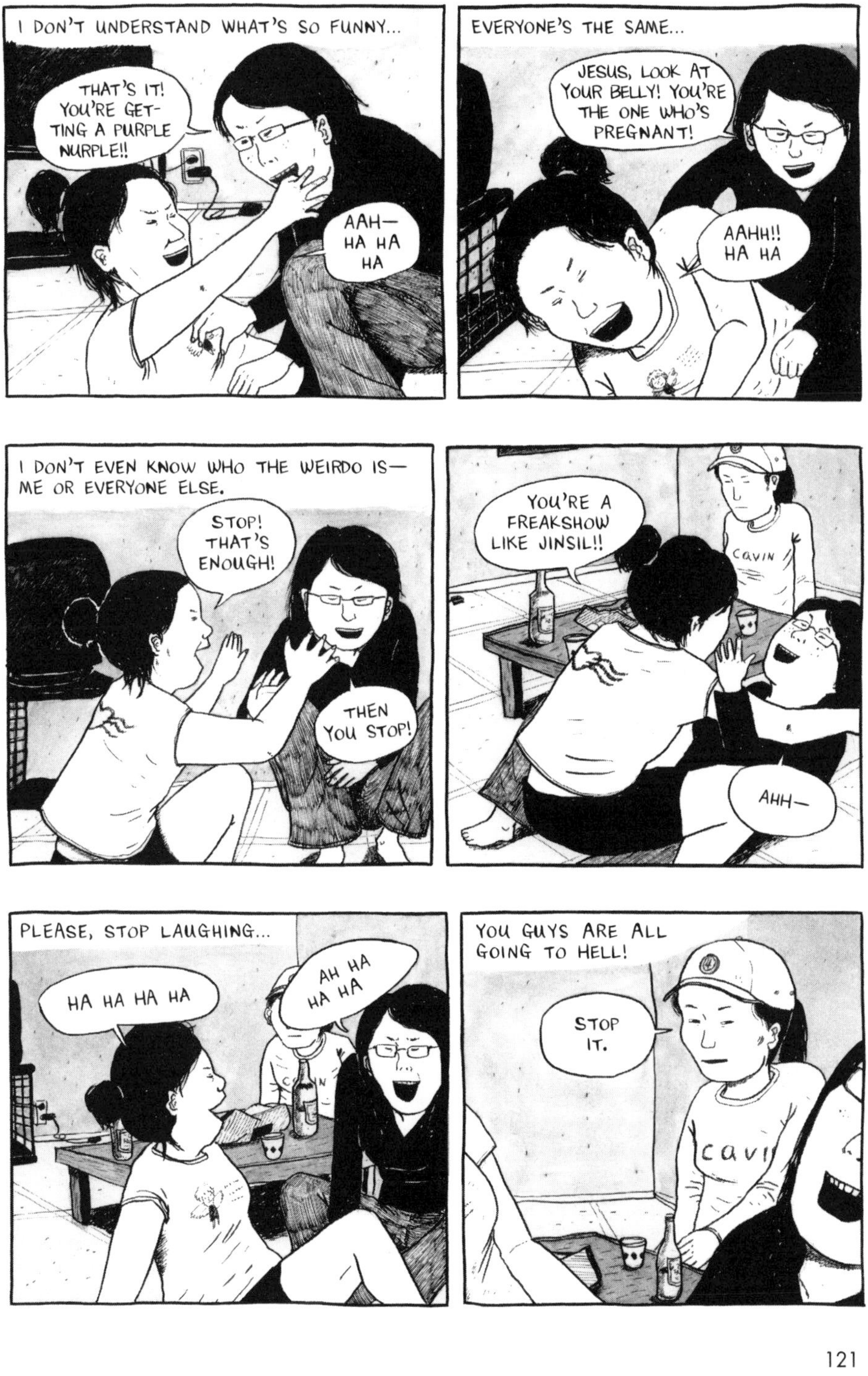
I DON'T UNDERSTAND WHAT'S SO FUNNY...
THAT'S IT! YOU'RE GET-TING A PURPLE NURPLE!!
AAH— HA HA HA
EVERYONE'S THE SAME...
JESUS, LOOK AT YOUR BELLY! YOU'RE THE ONE WHO'S PREGNANT!
AAHH!! HA HA
I DON'T EVEN KNOW WHO THE WEIRDO IS— ME OR EVERYONE ELSE.
STOP! THAT'S ENOUGH!
THEN YOU STOP!
YOU'RE A FREAKSHOW LIKE JINSIL!!
CAVIN
AHH—
PLEASE, STOP LAUGHING...
HA HA HA HA
AH HA HA HA
YOU GUYS ARE ALL GOING TO HELL!
STOP IT.
CAVI

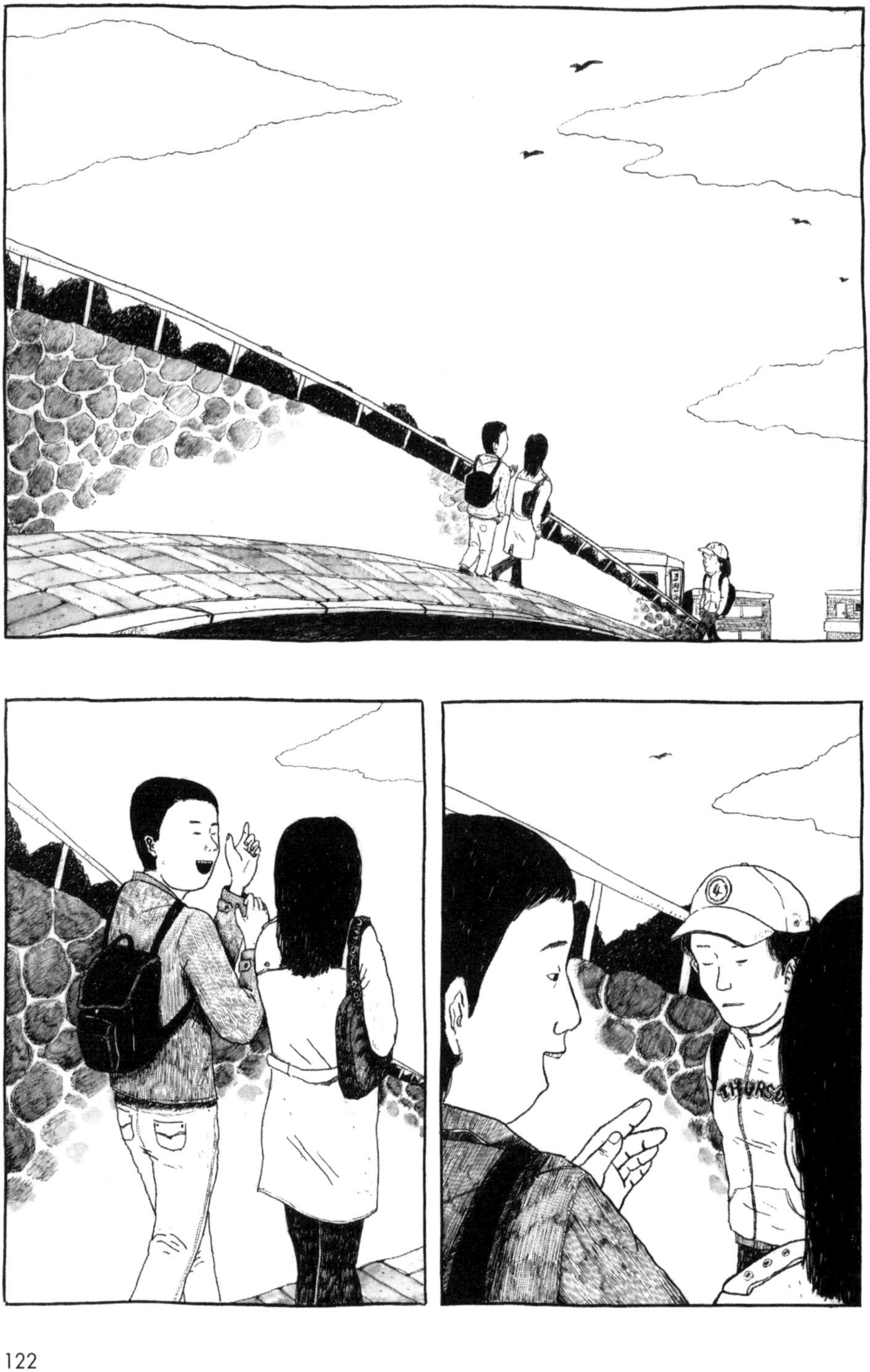

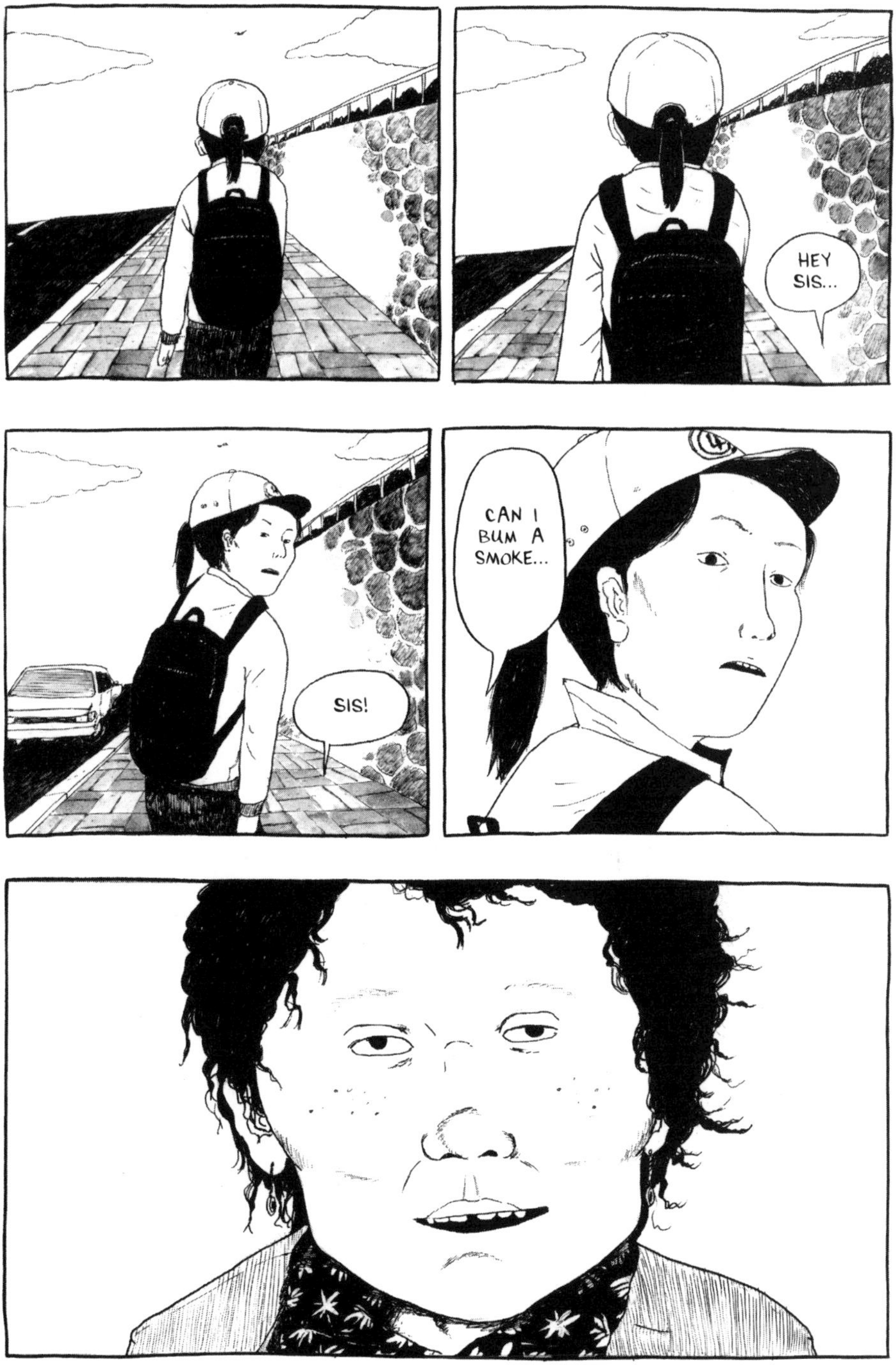
HEY SIS...
SIS!
CAN I BUM A SMOKE...

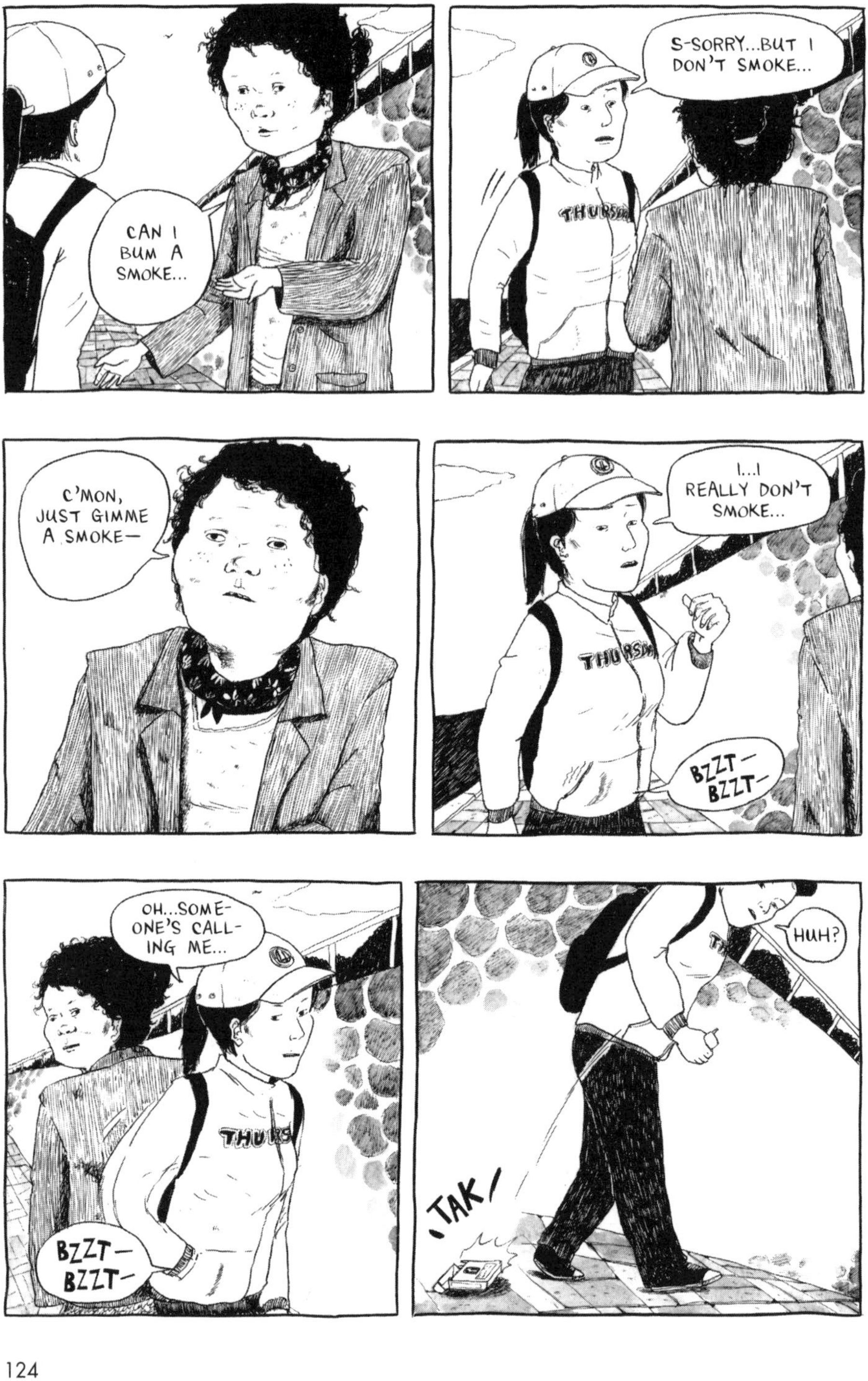
CAN I BUM A SMOKE...
S-SORRY...BUT I DON'T SMOKE...
THURSD
C'MON, JUST GIMME A SMOKE—
I...I REALLY DON'T SMOKE...
BZZT— BZZT—
OH...SOME-ONE'S CALL-ING ME...
BZZT— BZZT—
HUH?
TAK

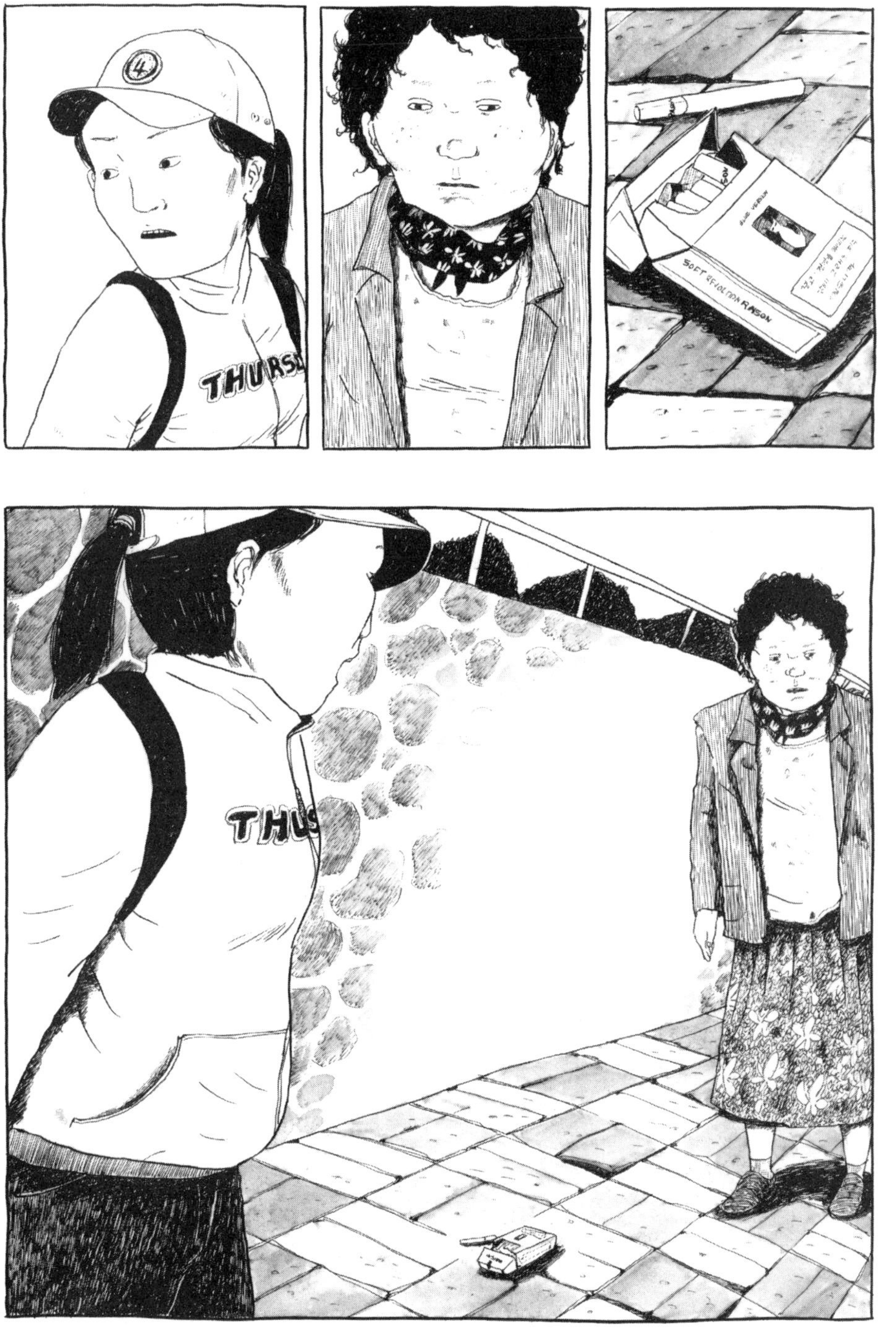
SOFT REVOLUTION RASON

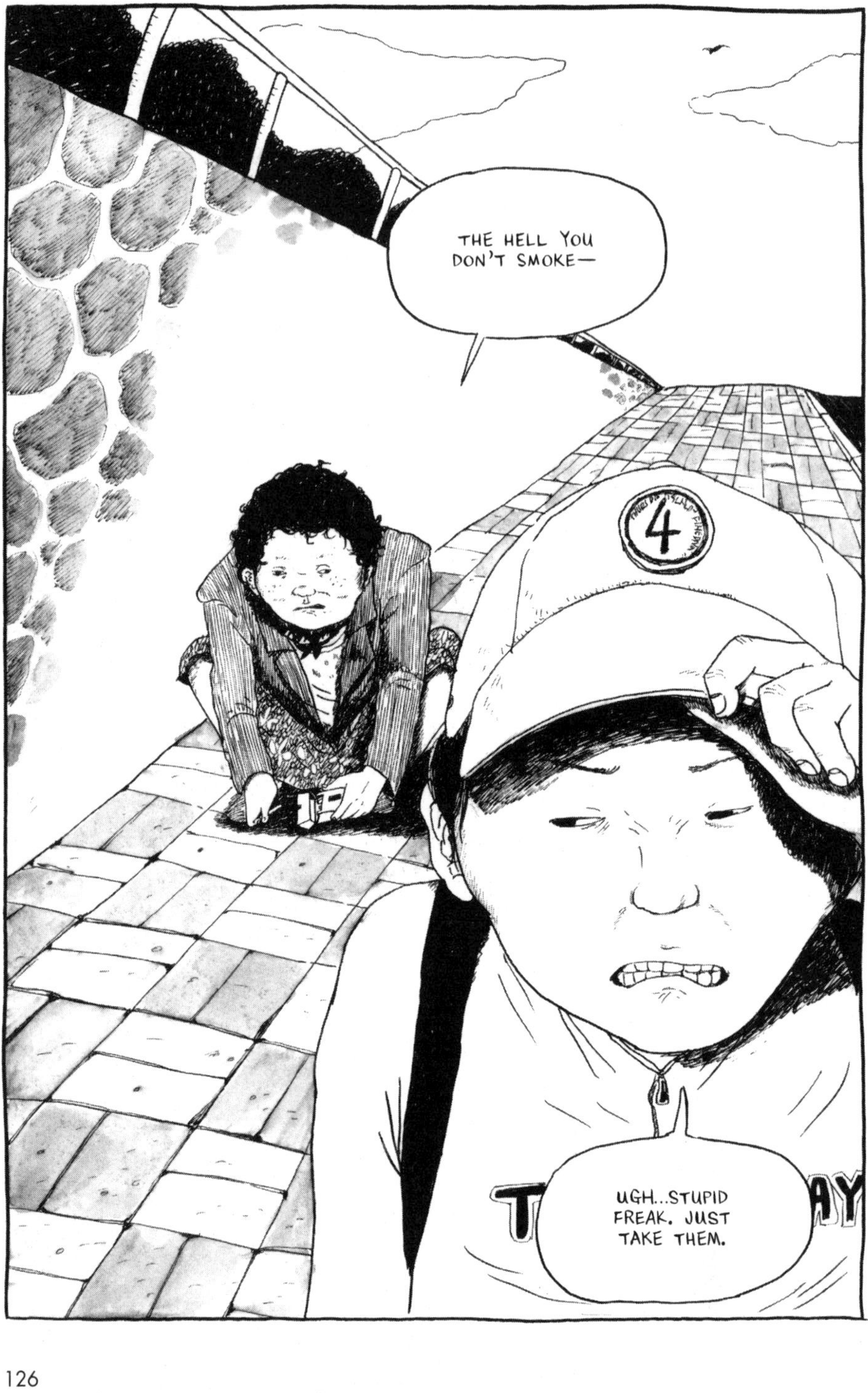
THE HELL YOU DON'T SMOKE—
UGH...STUPID FREAK. JUST TAKE THEM.

happy new year

TO MY SURPRISE,
I TURNED TWENTY-FOUR.

I THOUGHT BY THE
AGE OF TWENTY-FOUR,
I'D BE A YOUNG LADY,
LOOKING LIKE THIS...

TEE HEE,
ISN'T THAT
FUNNY—

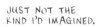

I BECAME A YOUNG
LADY ALL RIGHT...

QUIT
IT!

JUST NOT THE
KIND I'D IMAGINED.

*IN KOREA, PEOPLE TURN A YEAR OLDER ON NEW YEAR'S DAY, INSTEAD OF ON THEIR BIRTHDAYS.

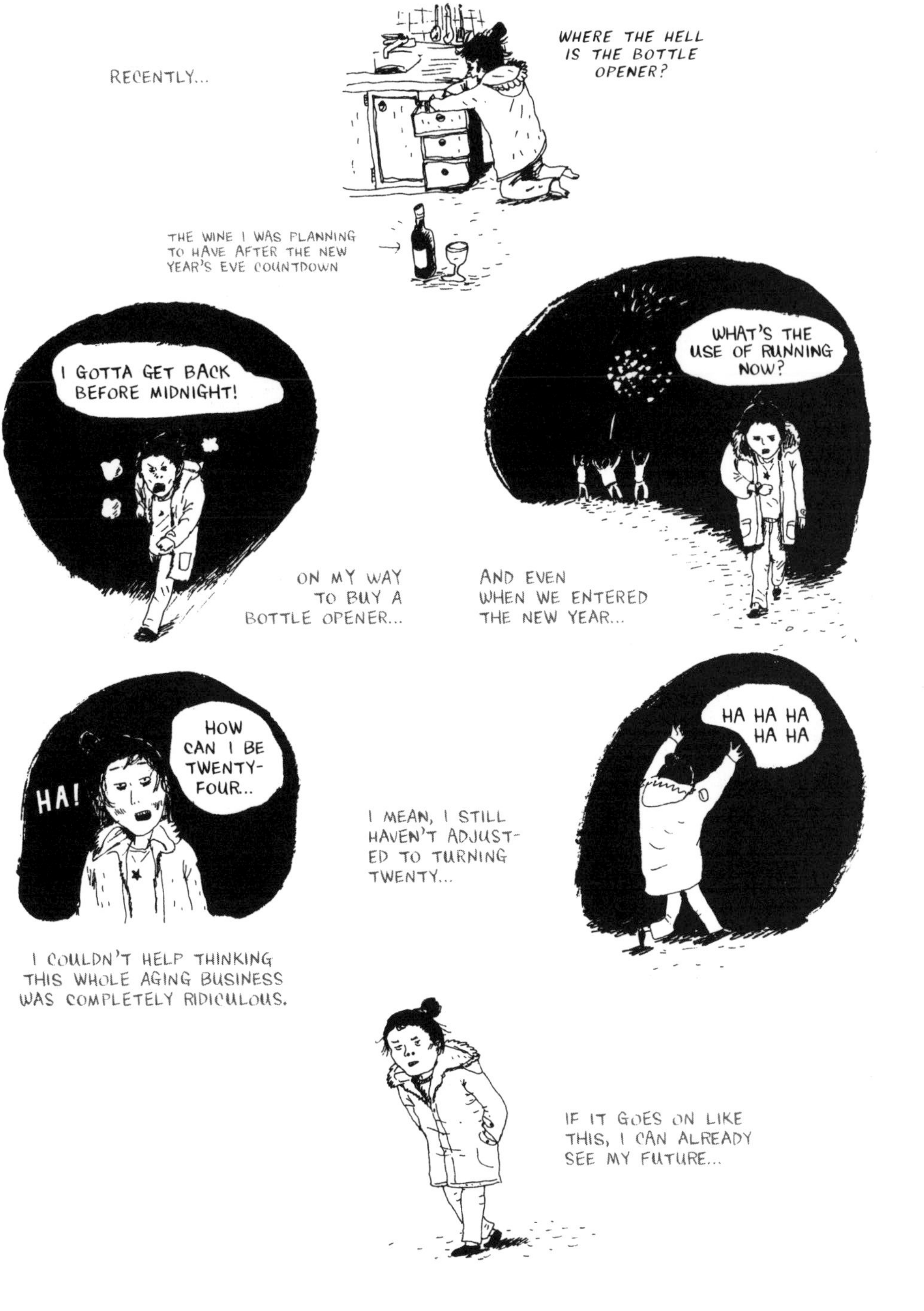

RECENTLY...
WHERE THE HELL IS THE BOTTLE OPENER?
THE WINE I WAS PLANNING TO HAVE AFTER THE NEW YEAR'S EVE COUNTDOWN
I GOTTA GET BACK BEFORE MIDNIGHT!
ON MY WAY TO BUY A BOTTLE OPENER...
AND EVEN WHEN WE ENTERED THE NEW YEAR...
WHAT'S THE USE OF RUNNING NOW?
HA!
HOW CAN I BE TWENTY-FOUR..
I COULDN'T HELP THINKING THIS WHOLE AGING BUSINESS WAS COMPLETELY RIDICULOUS.
I MEAN, I STILL HAVEN'T ADJUST-ED TO TURNING TWENTY...
HA HA HA HA HA
IF IT GOES ON LIKE THIS, I CAN ALREADY SEE MY FUTURE...

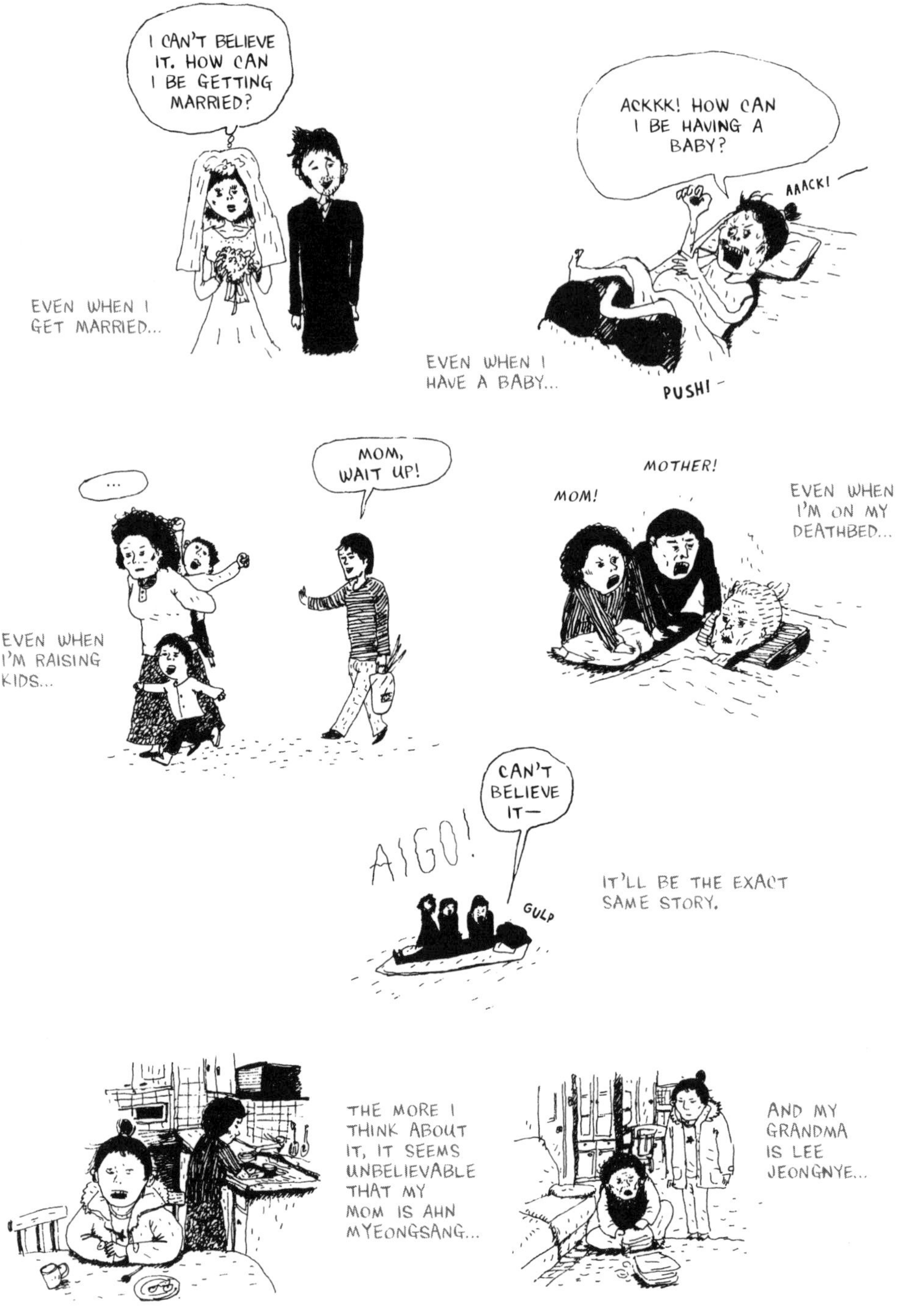
I CAN'T BELIEVE IT. HOW CAN I BE GETTING MARRIED?
EVEN WHEN I GET MARRIED...
ACKKK! HOW CAN I BE HAVING A BABY?
AAACK!
PUSH!
EVEN WHEN I HAVE A BABY...
...
MOM, WAIT UP!
EVEN WHEN I'M RAISING KIDS...
MOTHER!
MOM!
EVEN WHEN I'M ON MY DEATHBED...
AIGO!
CAN'T BELIEVE IT—
GULP
IT'LL BE THE EXACT SAME STORY.
THE MORE I THINK ABOUT IT, IT SEEMS UNBELIEVABLE THAT MY MOM IS AHN MYEONGSANG...
AND MY GRANDMA IS LEE JEONGNYE...

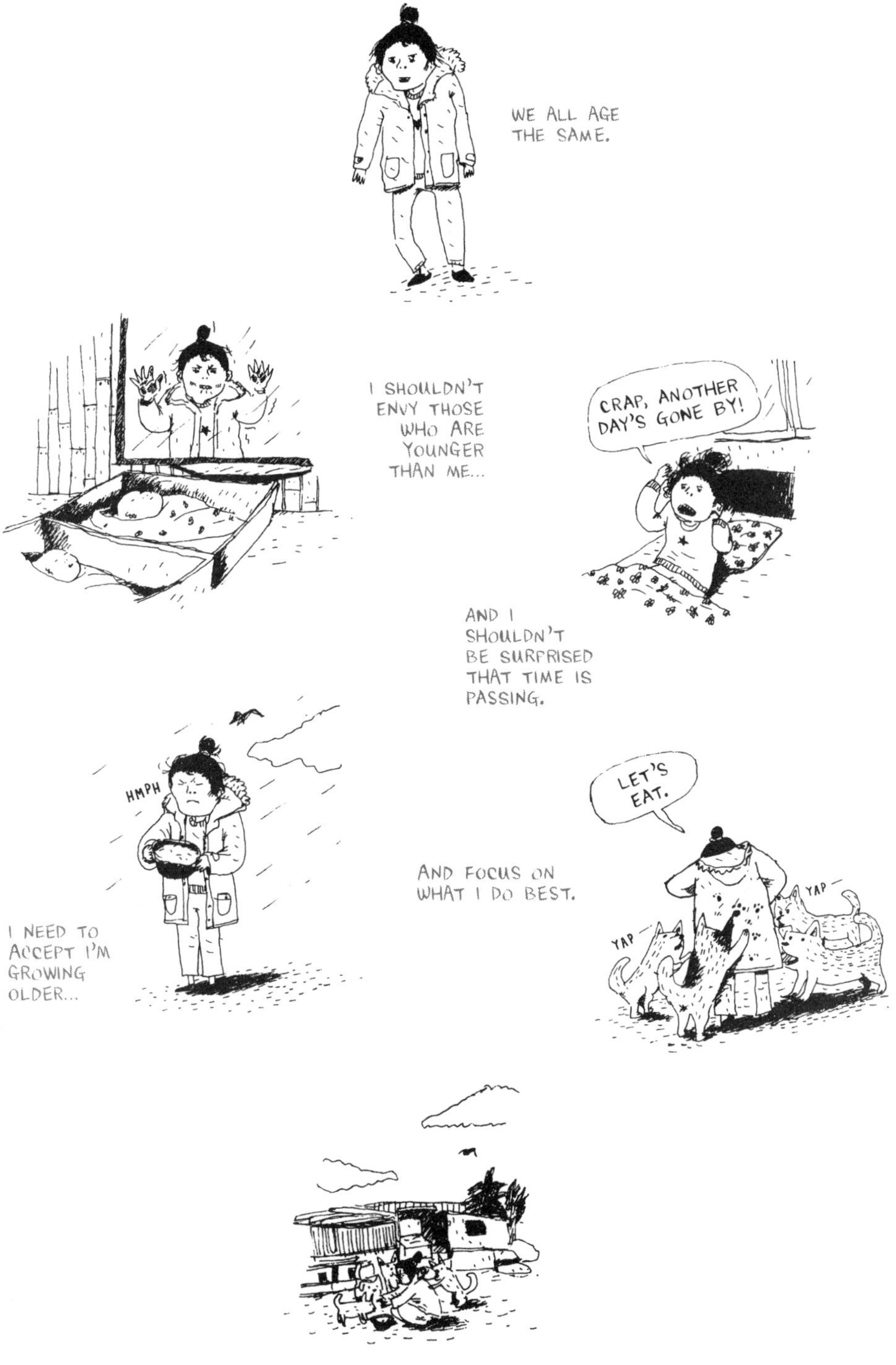
WE ALL AGE THE SAME.
I SHOULDN'T ENVY THOSE WHO ARE YOUNGER THAN ME...
CRAP, ANOTHER DAY'S GONE BY!
AND I SHOULDN'T BE SURPRISED THAT TIME IS PASSING.
HMPH
I NEED TO ACCEPT I'M GROWING OLDER...
AND FOCUS ON WHAT I DO BEST.
LET'S EAT.
YAP
YAP

dog

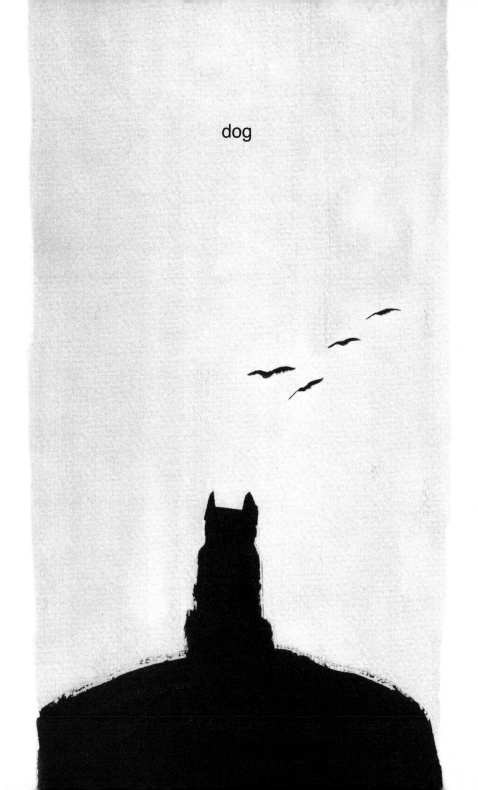

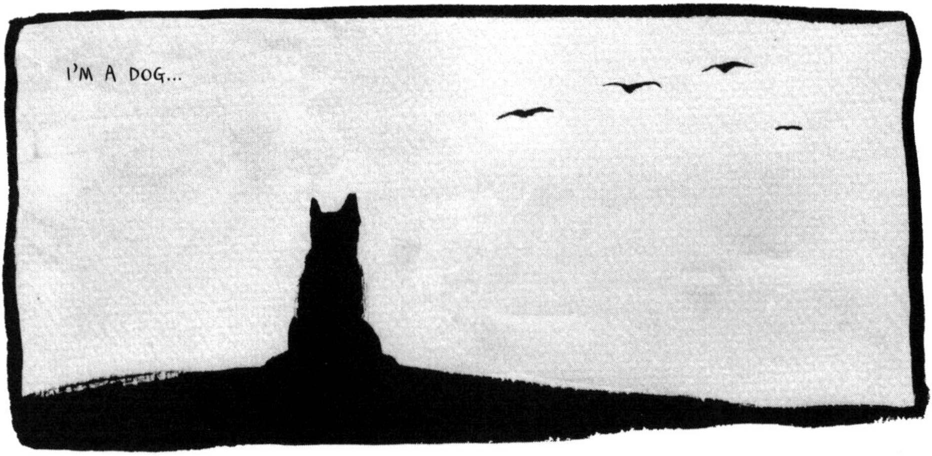
I'M A DOG...

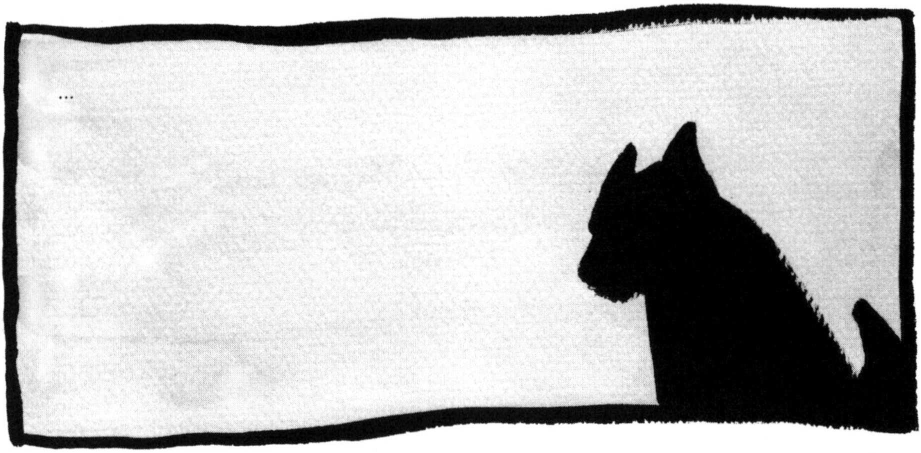
...

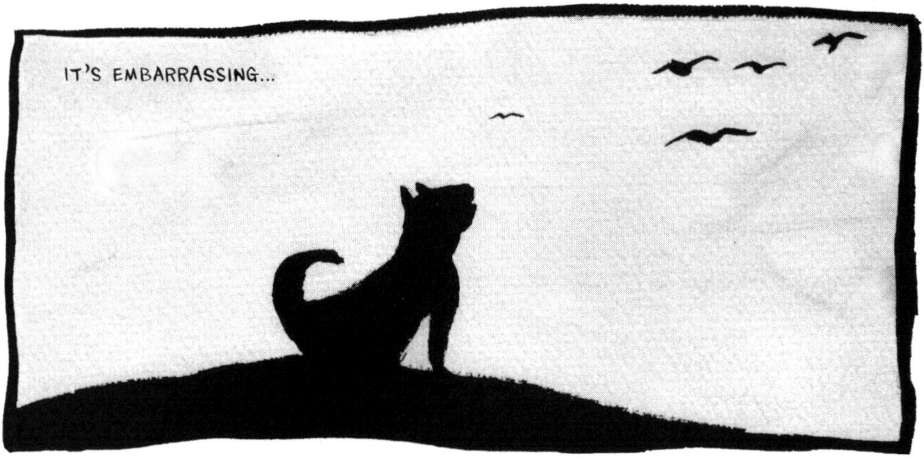
IT'S EMBARRASSING...

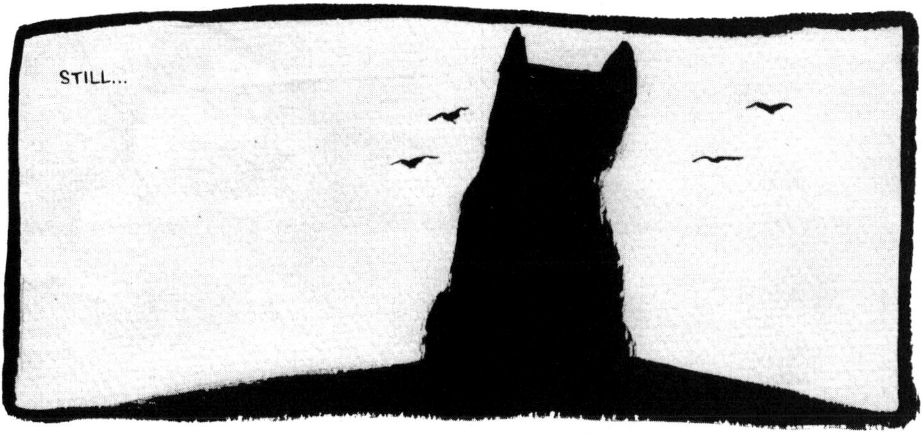
STILL...

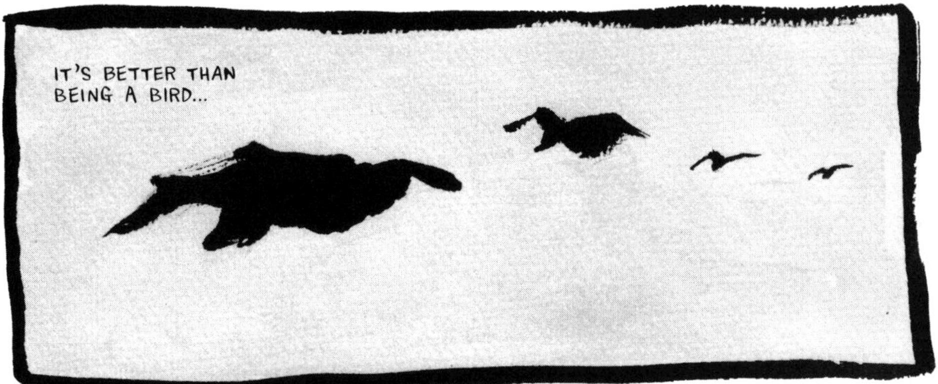
IT'S BETTER THAN
BEING A BIRD...

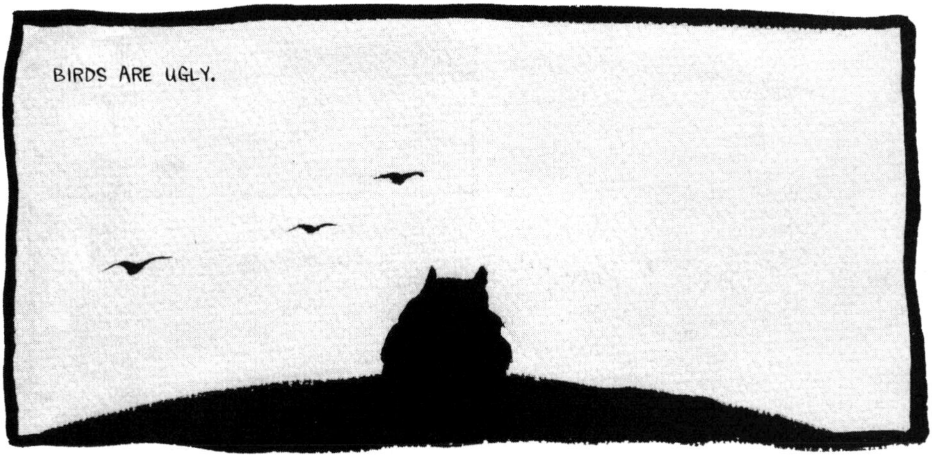
BIRDS ARE UGLY.

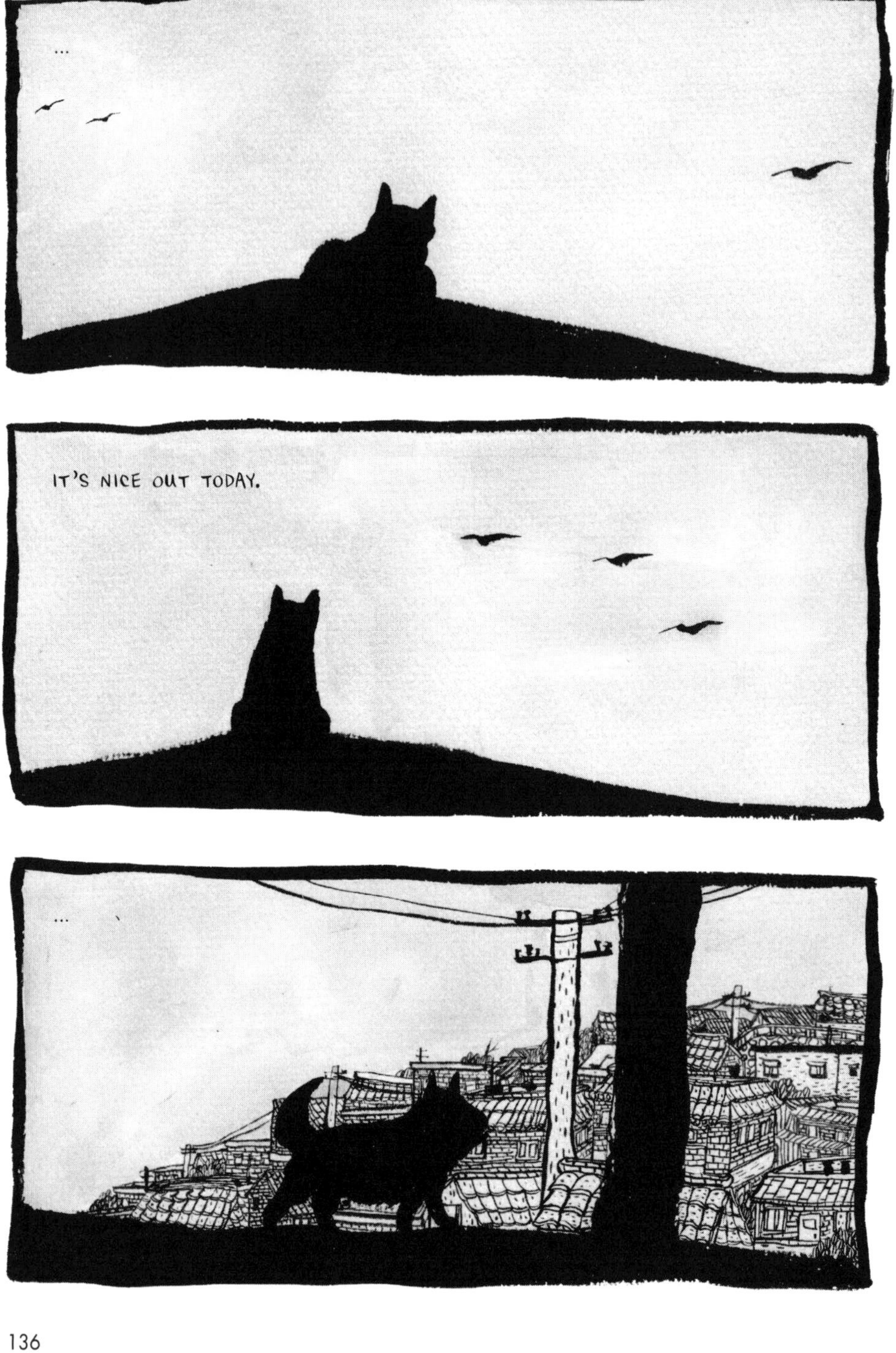
...
IT'S NICE OUT TODAY.
...

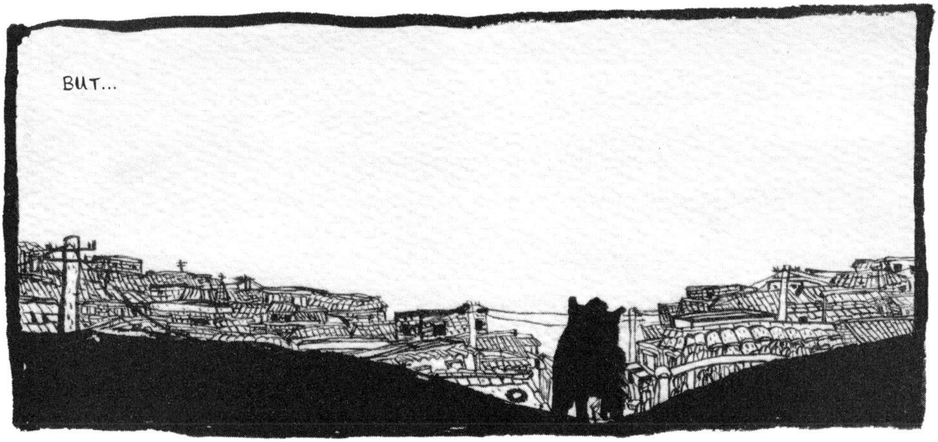
BUT...

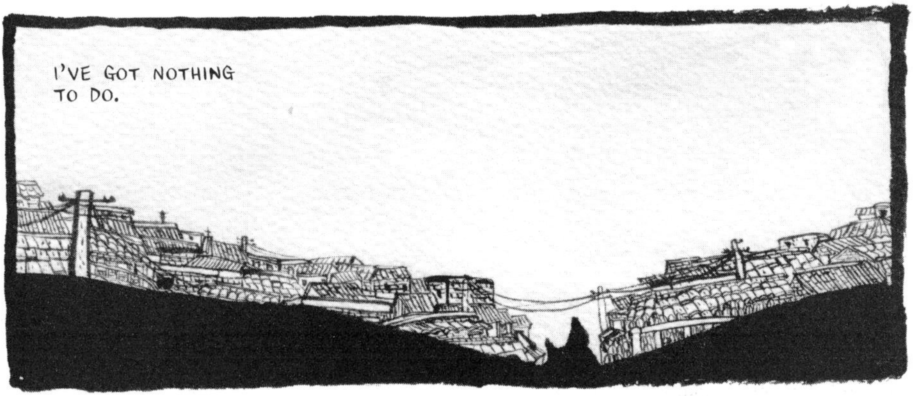
I'VE GOT NOTHING
TO DO.

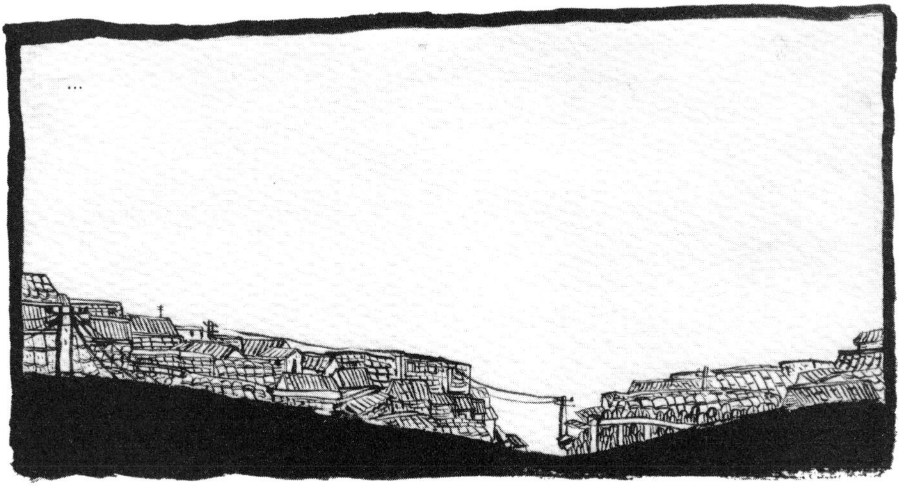
...

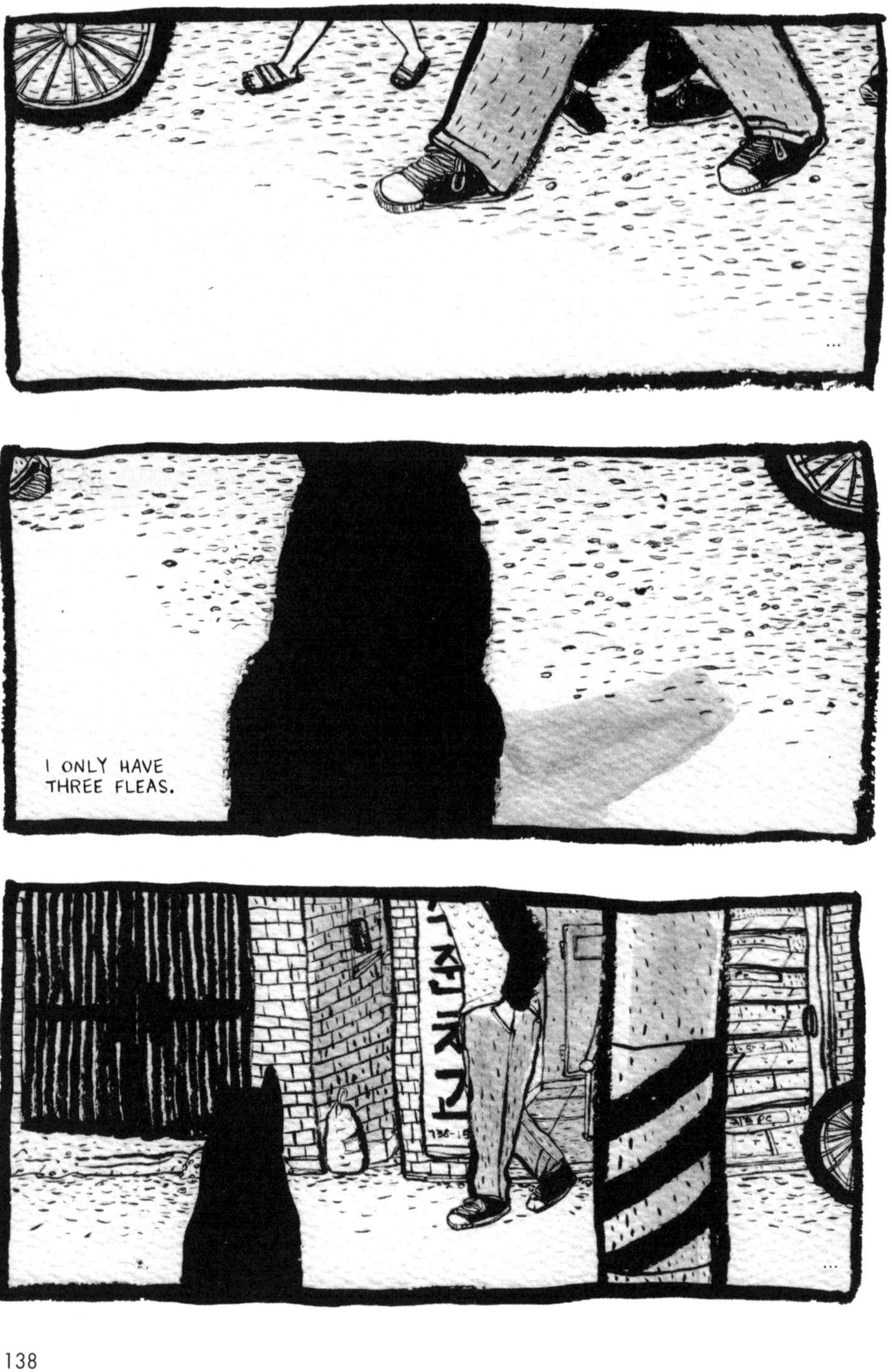
...
I ONLY HAVE
THREE FLEAS.
...

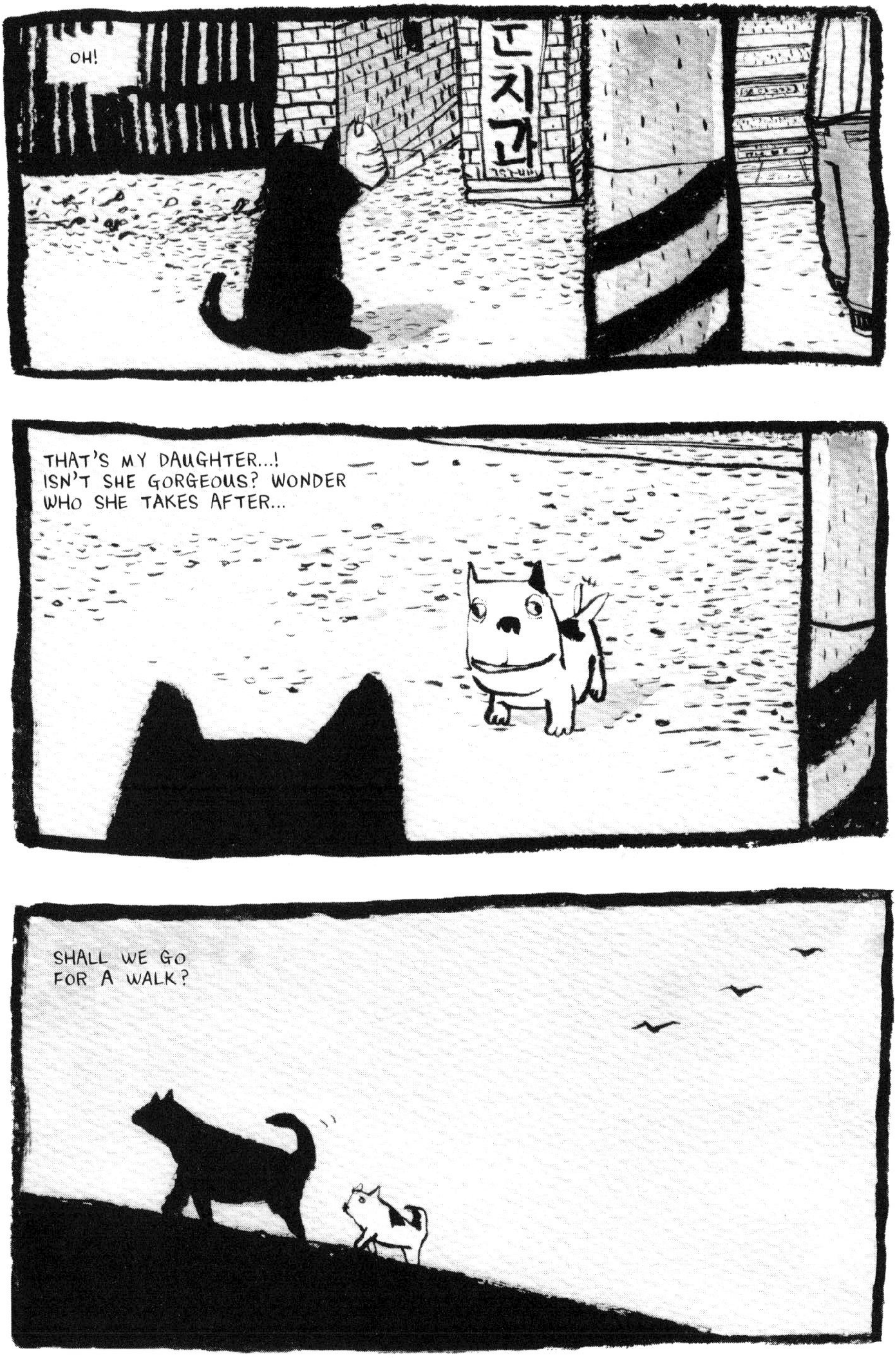
OH!
THAT'S MY DAUGHTER...! ISN'T SHE GORGEOUS? WONDER WHO SHE TAKES AFTER...
SHALL WE GO FOR A WALK?

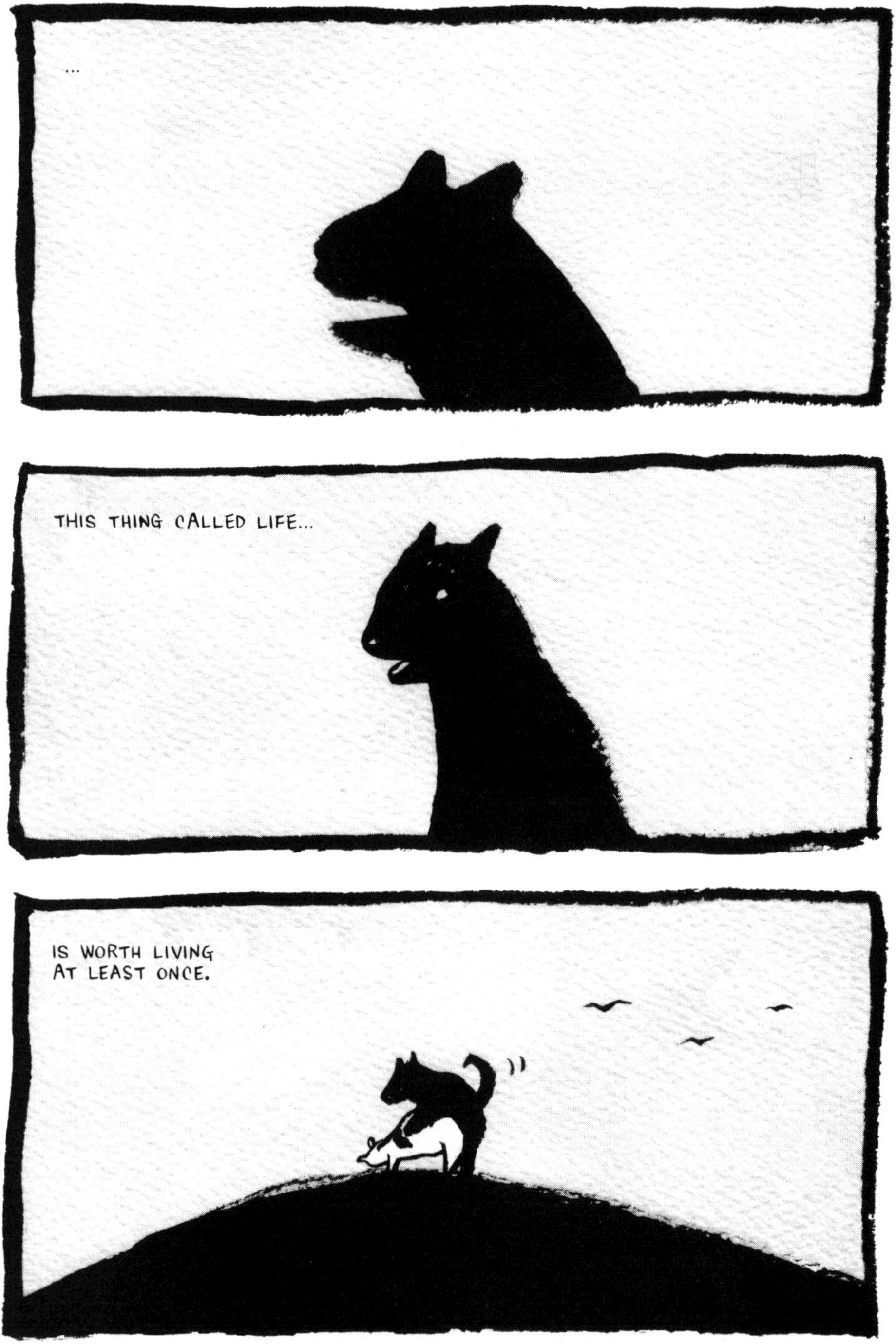
...
THIS THING CALLED LIFE...
IS WORTH LIVING
AT LEAST ONCE.

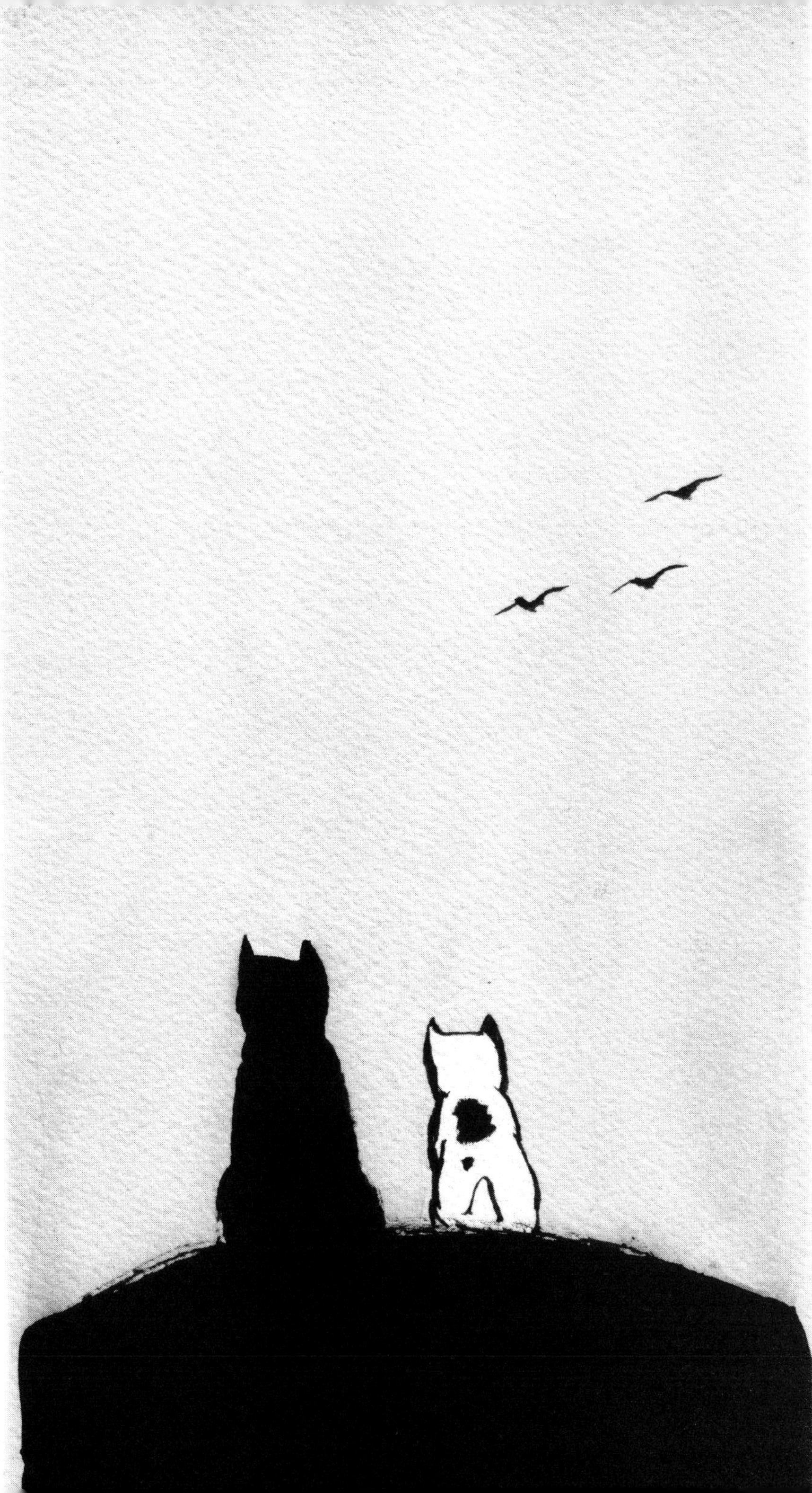

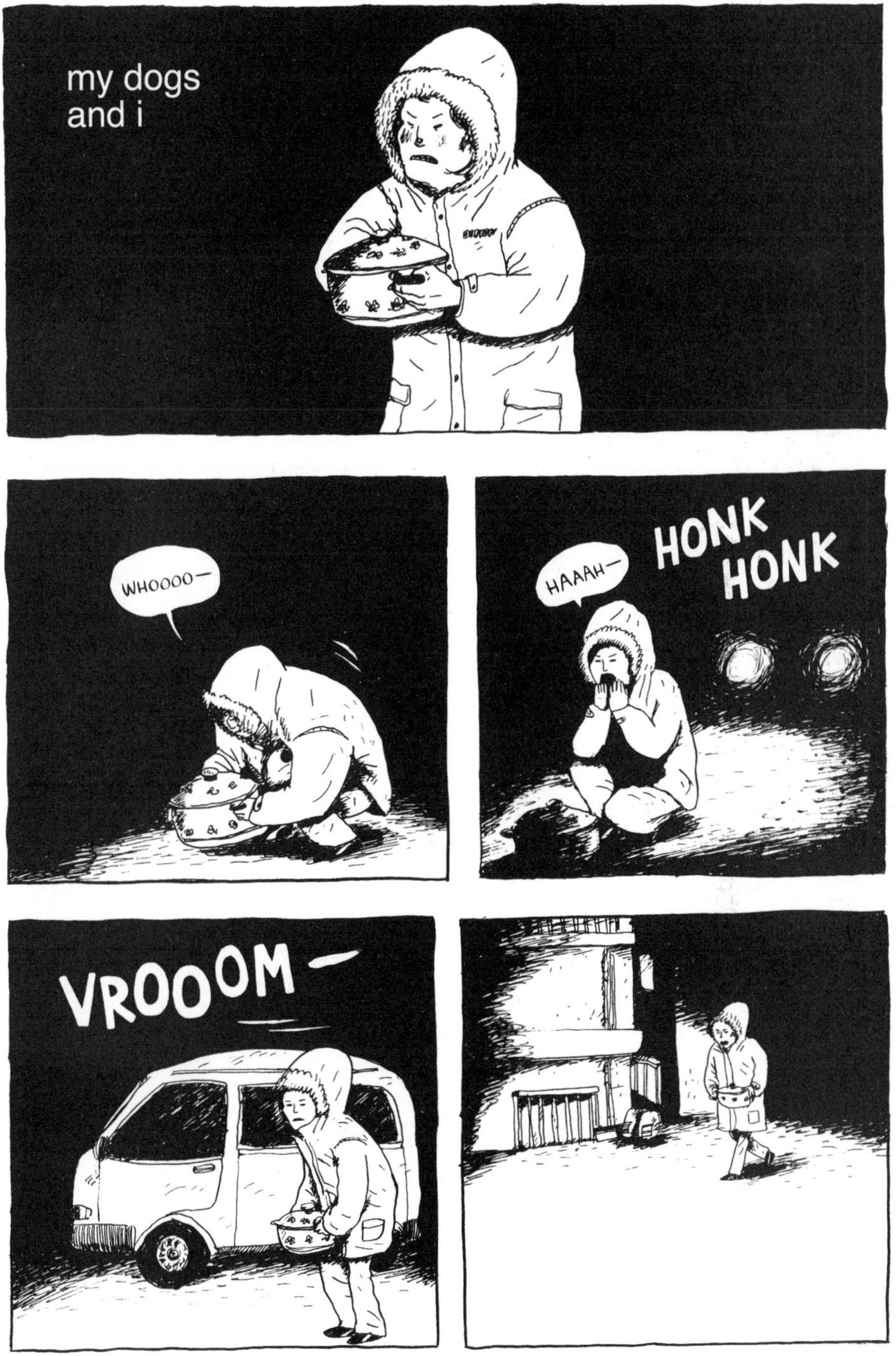
my dogs
and i
WHOOOO—
HAAAH—
HONK
HONK
VROOOM—

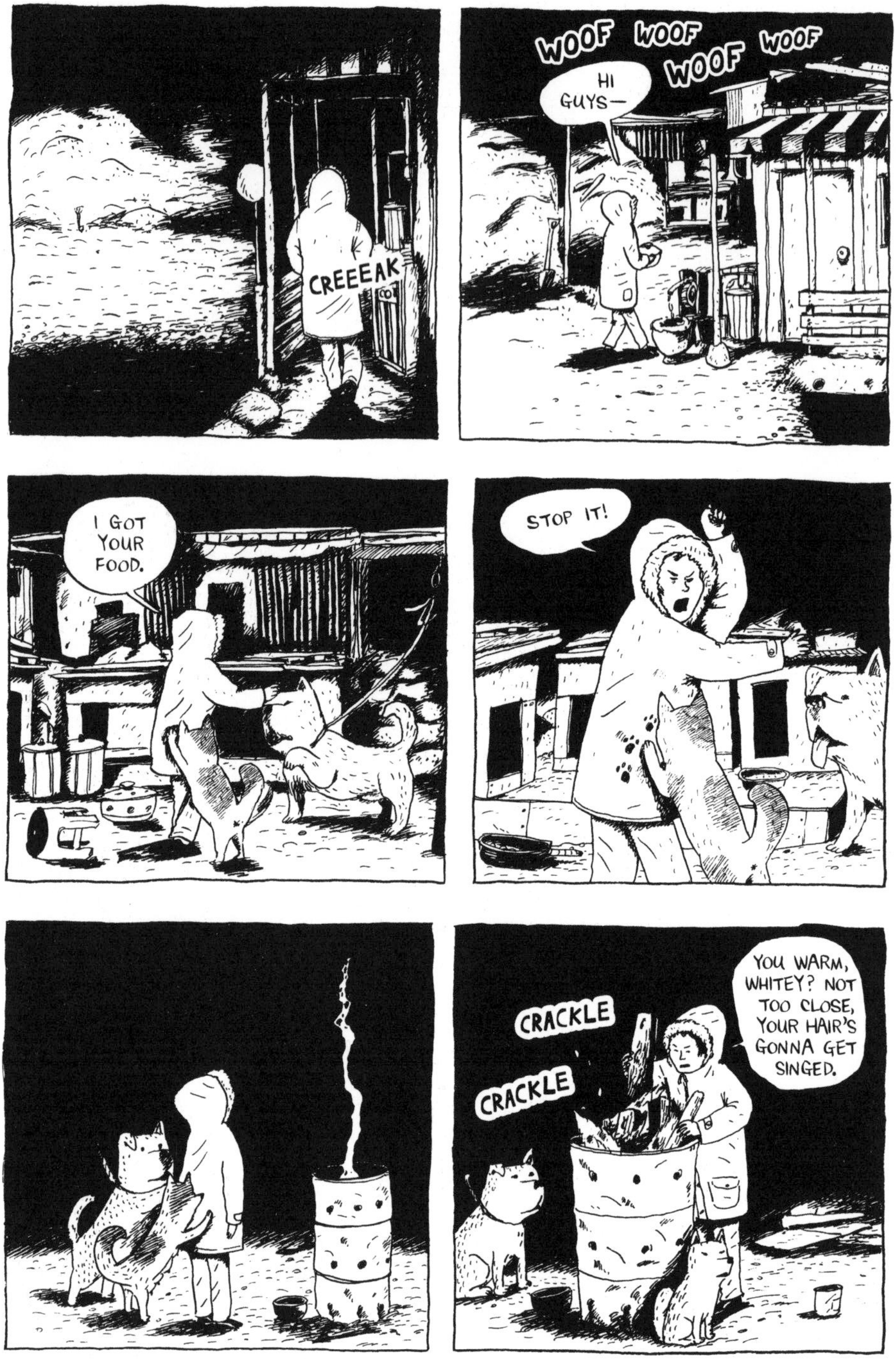
CREEEAK
WOOF WOOF
WOOF WOOF
HI GUYS—
WOOF
I GOT YOUR FOOD.
STOP IT!
CRACKLE
CRACKLE
YOU WARM, WHITEY? NOT TOO CLOSE, YOUR HAIR'S GONNA GET SINGED.

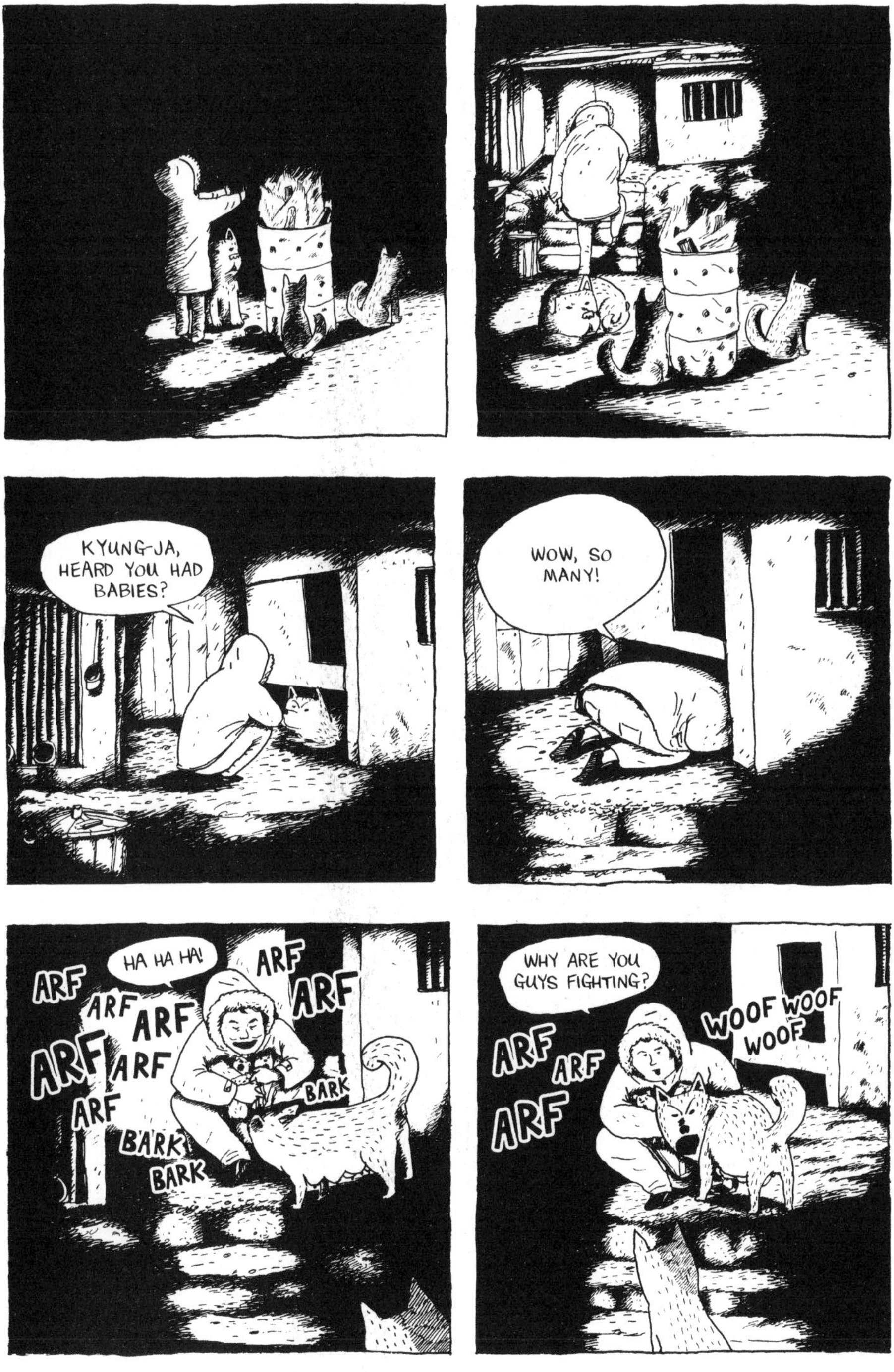
KYUNG-JA, HEARD YOU HAD BABIES?
WOW, SO MANY!
HA HA HA!
ARF
ARF
ARF ARF
ARF
ARF
ARF
ARF
BARK
BARK
BARK
WHY ARE YOU GUYS FIGHTING?
ARF
ARF
ARF
WOOF WOOF
WOOF

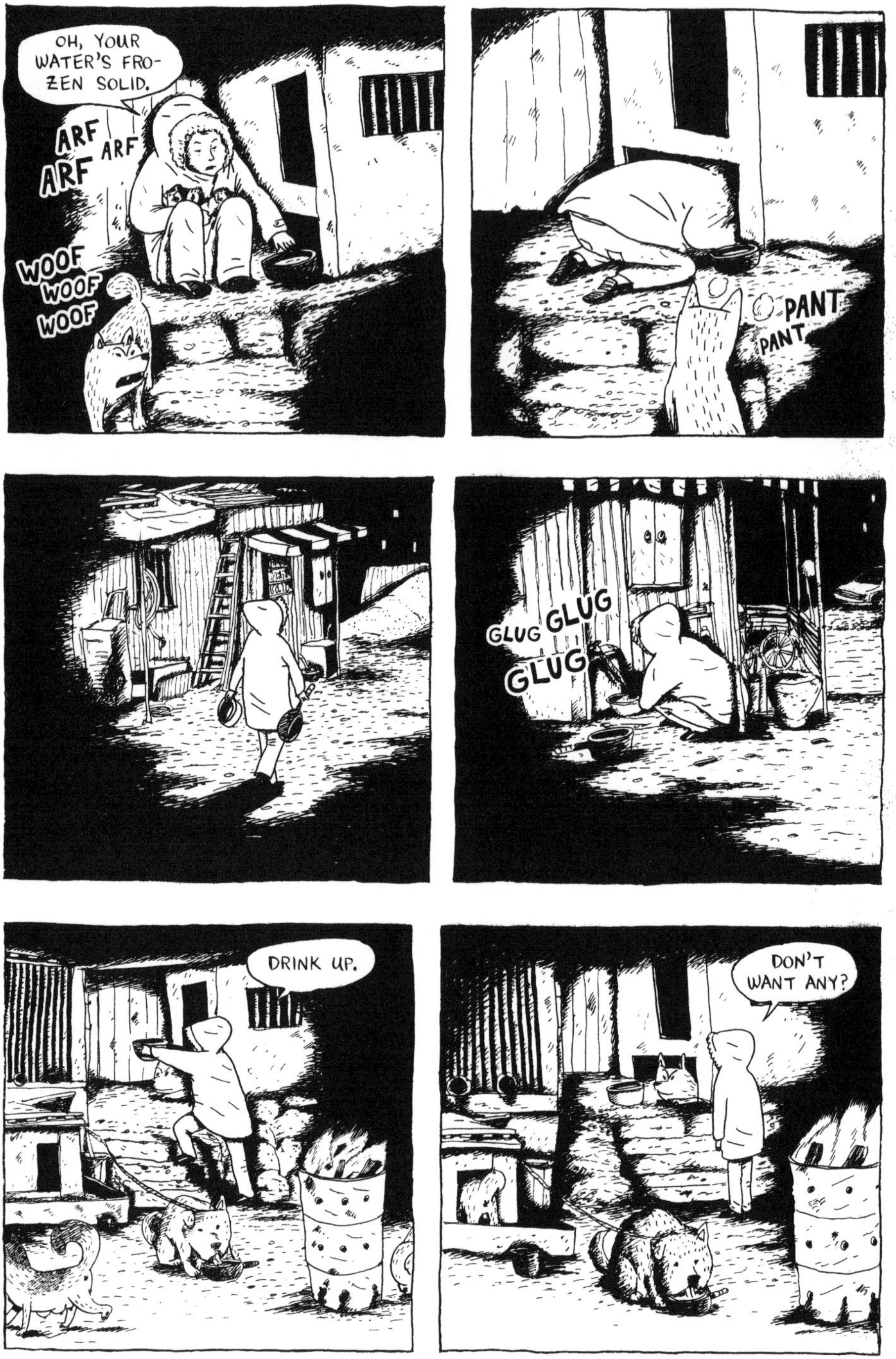
OH, YOUR WATER'S FRO-ZEN SOLID.
ARF ARF ARF
WOOF WOOF WOOF
PANT PANT
GLUG GLUG GLUG
DRINK UP.
DON'T WANT ANY?

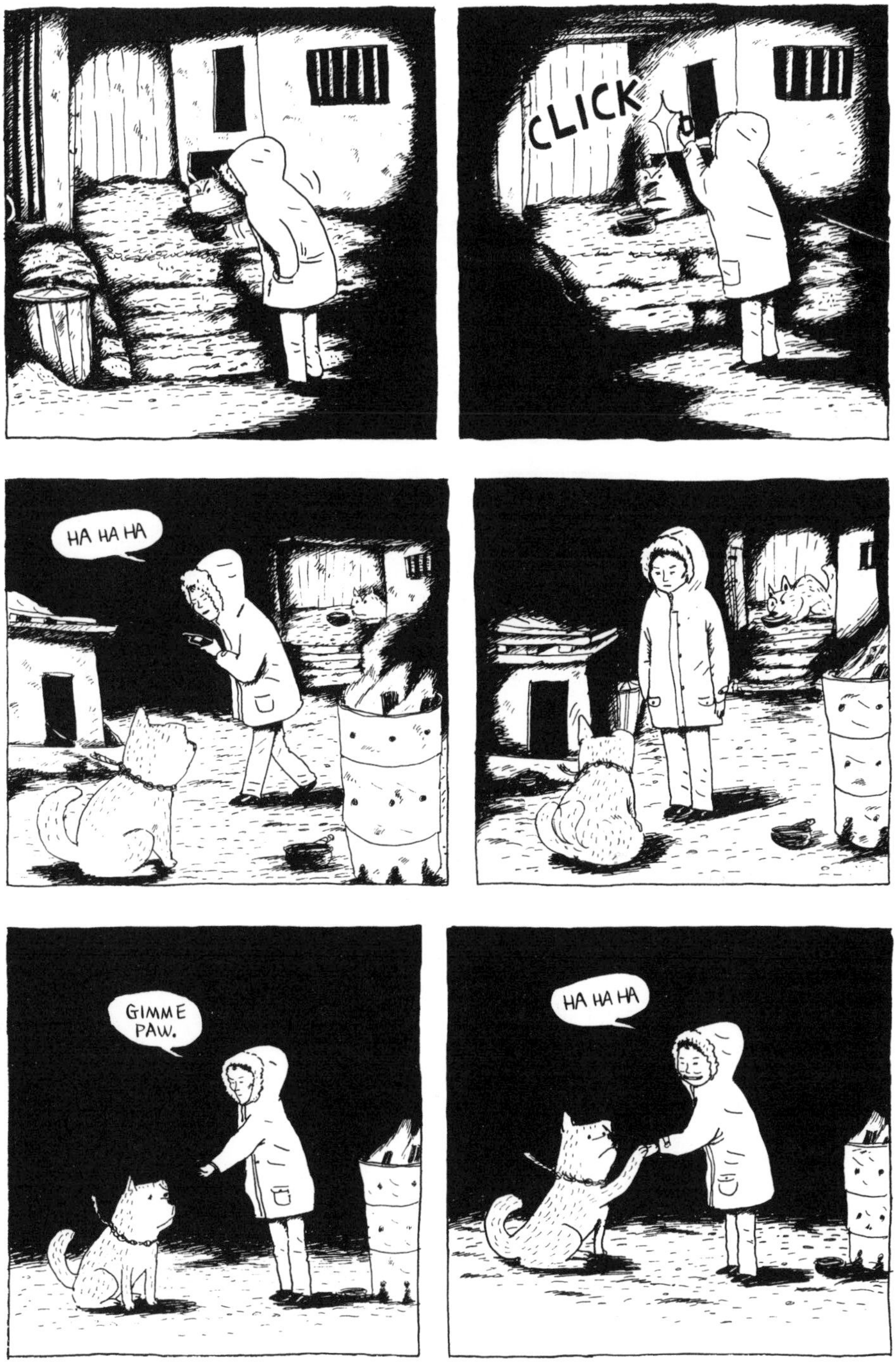
CLICK
HA HA HA
GIMME PAW.
HA HA HA

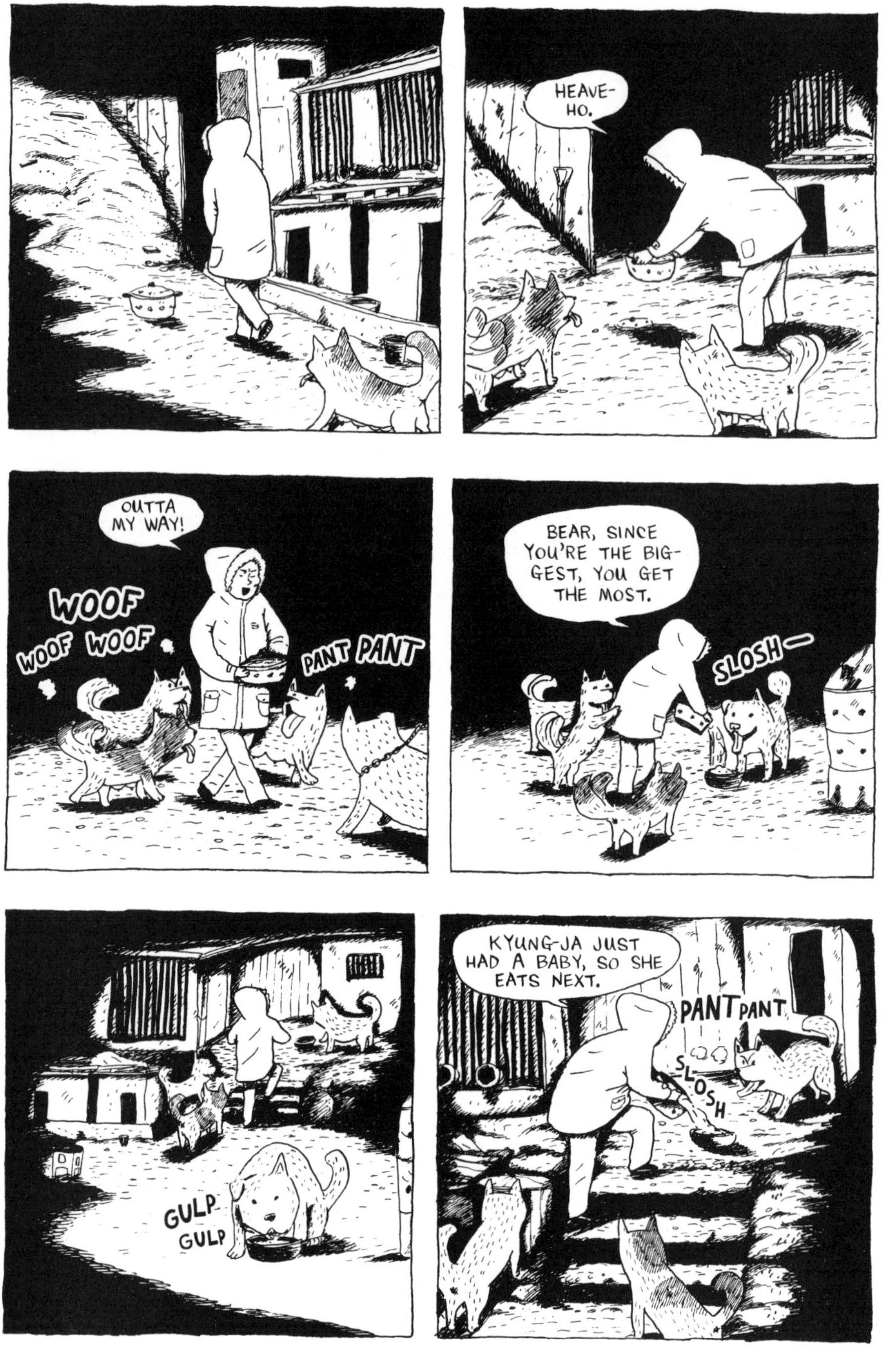
HEAVE-HO.
OUTTA MY WAY!
WOOF
WOOF WOOF
PANT PANT
BEAR, SINCE YOU'RE THE BIG-GEST, YOU GET THE MOST.
SLOSH—
GULP
GULP
KYUNG-JA JUST HAD A BABY, SO SHE EATS NEXT.
PANT PANT
SLOSH

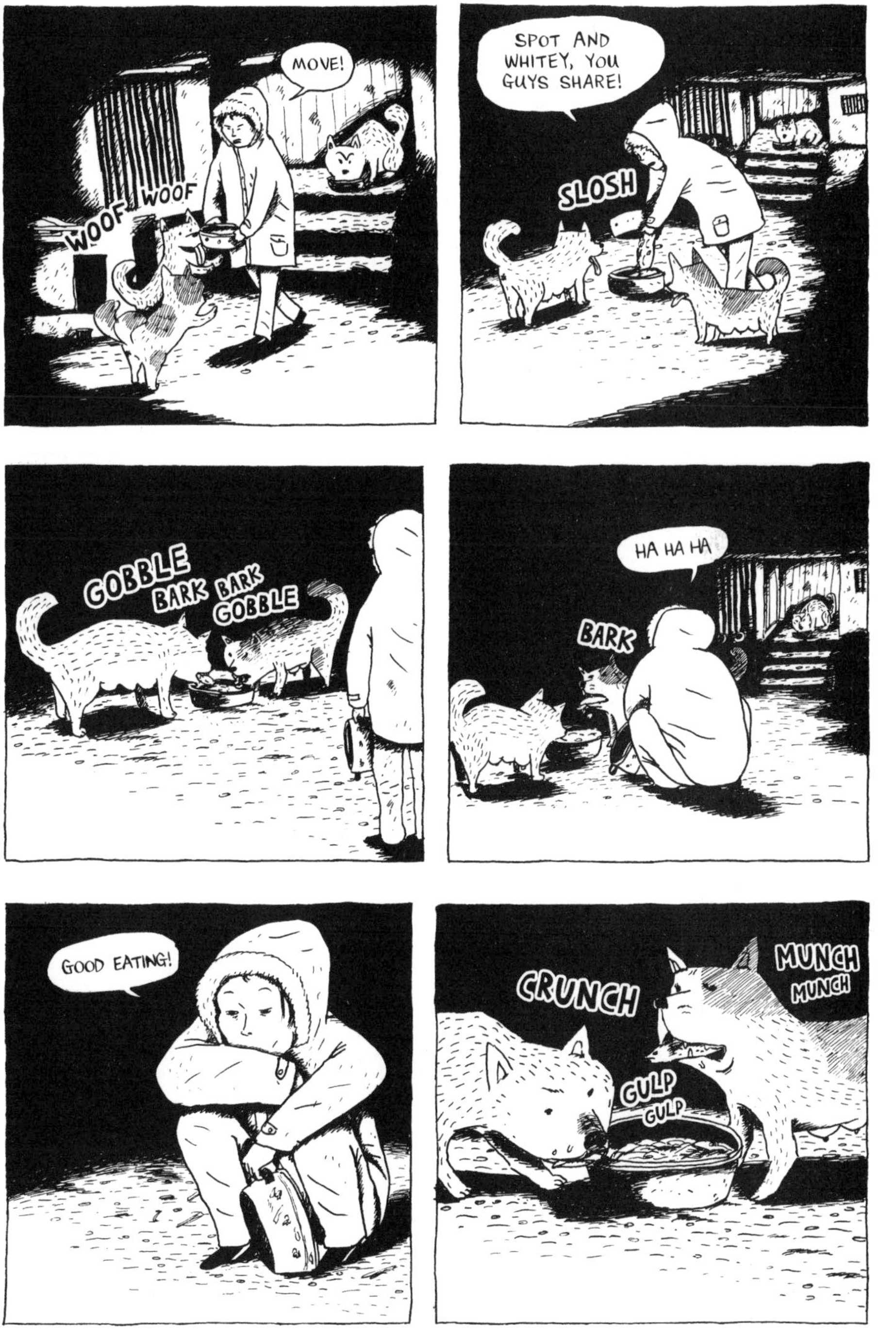
MOVE!
WOOF WOOF
SPOT AND WHITEY, YOU GUYS SHARE!
SLOSH
GOBBLE
BARK BARK
GOBBLE
HA HA HA
BARK
GOOD EATING!
CRUNCH
MUNCH
MUNCH
GULP
GULP

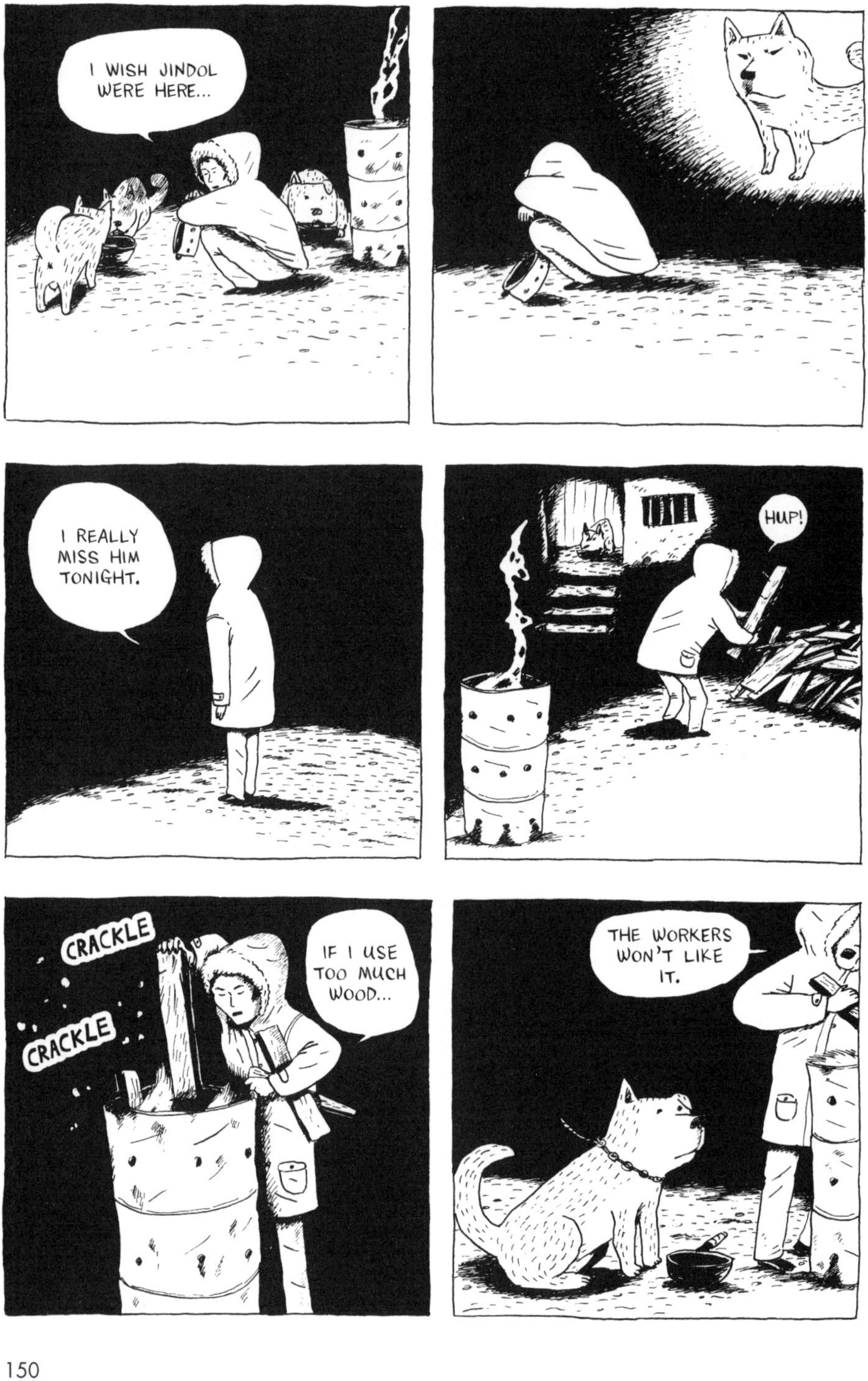
I WISH JINDOL WERE HERE...
I REALLY MISS HIM TONIGHT.
HUP!
CRACKLE
CRACKLE
IF I USE TOO MUCH WOOD...
THE WORKERS WON'T LIKE IT.

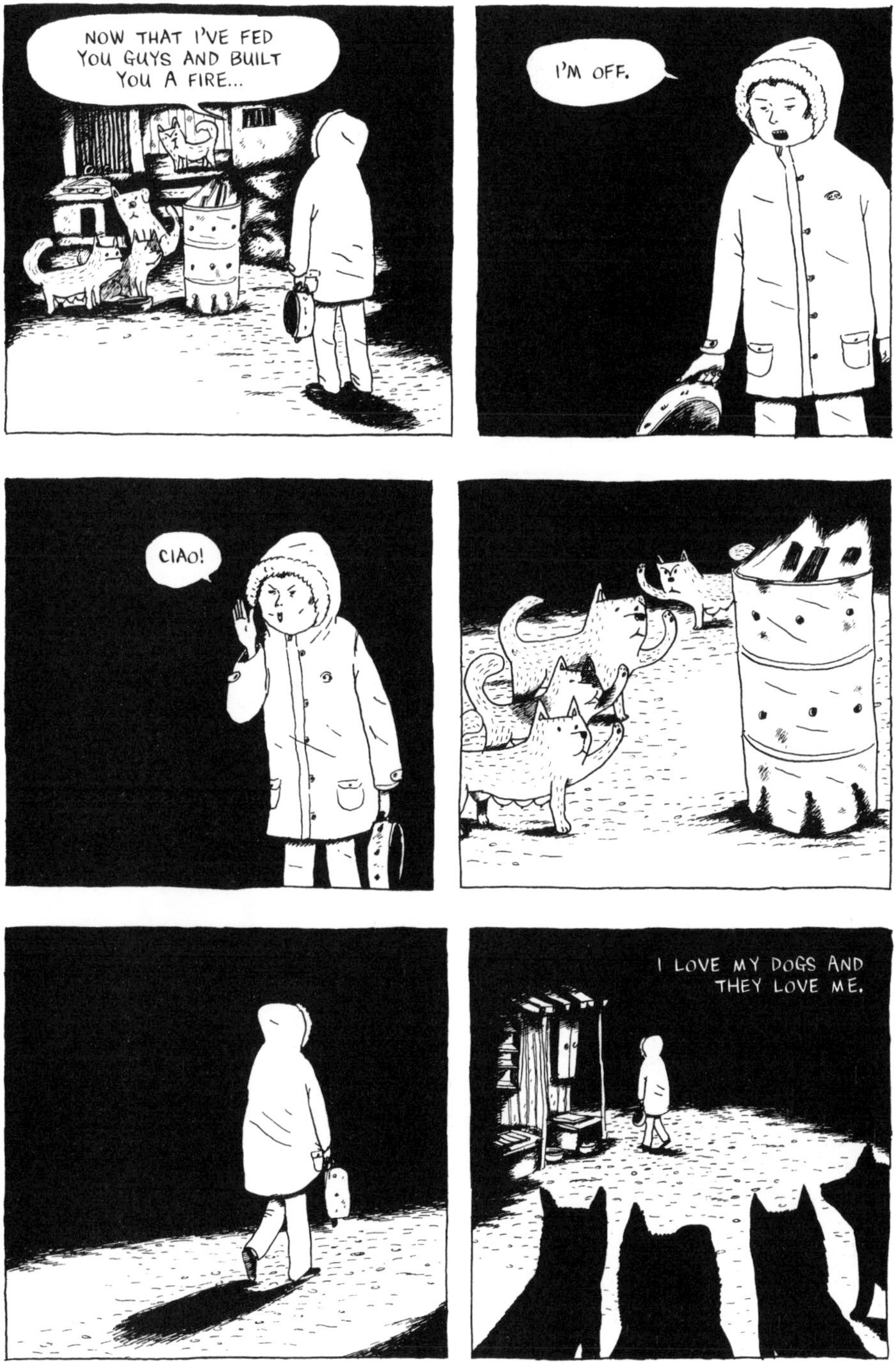
NOW THAT I'VE FED YOU GUYS AND BUILT YOU A FIRE...
I'M OFF.
CIAO!
I LOVE MY DOGS AND THEY LOVE ME.

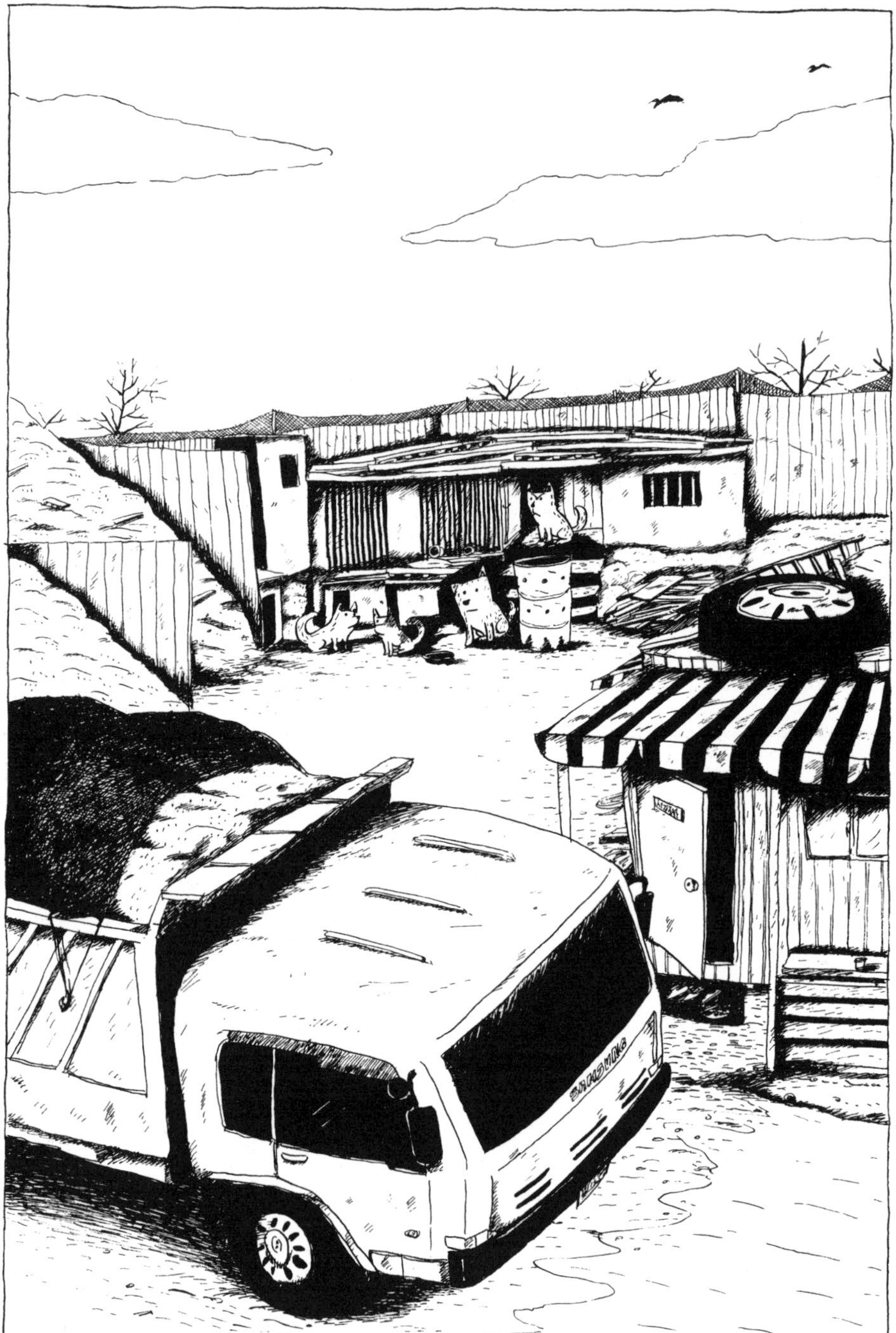

me and my guitar

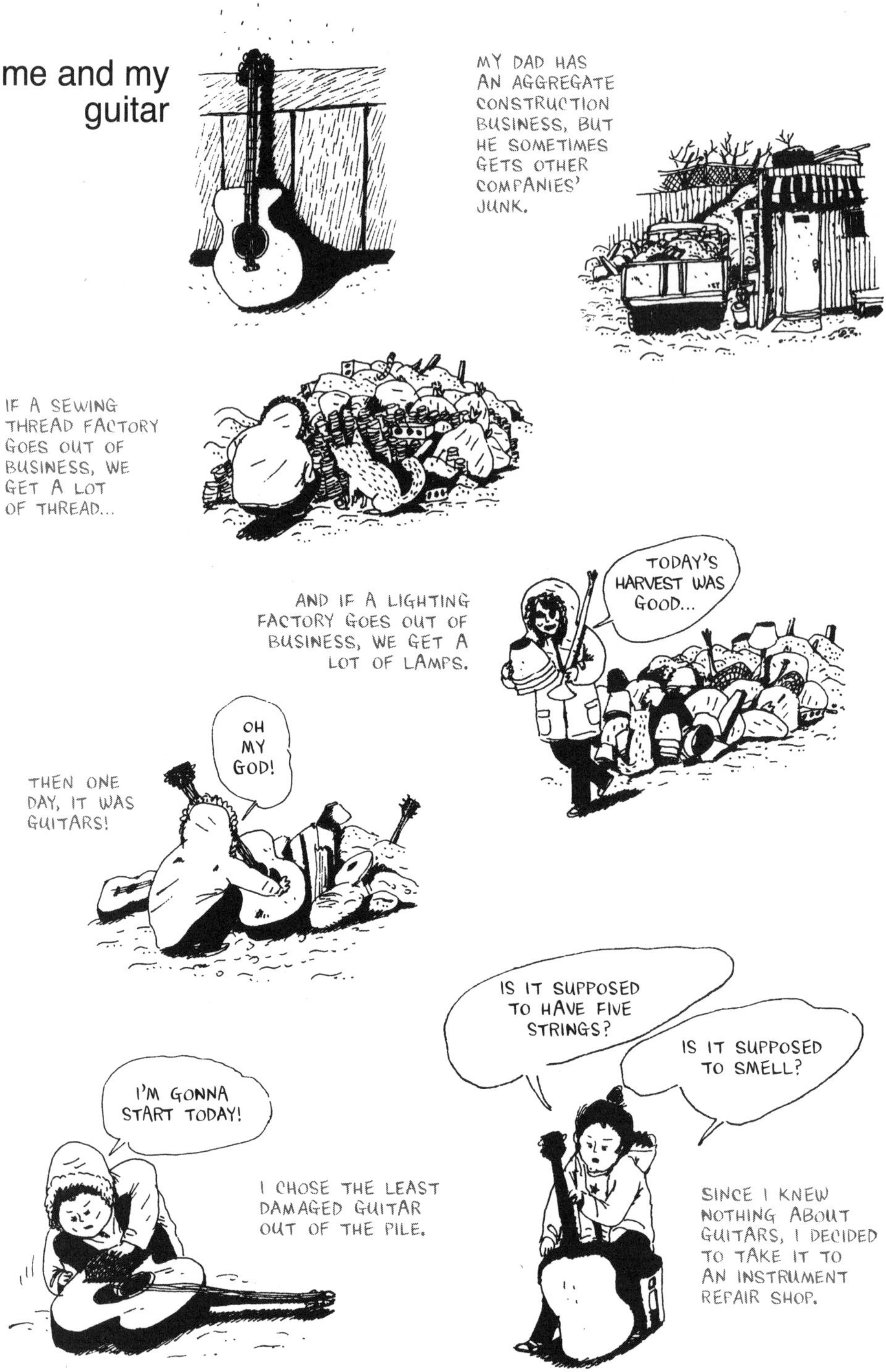

MY DAD HAS AN AGGREGATE CONSTRUCTION BUSINESS, BUT HE SOMETIMES GETS OTHER COMPANIES' JUNK.
IF A SEWING THREAD FACTORY GOES OUT OF BUSINESS, WE GET A LOT OF THREAD...
AND IF A LIGHTING FACTORY GOES OUT OF BUSINESS, WE GET A LOT OF LAMPS.
TODAY'S HARVEST WAS GOOD...
THEN ONE DAY, IT WAS GUITARS!
OH MY GOD!
I'M GONNA START TODAY!
I CHOSE THE LEAST DAMAGED GUITAR OUT OF THE PILE.
IS IT SUPPOSED TO HAVE FIVE STRINGS?
IS IT SUPPOSED TO SMELL?
SINCE I KNEW NOTHING ABOUT GUITARS, I DECIDED TO TAKE IT TO AN INSTRUMENT REPAIR SHOP.

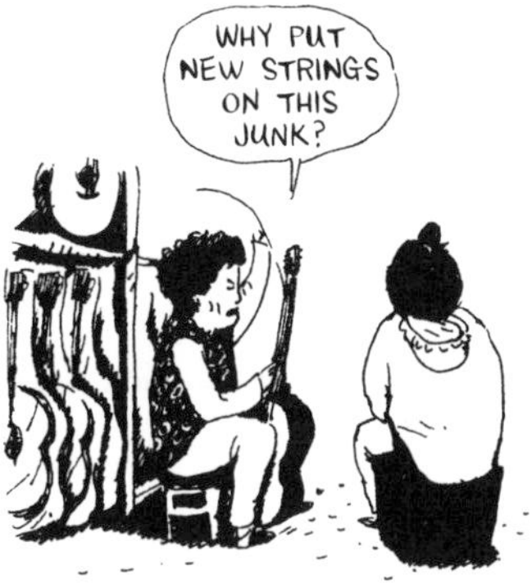
WHY PUT NEW STRINGS ON THIS JUNK?

AS SHE CHANGED THE STRINGS, THE LADY SAID THE GUITAR WAS CHEAP, OLD, AND DAMAGED...

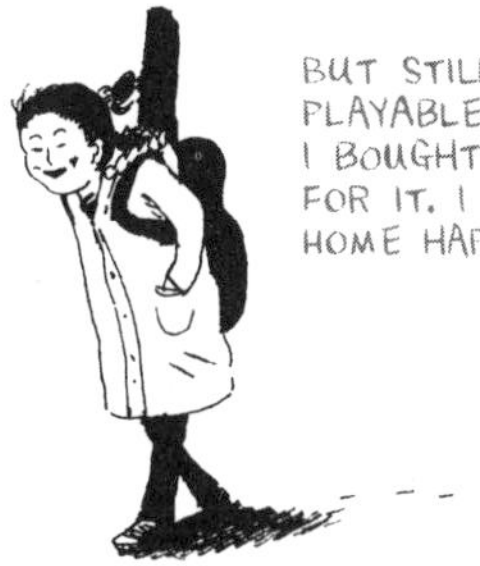

BUT STILL PLAYABLE. SO I BOUGHT A BAG FOR IT. I WENT HOME HAPPY.

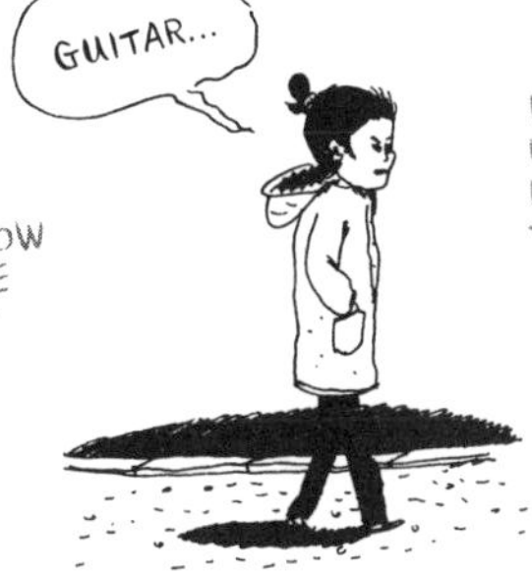
GUITAR...

EVERY DAY, I WONDERED HOW I WAS GOING TO LEARN...

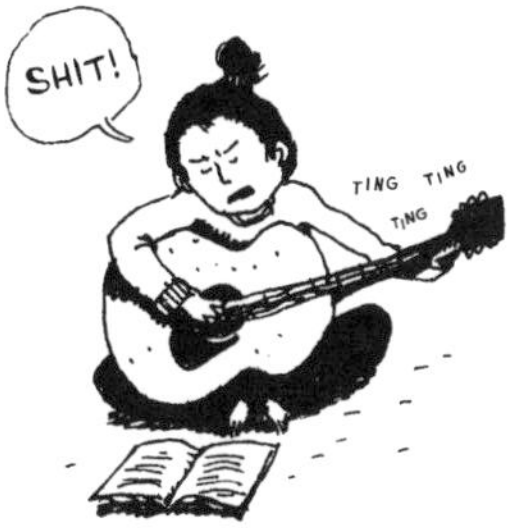
SHIT!
TING TING TING

I TRIED TO FOLLOW ALONG WITH THE MANUAL, BUT IT WASN'T EASY.

UNTIL I MADE A GREAT DISCOVERY!

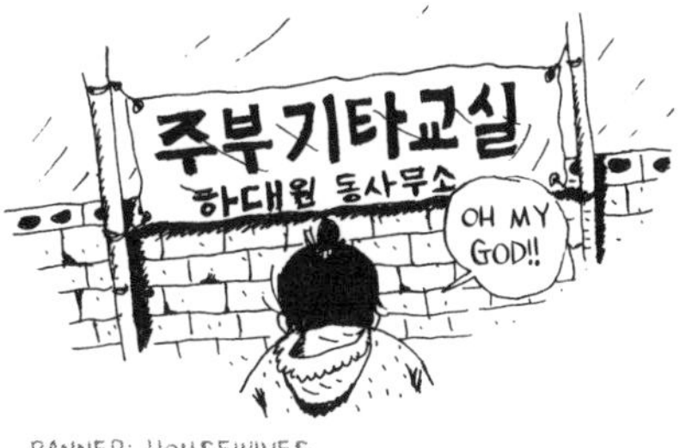
주부기타교실
하대원 동사무소
OH MY GOD!!

BANNER: HOUSEWIVES GUITAR CLUB/HADAEWON COMMUNITY CENTER

I WENT TO THE COMMUNITY CENTER TO ENROLL IN THE FREE CLASS...

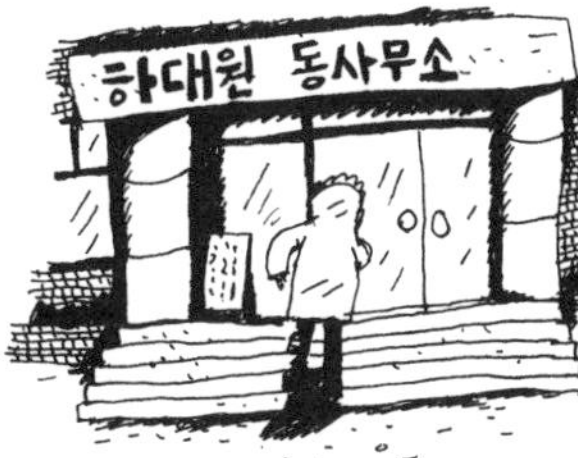
하대원 동사무소

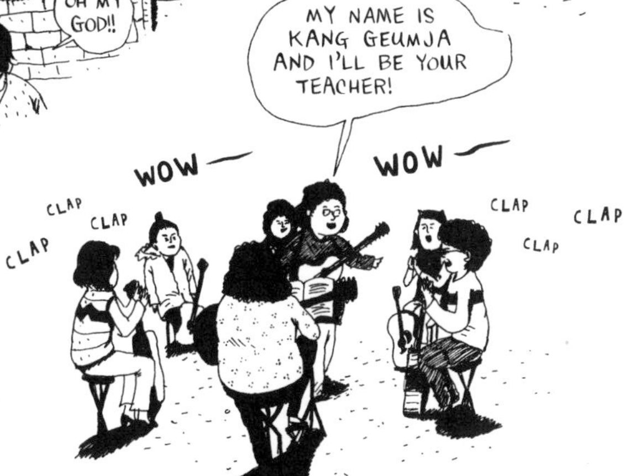
MY NAME IS KANG GEUMJA AND I'LL BE YOUR TEACHER!
WOW—
WOW—
CLAP
CLAP
CLAP
CLAP
CLAP
CLAP

AND JOINED THE HOUSEWIVES GUITAR CLUB!

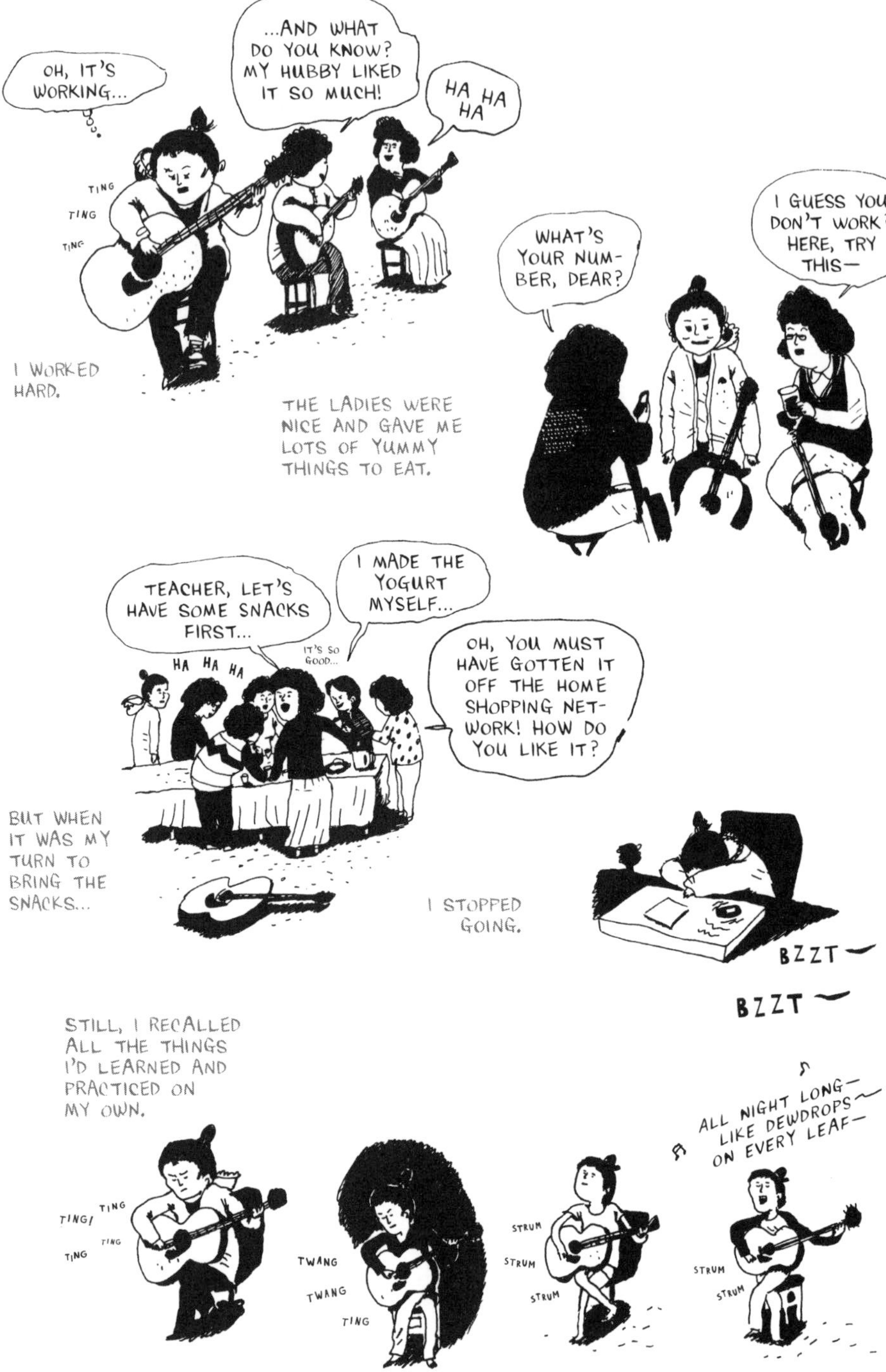
OH, IT'S WORKING...
...AND WHAT DO YOU KNOW? MY HUBBY LIKED IT SO MUCH!
HA HA HA
TING
TING
TING
I WORKED HARD.
THE LADIES WERE NICE AND GAVE ME LOTS OF YUMMY THINGS TO EAT.
WHAT'S YOUR NUMBER, DEAR?
I GUESS YOU DON'T WORK? HERE, TRY THIS—
TEACHER, LET'S HAVE SOME SNACKS FIRST...
I MADE THE YOGURT MYSELF...
IT'S SO GOOD...
HA HA HA
OH, YOU MUST HAVE GOTTEN IT OFF THE HOME SHOPPING NETWORK! HOW DO YOU LIKE IT?
BUT WHEN IT WAS MY TURN TO BRING THE SNACKS...
I STOPPED GOING.
BZZT—
BZZT—
STILL, I RECALLED ALL THE THINGS I'D LEARNED AND PRACTICED ON MY OWN.
TING! TING
TING TING
TWANG
TWANG
TING
STRUM
STRUM
STRUM
ALL NIGHT LONG— LIKE DEWDROPS— ON EVERY LEAF—
STRUM
STRUM

AND NOW, ONE YEAR LATER...

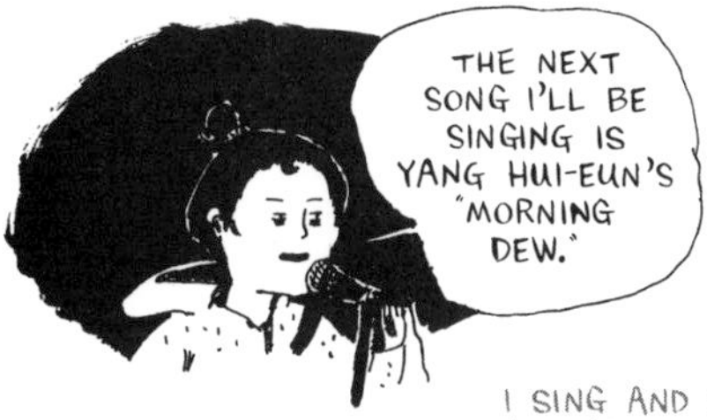
THE NEXT SONG I'LL BE SINGING IS YANG HUI-EUN'S "MORNING DEW."

I SING AND PLAY THE GUITAR IN THE CORNER OF MY STUDIO WHERE I'VE SET UP A LIVE CAFÉ.

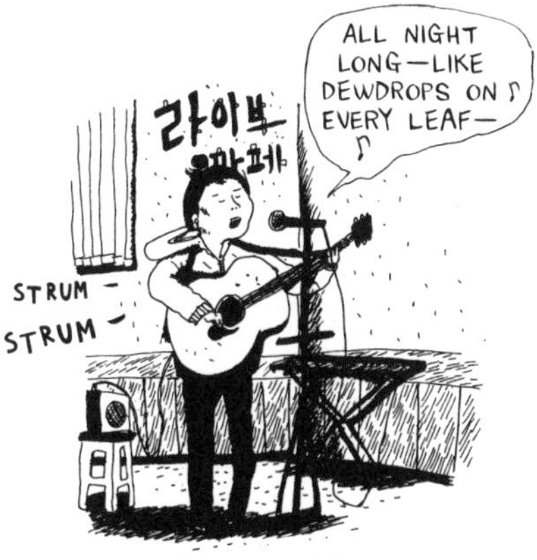
ALL NIGHT LONG—LIKE DEWDROPS ON EVERY LEAF—
STRUM
STRUM

SIGN: LIVE CAFÉ

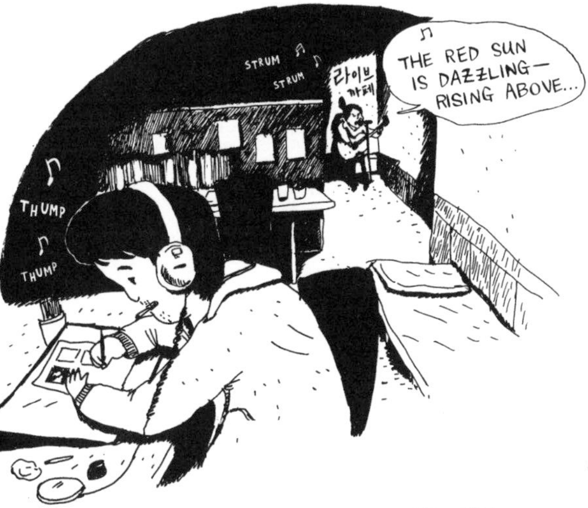
THE RED SUN IS DAZZLING—RISING ABOVE...
STRUM
STRUM
라이브
카페
THUMP
THUMP

THOUGH NO ONE IS LISTENING...

I'M VERY HAPPY.

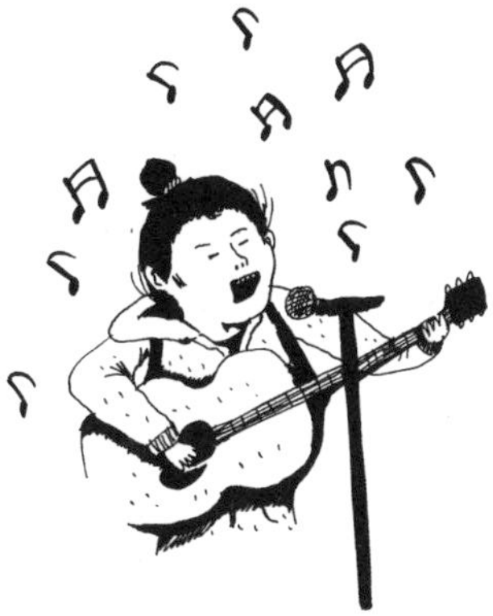

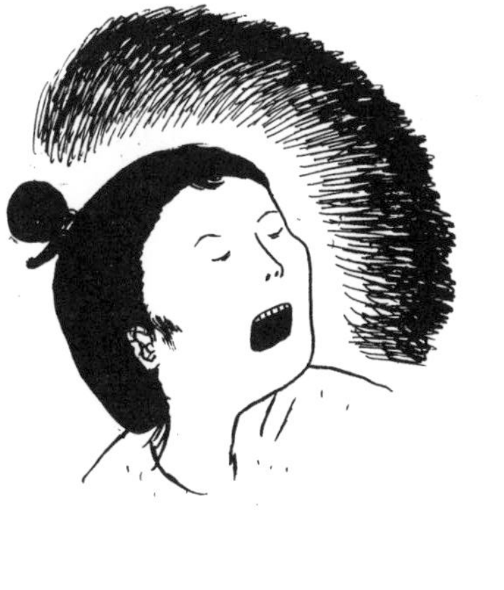

I LOOK FORWARD TO THE DAY I CAN SING AND PLAY IN FRONT OF AN AUDIENCE.

wild roses

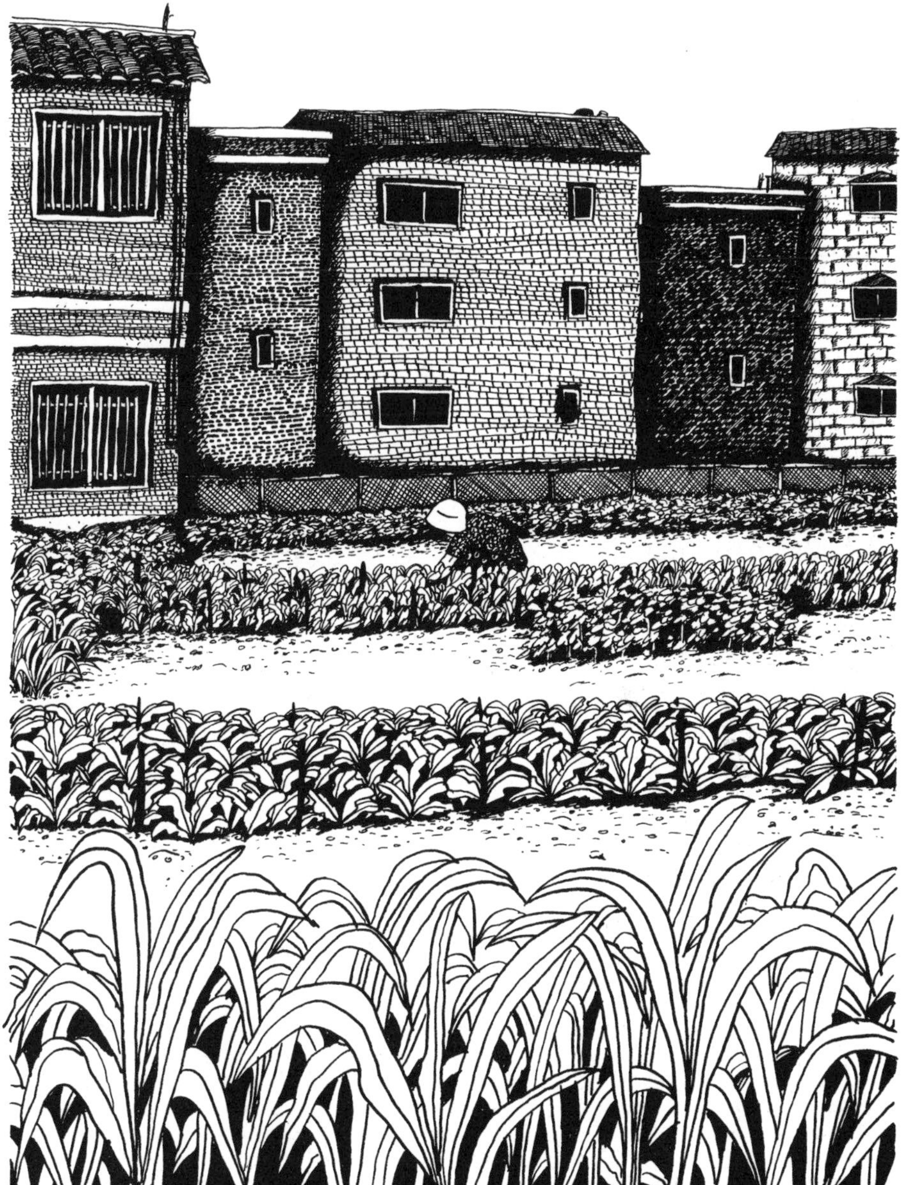

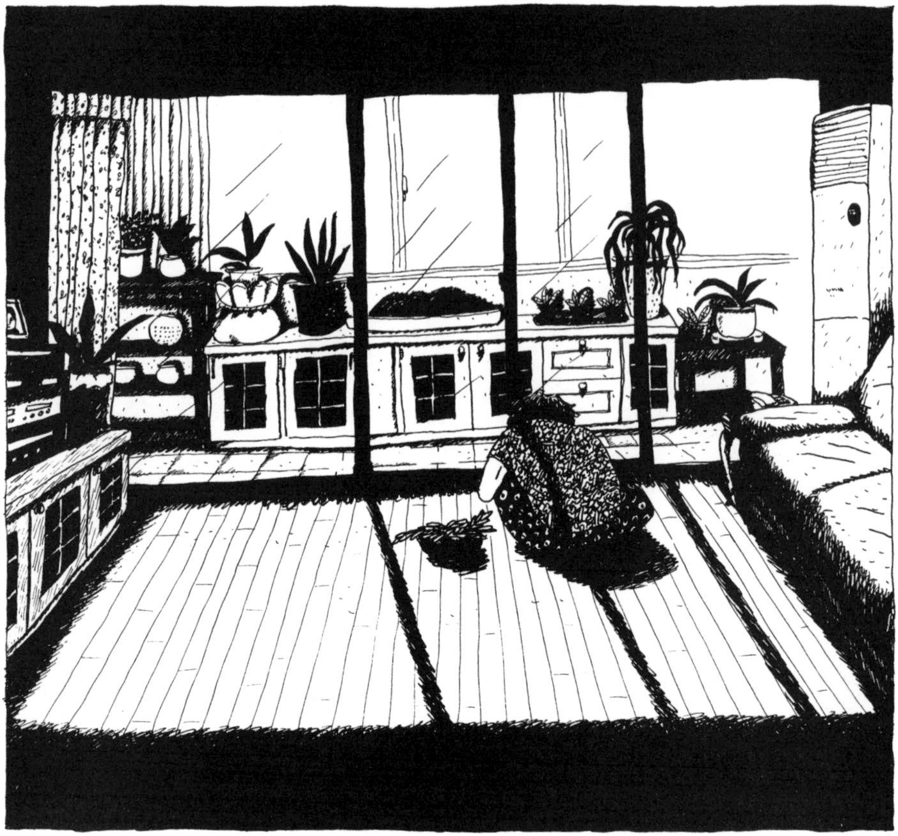

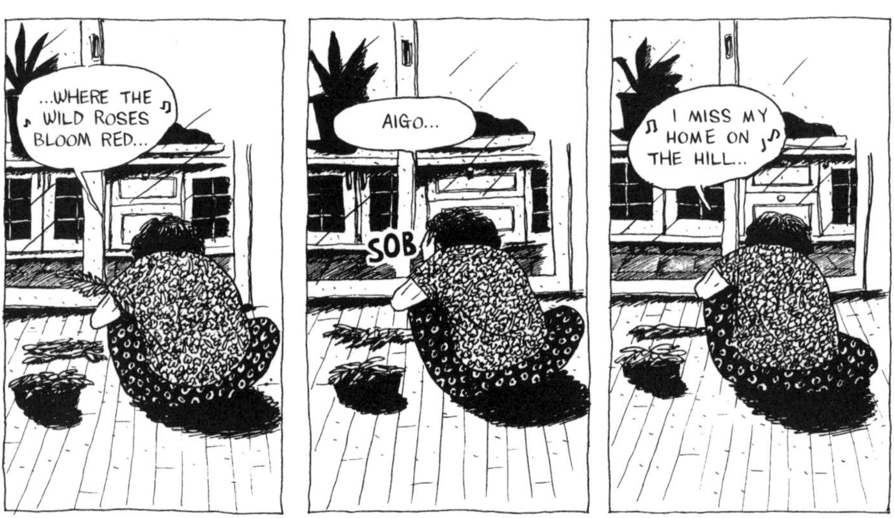
...WHERE THE WILD ROSES BLOOM RED...
SOB
AIGO...
I MISS MY HOME ON THE HILL...

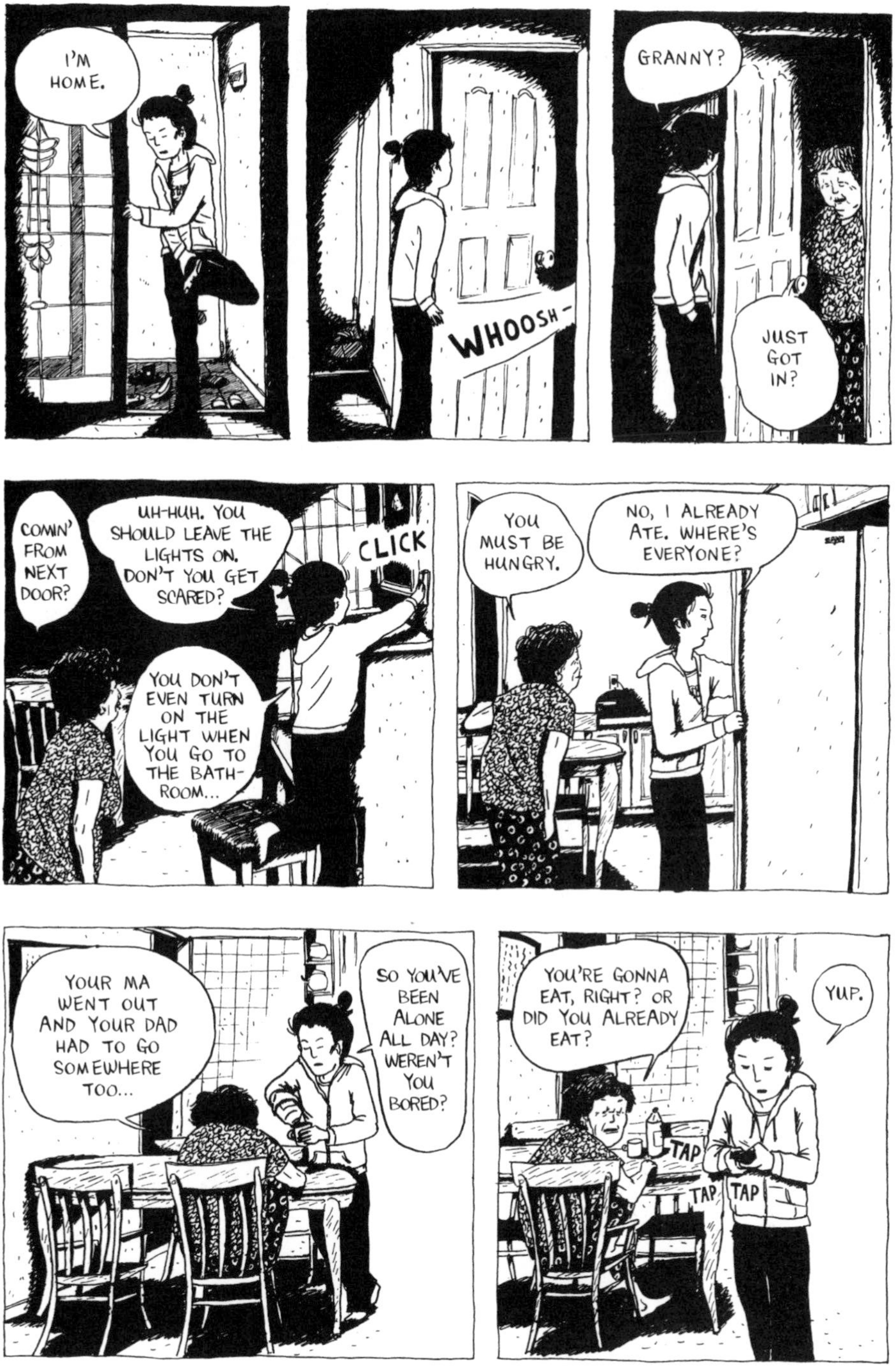
I'M HOME.
WHOOSH-
GRANNY?
JUST GOT IN?
COMIN' FROM NEXT DOOR?
UH-HUH. YOU SHOULD LEAVE THE LIGHTS ON. DON'T YOU GET SCARED?
CLICK
YOU DON'T EVEN TURN ON THE LIGHT WHEN YOU GO TO THE BATH-ROOM...
YOU MUST BE HUNGRY.
NO, I ALREADY ATE. WHERE'S EVERYONE?
YOUR MA WENT OUT AND YOUR DAD HAD TO GO SOMEWHERE TOO...
SO YOU'VE BEEN ALONE ALL DAY? WEREN'T YOU BORED?
YOU'RE GONNA EAT, RIGHT? OR DID YOU ALREADY EAT?
YUP.
TAP
TAP TAP

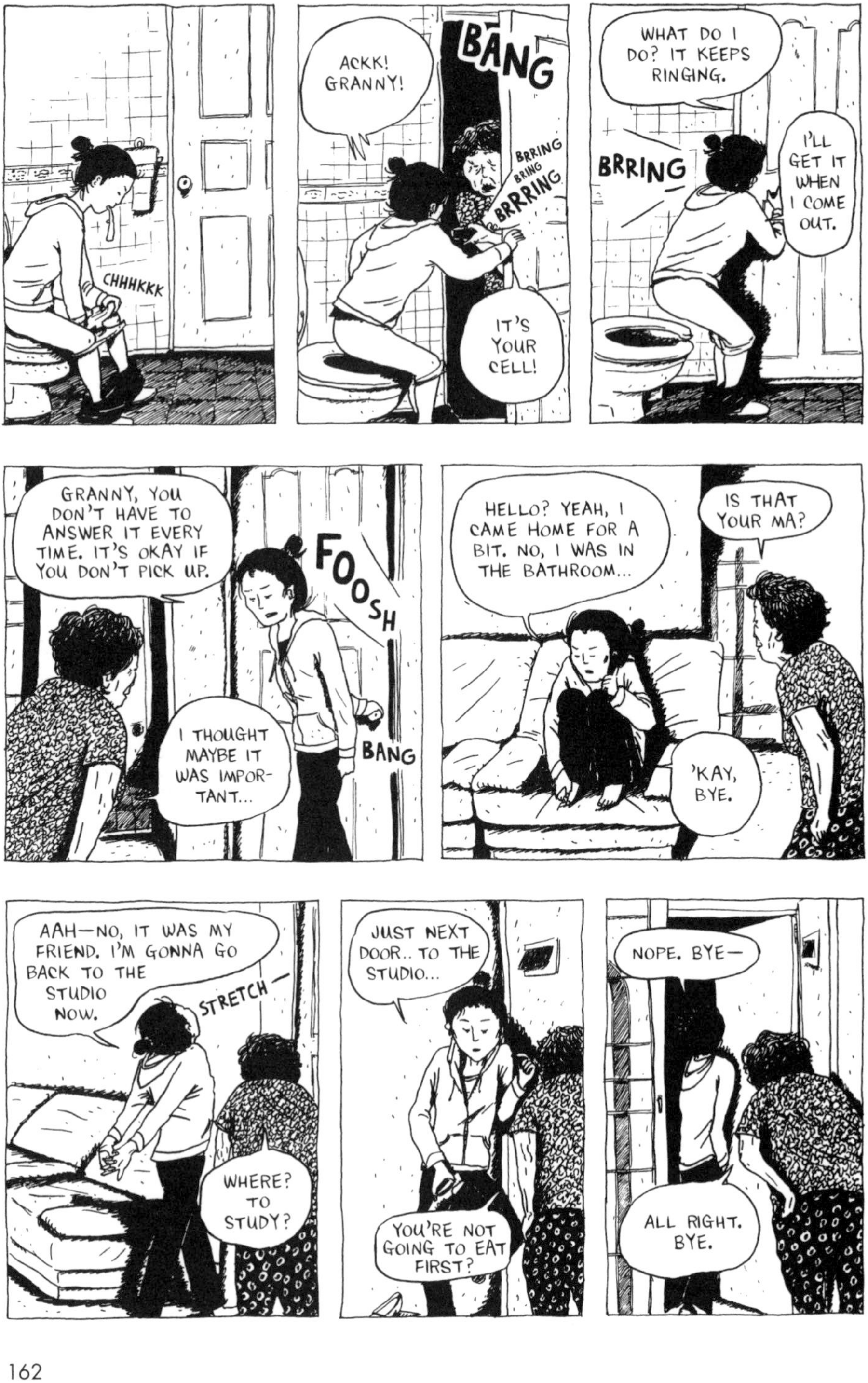
CHHHKKK
BANG
ACKK! GRANNY!
BRRING BRING BRRRING
IT'S YOUR CELL!
WHAT DO I DO? IT KEEPS RINGING.
BRRING
I'LL GET IT WHEN I COME OUT.
GRANNY, YOU DON'T HAVE TO ANSWER IT EVERY TIME. IT'S OKAY IF YOU DON'T PICK UP.
FOOSH
I THOUGHT MAYBE IT WAS IMPOR-TANT...
BANG
HELLO? YEAH, I CAME HOME FOR A BIT. NO, I WAS IN THE BATHROOM...
IS THAT YOUR MA?
'KAY, BYE.
AAH—NO, IT WAS MY FRIEND. I'M GONNA GO BACK TO THE STUDIO NOW.
STRETCH—
WHERE? TO STUDY?
JUST NEXT DOOR.. TO THE STUDIO...
YOU'RE NOT GOING TO EAT FIRST?
NOPE. BYE—
ALL RIGHT. BYE.

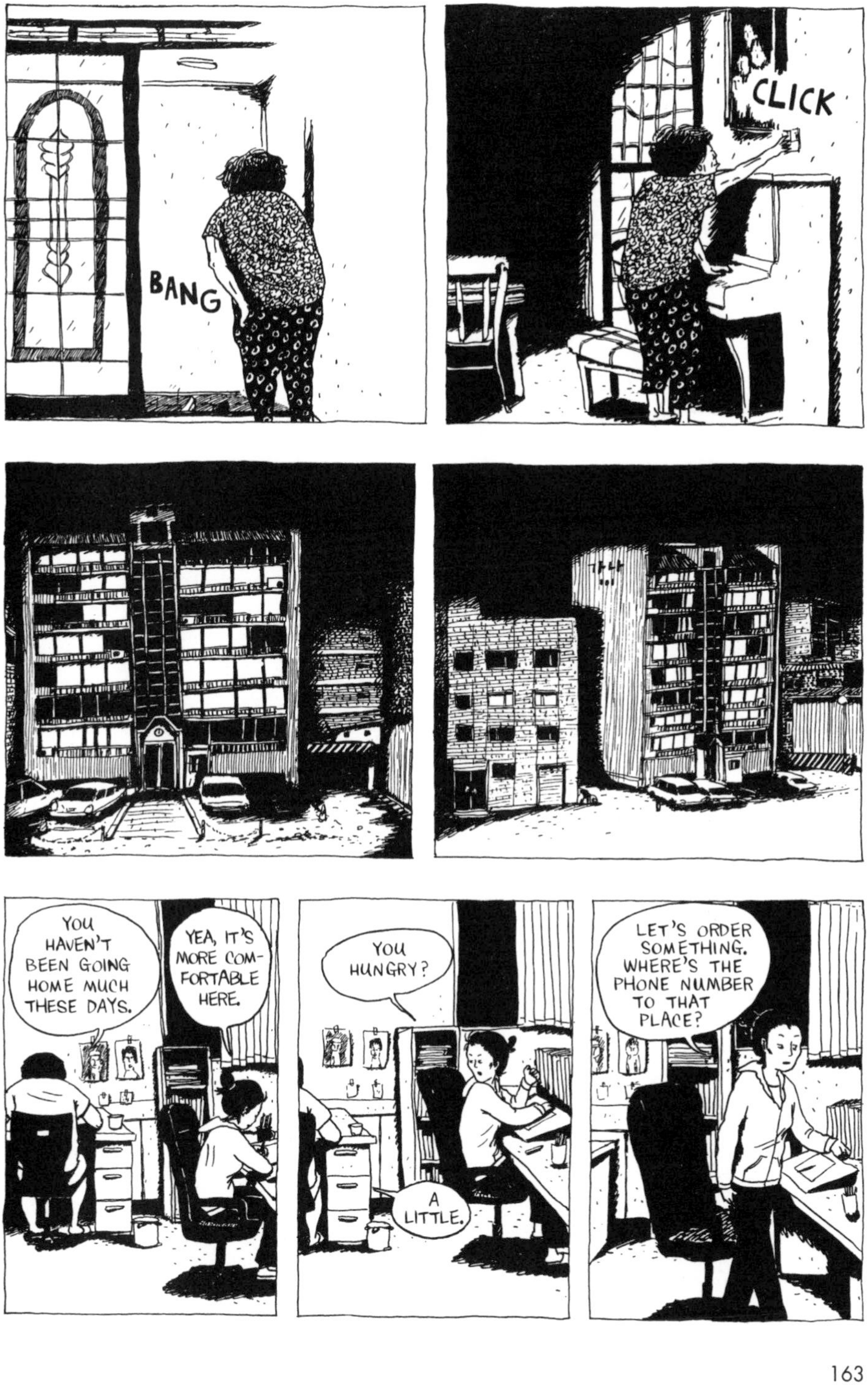
BANG
CLICK
YOU HAVEN'T BEEN GOING HOME MUCH THESE DAYS.
YEA, IT'S MORE COM-FORTABLE HERE.
YOU HUNGRY?
A LITTLE.
LET'S ORDER SOMETHING. WHERE'S THE PHONE NUMBER TO THAT PLACE?

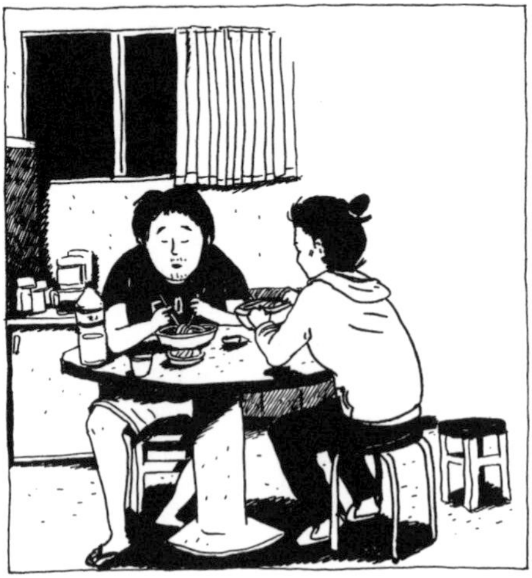

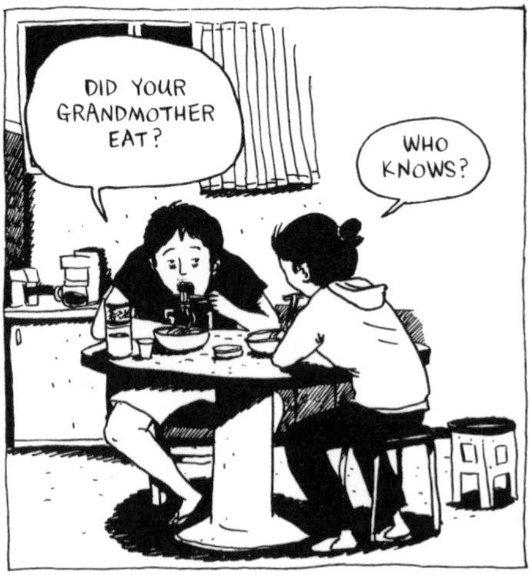
DID YOUR GRANDMOTHER EAT?
WHO KNOWS?

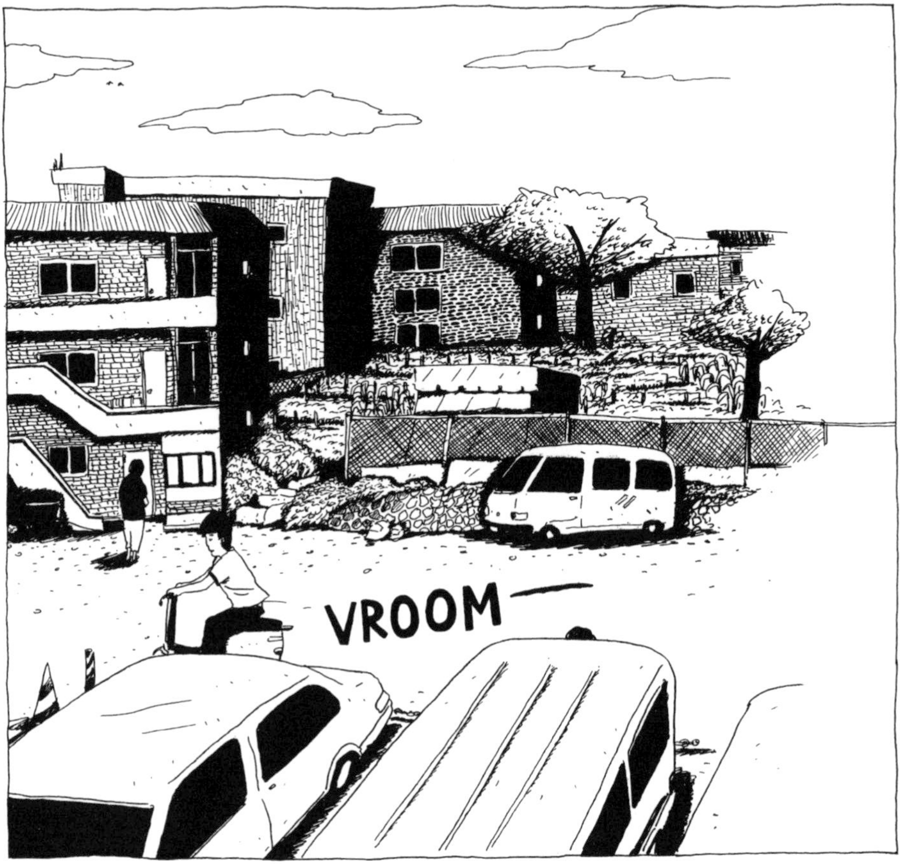
VROOM

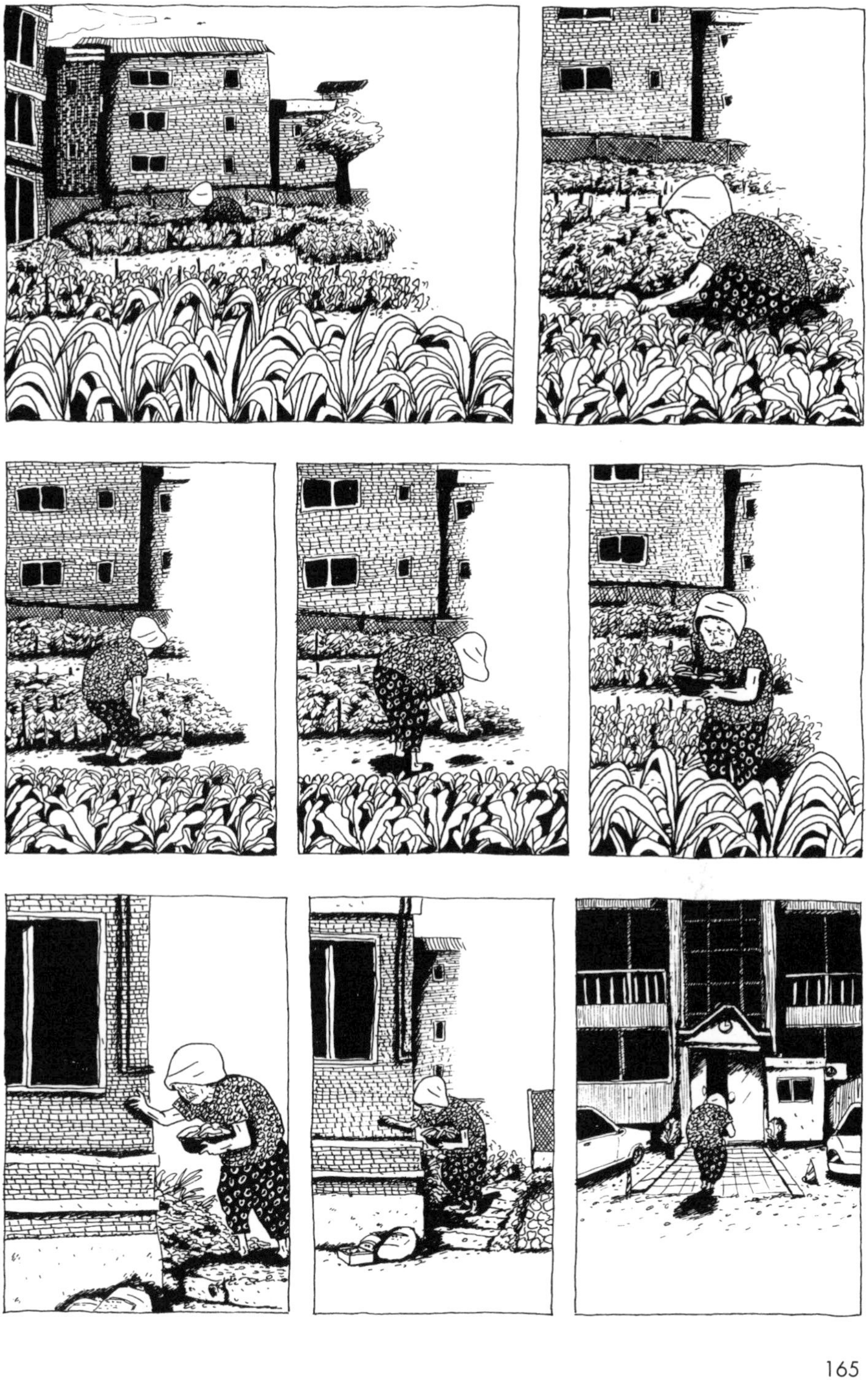

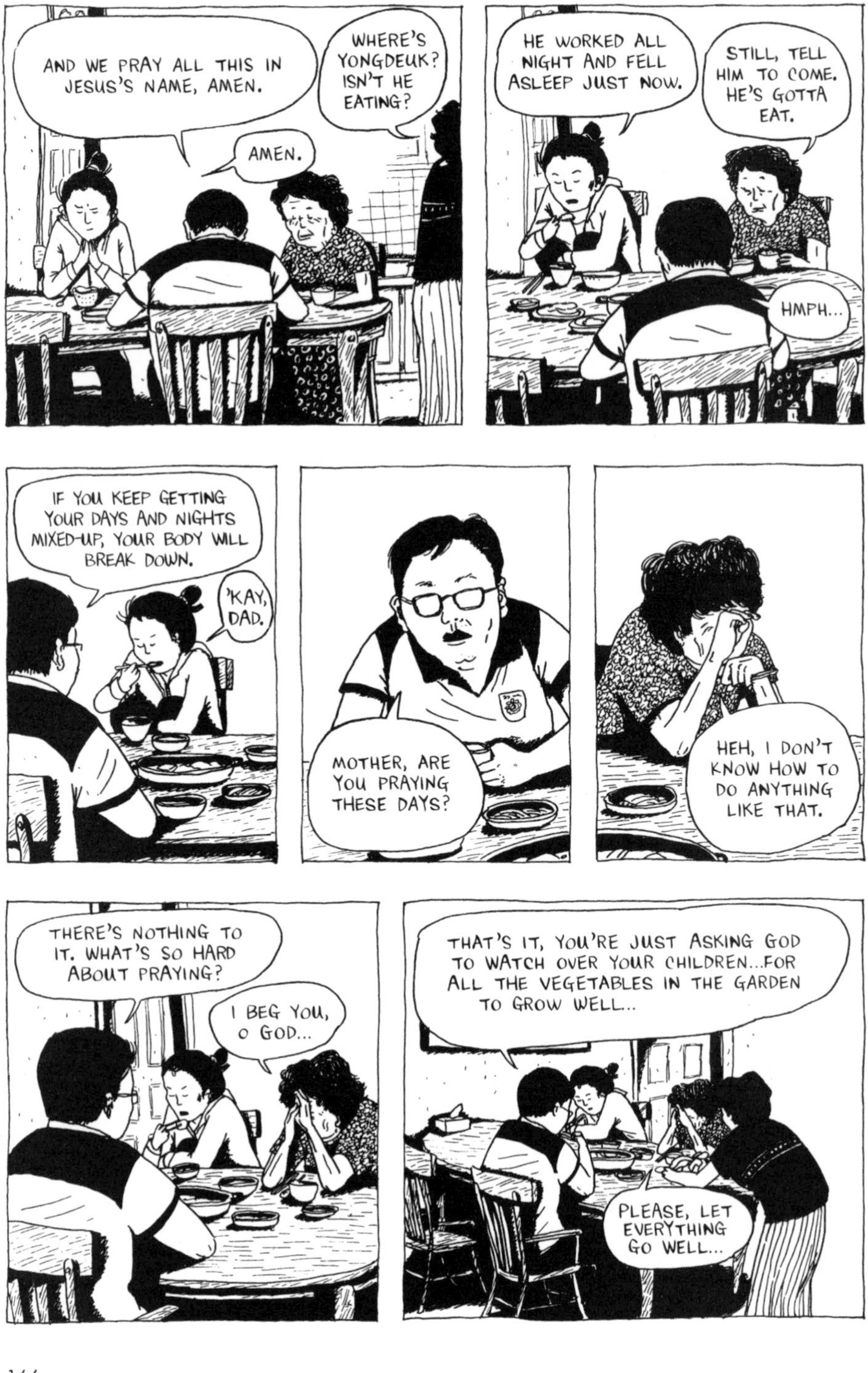
AND WE PRAY ALL THIS IN JESUS'S NAME, AMEN.
AMEN.
WHERE'S YONGDEUK? ISN'T HE EATING?
HE WORKED ALL NIGHT AND FELL ASLEEP JUST NOW.
STILL, TELL HIM TO COME. HE'S GOTTA EAT.
HMPH...
IF YOU KEEP GETTING YOUR DAYS AND NIGHTS MIXED-UP, YOUR BODY WILL BREAK DOWN.
'KAY, DAD.
MOTHER, ARE YOU PRAYING THESE DAYS?
HEH, I DON'T KNOW HOW TO DO ANYTHING LIKE THAT.
THERE'S NOTHING TO IT. WHAT'S SO HARD ABOUT PRAYING?
I BEG YOU, O GOD...
THAT'S IT, YOU'RE JUST ASKING GOD TO WATCH OVER YOUR CHILDREN...FOR ALL THE VEGETABLES IN THE GARDEN TO GROW WELL...
PLEASE, LET EVERYTHING GO WELL...

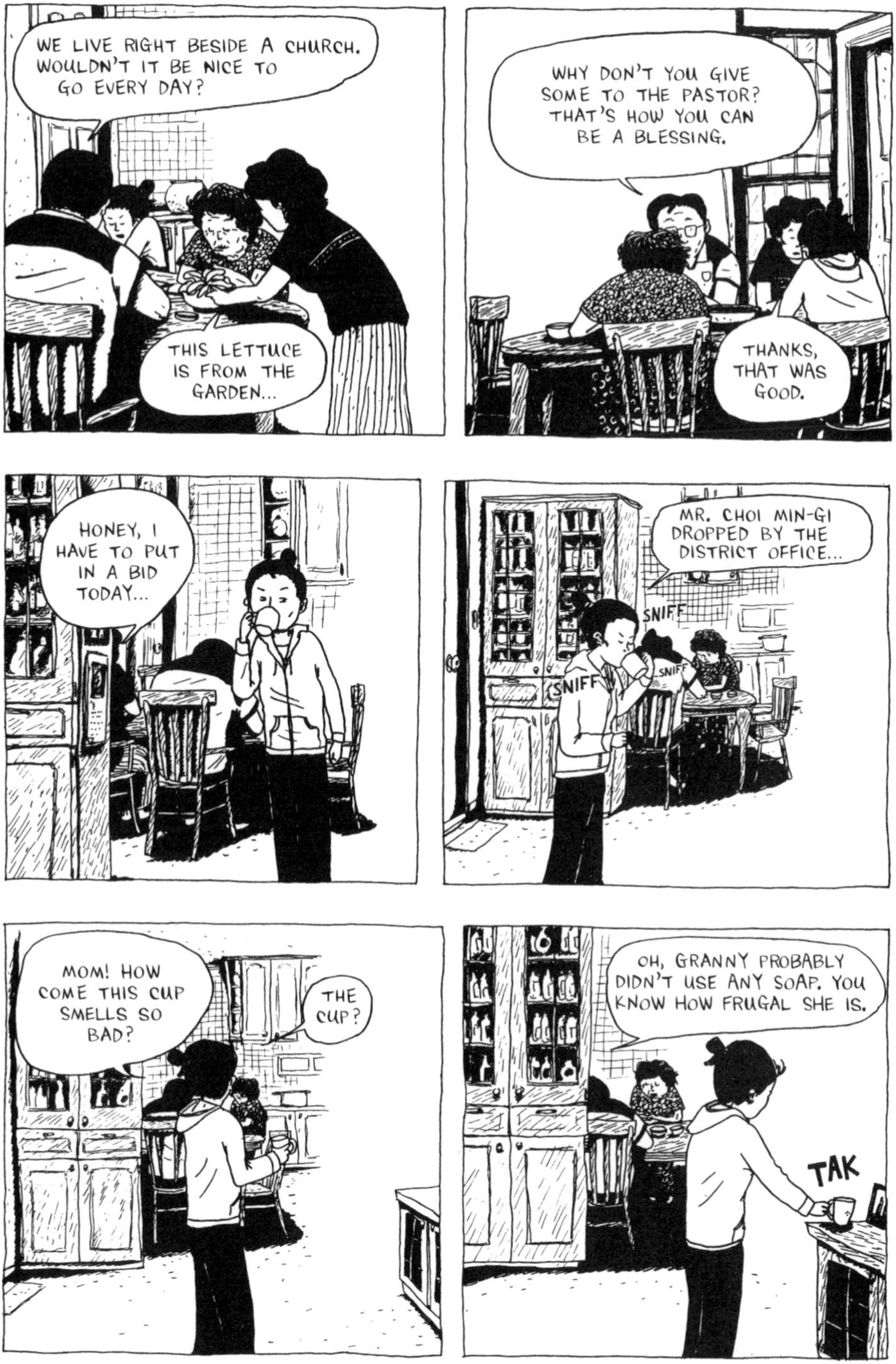
WE LIVE RIGHT BESIDE A CHURCH. WOULDN'T IT BE NICE TO GO EVERY DAY?
THIS LETTUCE IS FROM THE GARDEN...
WHY DON'T YOU GIVE SOME TO THE PASTOR? THAT'S HOW YOU CAN BE A BLESSING.
THANKS, THAT WAS GOOD.
HONEY, I HAVE TO PUT IN A BID TODAY...
MR. CHOI MIN-GI DROPPED BY THE DISTRICT OFFICE...
SNIFF
SNIFF
SNIFF
MOM! HOW COME THIS CUP SMELLS SO BAD?
THE CUP?
OH, GRANNY PROBABLY DIDN'T USE ANY SOAP. YOU KNOW HOW FRUGAL SHE IS.
TAK

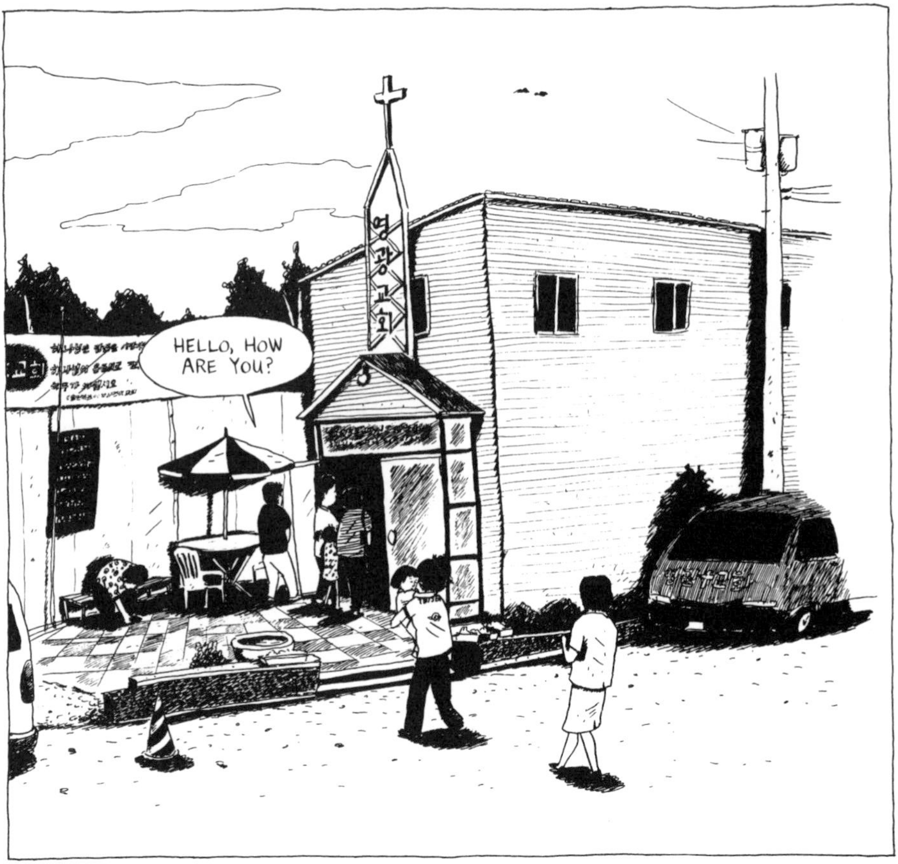
HELLO, HOW ARE YOU?

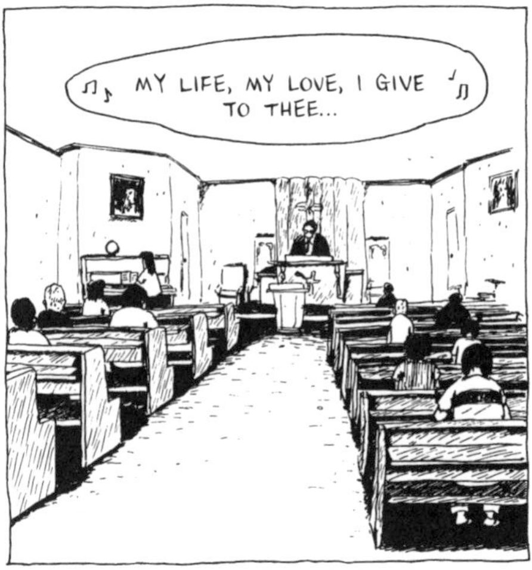
MY LIFE, MY LOVE, I GIVE TO THEE...

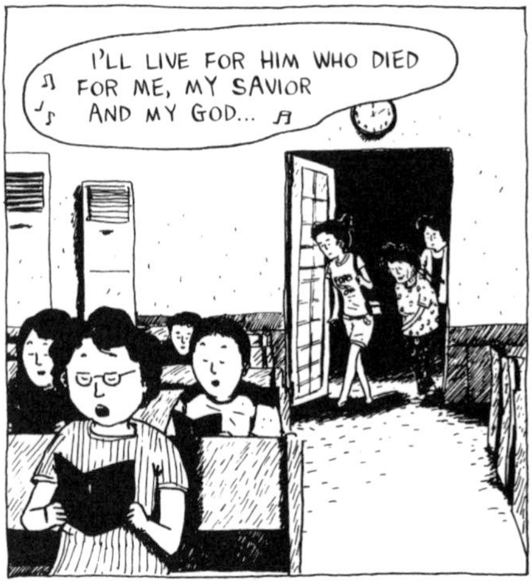
I'LL LIVE FOR HIM WHO DIED FOR ME, MY SAVIOR AND MY GOD...

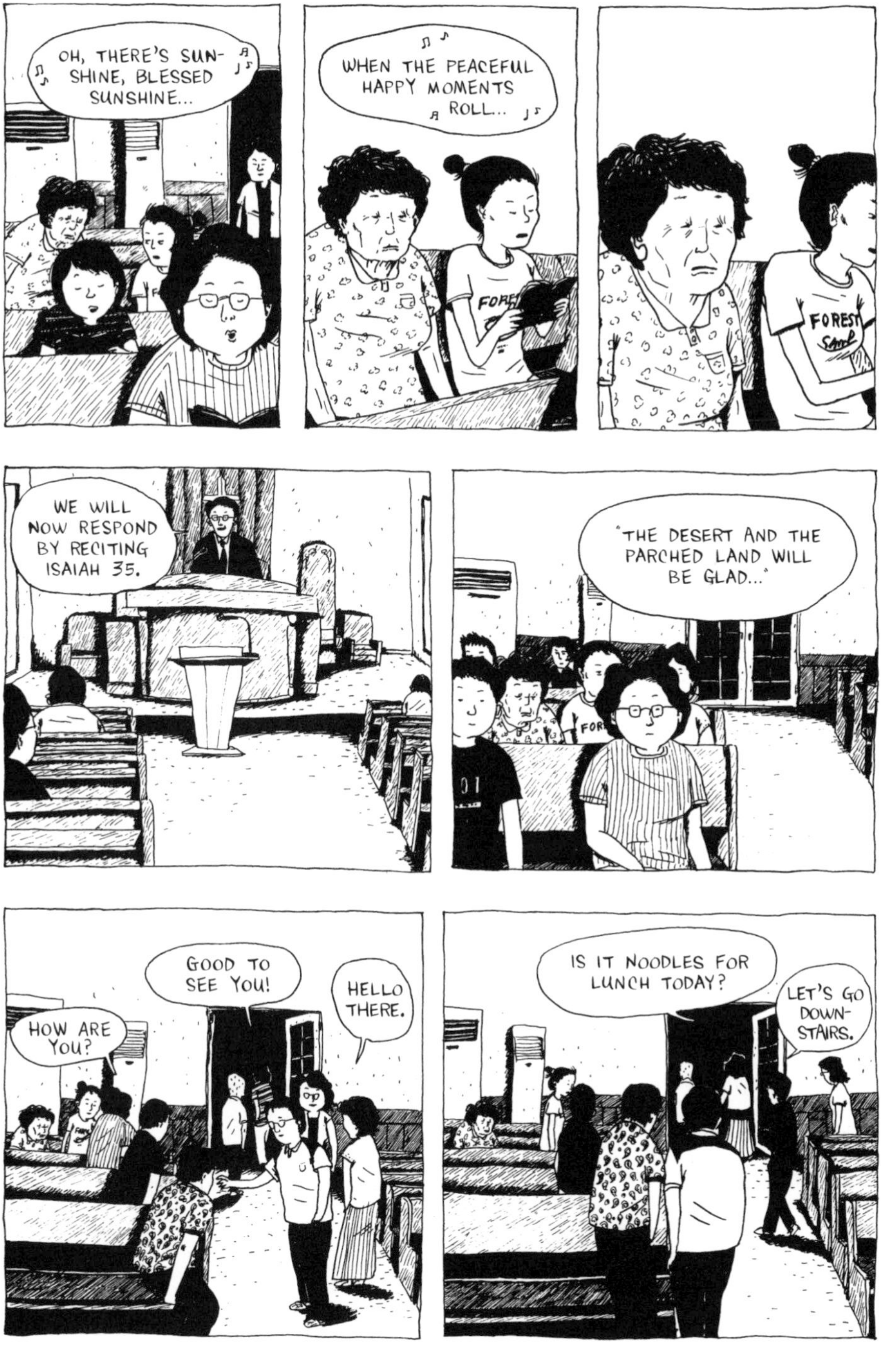
OH, THERE'S SUN-SHINE, BLESSED SUNSHINE...
WHEN THE PEACEFUL HAPPY MOMENTS ROLL...
FOREST
WE WILL NOW RESPOND BY RECITING ISAIAH 35.
"THE DESERT AND THE PARCHED LAND WILL BE GLAD..."
HOW ARE YOU?
GOOD TO SEE YOU!
HELLO THERE.
IS IT NOODLES FOR LUNCH TODAY?
LET'S GO DOWN-STAIRS.

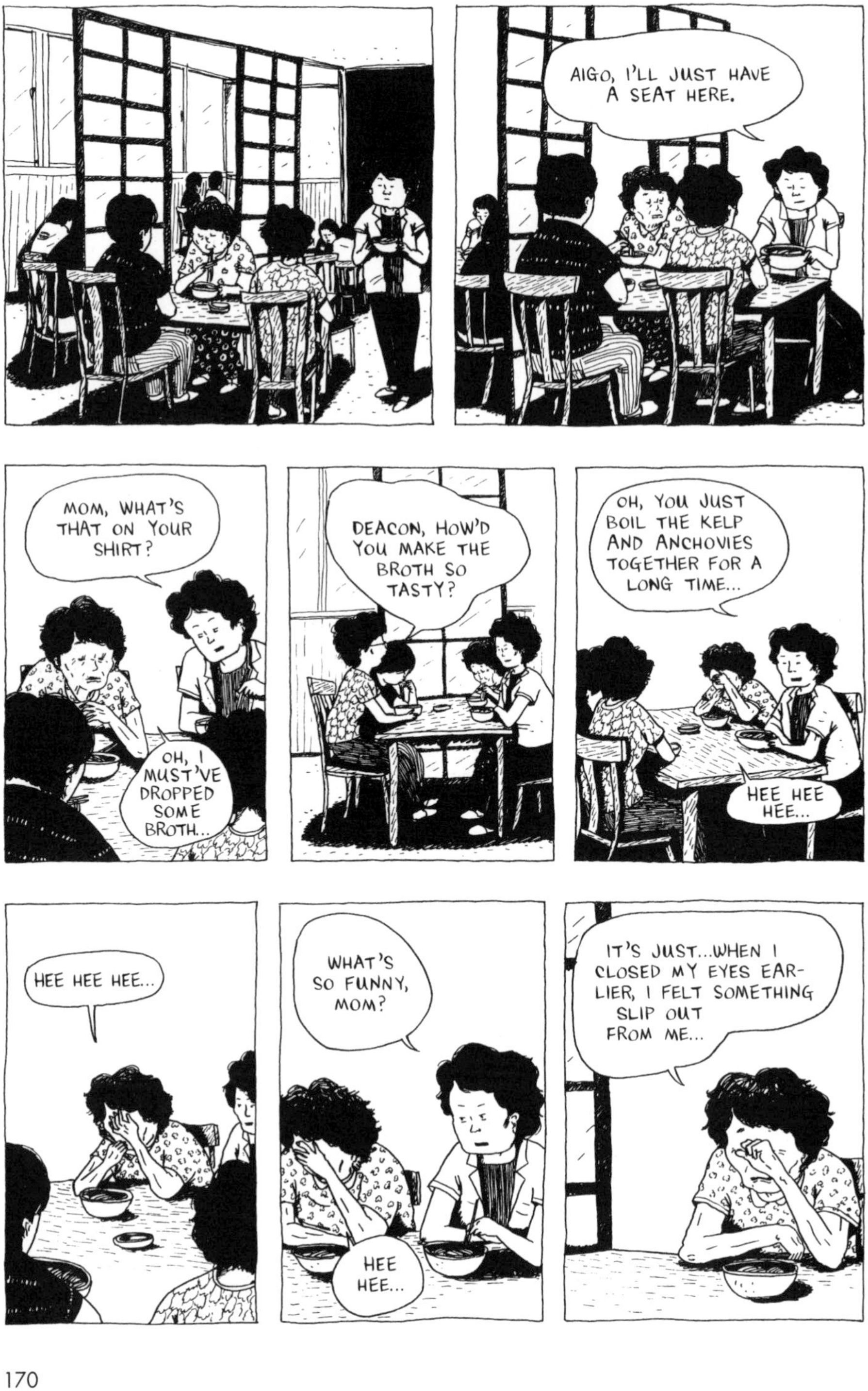
AIGO, I'LL JUST HAVE A SEAT HERE.
MOM, WHAT'S THAT ON YOUR SHIRT?
OH, I MUST'VE DROPPED SOME BROTH...
DEACON, HOW'D YOU MAKE THE BROTH SO TASTY?
OH, YOU JUST BOIL THE KELP AND ANCHOVIES TOGETHER FOR A LONG TIME...
HEE HEE HEE...
HEE HEE HEE...
WHAT'S SO FUNNY, MOM?
HEE HEE...
IT'S JUST...WHEN I CLOSED MY EYES EAR-LIER, I FELT SOMETHING SLIP OUT FROM ME...

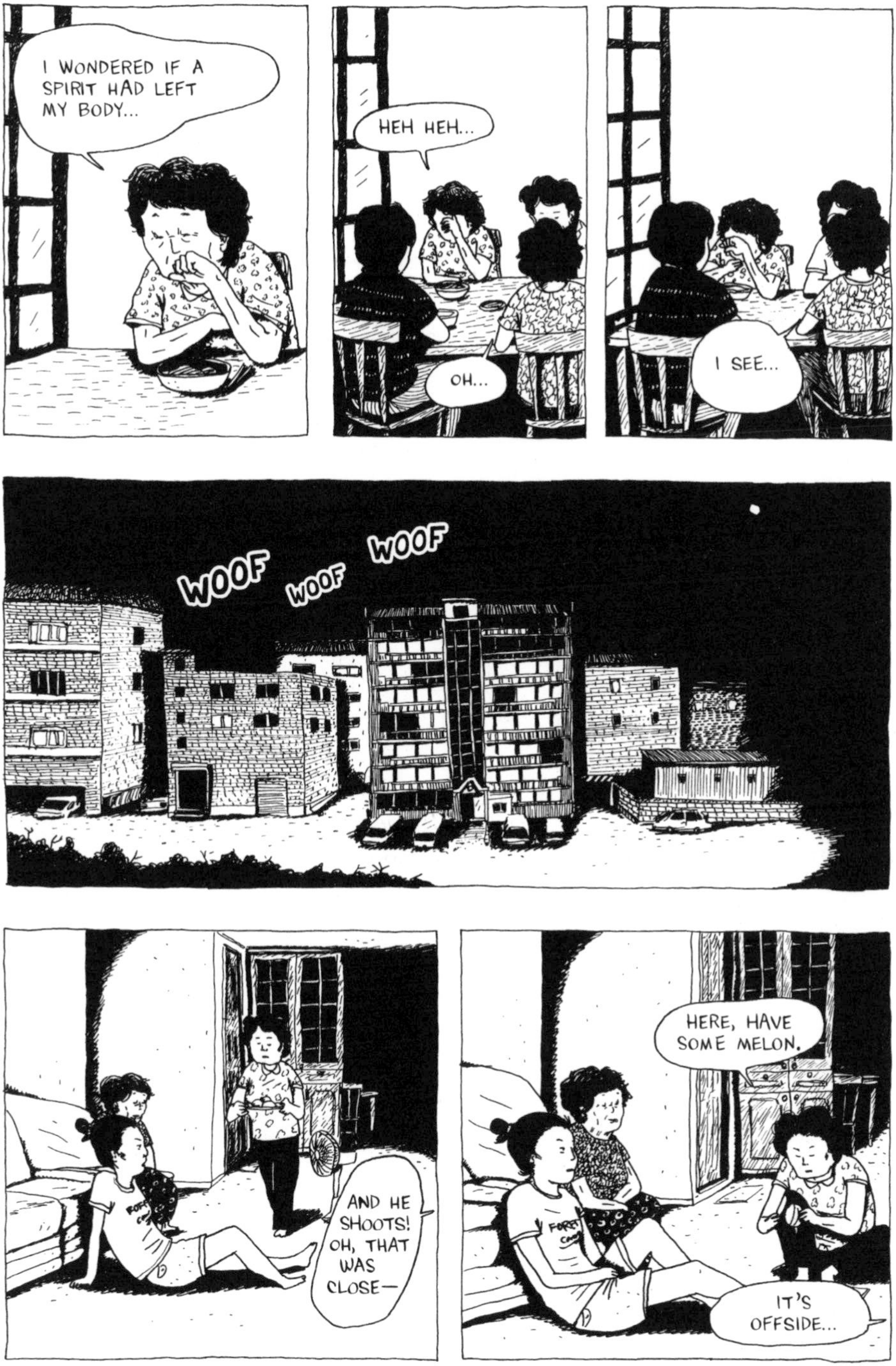
I WONDERED IF A SPIRIT HAD LEFT MY BODY...
HEH HEH...
OH...
I SEE...
WOOF
WOOF
WOOF
HERE, HAVE SOME MELON.
AND HE SHOOTS! OH, THAT WAS CLOSE—
IT'S OFFSIDE...

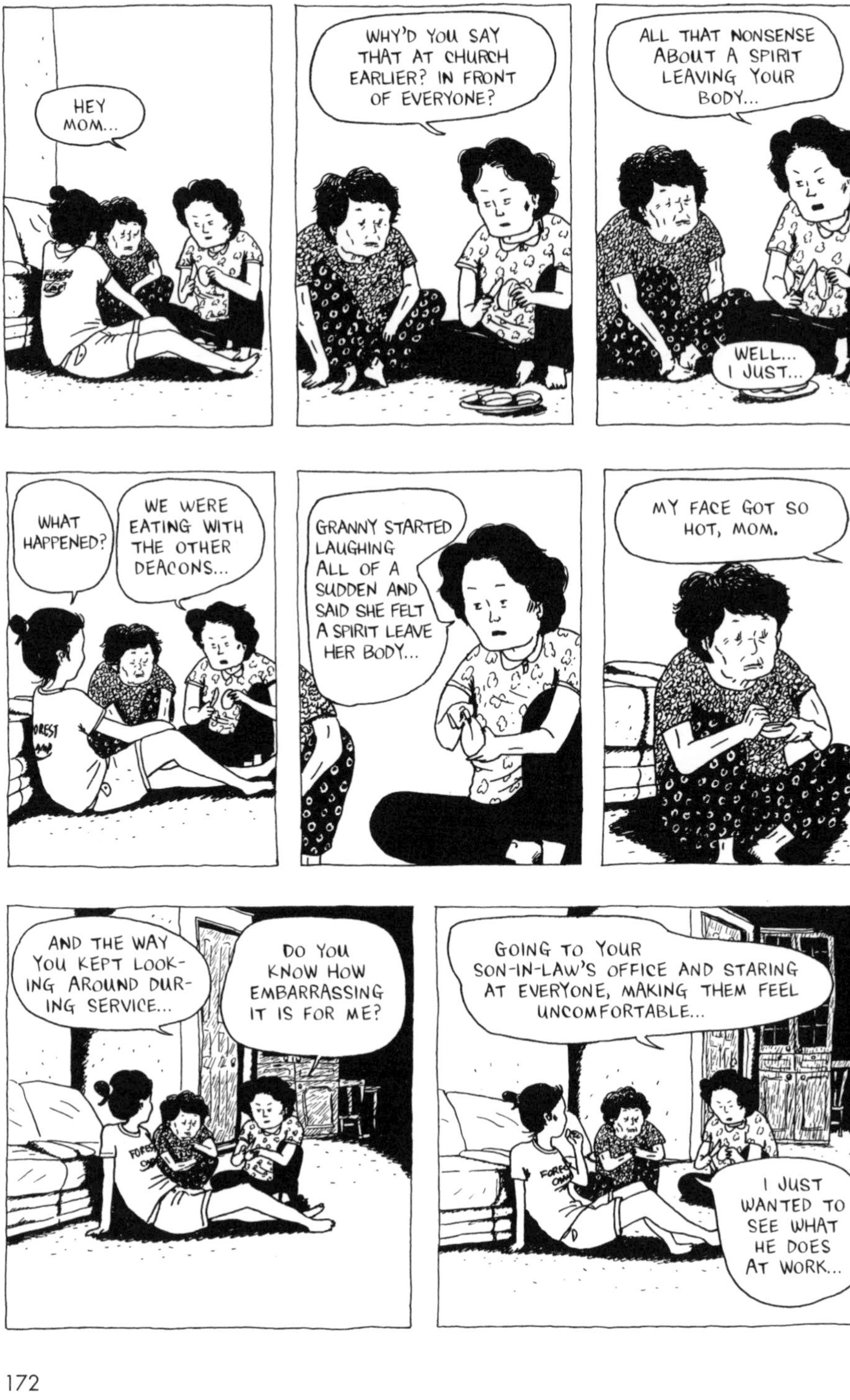
HEY MOM...
WHY'D YOU SAY THAT AT CHURCH EARLIER? IN FRONT OF EVERYONE?
ALL THAT NONSENSE ABOUT A SPIRIT LEAVING YOUR BODY...
WELL... I JUST...
WHAT HAPPENED?
WE WERE EATING WITH THE OTHER DEACONS...
GRANNY STARTED LAUGHING ALL OF A SUDDEN AND SAID SHE FELT A SPIRIT LEAVE HER BODY...
MY FACE GOT SO HOT, MOM.
AND THE WAY YOU KEPT LOOK-ING AROUND DUR-ING SERVICE...
DO YOU KNOW HOW EMBARRASSING IT IS FOR ME?
GOING TO YOUR SON-IN-LAW'S OFFICE AND STARING AT EVERYONE, MAKING THEM FEEL UNCOMFORTABLE...
I JUST WANTED TO SEE WHAT HE DOES AT WORK...

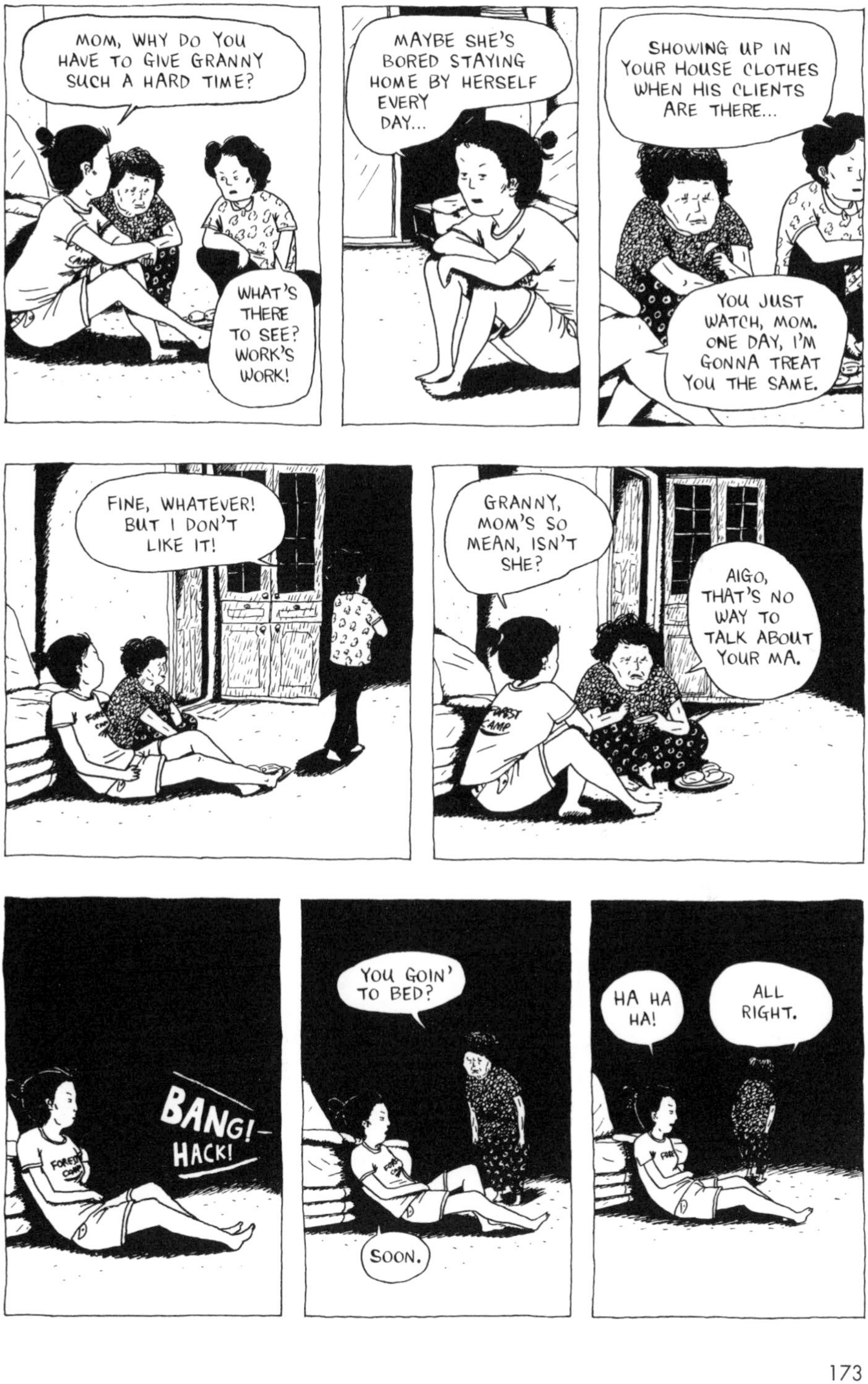

MOM, WHY DO YOU HAVE TO GIVE GRANNY SUCH A HARD TIME?
WHAT'S THERE TO SEE? WORK'S WORK!
MAYBE SHE'S BORED STAYING HOME BY HERSELF EVERY DAY...
SHOWING UP IN YOUR HOUSE CLOTHES WHEN HIS CLIENTS ARE THERE...
YOU JUST WATCH, MOM. ONE DAY, I'M GONNA TREAT YOU THE SAME.
FINE, WHATEVER! BUT I DON'T LIKE IT!
GRANNY, MOM'S SO MEAN, ISN'T SHE?
AIGO, THAT'S NO WAY TO TALK ABOUT YOUR MA.
BANG!
HACK!
YOU GOIN' TO BED?
SOON.
HA HA HA!
ALL RIGHT.

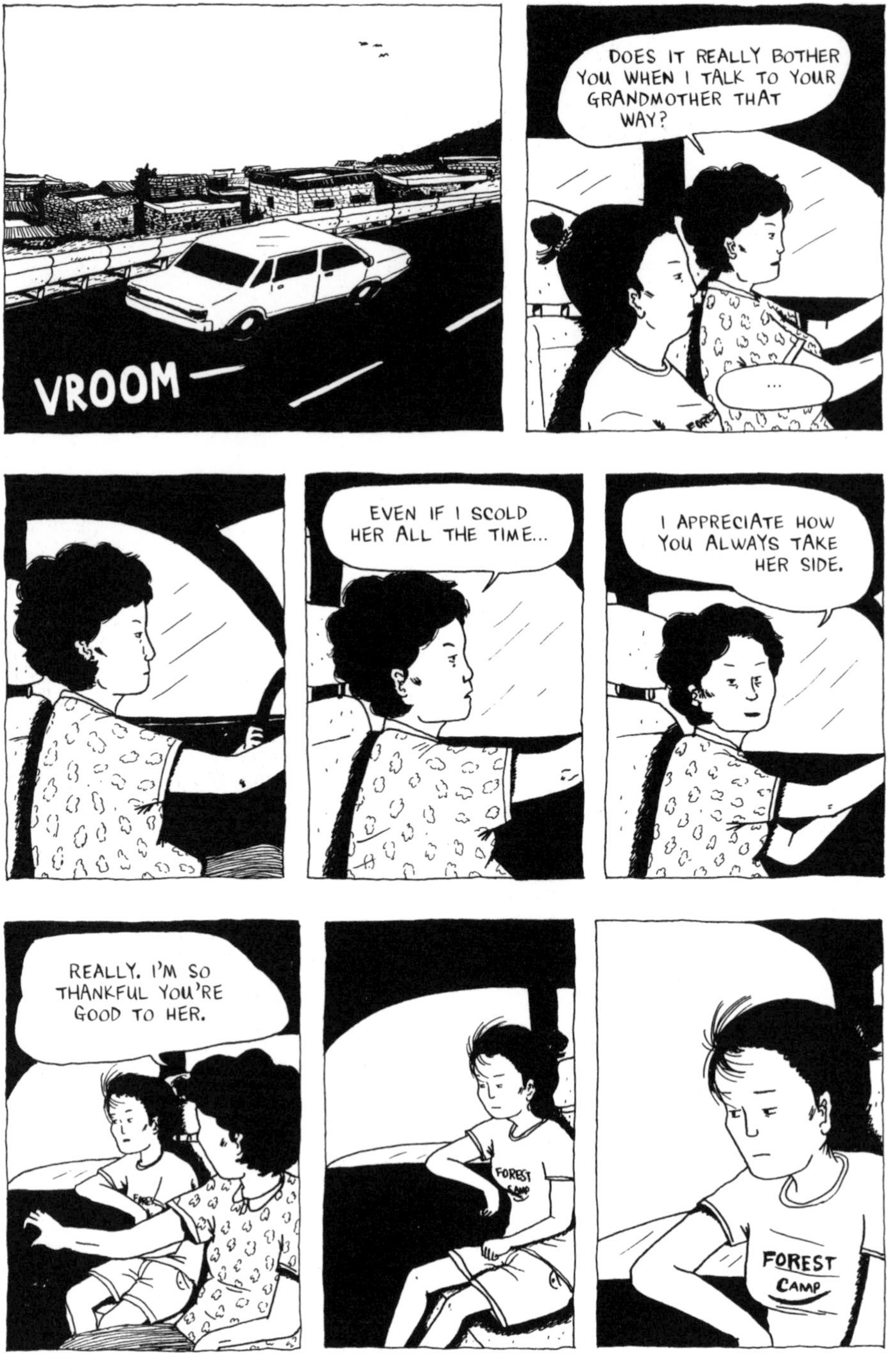
VROOM
DOES IT REALLY BOTHER YOU WHEN I TALK TO YOUR GRANDMOTHER THAT WAY?
...
EVEN IF I SCOLD HER ALL THE TIME...
I APPRECIATE HOW YOU ALWAYS TAKE HER SIDE.
REALLY. I'M SO THANKFUL YOU'RE GOOD TO HER.
FOREST CAMP
FOREST CAMP

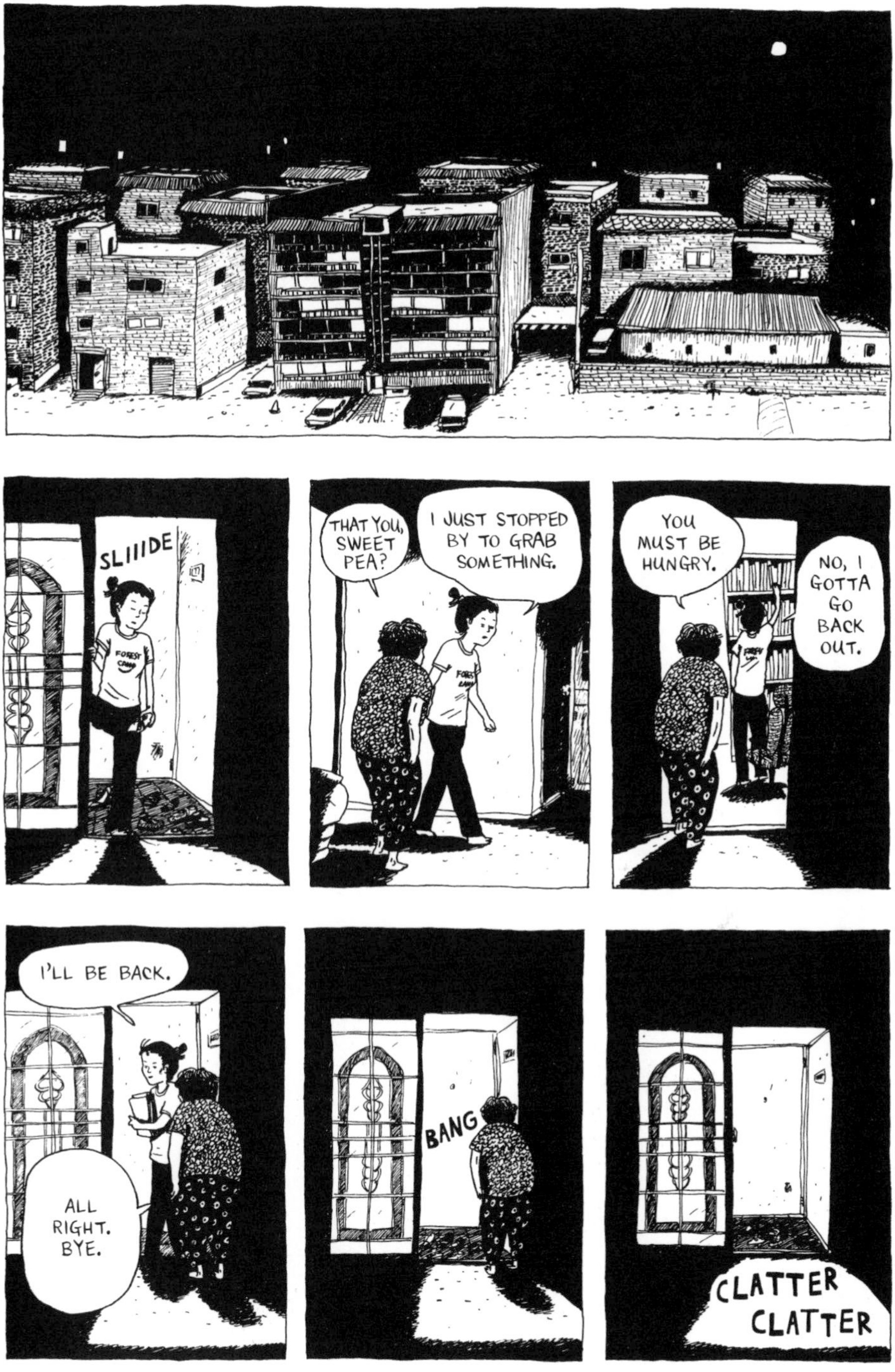
SLIIIDE
THAT YOU, SWEET PEA?
I JUST STOPPED BY TO GRAB SOMETHING.
YOU MUST BE HUNGRY.
NO, I GOTTA GO BACK OUT.
I'LL BE BACK.
ALL RIGHT. BYE.
BANG
CLATTER CLATTER

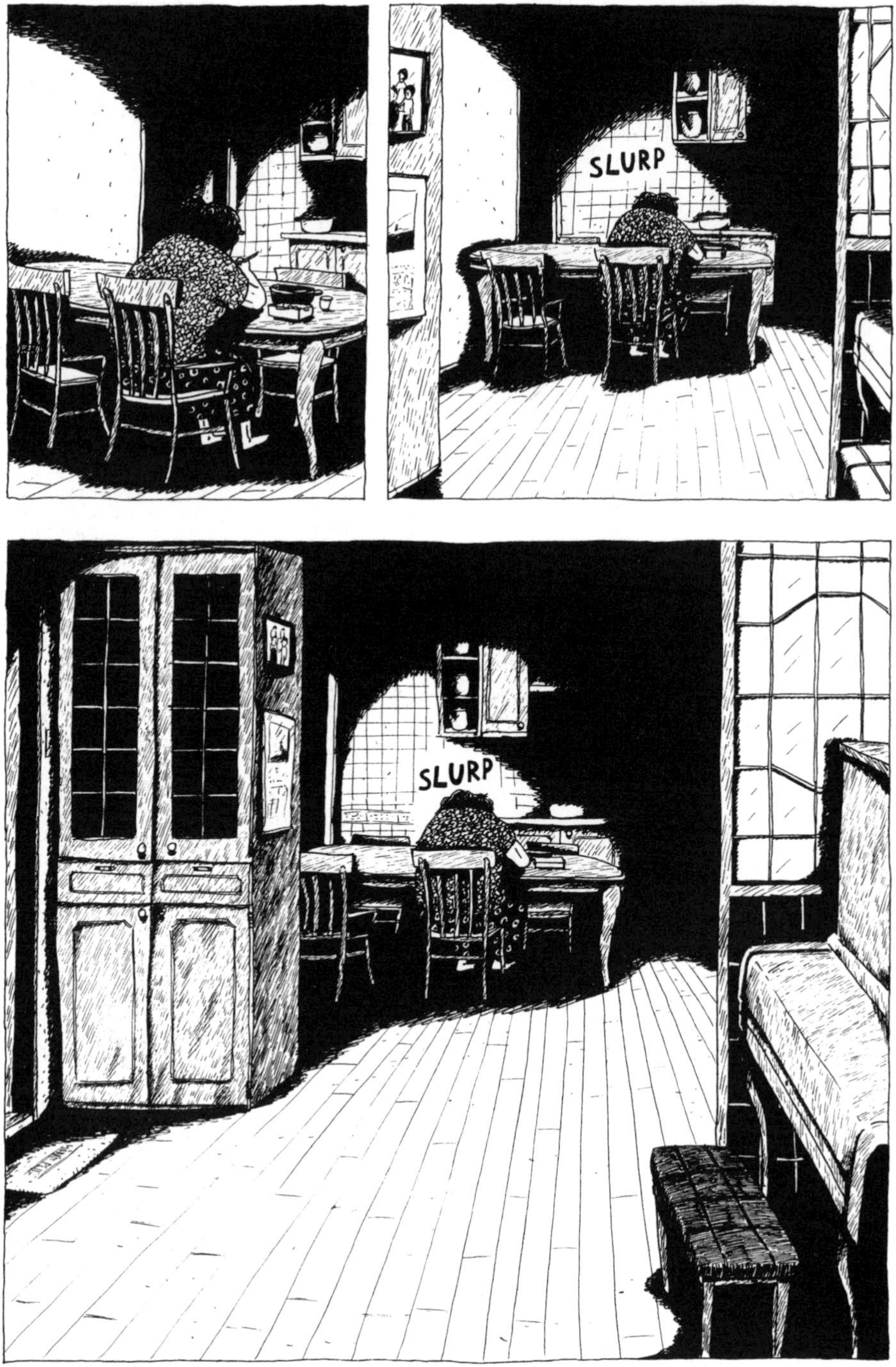
SLURP
SLURP

i'm off to geomun island

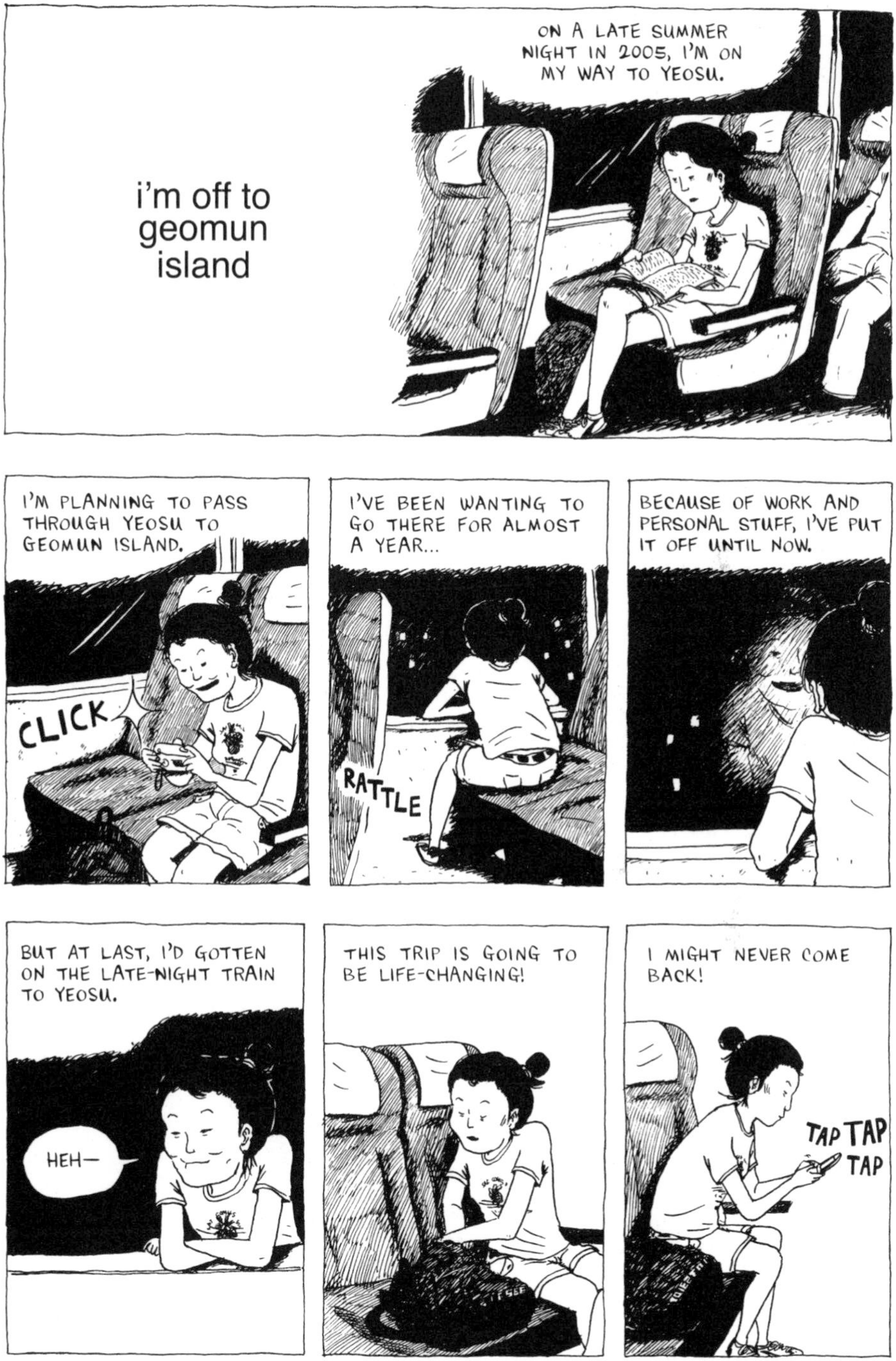

ON A LATE SUMMER NIGHT IN 2005, I'M ON MY WAY TO YEOSU.
I'M PLANNING TO PASS THROUGH YEOSU TO GEOMUN ISLAND.
CLICK
I'VE BEEN WANTING TO GO THERE FOR ALMOST A YEAR...
RATTLE
BECAUSE OF WORK AND PERSONAL STUFF, I'VE PUT IT OFF UNTIL NOW.
BUT AT LAST, I'D GOTTEN ON THE LATE-NIGHT TRAIN TO YEOSU.
HEH—
THIS TRIP IS GOING TO BE LIFE-CHANGING!
I MIGHT NEVER COME BACK!
TAP TAP TAP

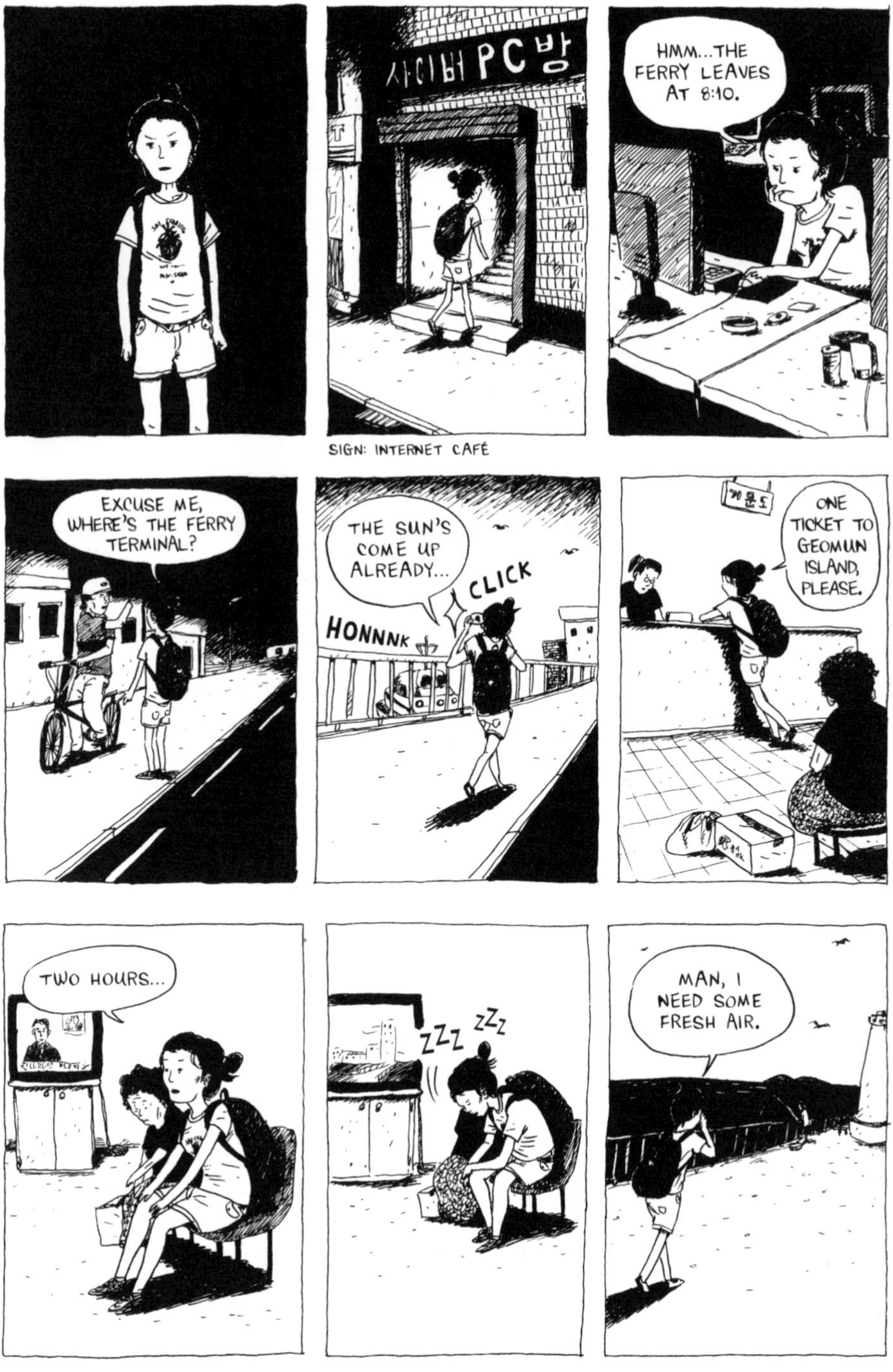
사이버 PC방
SIGN: INTERNET CAFÉ
HMM...THE FERRY LEAVES AT 8:10.
EXCUSE ME, WHERE'S THE FERRY TERMINAL?
THE SUN'S COME UP ALREADY...
CLICK
HONNNK
ONE TICKET TO GEOMUN ISLAND, PLEASE.
TWO HOURS...
ZZZ ZZZ
MAN, I NEED SOME FRESH AIR.

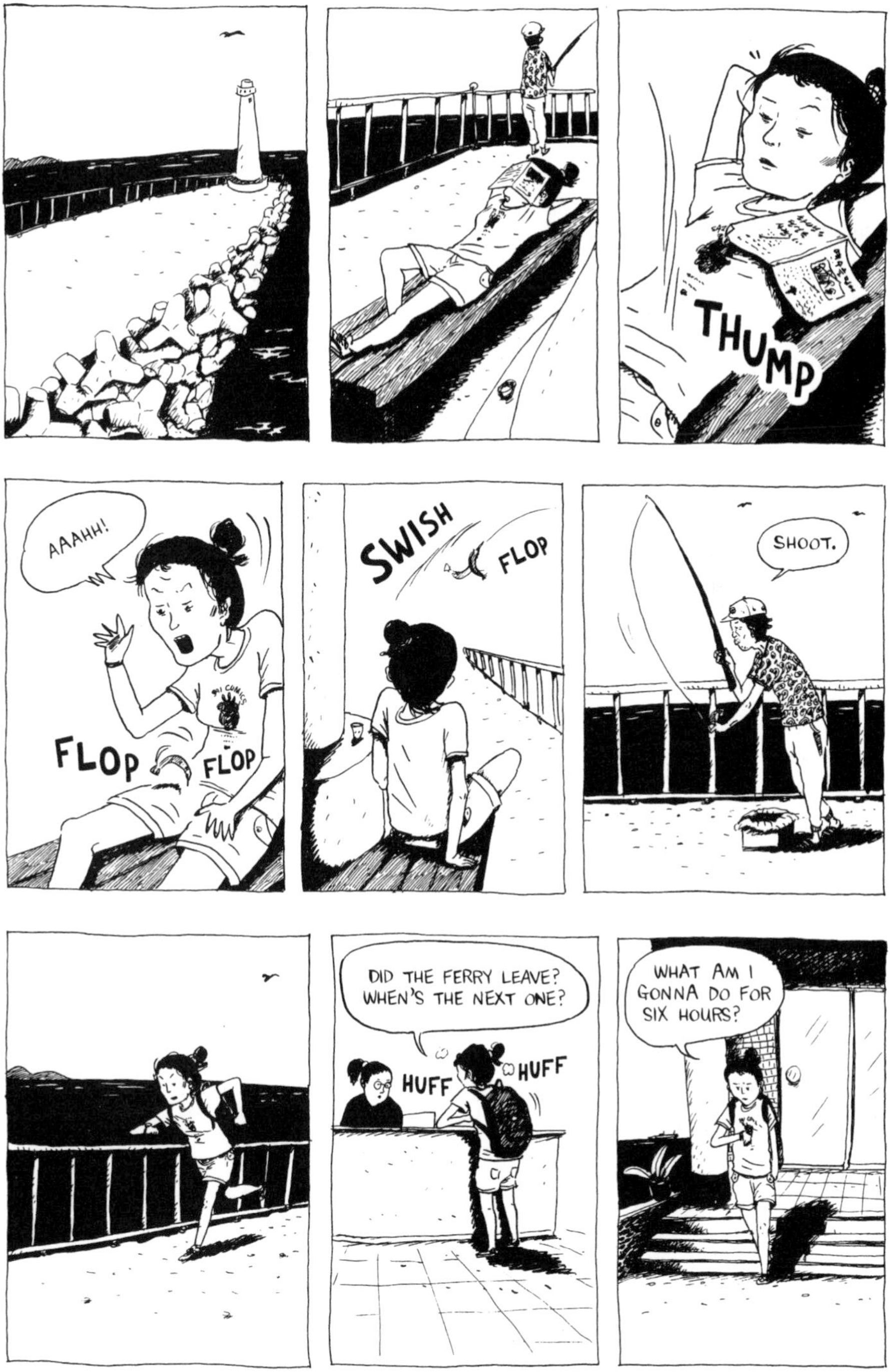
THUMP
AAAHH!
FLOP
FLOP
SWISH
FLOP
SHOOT.
DID THE FERRY LEAVE? WHEN'S THE NEXT ONE?
HUFF
HUFF
WHAT AM I GONNA DO FOR SIX HOURS?

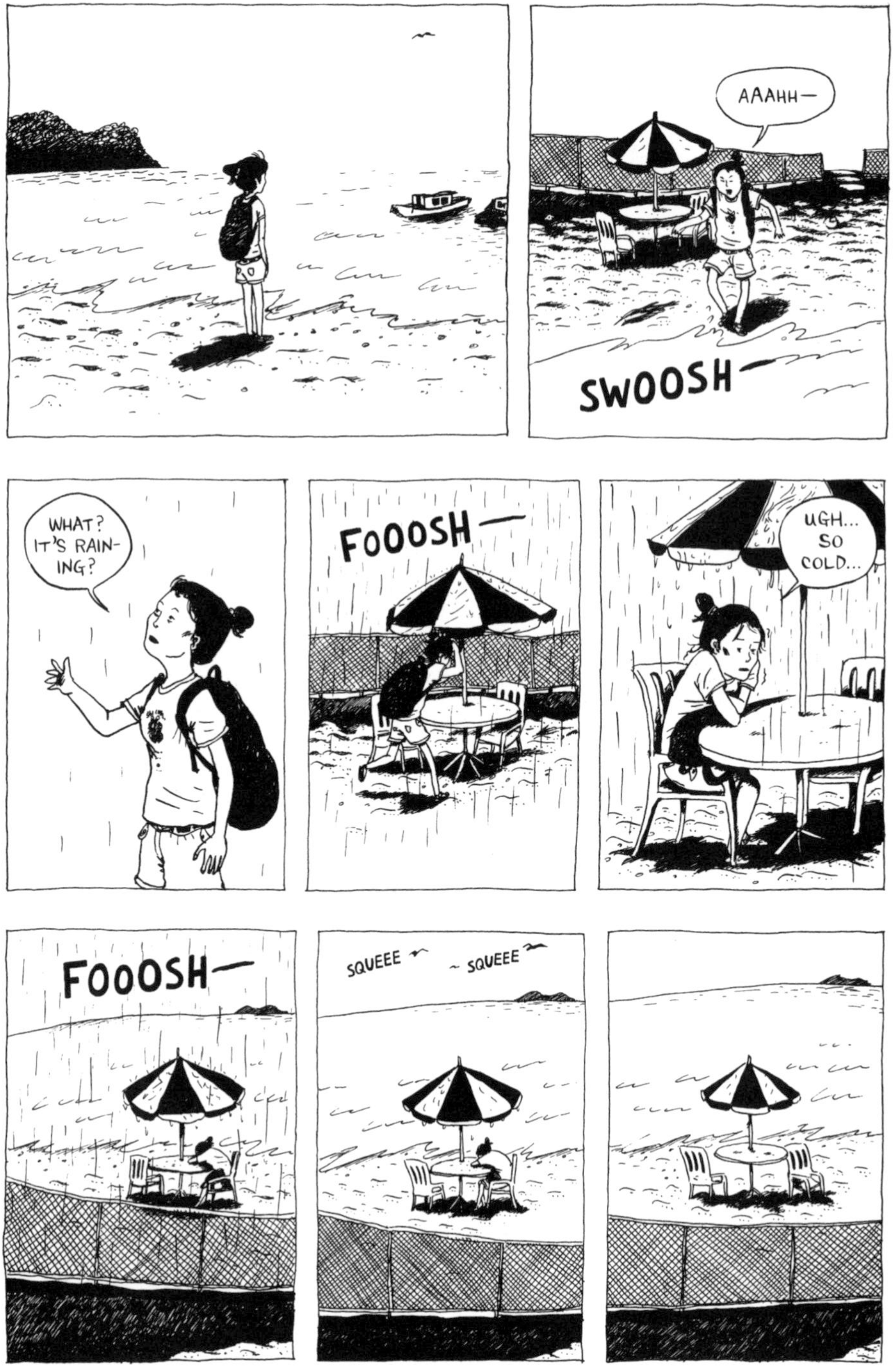
AAAHH—
SWOOSH—
WHAT? IT'S RAIN-ING?
FOOOSH—
UGH... SO COLD...
FOOOSH—
SQUEEE
SQUEEE

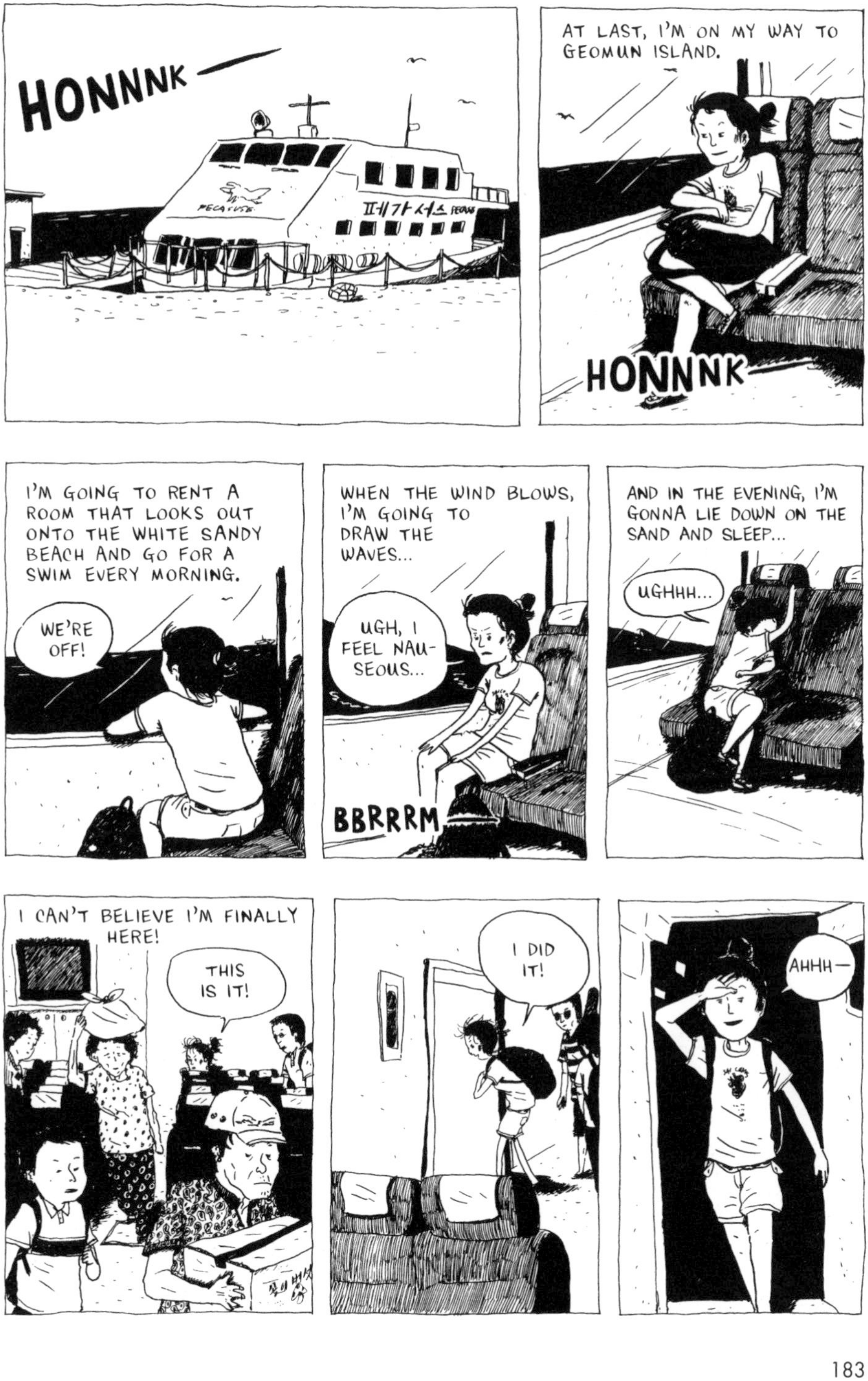
HONNNK
AT LAST, I'M ON MY WAY TO GEOMUN ISLAND.
HONNNK
I'M GOING TO RENT A ROOM THAT LOOKS OUT ONTO THE WHITE SANDY BEACH AND GO FOR A SWIM EVERY MORNING.
WE'RE OFF!
WHEN THE WIND BLOWS, I'M GOING TO DRAW THE WAVES...
UGH, I FEEL NAU-SEOUS...
BBRRRM
AND IN THE EVENING, I'M GONNA LIE DOWN ON THE SAND AND SLEEP...
UGHHH...
I CAN'T BELIEVE I'M FINALLY HERE!
THIS IS IT!
I DID IT!
AHHH—

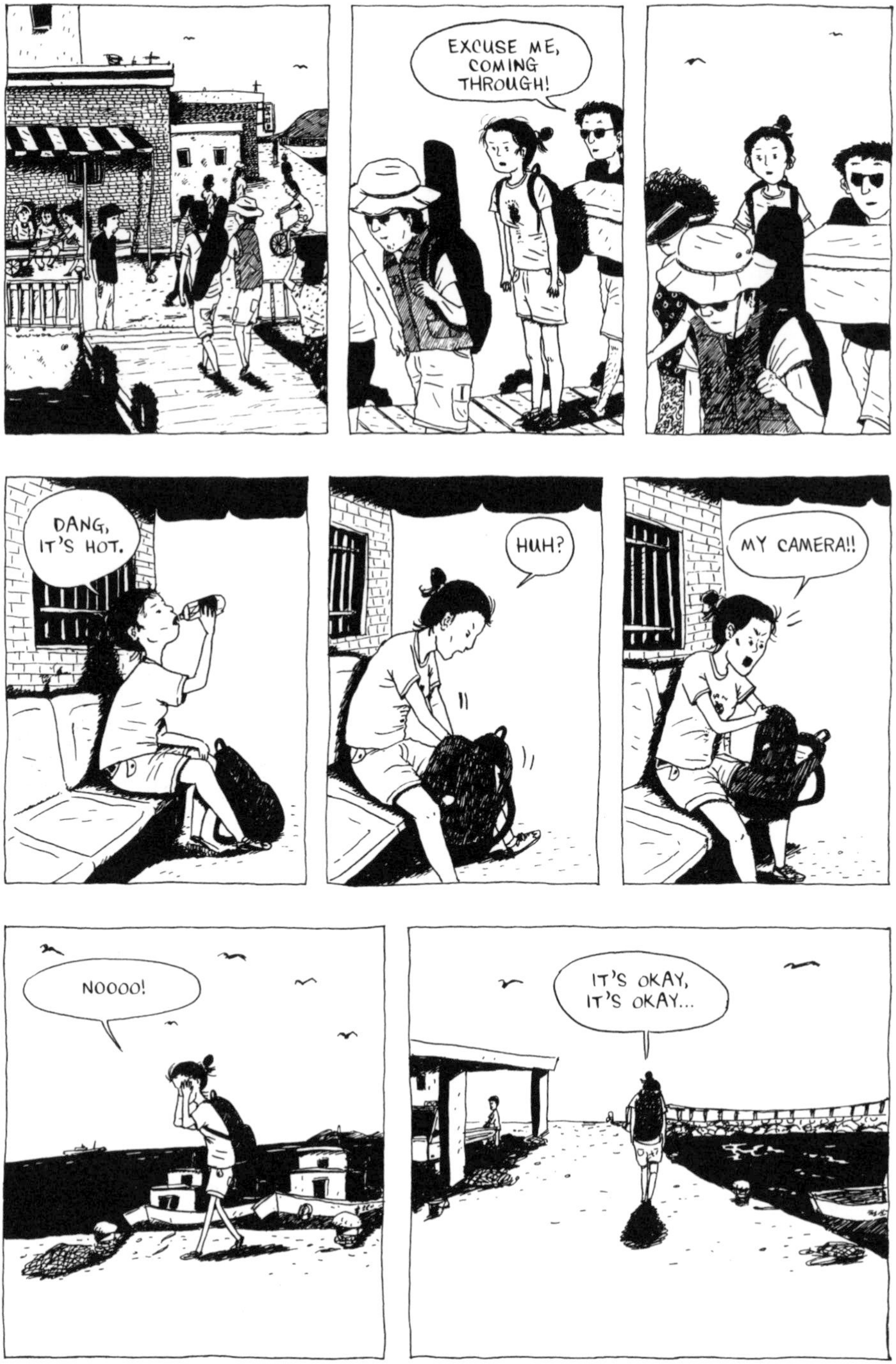
EXCUSE ME, COMING THROUGH!
DANG, IT'S HOT.
HUH?
MY CAMERA!!
NOOOO!
IT'S OKAY, IT'S OKAY...

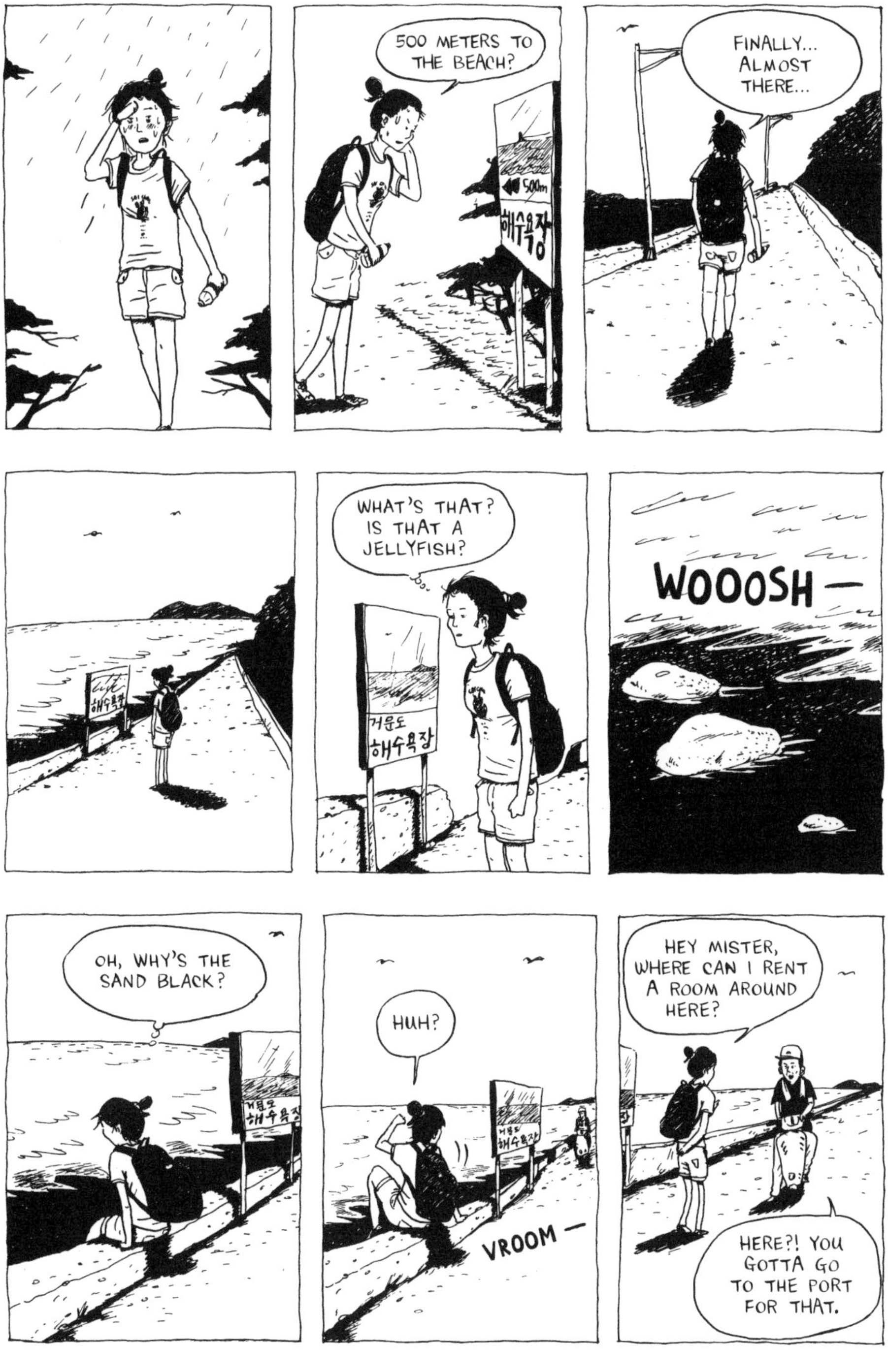
500 METERS TO THE BEACH?
500m
해수욕장
FINALLY... ALMOST THERE...
해수욕장
WHAT'S THAT? IS THAT A JELLYFISH?
거문도
해수욕장
WOOOSH —
OH, WHY'S THE SAND BLACK?
거문도
해수욕장
HUH?
거문도
해수욕장
VROOM —
HEY MISTER, WHERE CAN I RENT A ROOM AROUND HERE?
HERE?! YOU GOTTA GO TO THE PORT FOR THAT.

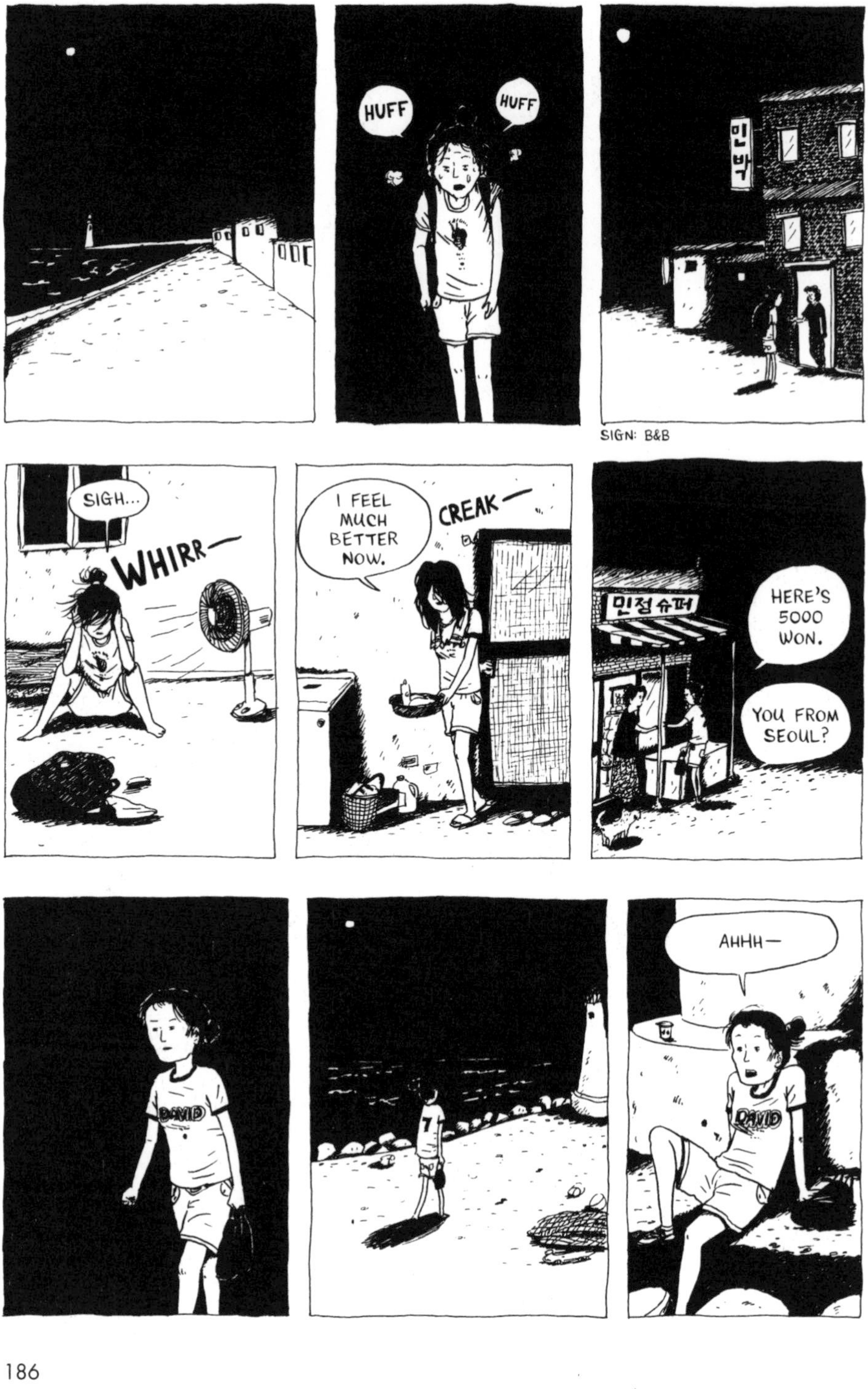
HUFF
HUFF
민박
SIGN: B&B
SIGH...
WHIRR—
I FEEL MUCH BETTER NOW.
CREAK—
민정슈퍼
HERE'S 5000 WON.
YOU FROM SEOUL?
DAVID
7
DAVID
AHHH—

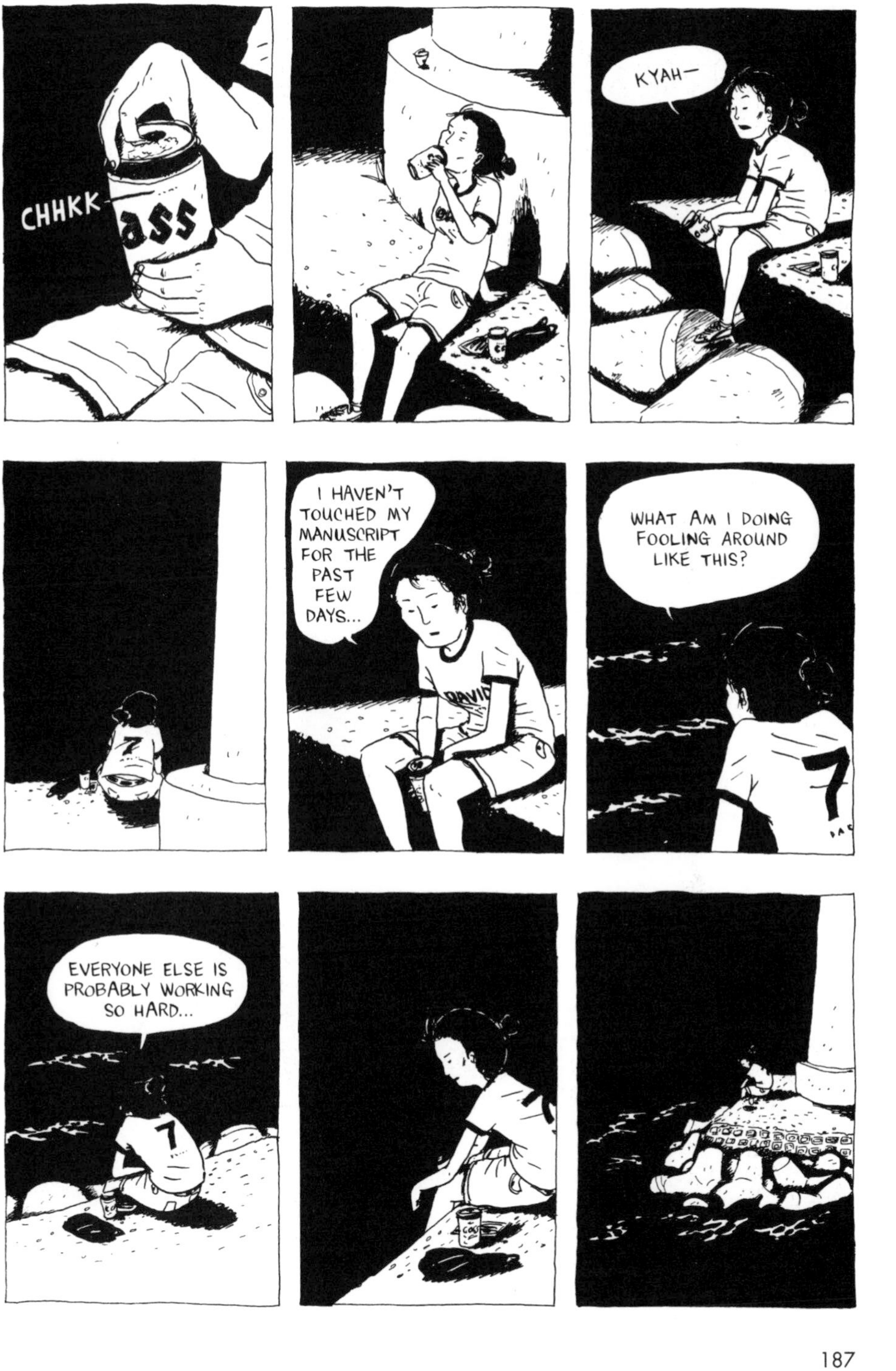
CHHKK
KYAH—
I HAVEN'T TOUCHED MY MANUSCRIPT FOR THE PAST FEW DAYS...
WHAT AM I DOING FOOLING AROUND LIKE THIS?
EVERYONE ELSE IS PROBABLY WORKING SO HARD...

NOTE: GEOMUN ISLAND / COME AGAIN

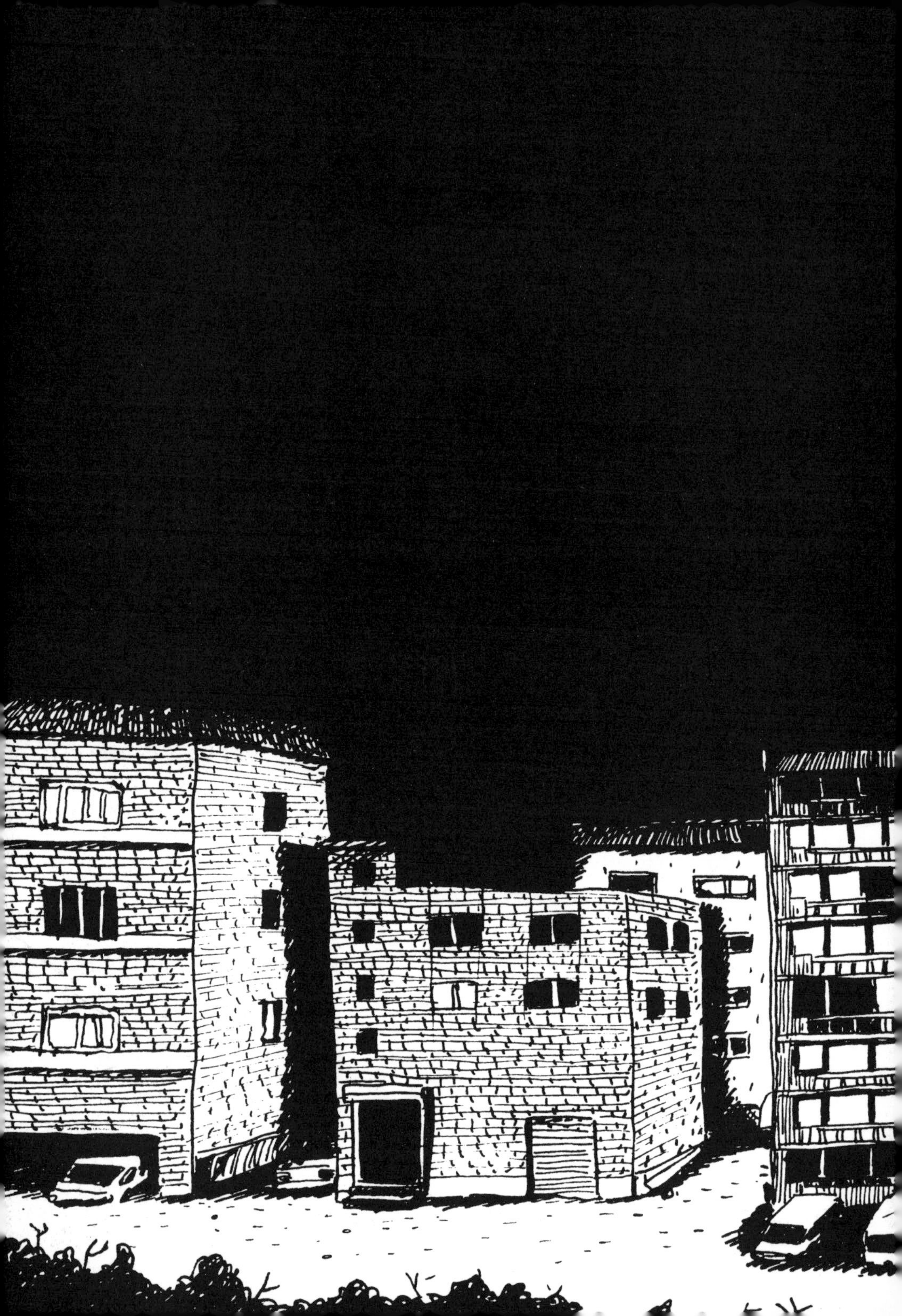